*Engelhart/Roksandić Vidlička* (eds.)

Dealing with Terrorism

Research Series of the Max Planck Institute for
Foreign and International Criminal Law

# Reports on Research in Criminal Law

Edited by Ulrich Sieber

Volume S 165

Schriftenreihe des Max-Planck-Instituts für
ausländisches und internationales Strafrecht

# Strafrechtliche Forschungsberichte

Herausgegeben von Ulrich Sieber

Band S 165

Max-Planck-Institut für ausländisches
und internationales Strafrecht

# Dealing with Terrorism

## Empirical and Normative Challenges of Fighting the Islamic State

Edited by

Marc Engelhart • Sunčana Roksandić Vidlička

Duncker & Humblot • Berlin

Bibliografische Information der Deutschen Nationalbibliothek

Die Deutsche Nationalbibliothek verzeichnet diese Publikation in der Deutschen Nationalbibliografie; detaillierte bibliografische Daten sind im Internet über <http://dnb.d-nb.de> abrufbar.

Editorial office: Dorothea Borner-Burger, Petra Lehser
English language reviser: Yvonne Shah-Schlageter


c/o Max-Planck-Institut für ausländisches und internationales Strafrecht
Günterstalstraße 73, 79100 Freiburg i.Br., Germany
http://www.mpicc.de

Distribution in cooperation with/Vertrieb in Gemeinschaft mit
Duncker & Humblot GmbH, Berlin
http://www.duncker-humblot.de

Cover photo/Umschlagbild: IS Propaganda Foto
Print/Druck: Stückle Druck und Verlag, Stückle-Straße 1, 77955 Ettenheim
Printed in Germany

ISSN 1860-0093
ISBN 978-3-86113-777-1 (Max-Planck-Institut)
ISBN 978-3-428-15799-0 (Duncker & Humblot)
DOI https://doi.org/10.30709/978-3-86113-777-1
Gedruckt auf alterungsbeständigem (säurefreiem) Papier
entsprechend ISO 9706

# Preface

This book is the collaborative work product of a community of international legal and criminological scholars and practitioners. Their research results were first presented and discussed at two international courses entitled 'ISIS as a Threat and Legal Challenge and the Prevention of Recruitment' and 'Fight Against Terrorism through Prevention of Financing and Recruitment' held at the Inter-University Centre Dubrovnik in 2016 and 2017. The contributions in this book focus on distinctive aspects of national, transnational, and international crime control systems in the field of counter-terrorism measures regulated in criminal and security law.

The present contributions originated in the 'International Spring Course on EU Substantive Criminal Law and the Protection of Victims', which was started in 2014 and has been co-organised by the Max Planck Institute for Foreign and International Criminal Law in Freiburg (Germany) and the University of Zagreb, Faculty of Law (Croatia). In 2017 and 2018 it was also supported by funding from the European Commission as a Jean Monnet Project ('Advanced Issues in Criminal Law and Policy').

The course addressed topics covering current issues of European criminal and security law, often influenced by international developments such as UN legislation or initiatives. While it is focused on the European Countries, with an emphasis on the Balkan region, the course also deals with important developments in countries such as the USA or Russia. It serves to promote the interdisciplinary exchange of knowledge and the networking of scientists and practitioners from the judiciary, police, companies, as well as international institutions and non-governmental organisations. Its aim is to create a platform for the development and discussion of new legal and policy approaches. Due to the fact that advanced students (especially in the context of a doctorate) are also offered the possibility to be active participants, this forum brings together both experienced experts and junior scholars in the sciences and the law to their mutual benefit.

The editors of this volume would like to thank the authors for their very topical and critical contributions, as well as for their highly instructive presentations at the Dubrovnik course. We also wish to thank our co-course directors, Professor *Ksenija Turković*, Judge of the European Court of Human Rights, and Associate Professor *Maja Munivrana Vajda* for devoting so much time and effort to the organisation and realisation of the courses.

We are also very grateful to Professor *Ulrich Sieber* and Professor *Hans-Jörg Albrecht*, Directors of the Max Planck Institute for Foreign and International Criminal Law, for their continued support and guidance. We thank all our collaborators from the Max Planck Institute and the University of Zagreb who contributed to the courses and assisted in finalising this publication. Our sincere thanks are due to the Max Planck Institute collaborators Ms *Yvonne Shah-Schlageter* and Dr *Christopher Murphy* for the linguistic revisions of the papers, Ms *Dorothea Borner-Burger*, Ms *Ines Hofmann*, and Ms *Petra Lehser* for the layout of the text and for preparing it for publication.

Freiburg i.Br. and Zagreb, April 2019 The editors

# Table of Contents

## Part 2 – National Legal Answers to Terrorism and Recruitment



## Part 3 – Summary

## List of Abbreviations

| | |
|---|---|
| ACHR | American Convention on Human Rights |
| AEDH | European Association for the Defence of Human Rights |
| AJCL | The American Journal of Criminal Law |
| AJIL | The American Journal of International Law |
| AP | Additional Protocol |
| App. No. | Application Number |
| ATD | Antiterrordatei (Anti-Terrorism File) |
| BfV | Bundesamt für Verfassungsschutz (Federal Office for the Protection of the Constitution) |
| BGBl. | Bundesgesetzblatt (Federal Law Gazette) |
| BKA | Bundeskriminalamt (Federal Police Office) |
| BND | Bundesnachrichtendienst (Federal Intelligence Agency) |
| Brit. J. Criminol. | The British Journal of Criminology |
| BVerfGE | Entscheidungen des Bundesverfassungsgerichts (Federal Constitutional Court Decisions) |
| CAH | crimes against humanity |
| Case W. Res. J. Int'l L | Case Western Reserve Journal of International Law |
| CETS | Council of Europe Treaty Series |
| CIA | Central Intelligence Agency |
| CT | Counter-Terrorism |
| EAW | European arrest warrant |
| ECLI | European Case Law Identifier |
| ECHR | European Convention on Human Rights |
| ECtHR | European Court of Human Rights |
| ECTC | European Counter Terrorism Centre |
| EP | European Parliament |
| ETA | Euskadi Ta Askatasuna (Basque Homeland and Liberty) |
| EU | European Union |
| EU CTC | European Union Counter-Terrorism Coordinator |
| EU IRU | European Union Internet Referral Unit |
| EWCA Crim | Court of Appeal (Criminal Division) for England and Wales |

| | |
|---|---|
| FATF | Financial Action Taskforce |
| FBI | Federal Bureau of Investigation |
| FTFs | Foreign Terrorist Fighters |
| GAL | Grupos Antiterroristas de Liberación (Antiterrorist Liberation Groups) |
| GCC | Gulf Cooperation Council |
| GCSD | Georgian Center for Strategy and Development |
| GG | Grundgesetz (Basic Law) |
| GPS | Global Positioning System |
| GV.NW | Gesetz- und Verordnungsblatt für das Land Nordrhein-Westfalen (Official Gazette of North Rhine-Westphalia) |
| ICC | International Criminal Court |
| ICCT | International Centre for Counter-Terrorism |
| ICJ | International Court of Justice |
| ICL | International Criminal Law |
| ICRC | International Committee of the Red Cross |
| ICTR | International Tribunal for Rwanda |
| ICTY | International Criminal Tribunal for the former Yugoslavia |
| i.e. | id est |
| IHL | International Humanitarian Law |
| ILSA | International Law Students Association |
| IMRO | Internal Macedonian Revolutionary Organization |
| Int'l J.L. & Info. Tech. | International Journal of Law and Information Technology |
| IRA | Irish Republican Army |
| IS | Islamic State |
| ISIL | Islamic State in Iraq and the Levant |
| ISIS | Islamic State of Iraq and Syria |
| JHA | Justice and Home Affairs |
| JIT | Joint Investigation Team |
| LCC | Lebanese Criminal Code |
| LfV | Landesbehörden für Verfassungsschutz (State Offices for the Protection of the Constitution) |
| LIBE | (European Parliament's) Committee on Civil Liberties, Justice and Home Affairs |
| LTTE | Liberation Tigers of Tamil Eelam |

| | |
|---|---|
| MENA | Middle East and North Africa |
| NGO | Non-Governmental Organization |
| NSA | National Security Agency |
| O.J. | Official Journal |
| OTP | Office of the Prosecutor (at the ICC) |
| PhD | Doctor of Philosophy |
| PIU | Passenger Information Unit |
| PKK | Partiya Karkerên Kurdistanê (Kurdistan Workers' Party) |
| PNR | Passenger Name Record |
| PSOE | Partido Socialista Obrero Español (Spanish Socialist Workers' Party) |
| PSR | Party of Socialists-Revolutionaries |
| Rn. | Randnummer (margin number) |
| RULAC | Rule of Law in Armed Conflicts |
| SA | Sturmabteilung (Stormtrooper) |
| SC | Security Council |
| SCSL | Special Court for Sierra Leone |
| STL | Special Tribunal for Lebanon |
| TEK | Anti-Terrorism Task Force |
| TE-SAT | European Union Terrorism Situation and Trend Report |
| UDHR | Universal Declaration of Human Rights |
| UK | United Kingdom |
| UN | United Nations |
| US | United States |
| v. | versus |
| VN | Vereinte Nationen |
| Wm. & Mary L. Rev. | William and Mary Law Review |

# List of Contributors

STEVEN W. BECKER is an Attorney at Law and Founding Member of the Law Office of Steven W. Becker LLC, Chicago, Illinois (USA).

CENAP ÇAKMAK is a former Professor in the Department of International Relations at the Eskişehir Osmangazi University, Eskişehir (Turkey).

PETER B. CAMPBELL is a Maritime Archaeologist and an Assistant Director for Archaeology at the British School at Rome (Italy).

ELIKO CIKLAURI-LAMMICH is a Senior Research Fellow at the Max Planck Institute for Foreign and International Criminal Law, Freiburg (Germany).

DAVOR DERENČINOVIĆ is a Professor of Criminal Law and Head of Chair for Criminal Law, Faculty of Law, University of Zagreb (Croatia).

MARK DRUMBL is the Class of 1975 Alumni Professor of Law at Washington and Lee University, School of Law, and the Director of the Transnational Law Institute, Lexington, Virginia (USA).

MARC ENGELHART is a Senior Research Fellow and Head of an Otto Hahn Research Group at the Max Planck Institute for Foreign and International Criminal Law, Freiburg (Germany).

MAXIME LASSALLE is a Junior Research Fellow at the Faculty of Law, Economics and Finance, University of Luxembourg (Luxembourg).

KATALIN LIGETI is a Professor of European and International Criminal Law at the Faculty of Law, Economics and Finance, University of Luxembourg (Luxembourg).

DAVID LOWE is the Founder of Dr David Lowe Consultancy and a former police officer and principal lecturer at Liverpool John Moores University's Law School (UK).

ALEKSANDAR MARSAVELSKI is an Assistant Professor at the Department of Criminal Law, Faculty of Law, University of Zagreb (Croatia).

RUSSELL A. MILLER is the J.B. Stombock Professor of Law at Washington and Lee University, School of Law, Lexington, Virginia (USA).

MAJA MUNIVRANA VAJDA is an Associate Professor at the Department of Criminal Law, Faculty of Law, University of Zagreb (Croatia).

KATIE A. PAUL is an Anthropologist and Archaeologist and is a Co-Director of the ATHAR Project, Washington, DC (USA).

CHRISTOPHE PAULUSSEN is a Senior Research Fellow at the T.M.C. Asser Instituut, Research Department, The Hague (The Netherlands).

MAJA SERAFIN is a Junior Research Fellow at the Max Planck Institute for Foreign and International Criminal Law, Freiburg (Germany).

SUNČANA ROKSANDIĆ VIDLIČKA is an Assistant Professor at the Department of Criminal Law, Faculty of Law, University of Zagreb (Croatia).

JOHN VERVAELE is a Professor of Economic and European Criminal Law at Utrecht Law School (the Netherlands) and a Professor of European Criminal Law at the College of Europe in Bruges (Belgium).

# Part 1
# International and European Framework for Fighting Terrorism

# Europe at a Crossroads – Countering Terrorism in the Surveillance Society

*Davor Derenčinović**

"Nothing changes instantaneously:
in a gradually heating bathtub
you'd be boiled to death before you knew it."

*Margaret Atwood*, The Handmaid's Tale

## I. Introduction

"It was after the catastrophe, when they shot the president and machine-gunned the Congress and the army declared a state of emergency. They blamed it on the Islamic fanatics at the time. I was stunned. Everyone was, I know that. It was hard to believe, the entire government gone like that. How did they get in, how did it happen? That was when they suspended the Constitution. They said it would be temporary." This is a quote from *Margaret Atwood's* dystopian novel "The Handmaid's Tale," the story of the Republic of Gilead, formerly the United States of America, where a staged terrorist attack (blamed on Islamic extremists) paved the way for ecological disaster and a theocratic new order. The Republic is surveilled by the Eyes of God, the menacing secret police.[1]

Although published back in 1985, this dystopian scenario anticipated, at least to a certain extent, some of the real events the world has been facing since the terrorist attacks on New York and Washington in 2001. These attacks were used by the executive as a pretext for unprecedented restrictions on constitutional rights of citizens.[2] A well-established system of checks and balances was then radically redefined in favor of the executive branch. Declining constitutional protection took many faces. For instance, through administrative preventive detention persons under suspicion of terrorist activities were deprived of their right to be imprisoned or taken into

---

* Prof.dr.sc. *Davor Derenčinović*, Full Professor of Criminal Law, Zagreb Faculty of Law; President of the Croatian Academy of Legal Sciences. This paper was written as part of the research on the Zagreb Faculty of Law project "New Croatian Legal System."

1 https://timeline.com/handmaids-tale-dystopian-relevant-6ffbb4c839be [last visited 5 February 2018].

2 In general, see *Becker*, in: Becker/Derenčinović (eds.), International Terrorism, pp. 1–23.

custody only upon decision by an impartial court. They were kept *incommunicado* and without the right to hire a lawyer and to access the court. Those captured in the zones of active hostilities (in Afghanistan or Iraq) were considered enemy combatants and therefore deprived of the rights that prisoners of war enjoy under the Geneva conventions of 1949 and Protocols thereto.[3] Prohibition of torture and inhuman or degrading treatment that is considered as an absolute right under human rights conventions was mitigated by the authorities through legal interpretations. For instance, to justify the practice of keeping imprisoned suspected terrorists sleepless for days, authorities denied criticism that this amounted to "sleep deprivation" but rather called it "modification of a sleep regime," which is not prohibited under international human rights law.[4] Moreover, such extreme measures were justified on the grounds they were taken outside the boundaries of domestic jurisdiction and against foreigners who are not entitled to constitutional protection clauses. In addition to these measures taken against suspected terrorists who were considered not only perpetrators of criminal offences but a genuine threat to national security, some of the counterterrorist measures also seriously affected ordinary citizens who had nothing to do with terrorism. These include measures such as mass surveillance and interception of telecommunications, of email correspondence, of social networks, measures of so-called racial profiling, etc.

The public reaction to the implementation of these intrusive measures by the authorities was very lukewarm. With a few exceptions of several human rights NGOs who raised their voices, citizens mostly remained silent on emerging trends in restricting their fundamental freedoms. This may be easily explained by two sets of reasons. Firstly, raising awareness in the general public about a common enemy to mankind and to most fundamental constitutional rights and liberties, i.e., terrorists, resulted in a psychological mobilization against that common threat. Furthermore, this lack of response may also be understood from the perspective of Maslow's hierarchy of needs. Maslow distinguishes between basic, psychological, and self-fulfillment needs.[5] Safety/security is a basic human need (along with biological and physiological needs) that must be satisfied before any other need is satisfied (for instance, the need of having an intimate relationship and/or friendship).[6] This motivational circle of different human needs offers a good explanation for why curtailing other constitutional rights that embody other human needs whose satisfaction is of secondary importance [to the public in general] went almost without a response by the silent majority.

---

3 See *Goldman/Tittemore*, Unprivileged Combatants, p. 3.

4 On sleep deprivation in general, see *Scharf*, 20 Duke J. Comp. & Int'l L. 389–412 (2010).

5 https://www.simplypsychology.org/maslow.html [last visited 5 February 2018].

6 *Ibid.*

The same pattern of governmental action followed by public non-reaction occurred in Europe after the recent wave of terrorist attacks in Madrid, Moscow, London, Brussels, and Paris, to mention a few. These attacks resulted in massive casualties and brought a sense of insecurity to the citizens of the European states. The immediate responses to these attacks by many European governments have not been very different from the reaction of the United States government in the close aftermath of the 9/11 attacks. Claiming the constitutional duty to protect all those under their jurisdiction, executive branches of government in some of the well-established European democracies governed by the rule of law, in response to a threat of terrorism, took control over the design and the implementation of counter-terrorist measures. By terminating or at least suspending checks and balances in emergency situations, the executive branch continued to restrict the most fundamental human rights, and those affected were not only suspected terrorists but also ordinary citizens.

As a phenomenon that remains without a universal definition, terrorism *per se* poses a threat to most human rights. On one hand, terrorism denies human rights, and terrorist attacks threaten human rights (the right to life, to personal freedom and security, etc.) of real and/or potential victims. On the other hand, unfortunately, in the fight against terrorism, the fundamental human rights of suspected terrorists also come under threat. Unlike situations when the state justifies the restriction or suspension of fundamental human rights in suppression of crime only in cases where there is well-grounded evidence against the suspect, some recent trends of contemporary anti-terrorism justify interventions into the domain of human rights even when such evidence is insufficient.[7]

Among the rights more exposed than others to potential violations in the fight against terrorism are the privacy rights. This is because the threshold for limiting privacy rights in legal proceedings is very low, and in cases of so-called regulatory checks (for instance at airports) there is no threshold for carrying out these measures at all. In Europe, respect for the privacy rights of citizens and other subjects who can appear as applicants before the European Court of Human Rights (ECtHR) by the governments is guaranteed under Article 8 of the European Convention on Human Rights and Fundamental Freedoms (ECHR). Privacy rights protected under this provision (private life, family life, home, and correspondence) are not absolute. There has been a certain margin of appreciation for the parties to interfere with privacy rights when it is in accordance with the law and necessary in a democratic society in the interests of national security, public safety, or the economic well-being of the country, for the prevention of disorder or crime, for the protection of health or morals, or for the protection of the rights and freedoms of others.

[7] *Derenčinović*, in: Rimmington (ed.), International Terrorism, p. 16.

The ECtHR repeatedly stressed that the margin of appreciation in application of Article 8 ECHR is rather broad when restriction of privacy rights is justified for preventing terrorism. For instance, the taking and retention of a photograph of a suspected terrorist without consent was not disproportionate to the legitimate terrorist-prevention aims of a democratic society.[8] Likewise, the interests of national security and the fight against terrorism prevail over the applicants' interest in having access to information about them in the Security Police files.[9] Nevertheless, while recognizing the State's interest in protecting national security, the Court found that the absolute ban on returning the bodies of alleged terrorists did not strike a proper balance between the State and the Article 8 ECHR rights of the family members of the deceased.[10]

The protection of citizens from government surveillance is also enshrined in Article 8 ECHR. Exceptions relate to GPS surveillance of a suspected terrorist and the use of the data thus obtained.[11] According to the reasoned opinion of the Court expressed in the recent landmark case *Szabó and Vissy v. Hungary*, the mass surveillance of communications to pre-empt impending incidents should be allowed but legislation governing such operations must provide the necessary safeguards against abuse regarding the ordering and implementation of surveillance measures and any potential redress.[12] This recent case (2016) is very important for the appropriate establishment of a balancing test between efficient antiterrorism measures and the protection of privacy rights of those who might be affected by their implementation and will be discussed in more detail in section III. of this paper.

## II. Surveillance society and new antiterrorist legislation in Europe

*Jeremy Bentham* advocated a strengthening of the social control for the purposes of the utilitarian criminal policy. The utilitarian philosophy is based on the premise that morality means no less than happiness distributed to as many individuals as possible. The fundamental utilitarian principle seeks to provide that distribution by incapacitating those who threaten the collective harmony, including delinquents but also political opponents who might disturb the social peace (that is why Enlightenment era thinkers were very much in favor of capital punishment for political opposition). Discussing the method for achieving these utilitarian goals, *Bentham*

---

8 *Murray v. the United Kingdom* (ECtHR 1994), § 93, Guide on Article 8 of the European Convention on Human Rights, European Court of Human Rights, 2017, p. 26.

9 *Segerstedt-Wiberg and Others v. Sweden* (ECtHR 2006), § 91, *ibid.* p. 29.

10 *Sabanchiyeva and Others v. Russia* (ECtHR 2013), § 146, *ibid.* p. 22.

11 *Uzun v. Germany* (ECtHR 2010), § 81, *ibid.* p. 32.

12 *Szabó and Vissy v. Hungary* (ECtHR 2016), §§ 64, 68 and 78–81, *ibid.* p. 84.

established the concept of the *Panopticon* – a prison with a central unit from which all activities of prisoners can be easily monitored. This concept was further interpreted and developed by *Foucault*:

> We know the principle on which it was based: at the periphery, an annular building; at the centre, a tower; this tower is pierced with wide windows that open onto the inner side of the ring; the peripheric building is divided into cells, each of which extends the whole width of the building; they have two windows, one on the inside corresponding to the windows of the tower; the other, on the outside, allows the light to cross the cell from one end to the other. All that is needed, then, is to place a supervisor, in a central tower and to shut up in each cell a madman, a patient, a condemned man, a worker or a schoolboy. (*Foucault*, 1977:200)[13]

The concept of *Panopticon* was much more than just an idea on how to control convicts in the penitentiaries at that time. Although it was never turned from blueprint into reality, over time, the *Panopticon* became the model for the subsequent development of social control in modern society as a whole.[14] The idea of strengthening social control in form of central oversight over disorder and crime in general has been closely linked to the term "surveillance society." A historical overview of the introduction of this term into literature is provided by *Murakami Wood* who referred to *Garry Marx's* "very deliberate attempt to characterize the 'new surveillance' brought in by the digital" as well as to works by *Oscar Gandy* and *David Lyon*.[15] For him, surveillance society "would appear to be becoming as ubiquitous as surveillance itself."[16]

The development of technology and logistics in contemporary surveillance society has brought new approaches in preventing terrorism. These new features make surveillance over the movements and activities of suspected terrorists easier than ever before. Advanced surveillance techniques also improved preventive policing that can be defined as any action carried out by police with the intention of identifying and intervening to stop a specific crime or a type of crime before or while it is carried out.[17] However, the indiscriminate nature of some surveillance measures affect ordinary citizens and turn them into some sort of collateral suspects. The *Council of Europe Human Rights Commissioner* also recognized that

> we are rapidly becoming a surveillance society…this is partly the result of general technical and societal developments, but these trends are strongly reinforced by measures taken in the fight against terrorism…in the context of the fight against terrorism, this means individuals are at risk of being targeted for being suspected "extremists" or for being suspected of being "opposed to our constitutional legal order", even if they have not (yet) committed any criminal (let alone terrorist) offence… "targets" of this kind are moreover increasingly selected through computer "profiles". Even if some may be caught, there will always be relatively large numbers of "false

13 *Pratt*, 2 Social & Legal Studies 374 (1993).

14 *Ibid.* p. 374.

15 *Murakami Wood*, 6 Eur. J. Criminology 179 (2009).

16 *Ibid.*

17 *Sorell*, 30 Crim. Just. Ethics 2 (2011).

> negatives" – real terrorists who are not identified as such, and unacceptably high numbers of "false positives": large numbers of innocent people who are subjected to surveillance, harassment, discrimination, arrest - or worse. Freedom is being given up without gaining security.[18]

There are numerous examples of recently adopted antiterrorist legislation in Europe that are highly questionable from the human rights point of view for broadening the scope of the surveillance society under the pretext of countering terrorism. Hungarian legislation regulating the state of emergency allows "severe restrictions on freedom of movement and freezing of assets."[19] Recent antiterrorist legislation in France grants the authority to the ministers (interior, defense, and transport) to order the collection of data gathered by means of telecommunication. However, this cannot be applied to the "personal data that may reveal a person's racial or ethnic origin, religious or philosophical beliefs, political opinions, trade union membership, or data relating to the health or sexual life of the person concerned." French legislation has been criticized not only by human rights activists but also by the *Council of Europe Human Rights Commissioner* for allowing broad administrative discretion in setting up protective perimeters for searches and seizures. Legislation lacks clearly defined criteria for such administrative action and conditions for judicial oversight. The Commissioner also raised his concern about ordering electronic surveillance and house arrest on discretionary grounds.[20] Mass surveillance and interception through the web surface can also be authorized in many European countries including the United Kingdom, France, Germany, Poland, Hungary, Austria, Belgium, and the Netherlands. Polish legislation adopted in 2016 allows covert surveillance measures targeting foreign nationals, including wiretapping, monitoring of electronic communications, and the surveillance of telecommunications networks and devices without any judicial oversight for three months.[21]

At first sight, most of these new measures, adopted as a response to a threat of terrorism that are in accordance with EU counter-terrorist policies and activities might not, in cases of individual complaints, pass the proportionality test at the Strasbourg Court. As reminder of the elements considered by the Court in adjudicating cases concerning secret surveillance, some excerpts from the Court's landmark decisions on this issue are provided in section III.

---

18 Protecting the Right to Privacy in the Fight against Terrorism, CommDH/Issue Paper (2008) 3, p. 16.

19 https://www.amnesty.org/en/latest/news/2017/01/eu-orwellian-counter-terrorism-laws-stripping-rights-under-guise-of-defending-them/ [last visited 5 February 2018].

20 https://www.coe.int/hy/web/commissioner/-/the-commissioner-addresses-the-french-senate-on-surveillance-bill [last visited 5 February 2018].

21 Supra note 20.

## III. Protection of privacy rights while countering terrorism in the jurisprudence of the ECtHR

In general, the ECtHR has repeatedly stressed that parties have a certain margin of appreciation in restricting privacy rights in countering terrorism. However, they do not enjoy unlimited discretion to subject persons within their jurisdiction to secret surveillance. Powers of secret surveillance of citizens are tolerable only in so far as they are strictly necessary for safeguarding the democratic institutions.[22] Consequently, the existence of adequate and effective guarantees against abuses of the State's strategic monitoring powers makes an application inadmissible for being manifestly ill-founded.[23]

The powers of secret surveillance of citizens, characteristic as they are for the police state, are tolerable under the Convention only to the extent strictly necessary for safeguarding the democratic institutions. Noting, however, that democratic societies nowadays find themselves threatened by highly sophisticated forms of espionage and by terrorism, with the result that the State must be able, in order to effectively counter such threats, to undertake the secret surveillance of subversive elements operating within its jurisdiction, the Court considered that the existence of some legislation granting powers of secret surveillance over the mail, post, and telecommunications was, under exceptional conditions, necessary in a democratic society in the interests of national security and/or for the prevention of disorder or crime.[24]

Domestic legislation should be of "sufficient clarity, to provide adequate protection against abuse of power, the scope or manner of exercise of the very wide discretion conferred on the authorities to intercept and examine external communications."[25] In this regard, the Court found no violation in a case where there was no evidence of any significant shortcomings in the application and operation of the surveillance regime regarding the clarity of the procedures for the authorization and processing of interception warrants as well as the processing, communicating, and destruction of data collected.[26] The legislation on secret surveillance must have adequate and effective guarantees against arbitrariness and the risk of abuse inherent in any system of secret surveillance. This is of special importance in countries where the secret service and the police have direct access to telecommunications. These guarantees concern the threshold for ordering and conducting the measure, its duration, supervision of the interception, available effective remedies, etc. Rem-

22 *Weber and Saravia v. Germany* (ECtHR 2006), Mass Surveillance, European Court of Human Rights, 2017, p. 2.

23 *Ibid.*

24 *Klass and others v. Germany* (ECtHR 1978), *ibid.* p. 1.

25 *Liberty and Others v. the United Kingdom* (ECtHR 2008), *ibid.* p. 2.

26 *Kennedy v. the United Kingdom* (ECtHR 2010), *ibid.*

edies would not be considered as available if they were only available to persons able to submit proof of interception and that obtaining such proof was impossible in the absence of any notification system or possibility of access to information about an interception.[27]

In *Szabó and Vissy v. Hungary*,[28] the issue before the Court was whether the legislation that allows the executive to warrant secret intelligence gathering without the possibility to challenge such decision before an independent authority violates Article 8 of the Convention. In 2010, the Hungarian Parliament adopted Act no. CXLVII that defines combating terrorism as one of the tasks of the police. Within the force, a specific Anti-Terrorism Task Force (TEK) was established as of 1 January 2011. Its competence is defined in section 7/E of Act no. XXXIV of 1994 on the Police, as amended by Act no. CCVII of 2011 (the Police Act).[29] In case of secret surveillance linked to the investigation of certain specific crimes, the decision issued by the executive is subject to judicial authorization, which is not the case for secret surveillance within the framework of intelligence gathering for national security (in order to prevent terrorist acts or in the interests of Hungary's national security or to rescue Hungarian citizens from capture abroad in war zones or in the context of terrorist acts). Measures of secret surveillance can be ordered only if the necessary intelligence cannot be obtained in any other way (subsidiarity). These measures are valid for 90 days, which can be prolonged for another 90-day period by the minister, who has no right to know about the results of the ongoing surveillance when called on to decide on its prolongation. Once the surveillance is terminated, the law imposes no specific obligation on the authorities to destroy any irrelevant intelligence obtained.[30]

The applicants, two Hungarian NGO activists, were not personally subjected to the measures of secret surveillance, but they claimed in the constitutional complaint that the sweeping prerogatives under section 7/E (3) infringed their constitutional right to privacy.[31] They challenged the fact that the threshold for ordering the measure is not of sufficient clarity as well as the fact that it can be ordered by the executive without detailed reasoning and without obligation to inform persons subjected to the measure. In addition, the applicants pointed out that section 7/E (3) violates privacy rights because there is no guarantee of proper handling of collected but irrelevant information (unlike in cases of secret surveillance ordered on suspicion that a crime has been committed, where such information must be destroyed within eight days).

---

27 *Zakharov v. Russia* (ECtHR 2015), *ibid.* p. 3.

28 Supra note 12.

29 *Ibid.* § 8.

30 *Ibid.* § 12.

31 *Ibid.* § 13.

The Constitutional Court ruled that most of the complaints are unfounded because the scope of national security-related tasks was much broader than the scope of the tasks related to the investigation of a particular crime. However, the Court supported the applicants' claim that the decision of the minister ordering secret intelligence gathering had to be supported by reasons.[32]

On admissibility issues and applicants' alleged victim status, the ECtHR pointed out that an individual may claim to be a victim on account of the mere existence of legislation permitting secret surveillance, even if he or she cannot point to any concrete measures specifically affecting him or her.[33] This position was supported by ECtHR findings in *Klass and Others v. Germany* that was consistently followed through the case law of the Court. Therefore, the application was found admissible.

Before proceeding to its own assessment, the Court in the preliminaries referred to the 2013 Report of the United Nations Special Rapporteur on the promotion and protection of the right to freedom of opinion and expression who held that legal frameworks must ensure that communication surveillance measures:

(a) are prescribed by law, meeting a standard of clarity and precision that is sufficient to ensure that individuals have advance notice of and can foresee their application;

(b) are strictly and demonstrably necessary to achieve a legitimate aim; and

(c) adhere to the principle of proportionality and are not employed when less invasive techniques are available or have not yet been exhausted.[34]

The Report also underlined that individuals should have a legal right to be notified that they have been subjected to communications surveillance or that their communications data has been accessed by the State. Recognizing that advance or concurrent notification might jeopardize the effectiveness of the surveillance, individuals should nevertheless be notified once surveillance has been completed and have the possibility to seek redress in respect of the use of communications surveillance measures in their aftermath.

As to the merits of the case, while recognizing that parties enjoy a certain margin of appreciation in choosing the means for achieving the legitimate aim of protecting national security, ECtHR stressed that this margin is subject to European supervision embracing both legislation and decisions applying it. In view of the risk that a system of secret surveillance set up to protect national security may undermine or even destroy democracy under the cloak of defending it, the Court must be satisfied that there are adequate and effective guarantees against abuse. The assessment depends on all the circumstances of the case, such as the nature, scope,

---

32 *Ibid.* § 14.

33 *Ibid.* § 33.

34 *Ibid.* § 24.

and duration of the possible measures, the grounds required for ordering them, the authorities competent to authorize, carry out, and supervise them, and the kind of remedy provided by the national law.[35]

As to the lack of clarity of the legislation, the Court concluded that the relevant section allows authorities to subject to secret surveillance virtually any person in Hungary.[36] Regarding the strict necessity and proportionality test, the Court emphasized that there is no legal safeguard requiring TEK to produce supportive materials or, in particular, a sufficient factual basis for the application of secret intelligence gathering measures that would enable to evaluate the necessity of the proposed measure - and this on the basis of an individual suspicion regarding the target person. In a view expressed by the Court, the requirement "necessary in a democratic society" must be interpreted in this context as requiring "strict necessity" in two aspects. A measure of secret surveillance can be found as being in compliance with the Convention only if it is strictly necessary, as a general consideration, for the safeguarding of the democratic institutions and, moreover, if it is strictly necessary, as a particular consideration, for the obtaining of vital intelligence in an individual operation. In the Court's view, any measure of secret surveillance that does not correspond to these criteria will be prone to abuse by the authorities with formidable technologies at their disposal.[37] The Court also found that the provision on the duration of surveillance measures lacks sufficient clarity because it is not clear from the wording of the law – especially in the absence of judicial interpretation – if such a renewal of the surveillance warrant is possible only once or repeatedly, which is another element prone to abuse.[38]

The central issue in this case was the absence of the *ex post facto* review of the surveillance order by the independent authority. In this regard, the Court recalls that the rule of law implies, *inter alia*, that an interference by the executive authorities with an individual's rights should be subject to an effective control, which should normally be assured by the judiciary, at least in the last resort, judicial control offering the best guarantees of independence, impartiality, and a proper procedure. For the Court, supervision by a politically responsible member of the executive, such as the Minister of Justice, does not provide the necessary guarantees.[39] The Court also found that lack of subsequent notification of surveillance measures to those who were subjected to them amounts to a violation of privacy rights.[40]

Overall, the Court concluded that the challenged section of Hungarian legislation does not provide safeguards sufficiently precise, effective, and comprehensive on

35 *Ibid.* § 57.
36 *Ibid.* § 66.
37 *Ibid.* § 73.
38 *Ibid.* § 74.
39 *Ibid.* § 77.
40 *Ibid.* §§ 86–88.

the ordering, execution, and potential redressing of surveillance measures. Given that the scope of the measures could include virtually anyone, that the ordering is taking place entirely within the realm of the executive and without an assessment of strict necessity, that new technologies enable the Government to intercept masses of data easily concerning even persons outside the original range of operation, and given the absence of any effective remedial measures, let alone judicial ones, the Court concluded that there has been a violation of Article 8 of the Convention.[41]

## IV. Conclusion

In February 2003, *Osama Moustafa Hassan Nasr*, known as *Abu Omar*, an Egyptian imam who resided in Italy, was apprehended, as suspected terrorist, without a court issued warrant, by the Italian police in Milan. Under the secret rendition program, he was first transferred to the airbase in Aviano and then to Ramstein in Germany. From there he was taken by the CIA operatives to Egypt where he was, as suspected terrorist, kept in custody without charges, subjected to torture, and then released after four years.[42] This operation was considered illegal by the Italian criminal justice system. As a response, more than 20 persons, mostly CIA operatives and one air force officer as well as two Italian intelligence officers, were prosecuted and sentenced to prison terms. Some of the suspects were released on the grounds of diplomatic immunity. During the trial that took place in the absence of most of the defendants, the Italian Constitutional Court ruled that much of the evidence gathered during the trial was protected under Italy's official secrecy laws and could therefore not be used in court.[43] However, the trial continued and defendants were found guilty as charged based on the available evidence. Two convicts were subsequently pardoned by the Italian president, one in 2015 and one in 2017, just before being transferred from Portugal to Italy to serve the sentence, upon the granted European Arrest Warrant (EAW).[44] ECtHR found Italy responsible for a number of human rights violations in the *Abu Omar* case, including prohibition of torture.[45] The Court found that the Italian authorities were aware that the applicant had been a victim of an extraordinary rendition operation that had begun

41 *Ibid.* § 89.

42 https://www.theguardian.com/world/2009/nov/04/cia-guilty-rendition-abu-omar [last visited 5 February 2018].

43 *Ibid.*

44 https://www.npr.org/sections/thetwo-way/2017/03/01/517916196/italy-grants-partial-clemency-to-ex-cia-officer-over-extraordinary-rendition [last visited 5 February 2018].

45 http://www.telegraph.co.uk/news/worldnews/europe/italy/12170557/Italy-condemned-for-role-in-CIA-rendition-plot.html [last visited 5 February 2018].

with his abduction in Italy and had continued with his transfer abroad.[46] The Court also held that the legitimate principle of "state secrecy" had clearly been applied by the Italian executive in order to ensure that those responsible did not have to answer for their actions. The investigation and trial had not led to the punishment of those responsible, who had therefore ultimately been granted impunity.[47]

This case is a very illustrative example of the dynamic interplay between the executive and other branches of government, including the judiciary, in setting the limits of state action in the fight against terrorism. As was shown in this paper, the ECtHR in its jurisprudence, including the most recent one, established standards and safeguards for the protection of human rights while countering terrorism. These standards concerning privacy rights provide protection against the arbitrary secret surveillance of citizens by the government. ECtHR case law strictly prohibits secret surveillance in the form of the so-called "fishing expedition" or undertaking the operation without having, in advance, at least circumstantial evidence as a minimum threshold. Other criteria determining the threshold for undertaking legitimate and proportionate measures restricting the privacy of the citizens in countering terrorism can be found, in addition to the ECtHR jurisprudence, in the Report on the Democratic oversight of the Security Services adopted by the *Venice Commission* in 2007 at its 71st Plenary Session (and updated in 2015) that was extensively quoted in the ECtHR judgement *Szabó and Vissy v. Hungary* analyzed in section III. of this paper.[48] The *Venice Commission* concluded that, for a variety of reasons, there can be tension as regards national security policy, not only between the governing party and the political opposition in a State, but also constitutional tension between the executive and the legislative power, tension within a government (especially a coalition government), and tension between political masters and the staff of security intelligence agencies.[49] To address these tensions and secure protection from arbitrariness, several mechanisms should be put in place: internal and governmental controls as part of overall accountability systems, parliamentary accountability, judicial review and authorization, accountability to expert bodies, and complaint mechanisms.[50]

Threat and danger of terrorism is clear and present in Europe nowadays. States have rights but also responsibilities to protect those under their jurisdiction from this imminent threat. However, restrictions of the most fundamental human rights and liberties including right to privacy must be in accordance with three important

---

46 *Nasri and Ghali v. Italy* (ECtHR 2016), Secret detention sites, European Court of Human Rights, 2016, p. 2.

47 *Ibid.*

48 Report on the Democratic oversight of the Security Services, Venice Commission, 2007.

49 *Ibid.* § 82.

50 Supra note 12, pp. 16–18.

principles enshrined in the ECHR and in the ECtHR case law – legitimacy, necessity, and proportionality. Therefore, the governments, legislators, and constitutional courts in European countries have no other option but to follow the standards set by European human rights institutions and mechanisms explored in this paper. Otherwise, it is very likely that criticism from Strasbourg will tighten.

## Bibliography

### Books and articles

*Becker*, *Steven*, Closing the Door on Justice: Secret Evidence and the Lack of Transparency in Court Proceedings in the Wake of the "War on Terrorism". In: Steven Becker/ Davor Derenčinović (eds.), International Terrorism: the Future Unchained? Zagreb 2008, pp. 1–23.

*Derenčinović*, *Davor*, International Terrorism and Human Rights – Some Remarks on Rights and Limits of State Actions against Terrorism. In: Glynn Rimmington (ed.), Empire or Interdependence Conference. Wichita 2005, pp. 15–38.

*Goldman*, *Robert/Tittemore*, *Brian*, Unprivileged Combatants and the Hostilities in Afghanistan: Their Status and Rights Under International Humanitarian and Human Rights Law. The American Society of International Law, Task Force on Terrorism. Washington D.C. 2002, pp. 1–57.

*Murakami Wood*, *David*, The Surveillance Society. 6 European Journal of Criminology 179–194 (2009).

*Pratt*, *John*, This Is Not a Prison – Foucault, the Panopticon and Pentonville. 2 Social & Legal Studies 373–395 (1993).

*Scharf*, *Michael*, The Torture Lawyers. 20 Duke Journal of Comparative & International Law 389–412 (2010).

*Sorell*, *Tom*, Preventive Policing, Surveillance, and European Counter-Terrorism. 30 Criminal Justice Ethics 1–22 (2011).

### Reports

Guide on Article 8 of the European Convention on Human Rights, European Court of Human Rights, 2017.

Mass Surveillance, European Court of Human Rights, 2017.

Protecting the Right to Privacy in the Fight against Terrorism, CommDH/Issue Paper (2008) 3.

Report on the Democratic oversight of the Security Services, Venice Commission, 2007.

Secret detention sites, European Court of Human Rights, 2016.

### Case law

*Kennedy v. the United Kingdom* (ECtHR 2010).

*Klass and others v. Germany* (ECtHR 1978).

*Liberty and Others v. the United Kingdom* (ECtHR 2008).

*Murray v. the United Kingdom* (ECtHR 1994).

*Nasri and Ghali v. Italy* (ECtHR 2016).

*Sabanchiyeva and Others v. Russia* (ECtHR 2013).

*Segerstedt-Wiberg and Others v. Sweden* (ECtHR 2006).

*Szabó and Vissy v. Hungary* (ECtHR 2016).

*Uzun v. Germany* (ECtHR 2010).

*Weber and Saravia v. Germany* (ECtHR 2006).

*Zakharov v. Russia* (ECtHR 2015).

### Internet

https://timeline.com/handmaids-tale-dystopian-relevant-6ffbb4c839be

https://www.simplypsychology.org/maslow.html

https://www.amnesty.org/en/latest/news/2017/01/eu-orwellian-counter-terrorism-laws-stripping-rights-under-guise-of-defending-them/

https://www.coe.int/hy/web/commissioner/-/the-commissioner-addresses-the-french-senate-on-surveillance-bill

https://www.theguardian.com/world/2009/nov/04/cia-guilty-rendition-abu-omar

https://www.npr.org/sections/thetwo-way/2017/03/01/517916196/italy-grants-partial-clemency-to-ex-cia-officer-over-extraordinary-rendition

http://www.telegraph.co.uk/news/worldnews/europe/italy/12170557/Italy-condemned-for-role-in-CIA-rendition-plot.html

# Establishing ICC Jurisdiction Over Crimes Committed by ISIL – Did Humanity Fail the Countries of Syria and Iraq?

*Maja Munivrana Vajda** and *Sunčana Roksandić Vidlička**

## I. International community and the response to atrocities committed by ISIS

Core crimes are the gravest of all international crimes, *largo sensu*, "in terms of their impact on humankind."[1] They threaten the most fundamental values of the international community: international peace, security, and the well-being of the world. They are typically expressions of states' disregard for these values, which is why they fall within the jurisdiction of the International Criminal Court (hereinafter: ICC), based on the complementarity principle. Substantive justice, as such, demands that the acts that deeply harm society and all its members should be punished.[2] However, as *Schabas* pointed out in 2013,

> [i]nternational criminal justice has grown cyclically over the past century, with periods of intense developments punctuated by rather long stretches of dormancy. It is legitimate to ask whether we are now in the downturn of yet another cycle. The International Criminal Court has failed to live up to its own expectations. But the real challenge is the declining enthusiasm for the Court in Africa. Inevitably, the banality of international justice will also promote inertia and disaffection in civil society, whose momentum has been so important to international criminal justice over the past two decades. Right now international justice needs more Pinochets and fewer Habrés.[3]

According to many reports that deal with the so-called Islamic State in Iraq and the Levant (hereinafter: ISIL) phenomenon,[4] ISIL is a terrorist organization described in 2015 as an organization "with a net worth of over $2,000,000,000 [which] fund[ed] its reign of terror through a host of criminal activities, including smuggling stolen oil, looting banks, imposing taxes, kidnapping for ransom, engag-

---

* *Maja Munivrana Vajda*, Associate professor, Department of criminal law, University of Zagreb, Faculty of Law.

* *Sunčana Roksandić Vidlička*, Assistant professor, Department of criminal law, University of Zagreb, Faculty of Law.

1 The Preamble of the Rome Statute of the International Criminal Court.

2 *Roksandić Vidlička*, Prosecuting Serious Economic Crimes as International Crimes, p. 208.

3 *Schabas*, 11 Journal of International Criminal Justice 545 (2013).

4 Also referred to in this text as ISIS, IS, or Da'esh.

ing in protection rackets, selling stolen artifacts, extorting funds, exploiting natural resources, and controlling crops. As a result of these illicit and unprosecuted activities, the Islamic State is the most "financially endowed terrorist organization in history."[5] Furthermore, ISIL was estimated to have between 9,000 to 200,000 members, including more than 30,000 foreign fighters from over 100 different countries.[6]

In order to investigate this organization and its crimes, the Independent International Commission of Inquiry on the Syrian Arab Republic was established on 22 August 2011 by the United Nation's Human Rights Council through Resolution S-17/1. Its mandate is to investigate all alleged violations of international human rights law since March 2011 in the Syrian Arab Republic.[7] UN Resolution 2249 of 2015[8] stated that ISIL's violent extremist ideology, its terrorist acts, its continued gross systematic and widespread attacks directed against civilians, abuses of human rights and violations of international humanitarian law, its eradication of cultural heritage and trafficking of cultural property, its recruitment and training of foreign terrorist fighters whose threat affects all regions and Member States, constituted a global and unprecedented threat to international peace and security.[9] This Resolution also condemned "in the strongest terms the continued gross, systematic and widespread abuses of human rights and violations of humanitarian law, as well as barbaric acts of destruction and looting of cultural heritage carried out by ISIL also known as Da'esh."[10]

Many other reports continuously rendered by different UN bodies describe the atrocities committed, such as the Sixth Report of the Secretary General on the threat posed by ISIL to international peace and security and the range of the United Nations efforts in support of Member States in countering the threat;[11] the Report of the Office of the United Nations High Commissioner for Human Rights on the human rights situation in Iraq in the light of abuses committed by the so-called Islamic State in Iraq and the Levant and associated groups;[12] and the latest Report of

---

5 *Schemenauer*, Civilian Research Project: Using the Rule of Law to Combat the Islamic State, p. 2, citing *Pagliery*, Inside the $2 billion ISIS war machine, CNN Money, 11 December 2015, http://money.cnn.com/2015/12/06/news/isis-funding/index.html.

6 *Ibid.*

7 The Resolution was adopted at its 17th Special Session.

8 UN Security Council, S/RES/2249 (2015), 20 November 2015.

9 Emphasized also in the Civilian Research Project: Using the Rule of Law to Combat the Islamic State, by lieutenant colonel *Schemenauer*, US Army, 29 December 2017. http://www.jcs.mil/Portals/36/Documents/Doctrine/Education/jpme_papers/schemenaur_s.pdf?ver=2017-12-29-142155-737, p. 1. Also see the in-depth analysis, The financing of the 'Islamic State' in Iraq and Syria (ISIS), requested by the European Parliament's Committee on Foreign Affairs, 11 September 2017.

10 Para. 3 of the Resolution.

11 UN Security Council, S/2018/80, 31 January 2018.

12 Human Rights Council, 28th session, A/HRC/28/18, 13 March 2015.

the Independent International Commission of inquiry on the Syrian Arab Republic.[13] In the last mentioned Report, the plight of displaced persons was also emphasized, a situation which, after seven years of war, affects more than 5.5 million refugees who have fled the country and more than 6.5 million internally displaced civilians subsisting inside the Syrian Arab Republic.[14] The described situation clearly represents a global security issue, not only for Syria but for other countries as well, as also recognized in the 2016 EU Global Strategy for the European Union's foreign and security policy.[15]

Furthermore, the UN Independent International Commission of Inquiry claimed in 2016 that the violence committed by ISIL against the Yazidis constituted a case of genocide[16] as defined by the 1948 Convention on the Prevention and Punishment of the Crime of Genocide. Accordingly, the Commission emphasized in 2017 that the international community should recognize that ISIL was committing the crime of genocide against the Yazidis and take steps to refer the situation to justice, including to the ICC or an *ad hoc* tribunal with relevant geographic and temporal jurisdiction. It also called on states to dedicate resources to bringing cases before national courts, whether under the framework of universal jurisdiction or otherwise.[17]

All of the above raises several important questions. First, was it then and is it now reasonable to expect the ICC to establish its jurisdiction over genocide or some of the other above-mentioned crimes committed by ISIL or by other groups involved in the conflict in Syria and Iraq? Would the purpose of the ICC be confirmed by responding to some of the atrocities committed by ISIL or other actors in the situations of Syria and Iraq? Could one still claim that if the ICC fails to prosecute crimes committed by ISIL but other national, *ad hoc*, or hybrid courts do so, that international criminal justice is in a downturn? In 2017, by the terms of UN Resolution 2379 (2017], adopted unanimously, an independent investigative team was established to support domestic efforts to hold ISIL accountable for its actions in Iraq. The team collects, preserves, and stores evidence of acts that may amount to war crimes, crimes against humanity, and genocide committed by the terrorist group in Iraq, and supports domestic efforts to hold ISIL accountable for its actions in Iraq.[18]

---

13 Human Rights Council, 38th session, A/HRC/39/65, 10–28 September 2018.

14 *Ibid.*

15 EU Global Strategy, From Shared Vision to Common Action: Implementing the EU Global Strategy Year 1, A Global Strategy EU Global Strategy for the European Union's Foreign and Security Policy, 2017, p. 12.

16 They came to destroy: ISIS Crimes Against the Yazidis, 16 June 2016, A/HRC/32/CRP.2.

17 E.g. *Cetorelli/Sasson/Shabila/Burnham*, ISIS' Yazidi Genocide, Demographic Evidence of the Killings and Kidnappings, Foreign Affairs, 8 June 2017, https://www.foreignaffairs.com/articles/syria/2017-06-08/isis-yazidi-genocide [last visited 1 January 2019].

18 However, the prosecutions that are now taking place in Iraq are already under heavy criticism. *Chulov/al-Faour*, They deserve no mercy: Iraq deals briskly with accused "women

The UN's emphasis on national prosecutions may be seen as a response to the refusal by the ICC's Office of the Prosecutor (hereinafter: OTP) to open a preliminary examination over the crimes of ISIL. *Hansel* emphasized that, according to the OTP itself and many scholars, a key goal of preliminary examinations involves "the ending of impunity, by encouraging genuine national proceedings."[19] Yet, the OTP did not even open a preliminary examination. In April 2015, Chief ICC Prosecutor *Bensouda* publicly addressed the question of exercising jurisdiction over alleged crimes by ISIL, concluding that "the jurisdictional basis for opening a preliminary examination into [alleged crimes] [was] too narrow at this stage."[20]

This statement might have come as a surprise, especially taking into the account that just one month prior, the Report of the Office of the UN High Commissioner for Human Rights on the human rights situation in Iraq in the light of abuses committed by the so-called Islamic State in Iraq and the Levant and associated groups of 2015[21] had recommended the Human Rights Council to urge the Security Council to remain seized of and to address, in the strongest terms, information that points to genocide, crimes against humanity, and war crimes, and to call on the Security Council to consider referring the situation in Iraq to the ICC.[22] Alternatively, it was recommended to Iraq to accept ICC jurisdiction over the current situation under Article 12 (3).[23] The Report had further recommended the government of Iraq to ensure that all alleged crimes be investigated in line with international human rights standards, that perpetrators be brought to justice, and that Iraq become a party to the Rome Statute of the ICC and ensure that the international crimes defined in the Rome Statute be criminalized under its domestic law.

This back and forth exchange between different international actors resembles a ping pong game. One might initially conclude that *Bensouda* in her statement of 2015 turned a blind eye to the function of preliminary examinations.[24] However, in her statements she also pointed out that "the decision of non-Party States and the United Nations Security Council to confer jurisdiction on the ICC is, however,

of Isis," A Baghdad court has sentenced more than 40 foreign women to death after 10-minute hearings, 22 May 2018, The Guardian, https://www.theguardian.com/world/2018/may/22/they-deserve-no-mercy-iraq-deals-briskly-with-accused-women-of-isis [last visited 1 January 2019].

19 *Hansen*, 17 Transitional Justice Institute Research Paper (2017), available at SSRN: https://ssrn.com/abstract=2939139 [last visited 1 January 2019].

20 ICC, "Statement of the Prosecutor of the International Criminal Court, Fatou Bensouda, on the Alleged Crimes Committed by ISIS" (Press Release, 8 April 2015), https://www.icc-cpi.int/Pages/item.aspx?name=otp-stat-08-04-2015-1 [last visited 1 January 2019].

21 Human Rights Council, 28th session, A/HRC/28/18, 13 March 2015.

22 Para. 79 of the Report of the Human Rights Council.

23 *Ibid.*

24 Similarly, *Zakerhossein*, 16 International Criminal Law Review 624 (2016).

wholly independent of the Court." [25] This led some to believe that "this statement was an attempt by the Prosecutor to pressure States and, especially, the Security Council, to assume their responsibility and confer jurisdiction on the ICC over this situation."[26] It is common knowledge that the Security Council has not referred the situation to the ICC to this day.

Did humanity fail the test? As the Prosecutor noted in her statement, the atrocities allegedly committed by ISIL undoubtedly constitute serious crimes of concern to the international community and a threat to the peace, security, and well-being of the region and the world. They also occurred in the context of other crimes allegedly committed by other warring factions in Syria and Iraq. However, Syria and Iraq are not parties to the ICC. Although the ICC has no territorial jurisdiction over crimes committed on Syrian and Iraqi soil, it could have personal jurisdiction. The information gathered indicates that several thousand foreign fighters have joined the ranks of ISIS, including a significant number of State Party nationals from, *inter alia*, Tunisia, Jordan, France, the United Kingdom, Germany, Belgium, the Netherlands, and Australia. Some of these individuals, as emphasized by *Bensouda*, may have been involved in the commission of crimes against humanity and war crimes and a few have even publicized their heinous acts through social media. However, preliminary information also indicates that "ISIL is primarily led by nationals of Iraq and Syria."[27] Is under these circumstances personal jurisdiction enough to trigger ICC jurisdiction *proprio motu* in the absence of a state or the Security Council referral? As underlined by *Bergsmo/Pejić*, the exercise of discretion to initiate an investigation *proprio motu* must be guided by the principle reflected in the ICC Statute's emphasis on "the most serious crimes of international concern."[28] Consequently, "it is the seriousness of the alleged crimes that must lead the Prosecutor's exercise of discretion under Article 15(1) of the ICC Statute."[29]

The next part of this paper will deal with the legal requirements for opening a preliminary examination, taking into account the political context, in order to as-

---

[25] ICC, Statement of the Prosecutor of the International Criminal Court, Fatou Bensouda, on the Alleged Crimes Committed by ISIS (Press Release, 8 April 2015), https://www.icc-cpi.int/Pages/item.aspx?name=otp-stat-08-04-2015-1 [last visited 1 January 2019].

[26] *Galand* refers here to *Sander*, The Situation Concerning the Islamic State: Carte Blanche for the ICC if the Security Council Refers?, 27 May 2015, https://www.ejiltalk.org/the-situation-concerning-isis-carte-blanche-for-the-icc-if-the-security-council-refers/ [last visited 1 January 2019].

[27] ICC, Statement of the Prosecutor of the International Criminal Court, Fatou Bensouda, on the Alleged Crimes Committed by ISIS (Press Release, 8 April 2015), https://www.icc-cpi.int/Pages/item.aspx?name=otp-stat-08-04-2015-1 [last visited 1 January 2019].

[28] *Bergsmo/Pejić*, in: Triffterer (ed.), The Commentary on the Rome Statute, 2008, p. 586.

[29] *Ibid.*

sess whether passivity by the ICC can be seen as a failure of international justice and what should be done about it.

## II. Was ISIL manifestly outside the scope of a preliminary examination?

As already mentioned above, despite the abundance of UN reports alleging commission of core crimes, Chief ICC Prosecutor *Bensouda* concluded that there was no basis for even opening a preliminary examination. The ICC Statute does not elaborate in detail on the purpose or formal requirements for opening a preliminary examination. In fact, in the entire ICC Statute there is only one reference to the concept of "preliminary examination"; Article 15(6) mentions preliminary examination in the context of the so-called *proprio motu* investigation of the Prosecutor on the basis of information on crimes within the jurisdiction.[30] The context makes it clear that the only purpose of the preliminary examination is to establish whether there is a reasonable basis for initiating a formal investigation. "[A] preliminary examination is an analysis of information made available by multiple reliable sources, and not an investigation in which active measures are undertaken to obtain primary evidence to determine the truth."[31] Yet, to analyze the seriousness of the information received, the Prosecutor may seek additional information from states, organs of the United Nations, intergovernmental or non-governmental organizations, or other reliable sources (Art. 15(2)). "Such communications shall be analyzed in combination with open source information such as reports from the United Nations, nongovernmental organizations and other reliable sources for corroboration purposes" and should be considered "in context and not in isolation."[32] It seems that all the UN reports were done in vain, at least in the sense of invoking international criminal law mechanisms.

Despite the fact that preliminary examinations are mentioned solely in the context of *proprio motu* investigations by the Prosecutor, preliminary examinations can also be conducted on referral by a State Party[33] or even by the Security Coun-

---

30 It points to Article 15(1) and (2) of the Rome Statute.

31 OTP, Situation on Registered Vessels of the Union of the Comoros, the Hellenic Republic and the Kingdom of Cambodia, Public Redacted Version of Prosecution Response to the Application for Review of its Determination under article 53(1)(b) of the Rome Statute, 30 March 2015, ICC-01/13-14- Red, p. 12, para. 18.

32 OTP, Situation on Registered Vessels of the Union of the Comoros, the Hellenic Republic and the Kingdom of Cambodia, Notice of Appeal of "Decision on the request of the Union of the Comoros to review the Prosecutor's decision not to initiate an investigation" (ICC-01/13-34), 27 July 2015, ICC01/13-35, p. 9, para. 20.

33 Or a declaration accepting the exercise of jurisdiction by the Court by a State which is not a Party to the Statute, see Article 12(3) of the Rome Statute.

cil, and this has been concluded by the OTP itself.[34] In such circumstances the Prosecutor must also evaluate the information available in order to determine whether to proceed with the investigation.

As stated by the OTP in its Policy Paper on Preliminary Examinations, the Prosecutor will conduct a preliminary examination of all situations not "manifestly outside the jurisdiction of the Court."[35] The goal of this phase is to collect all relevant information necessary to reach a decision on whether there is a reasonable basis to proceed with an investigation. If the Office is satisfied that all the criteria established by the Statute for this purpose are met, it has a legal duty to open an investigation into the situation.[36]

What does it mean that a situation is manifestly outside the jurisdiction of the Court? According to Cambridge Dictionary, "manifestly" means "very obviously."[37] If a communication is not clearly outside the jurisdiction of the Court, a preliminary examination should formally be started. In the situation in the Republic of Côte d'Ivoire the OTP emphasized the need to carry out an independent and objective analysis – "the evaluation of sources [follows a] consistent methodology based on criteria such as relevance (usefulness of the information to determine the elements of a possible future case), reliability (refers to the trustworthiness of the provider of the information as such), credibility (refers to the quality of the information in itself, to be evaluated by criteria of immediacy internal consistency and external verification), and completeness (the extent of the source's knowledge or coverage vis-à-vis the whole scope of relevant facts)."[38] Following this line of reasoning, it is difficult to disregard all the reports prepared by the UN and other independent commissions tasked with assessing the potential *ratione materiae* jurisdiction of the ICC.

A preliminary assessment does not guarantee that an investigation will actually be opened. The Policy Paper on Preliminary Examinations stipulates that the purpose of Phase 1 is to "analyze and verify the seriousness of information received, filter out information on crimes that are outside the jurisdiction of the Court and identify those that appear to fall within the jurisdiction of the Court."[39] The preliminary examination is intended to review a plausible hypothesis, to collect information, and to assess at the end of such analysis whether the "reasonable basis" standard prescribed by the Statute for opening an investigation has been met. The only criterion in deciding whether to start a preliminary examination is jurisdiction,

---

34 This has also been highlighted by the OTP itself in the OTP's Policy Paper on Preliminary Examinations, November 2013, para. 4.

35 *Ibid.*, para. 2.

36 *Ibid.*

37 Cambridge Dictionary, https://dictionary.cambridge.org/ [last visited 1 January 2019].

38 See Pre-Trial Chamber III, No.: ICC-02/11, 23 June 2011, para. 24.

39 The OTP, The Policy Paper on Preliminary Examinations, 2013, p. 18, para. 75.

but it is not clear whether the notion of jurisdiction includes only *ratione materiae* jurisdiction, which is clearly present here, or other forms of jurisdiction as well (territorial, personal, and temporal). What is clear is that these other types of jurisdiction must be assessed during the preliminary examination. According to Rule 48 of the Rules of Procedure and Evidence,[40] in determining whether there is a reasonable basis to proceed with an investigation under Article 15, paragraph 3, the Prosecutor must consider the factors set out in Article 53, paragraph 1(a)–(c).[41] Although Article 53 does not specify what is meant by jurisdiction requirement,[42] the OTP Policy Paper on Preliminary Examinations specifies types of jurisdiction that need to be taken into account. This means that the Prosecutor must consider: a) jurisdiction (temporal, material, and either territorial or personal jurisdiction); b) admissibility (complementarity and gravity);[43] and c) the interests of justice.[44]

Considering everything above, the question is, do ISIL crimes manifestly outside the jurisdiction of the ICC not even warrant opening a preliminary investigation? At first glance, they do not. However, one could also conclude the opposite. Would it make sense to open a preliminary examination when subject matter jurisdiction exists but other criteria of Article 53 of the ICC may not be fulfilled? Maybe *Bensouda*'s statement is not that misplaced after all by throwing the ball back to individual states and the Security Council.

## III. Jurisdictional challenges

There are three ways in which the jurisdiction of the ICC can be triggered. According to Article 13 of the ICC Statute, the ICC can exercise jurisdiction (1) when a situation is referred to the Prosecutor by a State Party; (2) when it is referred by the Security Council acting under Chapter VII of the Charter of the United Nations; and (3) when the Prosecutor initiates an investigation on its own accord based on communications from other sources (the so-called *proprio motu* investigations).

40 Official Records of the Assembly of States Parties to the Rome Statute of the International Criminal Court, First session, New York, 3–10 September 2002 (ICC-ASP/1/3and Corr.1), part II.A, as amended.

41 Rule 48 of the Rules of Procedure and Evidence. This rule implicitly also ties preliminary examinations with *proprio motu* trigger mechanism as it refers to Article 15 (3) ICC Statute.

42 Article 53 (1) and (1a) ICC Statute.

43 At this point, where there is still no specific case, complementarity involves an examination of the existence of relevant national proceedings in relation to the potential cases being considered for investigation by the Office. See the OTP's Policy Paper on Preliminary Examinations, November 2013, para. 8.

44 OTP Policy Paper on Preliminary Examinations, November 2013.

In cases of state referral and *proprio motu* investigations, jurisdiction is limited to states on the territory of which the conduct in question occurred (principle of territoriality) or states of which the person accused of the crime is a national (principle of nationality).[45] Other jurisdictional principles can serve to establish ICC jurisdiction only when the situation is referred by the Security Council.

## A. Territorial jurisdiction

The first basis for establishing jurisdiction is the territoriality principle. When it comes to ISIL, establishing jurisdiction on this ground may appear to be difficult at first glance, since ISIL actions are predominantly centered in Syria, Iraq, and Libya– none of which are parties to the ICC Statute. Yet, this may have changed with the first terrorist attacks in the EU. As *Ambos* noted, "regarding the Paris attacks, the requirement of a sufficient territorial link to an ICC State Party – given the massive scale of the attack and the combination of acts and effects on French territory – should be satisfied."[46] The same can probably be said about the attacks in Brussels, Nice, etc. All of these ISIL-related attacks may not only give rise to investigations initiated *proprio motu* (Articles 13 (c), 15 Rome Statute) by the ICC prosecutor but also to investigations initiated on the basis of state referrals, as the affected states are State Parties to the ICC Statute (Articles 13 (a), 14 Rome Statute). Yet, in addition to the issue of legal qualification of these attacks as crimes against humanity,[47] the question most likely to arise in these cases is this: Would the investigation just be limited to the ISIL terrorist attacks committed on the territory of a particular state? If so, would these events reach the threshold criteria for admissibility prescribed in Article 53, namely complementarity and gravity? Still, if the only requirement for a preliminary examination were that of jurisdiction, this would be a non-issue at this stage, i.e., something to be considered only later in the context of a formal investigation.

## B. Personal jurisdiction

The principle of active personality is another possibility for establishing jurisdiction. The ICC may exercise personal jurisdiction over alleged perpetrators who are nationals of a State Party even in the absence of territorial jurisdiction. This is precisely the basis on which the ICC Prosecutor reviewed communications received

---

[45] Article 13 ICC Statute.

[46] *Ambos*, The new enemy of mankind: The Jurisdiction of the ICC over members of "Islamic State," published on 26 November 2015, https://www.ejiltalk.org/the-new-enemy-of-mankind-the-jurisdiction-of-the-icc-over-members-of-islamic-state/ [last visited 1 January 2019].

[47] *Ibid.*

alleging crimes committed by ISIL. In doing so, the Prosecutor explicitly emphasized the need "to focus on those most responsible for mass crimes"[48] when assessing the prospect of exercising personal jurisdiction over nationals of States Parties within the ranks of this organization. Information gathered by many reports indicates that several thousand foreign fighters have joined the ranks of ISIL, including a significant number of State Party nationals. Although some of them were very likely involved in the commission of crimes against humanity and war crimes, the ICC Prosecutor stated that available information indicated that ISIL was primarily led by nationals of Iraq and Syria.[49] Thus, *Bensouda* assessed the prospects of investigating and prosecuting those most responsible within the leadership of ISIL as limited. However, she disregarded the OTP's explicit Strategic Plan, which allows the OTP to expand its general prosecutorial strategy in appropriate cases to encompass mid- or high-level perpetrators, or even particularly notorious low-level perpetrators, with a view to building up cases to reach those most responsible for the most serious crimes.[50] This has since been reaffirmed in the new Policy on Case Selection and Prioritization, which similarly recognizes that in some cases the focus may shift to a limited number of mid-level perpetrators in order to ultimately build the evidentiary foundations for case(s) against those most responsible.[51]

Although Regulation 34(1) of the Regulations of the Office and the Prosecution's Strategic Plan direct the OTP to conduct its investigations towards ensuring that charges are brought against those persons who appear to be the most responsible for the identified crimes, in order to perform an objective and open-ended investigation, the OTP may often have to focus first on the crime base in order to identify the organizations (including their structures) and individuals responsible for their commission. That may entail the need to consider the investigation and prosecution of lower-level perpetrators to build the evidentiary foundations for case(s) against those most responsible.[52] Additionally, the OTP may also decide to prosecute lower-level perpetrators whose conduct was particularly grave or notorious.[53]

48 https://www.icc-cpi.int/Pages/item.aspx?name=otp-stat-08-04-2015-1 [last visited 1 January 2019], see also Policy Paper on Preliminary Examinations of November 2013, para. 8.

49 *Ibid.*

50 See ICC Office of the Prosecutor, OTP Strategic Plan (June 2012–2015), para. 22.

51 OTP, Policy Paper on Case Selection and Prioritization, 2016.

52 Critically about this possibility *Stahn*, Why the ICC Should Be Cautious to Use the Islamic State to Get Out of Africa: Part 2, https://www.ejiltalk.org/why-the-icc-should-be-cautious-to-use-the-islamic-state-to-get-out-of-africa-part-2/ [last visited 1 January 2019]. He argues that due to the limited scope of ICC active personality jurisdiction, the OTP might never be able to reach the top of the pyramid, so the "gateway to the most responsible would remain a fiction."

53 OTP Strategic Plan 2016–2018, para. 34, OTP, Policy Paper on Case Selection and Prioritization, 15 September 2016, para. 42.

The statement by the Prosecutor is generally confusing. By pointing out that the members of ISIL who are nationals of State Parties, are so-called low-level perpetrators, she conflated jurisdiction with admissibility (i.e., its gravity prong) and misconstrue the nature of this procedural phase in which individual perpetrators are not yet fully identified. The existence of specific suspects and their roles is assessed later, during the gravity evaluation. Furthermore, in the case of *Prosecutor v. Muthaura, Kenyatta and Ali*, Pre-Trial Chamber II determined that the argument that only cases against principals or direct perpetrators have sufficient gravity to justify action by the Court is legally unfounded.[54] Hence, it seems that the perpetrator's position in the hierarchy may enter into the analysis only later, when assessing the gravity, and even then it should not be determinative. Additionally, it has been argued that the Prosecution should consider information available about the activities of ISIL as a whole even though some of them may have been carried out by nationals of non-State Parties.[55] In situations in which crimes are committed by nationals of different states, of both State Parties and non-State Parties, "to the extent that the Chamber can disentangle the different forms of participation there is no reason why the Court's personal jurisdiction should not apply as a matter of law."[56]

## C. The Security Council referral – a feasible option?

In May 2014 France drafted a resolution referring Syria to the ICC, which was co-sponsored by 65 Member States but vetoed by China and Russia. All other Council members voted in favor of the referral.[57] Lithuania, Chile, and the UK representatives at the UN have continued to push for a Council referral of the situation in Syria to the ICC – but without success. The position of Russia and China on a referral of Syria has not changed.[58] Although this has so far not proven to be a via-

---

[54] ICC-01/09-02/11-338, 19 September 2011, PTCII, para 47. http://www.internationalcrimesdatabase.org/upload/documents/20160111T115040-Ochi%20ICD%20Format.pdf.

[55] ISIL: Nationals of ICC states parties committing genocide and other crimes against the Yazidis. Requesting the commencement of a preliminary examination in the situation involving genocide and other crimes committed against the Yazidis in Sinjar and Nineveh Plains since August 2014, September 2015, p. 38 https://www.freeyezidi.org/wp-content/uploads/Corr-RED-ISIL-commiting-genocide-ag-the-Yazidis.pdf [last visited 1 January 2019].

[56] *Rastan*, in: Stahn (ed.), The Law and Practice of the ICC, 2015, p. 153.

[57] See UN Meetings coverage: Referral of Syria to International Criminal Court Fails as Negative Votes Prevent Security Council from Adopting Draft Resolution, 22 May 2014, S/2014/348, https://www.un.org/press/en/2014/sc11407.doc.htm [last visited 1 January 2019].

[58] *Galand*, The Situation Concerning the Islamic State: Carte Blanche for the ICC if the Security Council Refers?, May 27, 2015, https://www.ejiltalk.org/the-situation-concerning-isis-carte-blanche-for-the-icc-if-the-security-council-refers [last visited 1 January 2019].

ble option for lack of political consensus, one important legal question is how to define the situation that would be referred.[59]

Is it possible to refer to the ICC a worldwide situation that relates to a group? Or must the situation referred be one occurring in a particular geographical location or in a particular state?[60] In other words, should the Security Council refer the situation in Syria and Iraq or perhaps the situation of ISIL as a group? The second option would enable the Prosecutor to charge members of ISIL not only for crimes committed in Syria or in Iraq but also for crimes committed elsewhere (in Libya, Yemen, Tunisia, France). Interestingly, while some existing resolutions of the UN Security Council (e.g., Resolutions 2170 and 2178) or the Human Rights Council (e.g., Resolution S-22/1) explicitly brand ISIL as a target of sanctions, most UN reports are focused on the crimes committed on the territory of Iraq and Syria.

Situations are ordinarily defined by "territorial, temporal and possibly personal parameters."[61] As far as territorial parameters are concerned, reference to a given territory means reference to particular geographical location or a particular state. The two Security Council referrals, of situations in Sudan and Libya, are also territorially focused. As *Schabas* underlined, personal parameters are more problematic – targeting is exactly what the drafters attempted to avoid by using the term situation.[62] Yet, it would not be totally unprecedented; within its preliminary examination on the situation in Nigeria, the OTP examined also the "Situation related to Boko Haram."[63] However, even though this situation was described with the name of a terrorist group, the words "related to" indicate that prosecution could extend to crimes committed by other actors as well. Furthermore, it has been persuasively argued that a one-sided referral of ISIL to the ICC could have a negative impact on the chance to achieve peace in the region as it would send a message to the other groups taking part in mass atrocities that they can continue to do so without fear of international prosecution.[64]

So, even if the Security Council referred the situation of ISIL as a group, it would be up to the ICC to define the situation. In the case of the Security Council referral in the situation of Darfur, the ICC emphasized "that the referring party, when referring a situation to the Court submits that situation to the entire legal

---

59 *Ibid.*

60 Similarly *Galand, ibid.*

61 ICC, Decision on the Prosecution's Application for a Warrant of Arrest against Omar Hassan Ahmad Al Bashir, ICC-02/05-01/09, 4 March 2009, para. 36, https://www.icc-cpi.int/CourtRecords/CR2009_01517.PDF [last visited 1 January 2019].

62 *Schabas*, ICC Commentary, 2010, p. 299.

63 OTP, Situation in Nigeria, Article 5 Report, 2013, p. 21.

64 *Kersten*, The ICC and ISIS, https://justiceinconflict.org/2015/06/11/the-icc-and-isis-be-careful-what-you-wish-for/ [last visited 1 January 2019].

framework of the Court, not to its own interests."[65] In *Mbarushimana Challenge to Jurisdiction*, Pre-Trial Chamber I held that "a referral cannot limit the Prosecutor to investigate only certain crimes, e.g. crimes committed by certain persons or crimes committed before or after a given date. As long as crimes are committed within the context of the situation of crisis that triggered the jurisdiction of the Court, investigations and prosecutions can be initiated."[66] With all that in mind, it is not surprising that the Security Council does not refer even a very narrowly tailored situation of ISIL as a group to the ICC.

## IV. Admissibility

As set out in Article 17(1) of the ICC and repeated in the OTP Policy on Case Selection and Prioritization, admissibility requires an assessment of complementarity and gravity in relation to a specific case.[67] Concerning complementarity, the OTP will determine whether any States Party is exercising its jurisdiction in relation to the same person for substantially the same conduct as that alleged before the ICC, and if so, whether the national proceedings concerned are vitiated by an unwillingness or inability to investigate or prosecute genuinely.[68] In *Lubanga*, the Pre-Trial Chamber I alluded to genuineness as an important dimension of the complementarity determination.[69] An assessment must be made in light of the proceedings as they exist at the national level at the time and is potentially subject to revision based on any change of facts.

When it comes to ISIL terrorist attacks in Europe, which might come under ICC territorial jurisdiction, the complementarity principle may not work in favor of the ICC at first glance, as these states are clearly interested in prosecuting and punishing those responsible themselves.[70] In addition, concerning the active personality

---

[65] In the footnote of *Mbarushimana Challenge to Jurisdiction*, mentioning the *Decision to Issue an Arrest Warrant against Al-Bashir*, as cited in *Galand*, The Situation Concerning the Islamic State: Carte Blanche for the ICC if the Security Council Refers?, 27 May 2015, https://www.ejiltalk.org/the-situation-concerning-isis-carte-blanche-for-the-icc-if-the-security-council-refers/ [last visited 1 January 2019].

[66] *Mbarushimana Challenge to Jurisdiction*, para. 27, *ibid*. Similarly in Uganda's referral of the "situation concerning the Lord's Resistance Army [LRA]," the Prosecutor eventually decided that "the scope of the referral encompasses all crimes committed in Northern Uganda in the context of the ongoing conflict involving the LRA," see Kony Status Conference, para. 5, *ibid*.

[67] Paras. 19–32.

[68] *Ibid*.

[69] *Williams/Schabas*, in: Triffterer, The Commentary on the Rome Statute, 2008, p. 617.

[70] In fact, in some of the affected states, the proceedings are ongoing. See 1st Paris terror attack suspect's trial starts despite protests, https://www.cbsnews.com/news/paris-attacks-jawad-bendaoud-france-trial-bataclan-terrorism/ [last visited 1 January 2019].

principle, European states, such as the U.K., have already enacted legislative measures to address their own citizens who joined ISIL as foreign fighters and have also initiated prosecutions against nationals alleged to have committed crimes.[71] However, prosecuting ISIL may also be considered a serious security concern and some states may be reluctant to prosecute. Additionally, ISIL constitutes a transnational criminal threat of such degree that piecemeal domestic prosecution may be viewed as unsuitable.[72]

Iraq has started prosecutions of ISIL members. However, Human Rights Watch's most recent report warns that Iraq's prosecutions of former ISIL fighters violate basic standards of due process and human rights,[73] calling into question Iraq's genuine ability to prosecute these crimes.[74] Available data indicate that Syria still has not started to deal with crimes committed by ISIL on any larger scale, and hence we could preliminarily conclude that, at least with respect to crimes committed in Syria, the situation would be admissible before the ICC.

Regarding gravity as a criterion for admissibility under Article 17(1)(d), the Appeals Chamber dismissed setting an overly restrictive legal bar that would hamper the deterrent role of the ICC.[75] The factors guiding the OTP's assessment of gravity include both quantitative and qualitative considerations relating to the scale, nature, manner of commission, and impact of the crimes. The scale of the crimes may be assessed in light of, *inter alia*, the number of direct and indirect victims, the extent of damage caused by the crimes, in particular the bodily or psychological harm to the victims and their families, or their geographical or temporal spread (high intensity crimes over a brief period or low intensity crimes over an extended period).[76] While certain terrorist attacks per se may not be seen as sufficiently grave, there are no doubts that ISIS violence in its totality is grave enough to warrant ICC scrutiny.[77]

---

71 *Brennan*, Prosecuting ISIL before the ICC, https://www.asil.org/insights/volume/19/issue/21/prosecuting-isil-international-criminal-court-challenges-and-obstacles [last visited 1 January 2019].

72 *Coman*, 33(84) Utrecht Journal of International and European Law 120–145 (2017].

73 *Both*, Holding ISIS Accountable in Iraq and Beyond, What do Iraq's prosecutions of ISIS members mean for transitional justice?, December 2017, http://www.mantlethought.org/international-affairs/holding-isis-accountable-iraq-and-beyond.

74 This raises another complex issue of whether such domestic violations should trigger the complementarity mechanism and jurisdiction of the ICC and to what extent the ICC should act as a human rights court.

75 OTP, Policy Paper of Case Selection and Prioritization, paras. 19–32.

76 *Ibid*., para. 38.

77 See UN Reports cited in Chapter 1 of this paper.

## V. Interests of justice

The OTP can decide not to initiate the investigation in the interests of justice; yet, it needs to be emphasized that this can be done only as an exception and that there is a strong presumption in favor of investigation and prosecution if other criteria are met.[78] The OTP's Policy Paper on the Interests of Justice affirms that the prosecutorial discretion has to be exercised in light of the Statute's object and purpose, and particularly in light of the goals of preventing further atrocities and guaranteeing lasting respect for and the enforcement of international justice – "significant touchstones" in the assessment of the interests of justice.[79] Hence, it would be very difficult to justify the decision of the OTP not to investigate and prosecute ISIL crimes in the interests of justice.

## VI. Conclusion

The UN Reports documented many crimes committed by ISIL that could be prosecuted either before the ICC or as core crimes in national jurisdictions. However, as far as the ICC is concerned, it seems that the Prosecutor perceived the prosecution of ISIL as too heavy a burden. In addition to the legal challenges of establishing jurisdiction and admissibility, there are also political challenges. Advocates of judicial deterrence have increasingly emphasized the importance of the capacity of tribunals to deter ongoing crimes in specific conflicts.[80] However, the decision not to enter the preliminary examination of ISIL-related violence in Syria and Iraq might demonstrate that the ICC is unable to intervene when the conflict is ongoing and, thus, unable to play a truly crucial role in the deterrence and prevention of conflicts. Without an enforcement mechanism, without the cooperation of Iraq and Syria, and without the support of the Security Council, it would be very difficult for the Prosecutor acting *proprio motu* to intervene in an ongoing conflict, capture ISIL members, and seize the evidence. The resulting ineffectiveness would perhaps further undermine the legitimacy of the ICC, which is clearly in the downturn. Even if the Security Council referred the situation of ISIL to the ICC, based on the above, there is no guarantee that the other actors and sides to the Syrian conflict would not be investigated. This could deter the Security Council from referring even the narrowly structured situation of ISIL.

---

[78] OTP, Policy Paper on the Interests of Justice, September 2007, p. 3. https://www.icc-cpi.int/nr/rdonlyres/772c95c9-f54d-4321-bf09-73422bb23528/143640/iccotpinterestsofjustice.pdf [last visited 1 January 2019].

[79] See more in *Varaki*, 15 Journal of International Criminal Justice 455–470 (2017).

[80] *Vinjamuri*, in: Stahn, The Law and Practice of the ICC, 2015, p. 16.

Concerning national jurisdictions, Iraq has begun prosecuting ISIL members. Thus, based on the complementary principle, Iraq has an advantage over the ICC unless it proves to be genuinely unable or unwilling, and the same would apply to Syria. If the national prosecutions prove to be genuine and in accordance with human rights standards, despite initial concerns already raised regarding prosecutions in Iraq, justice would be served nonetheless. Perhaps that would be the best possible solution and could be seen as a success of international criminal justice despite the ICC's inactivity. However, even though this scenario is most desirable, it is, at least at this time, unlikely to occur. If those most responsible for such mass atrocities committed on the territory of many states by organizations such as ISIL are not prosecuted for core crimes, one could pessimistically conclude that humanity failed again the countries of Syria and Iraq.[81]

## Bibliography

*Ambos, Kai*, The new enemy of mankind: The Jurisdiction of the ICC over members of "Islamic State", 26 November 2015, https://www.ejiltalk.org/the-new-enemy-of-mankind-the-jurisdiction-of-the-icc-over-members-of-islamic-state/ [last visited 1 January 2019].

*Bergsmo, Morten/Pejić, Jelena*, Article 15, Prosecutor. In: Otto Triffterer (ed.), The Commentary on the Rome Statute of the International Criminal Court. 2d ed. München/Oxford/Baden-Baden 2008, pp. 581–594.

*Brennan, Anna Marie*, Prosecuting ISIL before the International Criminal Court: Challenges and Obstacles, ASIL Insights, vol. 19, issue 21, 17 September 2015, https://www.asil.org/insights/volume/19/issue/21/prosecuting-isil-international-criminal-court-challenges-and-obstacles [last visited 1 January 2019].

*Both, Maxine*, Holding ISIS accountable in Iraq and beyond. What do Iraq's prosecutions of ISIS members mean for transitional justice? 11 July 2018, http://www.mantlethought.org/international-affairs/holding-isis-accountable-iraq-and-beyond

Cambridge Dictionary, https://dictionary.cambridge.org/ [last visited 1 January 2019].

*Cetorelli, Valeria/Sasson, Isaac/Nazar, Shabila/Burnham, Gilbert*, ISIS' Yazidi Genocide Demographic Evidence of the Killings and Kidnappings Forreign Affairs, 8 June 2017. https://www.foreignaffairs.com/articles/syria/2017-06-08/isis-yazidi-genocide [last visited 1 January 2019].

*Chulov, Martin/al-Faour, Nadia*, "They deserve no mercy": Iraq deals briskly with accused "women of Isis", A Baghdad court has sentenced more than 40 foreign women to death after 10-minute hearings. 22 May 2018. The Guardian https://www.theguardian.com/world/2018/may/22/they-deserve-no-mercy-iraq-deals-briskly-with-accused-women-of-isis [last visited 1 January 2019].

81 Using a similar expression here as *Tisdall*, The epic failure of our age: how the west let down Syria, 10 February 2018, The Guardian, https://www.theguardian.com/world/2018/feb/10/epic-failure-of-our-age-how-west-failed-syria [last visited 1 January 2019].

*Coman, Kenny*, Prosecuting Crimes of International Concern: Islamic State at the ICC? 33(84) Utrecht Journal of International and European Law 120–145 (2017).

EU Global Strategy, From Shared Vision to Common Action: Implementing the EU Global Strategy. Year 1, 2017.

European Parliament, Committee on Foreign Affairs, The financing of the 'Islamic State' in Iraq and Syria (ISIS), requested by the European Parliament, Study, 11 September 2017.

*Galand, Alexandre Skander*, The Situation Concerning the Islamic State: Carte Blanche for the ICC if the Security Council Refers?, 27 May 2015, https://www.ejiltalk.org/the-situation-concerning-isis-carte-blanche-for-the-icc-if-the-security-council-refers/.

*Hansen, Thomas Obel*, The Policy Paper on Preliminary Examinations: Ending Impunity Through 'Positive Complementarity'?, Transitional Justice Institute Research Paper No. 17-01, 2017, SSRN: https://ssrn.com/abstract=2939139 or http://dx.doi.org/10.2139/ssrn.2939139.

ICC, OTP, Policy Paper on Case Selection and Prioritization, 15 September 2016, https://www.icc-cpi.int/itemsDocuments/20160915_OTP-Policy_Case-Selection_Eng.pdf [last visited 1 January 2019].

ICC, OTP, Policy Paper on the Interests of Justice, September 2007, https://www.icc-cpi.int/nr/rdonlyres/772c95c9-f54d-4321-bf09-73422bb23528/143640/iccotpinterestsofjustice.pdf [last visited 1 January 2019].

ICC, OTP, Policy Paper on Preliminary Examinations, November 2013, http://www.legal-tools.org/en/doc/acb906/ [last visited 1 January 2019].

ICC, OTP, Strategic Plan 2016-2018, 16 November 2015, https://www.icc-cpi.int/iccdocs/otp/EN-OTP_Strategic_Plan_2016-2018.pdf [last visited 1 January 2019].

ICC, OTP, Strategic Plan June 2012-2015, 11 October 2013, https://www.icc-cpi.int/iccdocs/otp/OTP-Strategic-Plan-2013.pdf [last visited 1 January 2019].

*Kersten, Mark*, The ICC and ISIS: Be Careful What You Wish For, 11 June 2015, https://justiceinconflict.org/2015/06/11/the-icc-and-isis-be-careful-what-you-wish-for/.

*Ochi, Megumi*, Gravity Threshold Before the International Criminal Court: an Overview of the Court's Practice, ICD Brief 19 January 2016, http://www.internationalcrimesdatabase.org/upload/documents/20160111T115040-Ochi%20ICD%20Format.pdf.

*Pagliery, Jose*, Inside the $2 billion ISIS war machine. CNN Money, 11 December 2015: http://money.cnn.com/2015/12/06/news/isis-funding/index.html.

*Rastan, Rod*, Jurisdiction. In: Carsten Stahn (ed.), The Law and Practice of the International Criminal Court. Oxford 2015, pp. 141–178.

*Roksandić, Vidlička Sunčana*, Prosecuting Serious Economic Crimes as International Crimes, A New Mandate for the ICC? Berlin 2018.

*Schabas, William A.*, The Banality of International Justice. 11 Journal of International Criminal Justice 545–551 (2013).

*Schabas, William A.*, The International Criminal Court, A Commentary on the Rome Statute. Oxford 2010.

*Schemenauer, Stephen*, Civilian Reseach Project: Using the Rule of Law to Combat the Islamic State, US Army, 29 December 2017.

*Stahn, Carsten*, Why the ICC Should Be Cautious to Use the Islamic State to Get Out of Africa: Part 2, 4 December 2014, https://www.ejiltalk.org/why-the-icc-should-be-cautious-to-use-the-islamic-state-to-get-out-of-africa-part-2/.

*Tisdall, Simon*, The epic failure of our age: how the west let down Syria, The Guardian 10 February 2018, https://www.theguardian.com/world/2018/feb/10/epic-failure-of-our-age-how-west-failed-syria.

UN Security Council, Sixth Report of the Secretary General on the threat posed by ISIL to international peace and security and the range of the United Nations efforts in support of Member States in countering the threat, S/2018/80, 31 January 2018.

UN, Human Rights Council, Report of the Independent International Commission of inquiry on the Syrian Arab Republic. A/HRC/39/65, 10–28 September 2018.

UN, Human Rights Council, Report of the Office of the UN High Commissioner for Human Rights on the human rights situation in Iraq in the light of abuses committed by the so-called Islamic State in Iraq and the Levant and associated groups from 2015, A/HRC/28/18, 13 March 2015.

UN, Human Rights Council, The Report of the Office of the United Nations High Commissioner for Human Rights on the human rights situation in Iraq in the light of abuses committed by the so-called Islamic State in Iraq and the Levant and associated groups, A/HRC/28/18, 13 March 2015.

UN, Independent International Commission of Inquiry Report, "They came to destroy": ISIS Crimes Against the Yazidis, 16 June 2016, A/HRC/32/CRP.2.

*Varaki, Maria*, Revisiting the 'Interests of Justice' Policy Paper. 15 Journal of International Criminal Justice 455–470 (2017].

*Vinjamuri, Leslie*, The ICC and the Politics of Peace and Justice. In: Carsten Stahn (ed.), The Law and Practice of the International Criminal Court. Oxford 2015, pp. 13–29.

*Williams, Sharon A./William A. Schabas*, Article 17 Issues of Admissibility. In: Otto Triffterer (ed.), The Commentary on the Rome Statute of the International Criminal Court, 2d ed. München/Oxford/Baden-Baden 2008, pp. 605–627.

*Zakerhossein, Mohammad Hadi*, To Bury a Situation Alive – A Critical Reading of the ICC Prosecutor's Statement on the ISIS Situation. 16 International Criminal Law Review 613–641 (2016).

# Foreign (Terrorist) Fighters: Combatants and/or Terrorists or Just Enemies?

*John A.E. Vervaele**

## I. Mapping the problem

The term "foreign fighters" is increasingly being used to refer to persons of foreign nationality fighting in conflicts of all types.[1] Their involvement in armed conflicts can take many different forms, from mercenaries looking for private gain, political freedom fighters – such as the international brigades fighting against *Franco* in the Spanish Civil War in the 1930s – to religious fighters whose ultimate aim is to create a caliphate or engage in jihad.[2] Being a foreign fighter is as such not an offence under the existing legal framework. It is not a term of art in international criminal law (ICL) and is neither included in the Rome Statute of the International Criminal Court (ICC) nor in statutes of other international criminal tribunals.[3] Participating in a foreign conflict is as such not prohibited under International Humanitarian Law (IHL),[4] but when such persons participate as mercenaries they cannot then qualify under IHL for the status of a combatant or a prisoner of war in an international armed conflict. They can, however, be criminally liable under domestic criminal law for their participation in a foreign armed conflict. Until recently, "foreign fighters" was not a term of art in counterterrorism law either. The legal qualification of their status depends to a large extent on their conduct – not on their thoughts or beliefs. This means that it is important to clarify the distinctions between fighters on the battlefield of an armed conflict recognized under IHL and those who are simply terrorizing the civilian population or are spreading terror by means of rape, slavery and enforced prostitution or those that are unlawfully destroying cultural heritage. Even in the first case we have to make a further distinction between those who adhere to *ius in bello* and those who use weapons in an extreme, brutal and inhuman way, thereby violating IHL and committing war

---

* Professor of Criminal Law and Criminal Procedure, Utrecht Law School, The Netherlands; President of the Association Internationale de Droit Pénal, Paris.

1 *de Guttry* et al. (eds.), Foreign Fighters.

2 *Engelhart*, Heiliger Krieg.

3 *Heinsch*, in: de Guttry et al. (eds.), Foreign Fighters, pp. 161–186.

4 *Sommario*, in: de Guttry et al. (eds.), Foreign Fighters, pp. 141–160.

crimes and crimes against humanity (CAH) and even genocide. Finally, it can make a difference with regard to their status whether the armed conflict is international or non-international. In the ongoing conflicts in Syria and Iraq it has become clear that foreign fighters can commit war crimes, CAH and even genocide, and the extent to which this is done has been revealed, but they can also commit terrorist offences and thus become foreign terrorist fighters (FTFs). Much less clear, however, is when they qualify as lawful combatants and should be excluded from any criminal prosecution or whether they are criminally liable and for which offences (international crimes or terrorism) and under which jurisdictions they could be prosecuted.

Traditionally, the branches or bodies of international law which govern armed conflict[5] *(ius ad bellum)* and IHL[6] *(ius in bello)*, ICL (war crimes, CAH, genocide and aggression) and suppression treaties dealing with counterterrorism were fairly autonomous. There was a clear separation between conduct in a time of peace and conduct in times of war and a clear separation between armed conflict between states and violent actions by non-state actors. National jurisdictions did not have too much difficulty in defining jurisdiction and the applicable law when it came to lawful warfare, war crimes or ordinary crimes such as homicide or terrorism. In any case counterterrorism legislation had to apply national constitutional standards and international and regional human rights standards. In times of war counterterrorism legislation had to apply, moreover, *ius ad bellum* and *ius in bello*. As counterterrorism legislation and armed conflict were never envisaged as exclusive concepts, international conventions also regulated any overlap between them. The International Convention against the Taking of Hostages (1979) provides in its Article 12, for example, the total exclusion of its application in armed conflict situations:

> In so far as the Geneva Conventions of 1949 for the protection of war victims or the Protocols Additional to those Conventions are applicable to a particular act of hostage-taking, and in so far as States Parties to this Convention are bound under those conventions to prosecute or hand over the hostage-taker, the present Convention shall not apply to an act of hostage-taking committed in the course of armed conflicts as defined in the Geneva Conventions of 1949 and the Protocols thereto, including armed conflicts mentioned in article 1, paragraph 4, of Additional Protocol I of 1977, in which peoples are fighting against colonial domination and alien occupation and against racist régimes in the exercise of their right of self-determination, as enshrined in the Charter of the United Nations and the Declaration on Principles of International Law concerning Friendly Relations and Co-operation among States in accordance with the Charter of the United Nations.

---

5 The Hague Conventions of 1899 and 1907 on the conduct of warfare.

6 The Fourth Geneva Convention of 12 August 1949 relative to the Protection of Civilian Persons in Time of War expressly provides, in Article 33, that all measures of terrorism are prohibited. Similarly, see the Additional Protocols I and II to the Geneva Conventions of 12 August 1949, and relating to the Protection of Victims of International and Non-International Armed Conflicts, of 8 June 1977.

The lines of division between IHL and counterterrorism have blurred over the past few decades for several reasons, resulting in conflicting jurisdictions, both at the domestic level and between international criminal courts and domestic courts, as well as overlapping applicable law. This can lead to overcriminalization or to impunity.[7] There are several reasons for the increase in overlap and the growing number of conflicts between IHL and counterterrorism that are related to both the dynamics of armed conflict and IHL and the dynamics in counterterrorism legislation.

## II. Analysis of the increasing overlap and the conflict of law and jurisdiction

### A. Dynamics of armed conflict and IHL

First of all, the traditional definition of armed conflict under public international law has been expanded from international armed conflicts[8] between states to non-international armed conflicts between actors that can also include non-state actors, such as rebels and the military opposition. The latter are protracted armed confrontations occurring between governmental armed forces and the forces of one or more armed groups, or between such groups arising on the territory of a State that reach a minimum level of intensity and in which the parties involved in the conflict show a minimum degree of organization. We see a strong increase worldwide in conflicts in which non-state parties are engaged in a "continuous combat function". War crimes and even core international crimes can be committed by both parties in that situation. The direct intentional targeting of civilians by a military force is an international crime that any jurisdiction may punish. The "armed forces" as actors can also include non-state actors that could also qualify as terrorist organizations, such as for instance ISIS or Al-Qaeda. At present both IHL and ICL cover acts of terrorism carried out during an armed conflict.[9]

---

[7] *Paulussen*, Impunity for international terrorists? Key legal questions and practical considerations (ICCT Research Paper), available at http://www.icct.nl/download/file/ICCT-Paulussen-Impunity-April-2012.pdf; *Paulussen*, Testing the adequacy of the international legal framework in countering terrorism: the war paradigm (ICCT Research Paper), available at http://www.icct.nl/download/file/ICCT-Paulussen-Legal-Framework-for-Counter-Terrorism-August-2012.pdf.

[8] Common Article 2 to the Geneva Conventions of 1949; Additional Protocol I extends the definition of international armed conflict to include armed conflicts in which peoples are fighting against colonial domination, alien occupation or racist regimes in the exercise of their right to self-determination (wars of national liberation); *Fleck*, Humanitarian Law in Armed Conflicts.

[9] *Cassese*, 4 J Int Criminal Justice 943 (2006).

Second, the question of the armed conflict occurring in the territory of one of the contracting parties has lost its relevance, as the four Geneva Conventions have now been universally ratified and any armed conflict between governmental armed forces and armed groups or between such groups cannot but take place on the territory of one of the Parties to the Convention. However, the belligerent activity of armed forces is only recognized as an armed conflict under international law if there is a certain degree of intensity in the hostilities (the number of actions, the number of participants, the number of victims) in a certain area of controlled territory and if the parties have a certain level of structure or organization. This means that the geographical scope of the conflict is no longer important for triggering jurisdiction but it does define whether the notion of armed conflict does substantially apply and determines which actions have a nexus therewith and which do not. In the *Kunarac* case the ICTY Appeals Chamber underlined that:

> "The state of armed conflict is not limited to the areas of actual military combat but exists across the entire territory under the control of the warring parties."[10]

Third, the concept of an armed conflict is in itself in a state of clear metamorphosis.[11] Armed groups use, for instance, digital means, such as cyber hacking and undermining cyber security, as a military tool. As governmental armed forces intervene in local armed conflicts (as is the case in Syria, for instance), non-state actors also delocalize their belligerent activities to the territory of the allied forces of their enemy. At the same time they train and use citizens of the allied forces of their enemy to commit violent attacks in the territories of those allied forces and/or use them as foreign fighters in the conflict area. This means that the nexus between armed conflict and conduct by armed forces can be much more delocalized than previously and that an internal armed conflict can have a worldwide nexus.

## B. Dynamics in counterterrorism legislation

As stated above, the dynamics are not limited to IHL and ICL. There are also a number of reasons that are related to the dynamics in the counterterrorism field. First, both in public international law and in domestic criminal justice, counterterrorism legislation has been substantially expanded. Since the 1980s the counterterrorism narrative has completely changed, certainly in relation to persons and organizations that pretend to be acting in the name of Islam and/or are of Arab descent

---

[10] *Prosecutor v. Kunarac et al.*, IT-96-23 & IT-96-23/1-A, Judgement, 12 June 2002, § 64, and in the same vein, *Prosecutor v. Blaškić*, IT-95-14-T, Judgement, 3 March 2000, § 64.

[11] *Henckaerts/Doswald-Beck*, Customary International Humanitarian Law; *Pictet* (ed.), Commentary Geneva Conventions I-IV, ICRC Geneva 1994; *Pictet* (ed.), Commentary Additional Protocols to the Geneva Conventions, ICRC Geneva 1987.

and who refer to their duty to fight their enemies as part of their jihad.[12] After the Arab Spring, the rise of violent conflicts in Iraq, Afghanistan, Syria and Yemen and in particular the exodus of young Arabs and converts to conflict zones, especially Syria, has resulted in the international community increasingly concentrating on counterterrorism. The threats posed by the Taliban, ISIS, the Al-Nusra Front, etc. have justified an even wider criminal response. Violent attacks in the name of jihad are certainly not only being carried out in Muslim conflict areas, such as Syria, Iraq, Yemen, Libya and Afghanistan, but on an international and global scale. Organizations such as ISIS have made the internationalization, globalization and digitalization of their "holy war" their specific brand name. Moreover, they have linked them to the setting up of their own proper territory and state structure (the ISIS caliphate). The terrorist attacks in France, Belgium, Germany and Turkey are the most recent and visible forms of this expansion. With the aim of countering terrorism and investigating and punishing the responsible perpetrators, the international community and domestic legislators have considerably increased their legislative and operational actions. Despite the lack of unanimity in the international community over the role of criminal law in countering terrorism, there is no doubt that there is a clear expansion of criminal law in all 19 international UN conventions and UN resolutions of the Security Council. Not only do they prescribe the criminalization of violent and harmful conduct, but they also increasingly oblige the criminalization of preparatory and anticipative acts that consist of abstract or concrete endangerment, such as, for instance, certain acts of the glorification or financing of terrorism.[13]

Second, given the globalization and digitalization of terrorist activity and the interplay between conflict zones and terrorism, terrorism legislation has been expanded to include conduct committed in armed conflict zones. The result is an increasing overlap, which means that the same conduct, such as for instance the spreading of terror among the civilian population in armed conflicts, can fall within the scope of very different fields of law, i.e., legal warfare, international core crimes (war crimes or CAH) and terrorism. Resolution 2178, that was unanimously endorsed by the UN Security Council in 2014, based on Chapter VII of the Charter, is a very good example of this, as it deals explicitly with the threat posed by FTFs,[14] namely, those fighters travelling to a State other than their State of residence or nationality for the purpose of committing, planning or preparing terrorist

[12] Jihad means the duty for Muslims to maintain and spread Islam as a belief. This, of course, has to be distinguished from the form known as "violent jihad".

[13] The International Convention for the Suppression of the Financing of Terrorism (1999) is a good example.

[14] European Counter Terrorism Centre (ECTC) at the European Police Office (Europol), Changes in Modus Operandi of Islamic State (IS) revisited, December 2016, available at https://www.europol.europa.eu/publications-documents/changes-in-modus-operandi-of-islamic-state-revisited.

acts or participating therein, or providing or receiving training for the purposes of terrorism, including in connection with an armed conflict. The phenomenon of foreign fighters who travel abroad to fight alongside a non-state armed group in the territory of another State is a perfect case which illustrates the conflicting overlap between criminal legislation in the field of counterterrorism and the law of armed conflict/IHL. If the foreign fighters participate in the armed conflict, both IHL and counterterrorism law can apply. This is of course not without problems, as the basic principles are different, as are the jurisdiction rules, the substantive elements of illegal conduct, the penalties, the procedural rules and the relevant privilege exceptions. In an armed conflict it can be lawful to kill and combatants can be shielded under the "combatant's privilege" or the "privilege of belligerency" from criminal liability and prosecution. Due to this privilege, murder is converted into lawful killing under *ius in bello*. What is clearly an act of terrorism in times of peace can be lawful or count as a war crime/criminal violation of IHL in times of war. To the implementation of UN Resolution 2178 in Europe, the response was twofold. On the one hand, in 2015 the Council of Europe adopted the Additional Riga Protocol[15] to the Warsaw Convention of 2005, adding new offences, especially in relation to FTFs and their "passive training", their travelling to and from areas of conflict, and the funding and material support for these trips. The second, even more recent European initiative was launched by the EU and already reflects the wave of cruel attacks in France and Belgium. It encompasses a directive[16] that replaces Council Framework Decision 2002/475/JH. The phenomenon of FTFs lies at the heart of the new criminal intervention, since it refers not only to the matter of travelling for terrorist purposes (including receiving training), but also to the financing, organization and facilitation of such travelling, including logistical and material support, accommodation, means of transport, services, goods and merchandise. Some EU countries even want to go beyond this obligation and to criminalize the mere fact of travelling to conflict areas.

Third, the cross-references in IHL and criminal counterterrorism law are rather limited and do not really tackle the increasing conflicting overlap and the blurring of the conceptual differences. In reality, counterterrorism legislation seems to take the lead and tries to get around the limitations imposed by IHL. The directive only contains, for instance, a statement in the recitals, without further elaborating thereon:

> (37) This Directive should not have the effect of altering the rights, obligations and responsibilities of the Member States under international law, including under international humanitarian law. This Directive does not govern the activities of armed forces during

---

15 CETS No. 217. Although signed by many States it has not yet entered into force because of the lack of sufficient ratifications.

16 Directive (EU) 2017/541 of the European Parliament and of the Council of 15 March 2017 on combating terrorism and replacing Council Framework Decision 2002/475/JHA and amending Council Decision 2005/671/JHA.

periods of armed conflict, which are governed by international humanitarian law within the meaning of those terms under that law, and, inasmuch as they are governed by other rules of international law, activities of the military forces of a State in the exercise of their official duties.

The result remains that in national legislation and in judicial practice there is a clear problem of an overlap in jurisdiction and the applicable law, and thus in legal certainty and foreseeability. Terrorism is today not only a treaty crime (under the UN and regional suppression treaties), but can also qualify, under strict conditions, as a war crime (under domestic and international criminal jurisdictions), which means that it is committed by armed forces in an armed conflict, or as a crime against humanity, thus not necessarily linked to an armed conflict. Terrorism can thus be directly punishable under ICL. Terrorism could also be considered as a crime under customary international law, but there is certainly no unanimity in the *opinio juris*[17] on this.

Public international law takes a clear stance on terrorism in times of war. Article 33(1) of the Fourth Geneva Convention of 1949 prohibits all measures of terrorism against civilians. The two Additional Protocols also spell out the general prohibition of terrorism (Article 51(2) of the First Protocol and Article 13(2) of the Second Protocol). Notwithstanding these prohibitions, a clear division between ICL and terrorism is not provided. For instance, the financing of FTFs could be prosecuted under terrorism offences if it is aimed at financing terrorist acts carried out or planned in a foreign country where an armed conflict is underway if these acts are directed against persons not taking an active part in armed hostilities. *A contrario* the financing of groups solely aiming to attack enemy armed forces in the foreign country concerned would be lawful. This single example suffices to deduce how difficult it can be for a national jurisdiction to decide upon the link between financing and the concrete acts in an armed conflict. Every single jurisdiction applies its own criteria and the lack of a homogenous approach risks also undermining the rationale of IHL and the related privileges, such as the combatant's privilege, which is a real carve-out provision that precludes criminal prosecution for war crimes or terrorism if combatants qualify as armed forces in an armed conflict, as defined by public international law. In order to make use of this privilege and be considered armed forces, non-state actors must have a clear chain of command and an organization/structure, they must be involved in a continuous combat function and must be able to apply *ius in bello* and to sanction disciplinary violations thereof. Further, they must be involved in an armed conflict with a certain degree of hostility in which both parties are organized and structured and aim to gain military control over a certain geographical area. If foreign fighters belong to organized groups and units which are under a specific command which is ultimately responsible for the conduct of its subordinates and if their groups participate in the armed conflict on the battlefield, then the question arises whether FTFs, as part of the

[17] *Cassese*, 4 J Int Criminal Justice 945 (2006).

armed forces involved in an armed conflict, can rely on the combatant's privilege[18] in order to avoid criminal prosecution for terrorism and should not be prosecuted in the case of lawful warfare or whether they should be prosecuted for war crimes in cases of unlawful warfare or violations of IHL.[19]

Terror inflicted on the civilian population in an armed conflict is a special case which provides an exception to the rule that "terrorism" as such is not defined as, and does not constitute, a crime under international treaty law. As acts of terror in armed conflict are covered by IHL, most "Terrorism Conventions" purportedly do not apply in times of armed conflict, although the approach is irregular and remains controversial.[20] The UN Draft Comprehensive Convention against International Terrorism[21] only excludes from its scope of application actions by the "armed forces" of the state during the conflict, thereby leaving non-state parties whose acts may respect IHL vulnerable to prosecution for terrorism. By contrast, the UN International Convention for the Suppression of the Financing of Terrorism (1999) criminalizes acts in armed conflict as terrorism and provides the UN's clearest definition of terrorism for this purpose in Article 2(1):

> 1. Any person commits an offence within the meaning of this Convention if that person by any means, directly or indirectly, unlawfully and wilfully, provides or collects funds with the intention that they should be used or in the knowledge that they are to be used, in full or in part, in order to carry out:
>
> (a) An act which constitutes an offence within the scope of and as defined in one of the treaties listed in the annex; or
>
> (b) Any other act intended to cause death or serious bodily injury to a civilian, or to any other person not taking an active part in the hostilities in a situation of armed conflict, when the purpose of such act, by its nature or context, is to intimidate a population, or to compel a government or an international organization to do or to abstain from doing any act.

However, the Convention does not contain any reference to a "freedom fighters" exception or combatant's privilege, nor does it articulate on the relationship with IHL, thereby resulting in further potential confusion as to the interplay of norms.[22]

After the analysis of the reasons for the increasing interplay and the overlap between ICL and counterterrorism legislation, it is now time to look at judicial practice and to assess how it deals with this problem and which solutions are proposed.

---

18 *W.T. Mallison/S.V. Mallison*, 42(2) Law Contemp Probl 10 (Spring 1978).

19 *Werle*, Principles of International Criminal Law; *Cassese*, International Criminal Law; *Cassese/Gaeta*, International Criminal Law.

20 *Duffy*, The "War on Terror", p. 43.

21 Negotiations started in 2000 at the UN and were stalled in 2015; for the actual draft see https://www.ilsa.org/jessup/jessup08/basicmats/unterrorism.pdf.

22 *Duffy*, The "War on Terror", p. 44.

# III. Case law and an illustration of the problem

## A. Liberation Tigers of Tamil Eelam (LTTE)

The LTTE was involved in an "internal armed conflict" in Sri Lanka within the meaning of international law. The objective of the LTTE was aimed at the partial or total independence of the Tamil people and the LTTE had its own area and population over which it exercised effective control, its own forces, its own judiciary and its own taxation system. It actually possessed all the attributes of an independent state, subject to relevant international recognition. From Dutch territory it was involved in the financing of and recruitment for armed activity in this conflict. LTTE participants and leaders were prosecuted in the Netherlands for violations of ICL (war crimes and CAH as defined in the Dutch International Crimes Act), as well as for counts of terrorism under the Dutch Terrorism Act and for a violation of the Dutch Sanctions Statute (that implements the listing of terrorist organizations under EU Regulation No. 2580/2001). *In concreto* they were accused of a call to arms and/or participating in military service and/or the use of children under the age of 15 for active participation in hostilities during a non-international armed conflict in the territory of Sri Lanka. The court of first instance came to the conclusion[23] that for conduct related to a non-international armed conflict there can be no question of participating in an organization whose purpose was to commit terrorist offences. Prosecuting them for criminal liability would lead to a denial of their rights under the Geneva Conventions and Additional Protocol II. For acts that can be committed outside an armed conflict (such as the recruitment of child soldiers – a crime against humanity) there is, however, no incompatibility with IHL and a criminal prosecution is thus lawful.

The LTTE also sought to annul the EU regulation that formed the origin of these measures.

In its judgment of 16 October 2014[24] the EU General Court had to assess the compatibility of blacklisting the LTTE under Regulation No. 2580/2001 as an EU terrorist organization with IHL. The LTTE defended the opinion that the Regulation cannot apply to situations of armed conflict, since those conflicts – and therefore the acts committed in that context – could, in its opinion, only be governed by IHL. For the LTTE, listing as a terrorist organization and the related freezing of its funds constituted interference by a third party in an armed conflict, which contradicts the principle of non-interference under IHL. Contrary to what the LTTE claimed, the applicability of IHL to a situation of armed conflict and to acts committed in that context does not imply that the legislation on terrorism does not apply to those acts. That is true both of the provisions of EU law applied in this case,

---

[23] ECLI:NL:RBSGR:2011:BT8829, Rechtbank's-Gravenhage, 21 October 2011.

[24] Joined Cases T-208/11 and T-508/11, *LTTE v. Council of the European Union.*

in particular Common Position 2001/931 and Regulation No. 2580/2001, and of international law invoked by the LTTE. The Court underlined that the 1949 Geneva Convention (IV) relative to the Protection of Civilian Persons in Time of War expressly provides, in Article 33, that all measures of terrorism are prohibited. Similarly, Additional Protocols I and II to the Geneva Conventions, which seek to ensure better protection for those victims, provide that acts of terrorism are "prohibited at any time and in any place whatsoever" (Article 4(2) of Additional Protocol II) and that: "Acts or threats of violence the primary purpose of which is to spread terror among the civilian population are prohibited" (Article 51(2) of Additional Protocol I and Article 13(2) of Additional Protocol II). In the view of the court, it follows from the foregoing considerations that the perpetration of terrorist acts by participants in an armed conflict is expressly covered and condemned as such by IHL. Further, the existence of an armed conflict within the meaning of IHL does not appear to preclude, in the case of a terrorist act committed in the context of that conflict, the application of provisions of humanitarian law on breaches of the laws of war, nor of provisions of international law specifically relating to terrorism. Finally, the Court referred *expressis verbis* to the 1999 International Convention for the Suppression of the Financing of Terrorism that expressly regulates the commission of terrorist acts in the context of an armed conflict within the meaning of international law. In Article 2(1)(b) thereof, it renders unlawful "any other act intended to cause death or serious bodily injury to a civilian, or to any other person not taking an active part in the hostilities in a situation of armed conflict, when the purpose of such act, by its nature or context, is to intimidate a population, or to compel a government or an international organization to do or to abstain from doing any act". The convention confirms the fact that, even in an armed conflict within the meaning of IHL, there may be terrorist acts which are liable to be punished as such and not only as war crimes. Such acts include those intended to cause death or serious bodily injury to civilians.

The Court of Appeal[25] in the Dutch criminal proceedings reasoned along the same lines as the EU General Court, and by referring to the *Galić* decision of the ICTY Appeals Chamber[26] it overturned the decision of the first instance court. The Appeals Chamber considered this terrorist purpose, as element of the terrorist offence, to be unlawful in the armed conflict in question, as there was no direct connection with military operations and the actions did not target other combatants. In addition, acts of terror against the civilian population are contrary to IHL and are therefore punishable under national law.

25 ECLI:NL:GHDHA:2015:1082, Gerechtshof Den Haag, 30 April 2015.

26 See the analysis under section IV. infra.

## B. The Sharia4Belgium case

In Belgium 45 suspects were prosecuted for participation in or leadership of a terrorist organization, the glorification of terrorism or threatening terrorist attacks. The vast majority of them had also gone to Syria to join Jabhat Al-Nusra and Majlis Shura al-Mujahideen. At the first instance criminal trial[27] in Antwerp in February 2015 the accused contended that they could not be prosecuted and convicted of terrorist offences, as Article 141bis of the Belgian Criminal Code explicitly excluded these actions from its scope. Article 141bis states that the title on terrorist offences does not apply to the conduct of armed forces during an armed conflict as defined in and regulated by IHL, nor to the conduct of the armed forces of a State in the execution of their official duties, as far as they are regulated by other international law provisions.[28]

The question thus arose whether the accused who had joined organizations such as Jabhat Al-Nusra and Majlis Shura al-Mujahideen in Syria had to be considered as armed forces under IHL. The answer must of course be based on the applicable IHL, especially the four Geneva Conventions of 12 August 1949 and their additional Protocols I and II of 8 June 1977, taking into account that the First Protocol only applies to international armed conflicts and the Second Protocol applies to internal armed conflicts. However, Syria is not a party to the Second Protocol. Some of the suspects raised the argument that their conduct in Belgium was intrinsically linked with their conduct in Syria and that their conduct was part of an internal armed conflict in the sense of IHL. For all these reasons this should preclude the application of Article 141bis of the Belgian Criminal Code. Moreover, they argued that because of the non-applicability of the Second Protocol, certain conduct could eventually qualify as war crimes, for which the Belgian criminal tribunal had no competence. The tribunal underlined that the parties accepted that there is an internal armed conflict in Syria. However, movements such as Jabhat al-Nusra and Majlis Shura al-Mujahideen are foreign Al-Qaeda movements that became active in Syria and are not internal fighters, but foreign fighters. Moreover, in Belgium there is no internal armed conflict. Under Common Article 3 of the Geneva Conventions of 1949 the concept of internal conflict also applies to situations in which two or more organized belligerent groups are fighting each other. To qualify as an "armed conflict" a number of criteria must be met, including, for instance, a certain organizational and command structure, the intensity of the conflict and for how long the

---

27 Rechtbank van eerste aanleg Antwerpen, notitienummer FD35.98.47-12 – AN35.F1. 1809-12 – zaak I –, 11 February 2015.

28 The official text in the French language reads as follows: « Le présent titre ne s'applique pas aux activités des forces armées en période de conflit armé, tels que définis et régis par le droit international humanitaire, ni aux activités menées par les forces armées d'un Etat dans l'exercice de leurs fonctions officielles, pour autant qu'elles soient régies par d'autres règles de droit international. » For a comment see *Venet*, Infractions terroristes et droit humanitaire, Journal des Tribunaux, no 6387, 13 March 2010, pp. 169–172.

conflict has lasted. The belligerents must operate as private militias under military command, so that they are able and prepared to apply IHL. They must be recognizable as such (by their armaments and symbols) and respect the law of war.

The tribunal questioned whether fighters related to Jabhat al-Nusra and Majlis Shura al-Mujahideen can qualify as belligerents in the sense of IHL. It concluded that the suspects in the criminal terrorist case who were being prosecuted under Article 141bis of the Belgian Criminal Code could not rely on their preclusion from this article because of their belligerent status under IHL, as they did not belong to groups that have a clear organizational and command structure. As a second cumulative argument the tribunal underlined that Jabhat al-Nusra and Majlis Shura al-Mujahideen and their members are not able and not willing to comply with IHL and cannot therefore rely on its protection.

On appeal the lawyers representing *F. Belkacem* and *M. El Youssoufi* again relied on the exclusion clause under Article 141bis of the Belgian Criminal Code. The Court of Appeal[29] rejected the argument that the actions of members of Sharia4Belgium in Belgium are falling under the scope of IHL, as Belgium is a country in which there is no armed conflict. For the actions committed in Syria, the Court assessed the concept of an armed conflict under Common Article 3 of the 1949 Geneva Conventions and the relevant interpretation thereof. The Court referred to the *Tadić* case and the *Haradinaj* case of the ICTY and Article 8(2)(f) of the ICC Rome Statute and considered the time span and intensity of the conflict on the one hand and the command structure of the belligerents on the other. A command structure means a chain of command, disciplinary procedures, headquarters, central control over territory and over weapons and material and the capacity to speak as one organization. The Court was also not convinced that groups such as Majlis Shura al-Mujahideen and Jabhat al-Nusra can qualify as belligerents/organized military groups during an armed conflict in the sense of IHL. Based on a detailed factual analysis the Court came to the conclusion that these groups do not have a sufficient level of organization. They do not have a clear structure; the groups are also not able to control territory or to elaborate and execute a military strategy. In fact, and again in the opinion of the Court, their main activities have been looting, banditry, the deprivation of liberty and executions. Most of these activities have been carried out by local groups acting without much control or leadership. Finally, the groups also do not have a command structure by which they can impose and enforce – through disciplinary proceedings – the application of IHL. Throughout the area they form a clandestine network based on several cells, active in different regions, with a limited level of organization, but with the common aim of fighting with violent means against atheists, democracy, human rights and IHL.

---

[29] Hof van Beroep, Antwerpen – 2015/FP/1.

It is also interesting that the Court made a clear distinction between an organized group under IHL and under domestic terrorism legislation. The fact that Jabhat al-Nusra and Majlis Shura al-Mujahideen do not qualify as organized armed forces under IHL certainly does not mean that they cannot qualify as terrorist groups under domestic terrorism legislation, as the criteria are completely different.

Finally, the Belgian Supreme Court *(Cour de Cassation)* had to deal with the case. In its decision[30] the Court did not fully agree with the conceptual analysis of the court of first instance and the Court of Appeal. First, the fact that these organizations commit violations of IHL does not mean that the right to qualify as organized armed forces under IHL does not apply and that there is therefore no question of an internal armed conflict. Second, the fact that members do not carry arms openly or do not wear uniforms and do not dress as a recognizable force also does not determine whether they can be regarded as an organized armed force under IHL or not. Third, the Supreme Court also referred to the ICTY *Tadić* judgement, which required that at least one of the parties to a non-international armed conflict must be an organized armed group and the level of organization is not tied to strict criteria, but to a number of indicative criteria. Based on the preparatory works of the Geneva Conventions, the case law of international courts and legal doctrine, the Supreme Court stated that the formal ruling ignored a flexible assessment of the level of organization, on the basis of non-exhaustive criteria. But even then the Supreme Court came to the same conclusion as the Tribunal of first instance and the Court of Appeal. The conduct in Belgium was excluded from the concept of armed conflict and for the conduct in Syria the belligerents did not qualify as an organized armed group.

So it is clear from the analysis of all courts that domestic terrorism legislation can apply both to situations of international and non-international armed conflict. By deciding this way the Belgian courts did follow the case law of the Brussels Court of Appeal in the so-called "filières irakiennes" case.[31] Astonishing, however, is the extent to which Tribunal of first instance and the Court of Appeal took into account the objectives of the belligerents. The fact that they were fighting against democracy and the rule of law and wanted to establish a theocracy or a caliphate does not in any way exclude them from the application of IHL.

## C. R. v. Mohammed Gul (UK)

*M. Gul* had uploaded videos onto the internet, including scenes showing attacks by insurgents on soldiers of the Coalition forces in Iraq and Afghanistan. The videos were accompanied by *nasheeds*, praising the bravery of those carrying out the

[30] Hof van Beroep, Antwerpen – 2015/FP/1 – FD 35.9847-12.

[31] Brussels, 26 June 2008, not published.

attacks and their martyrdom and encouraging such attacks. He was charged with six counts of the dissemination of terrorist publications contrary to s. 2 of the Terrorism Act 2006. In this case the jury raised a set of questions on the relationship between the combatant exception/immunity under IHL and domestic terrorism legislation. These questions were answered by the judge at the Crown Court and this led to this appeal based on the way in which the judge had misdirected the jury in relation to the definition of terrorism. The contentions of the appellant *M. Gul* can be summarized as follows: Combatant immunity extended to immunity for those participating in acts against the military in an armed conflict. The effect of this was that individuals possessing that status were immune from domestic criminal law, provided that they did neither commit crimes unrelated to the armed conflict nor war crimes. Whether there was such an armed conflict giving rise to combatant immunity, was a question of fact for the jury to decide. The judge had misdirected the jury on a question of fact and on the meaning of the 2000 Terrorism Act as attacks on armed forces during a non-international armed conflict were not terrorism.

The Court of Appeal (Criminal Division) for England and Wales[32] first underlined that the combatant's privilege or immunity from prosecution does not apply in non-international armed conflicts. Second, for the Court there is a common understanding that in times of peace the concept of armed conflict is excluded and thus nothing stands in the way of the full application of the international crime of terrorism. The Court referred to the judgment of the Appeals Chamber of the Special Tribunal for Lebanon (STL): Interlocutory Decision on the Applicable Law: Terrorism, Conspiracy, Homicide, Perpetration, Cumulative Charging (16 February 2011) by Judge *Cassese*. At paragraph 107 of the judgment, Judge *Cassese* expressed the view of the Appeals Chamber:

> that, while the customary rule of an international crime of terrorism that has evolved so far only extends to terrorist acts *in times of peace*, a broader norm that would outlaw terrorist acts *during times of armed conflict* may also be emerging. As the ICTY and the SCSL have found, acts of terrorism can constitute war crimes, but States have disagreed over whether a distinct crime of terrorism should apply during armed conflict.

Even if the Criminal Division was convinced that there is, as yet, no such development in international law in order to state with sufficient certainty that an international crime of terrorism could be defined as being applicable during a state of armed conflict, it also concluded that:

> … an overwhelming majority of States currently takes the view that acts of terrorism may be repressed even in time of armed conflicts to the extent that such acts target civilians who do not take an active part in armed hostilities; these acts, in addition, could also be classified as war crimes (whereas the same acts, if they are directed against combatants or civilians participating in hostilities, may *not* be defined as either terrorist acts or war crimes, unless the requisite conditions for war crimes were met).

32 (2012) EWCA Crim 280, 22 February 2012.

The Criminal Division also concluded that although international law may well develop "through state practice or *opinio juris*[33] a rule restricting the scope of terrorism so that it excludes some types of insurgents attacking the armed forces of government from the definition of terrorism, the necessary widespread and general state practice or the necessary *opinio juris* to that effect has not yet been established". So for the Criminal Division "there is nothing in international law which either compels or persuades one to read the terms of the 2000 Terrorism Act in such a way as to exempt suspects from the definition in the Act".

## IV. Foreign (terrorist) fighters

The UN has been trying to deal with the phenomenon of terrorism in a comprehensive and integrated manner. This resulted in 2006 in a UN Global Counter-Terrorism Strategy and Plan of Action. In 2014 the UN Security Council unanimously endorsed, based on Chapter VII of the Charter, Resolutions 2170 and 2178. The latter deals specifically with the threat posed by FTFs and defines[34] them as persons "who travel to a State other than their States of residence or nationality for the purpose of the perpetration, planning, or preparation of, or participation in, terrorist acts or the providing or receiving of terrorist training, including in connection with armed conflict". Resolution 2178, which is binding on all States parties to the UN, thus endorses the new legal concept of FTFs:

> 5. *Decides* that Member States shall, consistent with international human rights law, international refugee law, and international humanitarian law, prevent and suppress the recruiting, organizing, transporting or equipping of individuals who travel to a State other than their States of residence or nationality for the purpose of the perpetration, planning, or preparation of, or participation in, terrorist acts or the providing or receiving of terrorist training, and the financing of their travel and of their activities;
>
> 6. *Recalls* its decision, in resolution 1373 (2001), that all Member States shall ensure that any person who participates in the financing, planning, preparation or perpetration of terrorist acts or in supporting terrorist acts is brought to justice, and *decides* that all States shall ensure that their domestic laws and regulations establish serious criminal offenses sufficient to provide the ability to prosecute and to penalize in a manner duly reflecting the seriousness of the offense:
>
> (a) their nationals who travel or attempt to travel to a State other than their States of residence or nationality, and other individuals who travel or attempt to travel from their territories to a State other than their States of residence or nationality, for the purpose of the perpetration, planning, or preparation of, or participation in, terrorist acts, or the providing or receiving of terrorist training;
>
> (b) the wilful provision or collection, by any means, directly or indirectly, of funds by their nationals or in their territories with the intention that the funds should be used, or in the knowledge that they are to be used, in order to finance the travel of individuals

[33] See for instance *Cassese*, 4 J Int Criminal Justice 933–958 (2006).

[34] In Paragraph 8 of the Preamble to the Resolution.

who travel to a State other than their States of residence or nationality for the purpose of the perpetration, planning, or preparation of, or participation in, terrorist acts or the providing or receiving of terrorist training; and,

(c) the wilful organization, or other facilitation, including acts of recruitment, by their nationals or in their territories, of the travel of individuals who travel to a State other than their States of residence or nationality for the purpose of the perpetration, planning, or preparation of, or participation in, terrorist acts or the providing or receiving of terrorist training.

As we can see the Resolution imposes far-reaching obligations to criminalize the conduct of FTFs under domestic law, but without resolving the legal interplay and overlap with human rights law and IHL.[35] As foreign fighters are labelled as FTFs, even in connection with an armed conflict, acts governed by IHL can be terrorist acts, even when these acts are not illegal under IHL. The mere fact, for instance, that a person joins a terrorist group involved in an armed conflict or gives material or financial support to such a terrorist group leads, under the Resolution, to mandatory criminal liability under domestic law. The Resolution does not impose obligations that are related to ICC core crimes, though. However, it is clear that violations of both the Hague and Geneva Conventions *(ius ad bellum – ius in bello)* can result in conduct that qualifies as international core crimes. Warfare that consists of intentional, direct attacks against the civilian population or against religious, educational or health-related buildings or that uses systematic slavery, rape and sexual abuse can qualify as war crimes under the Hague Conventions. Wilful killings, torture and inhuman treatment, the taking of hostages and the extensive destruction or appropriation of property can qualify as war crimes under the Geneva Conventions. Most of these forms of conduct also qualify as war crimes under Article 8 of the ICC Rome Statute, but it is important to underline that intent and knowledge are part of the constituent elements of these offences. Some of the conduct, such as murder, extermination, deportation and torture can also qualify as CAH under Article 7 of the ICC Rome Statute if it consists of widespread/systematic attacks against the civilian population. FTFs as non-state actors can commit these crimes if they have intent and knowledge of the attacks. Finally, some actions by FTFs could even qualify as a crime of genocide under Article 6 of the ICC Rome Statute if there is a specific plan and a direct intent *(dolus directus)* to destroy a national, ethnic, racial or religious group as such. In the case of Syria the Alawites, Christians, Kurdish and Yazidi minorities come to mind. Negligence, recklessness or *dolus eventualis* does not suffice in this case.

A specific and interesting category is the "spreading of terror among the civilian population", as this is also part of many of the domestic law definitions of "terrorist aim". It is very clear that no international court has explicit and direct jurisdiction over either "acts of terrorism" or the "spreading of terror among the civilian population" during an armed conflict. These acts can, however, qualify as war crimes

35 *de Guttry*, in: de Guttry et al. (eds.), Foreign Fighters, pp. 259–281.

(and eventually as CAH) and as violations of Article 3 common to the Geneva Conventions and of Additional Protocol II. In Article 4 of the Statute of the International Tribunal for Rwanda (ICTR Statute) and Article 3 of the Statute of the Special Court for Sierra Leone (SCSL Statute) this is clearly stipulated as a violation of Additional Protocol II. In the Statutes of the other international criminal courts these practices have been introduced through the Geneva Conventions and/or customary international law.

Many foreign (terrorist) fighters are involved in such practices. They do not participate directly in the hostilities, but spread terror through beheadings, rape, practices of sexual slavery, enforced prostitution, and the wilful destruction of cultural heritage and historic artefacts. Many legal questions have already arisen before the ICTY and its interpretative rulings thus provide important guidance when it comes to the applicable law, elements of crimes and jurisdiction. In the ICTY Appeals Chamber case of *Galić*,[36] *Galić* argued, under his seventh ground of appeal, that the Trial Chamber had violated the principle of *nullum crimen sine lege* in convicting him under count 1. In the present case he had been charged with and convicted of the crime of acts or threats of violence whose primary purpose was to spread terror among the civilian population, under Article 3 of the ICTY Statute, on the basis of Article 51(2) of Additional Protocol I and Article 13(2) of Additional Protocol II, both of which state:

> The civilian population as such, as well as individual civilians, shall not be the object of attack. Acts or threats of violence the primary purpose of which is to spread terror among the civilian population are prohibited.

He also argued that the International Tribunal had no jurisdiction over the crime of acts or threats of violence whose primary purpose is to spread terror among the civilian population as "there exists no international crime of terror". He submitted that the Trial Chamber had erred in considering treaty law to be sufficient to give jurisdiction to the Tribunal, which could only exercise jurisdiction over crimes under customary international law. The Prosecution first introduced the various counts. Under count 1 it alleged that General *Galić* "conducted a protracted campaign of shelling and sniping upon civilian areas of Sarajevo and upon the civilian population thereby inflicting terror and mental suffering upon its civilian population." In the view of the Prosecution the crime of terror is a purported violation of the laws or customs of war. It encompasses the intent to spread terror when committed by combatants in a period of armed conflict. The Prosecution further maintained that the prohibition against terrorizing the civilian population amounts to a rule of *customary* international law which is applicable to all armed conflicts. The Prosecution submitted that the following elements constitute the crime of terror:

---

[36] *Prosecutor v. Galić*, IT-98-29, Appeals Chamber Judgement, 30 November 2006, para. 89-89; see also *Prosecutor v. Tadić*, IT-94-1, Decision on the Defence Motion for Interlocutory Appeal on Jurisdiction, 2 October 1995, *Appeals Chamber Decision*, paras. 89, 98, 102.

1. Unlawful acts or threats of violence …
2. Which caused terror to spread among the civilian population.
3. The acts or threats of violence were carried out with the primary purpose of spreading terror among the civilian population.

In addition, according to the Prosecution's submission, there must be a nexus between the acts or threats of violence and the armed conflict, and the accused had to bear responsibility for the acts or threats under Article 7 of the ICTY Statute. The "special intent requirement" (element 3) is, according to the Prosecution, the distinguishing feature of the crime of terror. The Prosecution has interpreted "primary purpose" as requiring that "the infliction of terror upon the civilian population was the predominant purpose served by the acts or threats of violence. It need not be established that the broader campaign in the Sarajevo theatre had this as its sole or only objective." Where the special intent, or *mens rea*, cannot be directly proved, it may be "inferred from the nature, manner, timing, frequency and duration of the shelling and sniping of civilians."

For the majority of the Bench of the Appeals Chamber first the key question had to be addressed, namely when does a serious violation of the prohibition against terrorizing the civilian population entail, under customary or conventional law, the individual criminal responsibility of the person breaching the rule? The Chamber first dealt with the legal nature of the prohibition of terror against the civilian population in customary international law. The Appeals Chamber affirmed the finding of the Trial Chamber that the prohibition of terror, as contained in the second sentence of both Article 51(2) of Additional Protocol I and Article 13(2) of Additional Protocol II, amounts to "a specific prohibition within the general (customary) prohibition of an attack on civilians", which constitutes, in its entirety, an affirmation of the existing customary international law at the time of of the adoption of the Additional Protocols.

Second, in order to link the prohibition with criminalization and criminal liability, the Chamber reiterated that the conditions that must be satisfied in order to fulfil the requirements of Article 3 of the ICTY Statute are the four conditions generally known as the *Tadić* conditions:

(i) the violation must constitute an infringement of a rule of international humanitarian law;

(ii) the rule must be customary in nature or, if it belongs to treaty law, the required conditions must be met;

(iii) the violation must be "serious", that is to say, it must constitute a breach of a rule protecting important values, and the breach must involve grave consequences for the victim; and

(iv) the violation of the rule must entail, under customary or conventional law, the individual criminal responsibility of the person breaching the rule.

For an offence to be a violation of IHL, therefore, the Chamber needed to be satisfied that each of the alleged acts was in fact closely related to the hostilities. In order to give a positive answer to the fourth Tadić condition, i.e., the customary international law nature of the prohibition of terror against the civilian population in times of armed conflict, the Appeals Chamber referred to state practice:

> 94. With respect to national legislation, the Appeals Chamber notes that numerous States criminalise violations of international humanitarian law – encompassing the crime of acts or threats of violence the primary purpose of which is to spread terror among the civilian population – within their jurisdiction (…)
>
> 95. The Appeals Chamber also notes that numerous States have incorporated provisions as to the criminalisation of terror against the civilian population as a method of warfare in a language similar to the prohibition set out in the Additional Protocols.

The Appeals Chamber also referred to historic arguments, based on the 1919 Report of the Commission of Responsibilities and the 1948 work by the UN War Crimes Commission. They referred to systematic terrorism as a war crime.

Since all four conditions had now been satisfied, the majority found that serious violations of the second part of Article 51(2) of Additional Protocol I, and specifically the violations alleged in this case – the causing of death or injury – entailed individual criminal responsibility in 1992. The majority expressed no view as to whether the Tribunal also had jurisdiction over other types of violations of the rule, consisting for example only of threats of violence, or comprising acts of violence not causing death or injury. In conclusion, the crime of terror against the civilian population as it stood in the indictment constitutes elements which are common to offences falling under Article 3 of the ICTY Statute, as well as the following specific elements:

1. Acts of violence directed against the civilian population or individual civilians not taking direct part in hostilities causing death or serious injury to body or health within the civilian population.
2. The offender wilfully made the civilian population or individual civilians not taking direct part in hostilities the object of those acts of violence.
3. The above offence was committed with the primary purpose of spreading terror among the civilian population.

With respect to "acts of violence", these do not include legitimate attacks against combatants but only unlawful attacks against civilians. The majority were of the view that "acts of violence" include an offence which constitutes acts of violence which are wilfully directed against the civilian population or individual civilians causing death or serious injury to body or health within the civilian population with the primary purpose of spreading terror among the civilian population – namely the crime of terror as a violation of the laws or customs of war – and that this formed part of the law to which the accused and his subordinates were subject during the period relevant to the indictment. The accused knew or should have known that this was so as Article 142 of the 1964 Yugoslav Criminal Code criminalized such conduct:

> Whosoever, in violation of the rules of the international law during a war, an armed conflict or an occupation, orders the imposition of measures against the civilian population aimed at inducing fear and terror or whosoever commits any of the acts, shall be punished by imprisonment of not less than five years or by death.

Terror as a crime within IHL was made effective in this case by treaty law. The Tribunal thus had jurisdiction *ratione materiae* by way of Article 3 of the ICTY Statute to prosecute this act of terrorism as a war crime.

The ICTY Appeals Chamber came to the conclusion that the prohibition of terror against the civilian population – a breach of IHL, as enshrined in Article 51(2) of Additional Protocol I and Article 13(2) of Additional Protocol II – clearly belonged to customary international law from at least the time of its inclusion in those treaties and that it had jurisdiction *ratione materiae* by way of Article 3 of the ICTY Statute and could thus attach individual criminal responsibility for spreading terror among the civilian population.

Judge *Schomburg* dissented on several points. He first of all had doubts as to whether there was a standing state practice during the time that was relevant in the indictment which charged *Galić* with acts committed between 1992 and 1994. He also doubted the validity of the historic arguments. He accepted that the War Crimes Commission mentioned "systematic terrorism" on its list of recommended war crimes. However, it was uncertain, in his view, "what the Commission actually meant by "systematic terrorism" and whether their idea of the concept corresponds to Art. 51(2), 2nd Sentence of Additional Protocol I and Article 13(2), 2nd Sentence of Additional Protocol II." Moreover, the Judgement correctly stated that "the few trials in Leipzig did not elaborate on the concept of 'systematic terrorism.'" Judge *Schomburg* also recalled that there was no criminalization of "terrorization against a civilian population in either Nuremberg or the Tokyo Charters". He also "pointed out that the Rome Statute does not have a provision referring to terrorization against a civilian population. If indeed this crime was beyond doubt part of customary international law, in 1998 (!) states would undoubtedly have included it in the relevant provisions of the Statute or in their domestic legislation implementing the Statute."

Of interest, finally, is the Interlocutory Decision on the Applicable Law: Terrorism, Conspiracy, Homicide, Perpetration, Cumulative Charging, rendered by the Appeals Chamber of the Special Tribunal for Lebanon (STL) on 16 February 2011.[37]

---

[37] The Appeals Chamber of the Special Court for Sierra Leone (SCSL) has also dealt with the issue of the applicable law linked to the spreading of terror among civilian populations: *Prosecutor v. Brima, Alex Tamba et al.*, Judgment (Trial Chamber), SCSL-03-01-T, 20 June 2007, and *Prosecutor v. Charles Ghankay Taylor*, Judgment (Appeals Chamber), SCSL-03-01-A, 26 September 2013.

The Pre-Trial Judge of the STL posed several questions for the Appeals Chamber. Three of these questions dealt with the crime of terrorism: "(1) Should the Tribunal take into account international notions on terrorism even though Article 2 of the Statute only refers to the Lebanese Criminal Code ('LCC')? (2) If so, is there an international definition of 'terrorism' and how should it be applied? (3) If not, how is the Lebanese definition of 'terrorism' to be interpreted by the Chamber?"

The Appeals Chamber's point of departure in its reasoning was that the STL predominantly applied domestic Lebanese law, but that this domestic law had to be interpreted in accordance with international conventional and customary law that is binding on Lebanon, such as, for instance, the Arab Convention against Terrorism, which had been ratified by Lebanon, and customary international law on terrorism in times of peace. Relying on the notion of international custom as set out by the International Court of Justice in the *Continental Shelf* case, the Chamber was of the opinion that there is a determined practice concerning the punishment of acts of terrorism, as commonly defined, at least when they are committed in times of peace; in addition, this practice is evidence of a belief by States that the punishment of terrorism responds to a social necessity *(opinio necessitatis)* and is hence rendered obligatory by the existence of a rule requiring this *(opinio juris)*. Moreover, the customary rule is expressed, in the opinion of the Chamber, in terms of international rights and obligations, as it can be held (i) to impose on any State (as well as other international subjects such as rebels and other non-State entities participating in international dealings) the obligation to refrain from engaging through their officials and agents in acts of terrorism, as defined in the rule; (ii) to impose on any State (and other international subjects and entities endowed with the necessary structures and judicial machinery) the obligation to prevent and repress terrorism, and in particular to prosecute and try persons on its territory or in territory under its control who are allegedly involved in terrorism, as defined in the rule; (iii) to confer on any State (and other international subjects endowed with the necessary structures and judicial machinery) the right to prosecute and repress the crime of terrorism, as defined in the rule, perpetrated on its territory (or in a territory under its control) by nationals or foreigners, and an obligation on any other State to refrain from opposing or objecting to such prosecution and repression against their own nationals (unless they are high-level state agents enjoying personal immunities under international law).

Second, the Appeals Chamber acknowledged that the existence of a customary rule outlawing terrorism does not automatically mean that terrorism is a criminal offence under international law. According to the legal parameters suggested by the ICTY Appeals Chamber in the *Tadić* case with regard to war crimes, in order to give rise to individual criminal liability at the international level it is necessary for a violation of the international rule to entail the individual criminal responsibility of the person breaching the rule. In the case of terrorism, when demonstrating the requisite practice, *opinio juris* and *opinio necessitatis*, namely the legal view that it is necessary and indeed obligatory to bring to trial and punish the perpetrators of terrorist acts, in the opinion of the Chamber it was relatively easy to fulfil the necessary criteria, as the process of forming the international criminalization of terrorism is similar to that of war crimes.

Third, the Appeals Chamber took the view that while the customary rule of an international crime of terrorism that has so far evolved only extends to terrorist acts *in times of peace*, a broader norm that would outlaw terrorist acts *during times of armed conflict* may also be emerging. However, the Chamber was clearly aware of the fact that both within the drafting committee of the Comprehensive Convention on International Terrorism and in reservations to the UN Convention for the Suppression of the Financing of Terrorism, some members of the Islamic Conference had expressed a strong disagreement with the notion of considering the acts of "freedom fighters" in times of armed conflict (including belligerent occupation and internal armed conflict), which are directed against innocent civilians, to be terrorist acts. They insisted on both the need to safeguard the right of peoples to self-determination and the necessity to also punish "State terrorism".

The Appeals Chamber came to the conclusion that on the basis of treaties, UN resolutions and the legislative and judicial practice of States, there is convincing evidence that a customary rule of international law has evolved on terrorism in times of peace, requiring the following elements: (i) the intent *(dolus)* to commit the underlying crime and (ii) the special intent *(dolus specialis)* to spread fear or coerce authority; (iii) the commission of a criminal act, and (iv) that the terrorist act be transnational. It thus accepted that the definition of terrorism has a customary international law nature.

The conclusions of the Appeals Chamber have not been endorsed by all in the *opinio juris* and can be qualified as controversial in doctrine. In an "Amicus Curiae Brief on the Question of the Applicable Terrorism Offence with a Particular Focus on a "Special" Special Intent and/or a Special Motive as Additional Subjective Requirements", *Kai Ambos*[38] argued that under the ICC Rome Statute terrorism is clearly not an international ICC offence[39] and that under international law terrorism is at best "a particularly serious transnational, treaty-based crime which comes close to a 'true' international crime but has not yet reached this status". Notwithstanding this, the general elements of this crime can be inferred from the relevant sources of international law.

---

38 Available at https://papers.ssrn.com/sol3/papers.cfm?abstract_id=1972174.

39 See also *Arnold*, The ICC as a New Instrument, p. 3.

## V. Conclusions

Foreign fighters are not classic participants in classic armed conflicts and the phenomenon is not explicitly dealt with in any of the ICL statutes. First, their status, privileges and ICL criminal liability under *ius ad bellum* and *ius in bello* thus depends on the specific acts *(actus reus)* they have been involved in and their intent *(mens rea)*. ICL courts at the international and domestic levels have been searching for solutions to fit them into the categories of IHL and ICL. The reasoning used is not always convincing, as we have seen, and requires extensive interpretation in order to comply with the *nullum crimen, nulla poena sine lege* principle. A second problem is that their status, obligations and privileges differ between international armed conflicts and non-international armed conflicts. This historic distinction no longer makes much sense and ICL courts have already gone beyond it. It is also questionable whether the classification scheme of IHL is still adequate to accommodate the challenges of transnational armed conflicts with the participation of groups such as Al-Qaeda and ISIS.

There is thus a need for legislative renewal in this area of public international law. Unfortunately, in our time it does not seem that States very much agree upon the common standards that should be applied in any renewal of IHL.

Foreign fighters have also increasingly become FTFs. This means that their actions have been qualified, under international counterterrorism conventions or regional European conventions and EU law, as terrorist acts. The expansion of counterterrorism legislation into the proactive and anticipative field of the *iter criminis* has converted foreign fighters into FTFs from the very moment that they start to collect money to organize their travelling to conflict areas or are praising those who have already left on social media. The distinction between terrorist acts in times of peace and war crimes or other ICL crimes in times of armed conflict has become completely blurred.[40] Moreover, in times of armed conflict we can see an increasing use of all types of tools to spread terror among the civilian population that can also qualify as war crimes, CAH and (State) terrorism.

This means that, in practice, national criminal courts and ICL courts are struggling with the lines of division between the applicable law and jurisdictional issues. From an IHL point of view, a great deal depends on the type of conflict, the geographical scope of the hostilities, the (classic) organizational structure of belligerents, the tools they use, the combatant status in non-international armed conflicts, etc. From the counterterrorism law point of view, these criteria (aiming at lawful warfare and the protection of innocent civilians) are only of relative importance. By an extensive criminalization of foreign fighters both during their preparatory stage, execution stage and eventual return, the main aim is to prosecute and punish them for alleged criminal behaviour. Whether this behaviour was part of an international

---

[40] *Scharf*, 7 ILSA Journal of Int'l & Comparative Law 391–398 (2001).

or national armed conflict is of no relevance. Only the small circle of those involved in active participation in armed hostilities in an international armed conflict could eventually qualify for a ground for exclusion from prosecution if the FTFs qualify for the combatant's privilege under IHL. This is a rather small shield of protection that is not always clearly defined. What if non-state actors launch proportionate attacks on military objectives in an internal conflict, like in Syria or Iraq? These acts are not prohibited by IHL, but can nevertheless be criminalized and prosecuted as terrorism. It is questionable whether this does not undermine the rationale of IHL. Altogehter, for many acts foreign fighters can be prosecuted for ICL crimes and/or terrorism at the same time. This means that it would be beneficial for the legislators of counterterrorism conventions to define the interplay with IHL and to provide foreseeability concerning the applicable law and jurisdiction.

As it stands, terrorism can qualify as a particularly serious transnational, treaty-based crime that is on the brink of becoming a true international crime. However, due to the lack of precision concerning the constituent elements of its definition terrorism is not yet considered an international crime per se, not even under customary law.[41] As we have seen, ICL courts can nevertheless play an important role as they deal with terrorism to the extent that they do qualify it as an ICL crime. It is, however, difficult for them to draw a clear line of division between ICL crimes and domestic terrorism prosecutions. A solution might be that the ICC should be given competence to deal with conflicts of law in the case of ICL crimes and counterterrorism.[42] By means of a kind of preliminary ruling procedure the ICC could elaborate an equivalent and multilateral framework in which public international law and IHL are upheld against the expansion of counterterrorism legislation that qualifies any armed opposition whatsoever as enemies under criminal emergency law.

## Bibliography

Additional Protocol to the Council of Europe Convention on the Prevention of Terrorism of 2005, October 22, 2015, CETS No. 217.

Additional Protocols I and II to the Geneva Conventions of 12 August 1949, and relating to the Protection of Victims of International and Non-International Armed Conflicts, of 8 June 1977.

*Ambos, Kai*, Amicus Curiae Brief on the Question of the Applicable Terrorism Offence with a Particular Focus on a 'Special' Special Intent and/or a Special Motive as Addi-

[41] Some authors do, however, advocate an extensive interpretation of the actual Rome Statute of the ICC. For an overview see *Roksandić Vidlička*, Prosecuting Serious Economic Crimes as International Crimes; *Cohen*, 20 Mich. St. Int'l L. Rev. 219 (2013).

[42] *Olásolo/Pérez Cepeda*, Terrorismo Internacional.

tional Subjective Requirements, available at https://papers.ssrn.com/sol3/papers.cfm?abstract_id=1972174.

*Arnold, Roberta*, The ICC as a New Instrument for Repressing Terrorism. Ardsley, NY 2004.

*Cassese, Antonio*, The Multifaceted Criminal Notion of Terrorism in International Law. 4 Journal of International Criminal Justice 933–958 (2006).

– International Criminal Law. Oxford 2003.

*Cassese, Antonio/Gaeta, Paola* (eds.), International Criminal Law. 3rd ed. Oxford 2013.

*Cohen, Aviv*, Prosecuting Terrorists at the International Criminal Court: Reevaluating an unused Legal Tool to Combat Terrorism. 20 Michigan State University College of Law International Law Review 219–257 (2011-2012).

*de Guttry, Andrea*, The Role Played by the UN in Countering the Phenomenon of Foreign Terrorist Fighters. In: Andrea de Guttry et al. (eds.), Foreign Fighters under International Law and Beyond. The Hague 2016, pp. 259–282.

*de Guttry, Andrea/Capone, Francesca/Paulussen, Christophe* (eds.), Foreign Fighters under International Law and Beyond. The Hague 2016.

*Duffy, Helen*, The "War on Terror" and the Framework of International Law. Cambridge 2015.

*Engelhart, Marc*, Heiliger Krieg, heiliger Profit. Afrika als neues Schlachtfeld des internationalen Terrorismus. Berlin 2014.

European Counter Terrorism Centre (ECTC) at the European Police Office (Europol), Changes in Modus Operandi of Islamic State (IS) revisited, December 2016, available at https://www.europol.europa.eu/publications-documents/changes-in-modus-operandi-of-islamic-state-revisited.

*Fleck, Dieter*, The Handbook of Humanitarian Law in Armed Conflicts. Oxford 1995.

*Heinsch, Robert*, Foreign Fighters and International Criminal Law. In: Andrea de Guttry et al. (eds.), Foreign Fighters under International Law and Beyond. The Hague 2016, pp. 161–186.

*Henckaerts, Jean-Marie/Doswald-Beck, Louise*, Customary International Humanitarian Law, Cambridge 2010.

*Mallison, W. Thomas/Mallison, Sally V.*, The Juridical Status of Privileged Combatants under the Geneva Protocol of 1977 concerning International Conflicts. 42(2) Law and Contemporary Problems 4–35 (Spring 1978).

*Paulussen, Christophe*, Impunity for international terrorists? Key legal questions and practical considerations (ICCT Research Paper), available at http://www.icct.nl/download/file/ICCT-Paulussen-Impunity-April-2012.pdf.

*Paulussen, Christophe*, Testing the adequacy of the international legal framework in countering terrorism: the war paradigm (ICCT Research Paper), available at http://www.icct.nl/download/file/ICCT-Paulussen-Legal-Framework-for-Counter-Terrorism-August-2012.pdf.

*Pictet, Jean S.* (ed.), Commentary on the Geneva Conventions of August 12 1949, I-IV ICRC Geneva 1949.

*Pictet, Jean*, Commentary on the Additional Protocols of 8 June 1977 to the Geneva Conventions of 12 August 1949. ICRC/Geneva 1987.

Proposal for a Directive of the European Parliament and of the Council on combating terrorism and replacing Council Framework Decision 2002/475/JHA on combating terrorism, currently in the final phase of negotiation in the trilogue between the Council, the EP and the Commission, available at http://www.europarl.europa.eu/RegData/etudes/BRIE/2016/586628/EPRS_BRI(2016)586628_EN.pdf.

*Roksandić Vidlička, Sunčana*, Prosecuting Serious Economic Crimes as International Crimes. A New Mandate for the ICC? Berlin 2017.

*Scharf, Michael P.*, Defining Terrorism as the Peace Time Equivalent of War Crimes: A Case of Too Much Convergence Between International Humanitarian Law and International Criminal Law? 7(2) ILSA Journal of International and Comparative Law, 391–398 (2001).

*Sommario, Emanuele*, The Status of Foreign Fighters under International Humanitarian Law. In: Andrea de Guttry et al. (eds.), Foreign Fighters under International Law and Beyond. The Hague 2016, pp. 141–160.

UN Draft comprehensive convention against international terrorism, https://www.ilsa.org/jessup/jessup08/basicmats/unterrorism.pdf.

UN Security Council, Resolution 2170, August 15, 2014.

UN Security Council, Resolution 2178, September 24, 2014.

*Venet, O.*, Infractions terroristes et droit humanitaire: l'article 141bis du Code Pénal, Journal des Tribunaux, no 6387, 13 mars 2010, 169–172.

*Werle, Gerhard*, Principles of International Criminal Law. The Hague 2005.

# UN Regulations on Asset Freezing as a Countermeasure Against the Financing of ISIS

*Maja Serafin*, LL.M.

## I. Introduction

The Islamic State in Syria and Iraq (ISIS) is considered the world's richest terrorist organization.[1] The group is able to control acquired territories, build infrastructure, and establish a "state." According to the Report 2015 of the Financial Action Task Force (FATF), most of ISIS funding comes from exhausting occupied territory.[2] Illicit gains are derived from oil and gas reservoirs, and from taxes imposed on the population living within the territory. Nonetheless, due to the destruction of oil wells by the international coalition's bombing campaign and the recapture of territory by Iraq's army, ISIS has been deprived of some of its important income sources.[3] For this reason, the importance of other financing sources may increase in the future and if so, preventing external financing will represent an important task.

The prevention of terrorism financing became an international priority after 9/11.[4] Since terrorist organizations have been carrying out their actions across national borders, terrorism has become a global problem; thus, the response must also be global. With regard to terrorism financing, this means to make it impossible for them to use the international market to transfer funds for terrorist purposes. At the level of the United Nations (UN) it became necessary to act not only against state actors but also against individuals who support terrorism. The problem of individual supporters was addressed by targeted sanctions. Unlike traditional sanctions, which are imposed on state actors, targeted sanctions do not affect a country's entire population but only those individuals who take unlawful actions.[5] Among other

---

1 *Levallois/Cousseran*, The financing of ISIS, p. 8.

2 FATF, Report 2015; see also more recent studies *Levallois/Cousseran*, The financing of ISIS; *Heißner* et al., Caliphate in Decline, 2017.

3 *Levallois/Cousseran*, The financing of ISIS, p. 9; *Clarke* et al., RAND Corporation Workshop – Financial Futures of ISIL, pp. 11–12.

4 *Barrett*, Case W. Res. J. Int'l L. 2009, 7–10; *Levi*, Brit. J. Criminol. 2010, 645–652.

5 See *Tehrani*, Die "Smart Sanctions," pp. 36–42; *Beuren*, in: Odendahl (ed.), Die Bekämpfung des Terrorismus, pp. 177–178.

steps taken to undermine terrorism financing,[6] immediate actions appeared to be necessary to prevent terrorist attacks. One such immediate action is asset freezing, which can be imposed based on the suspicion that an individual or entity supports a terrorist group. The suspicion refers not to the use of particular funds but more generally to the person who holds it on the basis of his or her past actions.[7] However, this measure raises concerns about democratic values, as sanctions are imposed not based on a person's actions but based on a general suspicion.[8]

The aim of this paper is a brief analysis of the role of asset freezing in preventing the financing of ISIS. Asset freezing has been developed to target different types of terrorist organizations, which, due to the fact that they lack a "state-like" structure, depend mostly on external donations.[9] The question is whether and how those sanctions can be effectively used against ISIS financing. In my search for an answer, I will first outline the development of asset freezing as a targeted sanction of the UN, the procedure of imposing it, and protection mechanisms for persons and entities concerned. Then I will look at ISIS' financing structure, the changes that occurred over the past years, and expected future developments. Since the threat of Al-Qaida has been a trigger for developing targeted sanctions, and since ISIS differs significantly from Al-Qaida, the final part of this paper will discuss the effect that can be expected from applying these measures.

## II. Preventing terrorism financing with smart sanctions

Smart sanctions constitute a development of international diplomatic sanctions introduced to avoid targeting an entire country's population because of wrongdoings on the part of political decision-makers or wealthy, influential individuals. The smart sanctions imposed by the UN are asset freeze, travel ban, and arms embargo.[10] The aim of financial sanctions is the economic isolation of targeted persons or entities. To this end, not only their assets are subject to freezing but due to the listing decision any economic contact with them is also prohibited.

---

6 See *Barrett*, Case W. Res. J. Int'l L. 2009, 9–10.

7 On the detection of terrorist funding see *Bantekas*, AJCL 2003, 320–323.

8 See *Gearty*, in: English (ed.), Illusions of Terrorism and Counter-Terrorism, pp. 73–75.

9 See *Levitt*, Fletcher Forum of World Affairs 2003, p. 61; *Bantekas*, AJCL 2003, 316–320.

10 https://www.un.org/sc/suborg/en/sanctions/1267#sanction%20measures [last visited 1 January 2019].

## A. Development of asset freezing as a smart sanction

The general concept of smart sanctions is the result of several years of development. At the very beginning, decisions had to be taken on whether individuals may be the subject of UN sanctions in the first place and whether terrorism constitutes a threat to peace. These were questions of interpretation of Article 39 of the UN Charter[11] in a way that allows to concern individuals responsible for supporting terrorist organizations as a threat to peace. UN Security Council (SC) Resolution 748 (1992) resolved that terrorism consists in a threat to the peace under Article 39 and that sanctions can be imposed on individuals.[12]

The next important step was the adoption of the International Convention for the Suppression of the Financing of Terrorism by the General Assembly of the United Nations in 1999.[13] Article 2 of the Convention defines terrorism financing as providing or collecting funds with the intention or in the knowledge that they are to be used to carry out a terrorist act. The purpose of financing is illegal, the source of the funds can be both legal and illegal. Terrorism financing utilizes the monetary neutrality and globalization of the financial markets to obscure the purpose of the funds. The Convention requires State Parties to take appropriate measures to identify, detect, freeze, or seize terrorist-related funds. State Parties are obliged to monitor and license money transmission agencies. Identifying terrorist-related funds represents a problem since their sources may also be legitimate. In such cases, law enforcement has to figure out the destination of the legitimate financial resources.[14] In order to identify suspicious transactions, State Parties must impose obligations on financial institutions.[15]

After the Convention had been adopted, first steps were taken to address the problem of individual financial support for terrorist organizations. SC Resolution 1267 (1999) established the Al-Qaida Sanctions Committee responsible for listing terrorism suspects.[16] SC Resolution 1333 (2000) decided for the first time that financial sanctions can be imposed on non-state actors. This was the Council's response to a growing threat to the peace that may be caused by individual actions.[17]

---

11 Article 39 UN Charter: The Security Council shall determine the existence of any threat to the peace, breach of the peace, or act of aggression and shall make recommendations, or decide what measures shall be taken in accordance with Articles 41 and 42, to maintain or restore international peace and security.

12 See *Tehrani*, Die "Smart Sanctions," pp. 38–41.

13 See *Bantekas*, AJCL 2003, 323–325.

14 On financing terrorism by legitimate means see *Bantekas*, AJCL 2003, 320–323.

15 Further information on the "Know Your Customer" policy *Bantekas*, AJCL 2003, 325.

16 S/RES/1267 (1999); see also *Schmahl*, in: Odendahl (ed.), Die Bekämpfung des Terrorismus, pp. 121–125.

17 For further information on the development of smart sanctions see *Tehrani*, Die "Smart Sanctions," pp. 39–40; *Bantekas*, AJCL 2003, 315–316.

After 9/11, the Security Council decided that targeted sanctions can be imposed in the event of any act of international terrorism; a connection to a state action is not required. In addition, Member States were required to criminalize the act of providing financial support to terrorist groups and to take measures to freeze the assets that are going to be used to this end.[18] SC Resolution 1373 (2001), adopted just a few days after the attacks of 9/11, requires State Parties to freeze all funds or financial assets of persons and entities that are directly or indirectly used to commit terrorist acts or owned or controlled by persons engaged in or associated with terrorism.[19] To monitor Member States' actions taken to implement the Resolution, a Counter-Terrorism Committee was established.[20] SC Resolution 1390 (2002) authorized the Security Council to list individuals, groups, and entities in support of terrorism and to request Member States to comply with the sanctions imposed. Assets of listed individuals must be frozen and Member States must ensure that no economic resources be made available to them.[21] Preventing terrorism financing has become an important aspect of terrorism prevention ever since. Since financing is an area in which terrorist organizations need interact with non-terrorist actors, it should be controlled to prevent terrorism.[22] Since 2015 this has also applied to groups and individuals supporting ISIS.[23]

## B. Listing procedure

The Sanctions Committee is composed of 15 Security Council members and takes listing decisions by consensus.[24] It is responsible for imposing and overseeing individual sanctions for supporting terrorist organizations, such as Al-Qaida and ISIS.[25] The asset freeze is one of the sanctions. Any Member State may submit a listing request,[26] which must be supported by evidence and may consist in intelligence, law enforcement, judicial, or media information.[27] After receiving a request,

---

18 S/RES/1373 (2001) and S/RES/1390 (2002); see *Tehrani*, Die "Smart Sanctions," pp. 40–41.

19 *Barrett*, Case W. Res. J. Int'l L. 2009, 9–10.

20 https://www.un.org/sc/ctc/about-us/ [last visited 1 January 2019]. See *Schmahl*, in: Odendahl (ed.), Die Bekämpfung des Terrorismus, pp. 128–129.

21 See *Tehrani*, Die "Smart Sanctions," p. 49.

22 *Barrett*, Case W. Res. J. Int'l L. 2009, pp. 9–10.

23 S/RES/2253 (2015).

24 The Committee is operating pursuant to S/RES/1267 (1999), S/RES/1989 (2011), S/RES/2235 (2015).

25 https://www.un.org/sc/suborg/en/sanctions/1267#work%20and%20mandate [last visited 1 January 2019].

26 For further information see https://www.un.org/sc/suborg/en/sanctions/1267/aq_sanctions_list [last visited 1 January 2019].

27 It has been updated in paragraph 2 (a) of SC Resolution 2253(2015) and renewed most recently in paragraph 1 (a) of SC Resolution 2368 (2017].

the Committee will take a listing decision within ten working days. If the decision is positive, the name will be added to the sanctions list available on the Committee's website. The information is also passed to the authorities of the country where the listed individual or entity is believed to be located and the country of which the person concerned is a national. Once an individual or entity is listed, they are subject to the asset freeze. This means that all Member States are required to freeze, without delay, the funds and other financial assets or economic resources of any individual or entity on the list. Listed individuals and entities are also subject to further sanctions such as travel bans (no entry or transit through Member States' territory) and arms embargoes (direct or indirect supply, sale, and transfer of arms and related material of all types, also including spare parts, technical advice, assistance and training, no exemptions).[28]

## C. Controversies and delisting procedure

When the listing of non-state actors was first introduced,[29] listed persons or entities had no legal remedies. Listing was an arbitrary diplomatic procedure. Individuals as well as entities do not fall under the jurisdiction of the International Court of Justice (ICJ). It is also questionable whether the ICJ has jurisdiction over political decisions of the Security Council such as sanctions. Though asset freezing is a provisional measure, it is a significant restriction on the right to property and the freedom to enter into business relationships. In response to this criticism, a delisting procedure has been introduced.[30] Still, the lack of judicial control or something of a similar nature over the decisions has stirred controversies about the listing procedure. Furthermore, listing decisions may be based on media information, and the evidence only needs to provide "reasonable grounds" or a "reasonable base" to effect a listing.

This criticism was addressed by SC Resolution 1730 (2006), establishing a UN Focal Point where a person or entity concerned can file a delisting application.[31] Moreover, the Sanctions Committee must review the list on a regular basis and prove the actuality of the information underlying listing decisions.[32] Still, those

---

28 For further information see https://www.un.org/sc/suborg/en/sanctions/1267#sanction%20measures [last visited 1 January 2019].

29 S/RES/1373 (2001), S/RES/1390 (2002).

30 See *Tehrani*, Die "Smart Sanctions," pp. 112–115; *Schmahl*, in: Odendahl (ed.), Die Bekämpfung des Terrorismus, p. 131; *Rosand*, AJIL 2004, 748–753; *Mimler*, VN 2013, p. 212; *Ginsborg*, in: Saul (ed.), Research handbook, pp. 612–617; critical on listing as a decision which directly concerns individual rights and their legitimation *Beuren*, in: Odendahl (ed.), Die Bekämpfung des Terrorismus, pp. 180–181.

31 See *Tehrani*, Die "Smart Sanctions," pp. 113–115; *Schmahl*, in: Odendahl (ed.), Die Bekämpfung des Terrorismus, p. 142.

32 See *Schmahl*, in: Odendahl (ed.), Die Bekämpfung des Terrorismus, p. 142.

changes did not guarantee a protection that meets the standard of independent judicial control of the questioned decision. A turning point came with a decision of the European Court of Human Rights in 2008. In the case of *Kadi v. Council of the EU and Commission of the European Communities*, the appellant, Mr. *Yassin Abdullah Kadi*, challenged the freezing of his and his charity's assets as unlawful and as a violation of human rights.[33] In 2009 the Sanctions Committee established the Office of the Ombudsperson to represent the rights of listed individuals and entities.[34] Anyone subject to a listing decision may submit a delisting request.[35] This can be done directly by the Committee or through the Office of the Ombudsperson. The petitioner is also required to submit evidence proving that he or she never met or does no longer meet the listing criteria. In other words, the listed person or entity has to counter the reasons for the listing decision. Even though the established delisting procedure still fails to meet the standard of independent judicial control, it does give those listed the protection of an independent arbitrator.[36]

Compared to the listing procedure, the delisting procedure is more complicated; processing a delisting application takes several months.[37] The decision has to be taken by consensus of the Committee or the application is passed from the Committee to be decided by the Security Council. First, evidence needs to be gathered; subsequently, the dialogue and report phase starts. If the listed individual or entity is represented by the Ombudsperson, the Committee has to review his or her official report. In a case where delisting has been recommended and the Committee does not decide by consensus in favor of keeping the name on the list, it has to be removed from the sanctions list within 60 days. Since the Ombudsperson's Office has been established until February 2018, it has received 80 cases, 74 of which have been fully completed; of these, 57 resulted in delisting, and in 17 applications, delisting was refused.[38] The vast majority of cases involved listings of individuals.

## III. Targeting ISIS' financing structure

Asset freezing is a countermeasure against individual financial support of terrorist organizations. In the following the current and the expected role of this funding source for ISIS will be examined.

---

33 *Kadi v. Council and Commission*, C-402 and 415/05, (2008) ECR I-6351.

34 *Beuren*, in: Odendahl (ed.), Die Bekämpfung des Terrorismus, p. 179.

35 S/RES/2253 (2015).

36 *Schmahl*, in: Odendahl (ed.), Die Bekämpfung des Terrorismus, p. 143.

37 For detailed information on the delisting procedure see https://www.un.org/sc/suborg/en/ombudsperson/procedure [last visited 1 January 2019].

38 S/2018/120, p. 4.

## A. Main funding sources

As already mentioned above, the majority of ISIS' funds comes from the occupied territory, which is ruled like a state.[39] These illegal proceeds derive from the following activities: taking control of oil and gas reservoirs, extorting agriculture (money and crops from farmers), bank looting, illicit taxation of goods and cash for the transit of territory in which ISIS operates, and selling cultural artefacts. Further, ISIS occupies many archeological sites, some of them UNESCO world heritage sites. Cultural artefacts traded on the black market represent a source of revenue of unknown amounts.[40] Foreign terrorist fighters have also provided some monetary support, but these contributions are relatively small. ISIS has also used modern communication networks to generate financial contributions from outside the occupied territory.[41]

Oil revenues have become one of the most important funding sources since ISIS took control over about 60 percent of Syria's and about 10 percent of Iraq's petrol production. This, together with the smuggling system already existing in the region, provided significant financial gains.[42] However, the importance of taxes and the confiscation of goods and bank money have increased since 2016 due to the international coalition's bombing campaign.[43] Military operations against ISIS led to the destruction of many oil wells. In addition, still existing facilities are aging and there is a lack of maintenance personnel. Military efforts combined with a drop in the oil price over the past years have led to a decline in ISIS' oil revenues.[44] The armed conflict also impacted the energy-generating potential of controlled water stocks.[45] In this situation, agricultural resources have become crucial for the organization. Private financial contributions still account only for a small percentage of ISIS resources.[46]

---

39 For further information see *Levallois/Cousseran*, The financing of ISIS, pp. 7–8.

40 See *Heißner* et al., Caliphate in Decline, pp. 8–9.

41 See Financial Action Task Force (FATF), Report 2015, pp. 12–18; *Clarke* et al., RAND Corporation Workshop – Financial Futures of ISIL, pp. 8–9; *Heißner* et al., Caliphate in Decline, pp. 7–12; on Al-Qaida finances, also including taxes and extorting local population, see *Barrett*, Case W. Res. J. Int'l L. 2009, 16.

42 *Levallois/Cousseran*, The financing of ISIS, p. 10.

43 *Levallois/Cousseran*, The financing of ISIS, pp. 10, 15; *Clarke* et al., RAND Corporation Workshop – Financial Futures of ISIL, p. 9.

44 *Levallois/Cousseran*, The financing of ISIS, p. 9.

45 *Levallois/Cousseran*, The financing of ISIS, p. 10.

46 *Levallois/Cousseran*, The financing of ISIS, p. 11.

## B. Meaning of individual financial support

The International Centre for the Study of Radicalisation reports that, between 2014 and 2016, donations were insignificant compared to the other revenue sources.[47] Unlike Al-Qaida , ISIS does not rely on donations as the main source of funding.[48] In terms of private donors, there is information that ISIS was financed by donors from the Gulf monarchies at the very beginning of its existence.[49] This seems unlikely in view of the fact that the organization carried out some attacks on Saudi soil. On the other hand, the purchasing of ISIS protection by some regimes cannot be excluded.[50] In 2014 Gulf monarchies started to introduce legislation to hamper the collection of funds for jihadist organizations and to monitor charity organizations. Nevertheless, loopholes in their legislation and control systems continue to exist.[51] The giving to charity *(zakat)*, one of the five pillars of Islam, plays an important role in this context as it has been misused by terrorist organizations ostensibly engaged "for the common good of a particular Muslim society,"[52] causing unsuspecting individuals to make financial contributions for terrorist purposes.[53] Another problem are the private charities in Syria and Iraq that are forced to use unofficial ways to transfer funds as a result of the difficulties they face when using the official network due to conflicts of interests of parties involved and military operations on the ground. Using unofficial ways puts funds at risk of being stolen and used for terrorism financing.[54]

## C. Expected development

The financial future and evolution of ISIS is uncertain and disputed.[55] Oil, extortion, and taxes remain the main financial resources.[56] Together, they represent 70–80 percent of the organization's revenue. Due to the military conflict and the ensuing loss of ISIS-controlled territory, taxation has become less profitable but

---

47 *Heißner* et al., Caliphate in Decline, p. 9.

48 See *Clarke* et al., RAND Corporation Workshop – Financial Futures of ISIL, p. 14; Financial Action Task Force (FATF), Report 2015, pp. 12–20; *Heißner* et al., Caliphate in Decline, p. 12; to compare with the Al-Qaida funding structure see *Barrett*, Case W. Res. J. Int'l L. 2009, 12–16.

49 Financial Action Task Force (FATF), Report 2015, p. 18; *Clarke* et al., RAND Corporation Workshop – Financial Futures of ISIL, p. 9; *Heißner* et al., Caliphate in Decline, p. 8.

50 *Levallois/Cousseran*, The financing of ISIS, p. 13.

51 *Levallois/Cousseran*, The financing of ISIS, p. 13.

52 *Bantekas*, AJCL 2003, 322.

53 See *Bantekas*, AJCL 2003, 322; *Levi*, Brit. J. Criminol. 2010, 657.

54 *Levallois/Cousseran*, The financing of ISIS, p. 13.

55 See *Clarke* et al., RAND Corporation Workshop – Financial Futures of ISIL, pp. 21–26.

56 *Clarke* et al., RAND Corporation Workshop – Financial Futures of ISIL, p. x.

also more important.[57] On the one hand, the support by foreign donors is expected to increase.[58] On the other hand, the search for foreign donors remains uncertain and contested.[59] Another scenario suggests that revenues from extortion and illicit trade will continue to be the principal revenue sources in the future.[60]

Even if current estimates about ISIS' future suggest that its territory will continue to shrink, and the ability to resist military actions will continue to decrease,[61] the report presented by the Secretary General to the UN on 2 February 2017 provides no indication that ISIS does not represent a serious threat.[62] ISIS has proven its ability to adapt to changes.[63] As the report says, ISIS' financial situation continues to deteriorate, but because of the group's weakening, the priorities have shifted by engaging in armed conflicts in Syria and Iraq. There has also been information that ISIS is trying to diversify its financial sources by speculating in the stock market.[64]

From the European perspective, there is yet another aspect to the current situation in the Middle East: the prevention of terrorist acts carried out outside ISIS-held territory. The situation on the ground does not correspond to what foreign fighters have been promised and leads to home returns of those who are willing to carry out attacks on their own.[65] Considering the fact that such attacks do not require much funding, they cannot be effectively prevented by financial sanctions. Also, while the Security Council encourages Member States to control the bank accounts of foreign fighters, the effectiveness of this measure is questionable.[66]

## IV. Conclusions

ISIS' revenue sources are unstable, and the organization's income has declined significantly over the last two years. However, this does not come as a result of traditional "counter terrorism measures" but mostly due to the successful military

57 *Levallois/Cousseran*, The financing of ISIS, p. 17; *Heißner* et al., Caliphate in Decline, p. 10.

58 Financial Action Task Force (FATF), Report 2015, p. 19; *Clarke* et al., RAND Corporation Workshop – Financial Futures of ISIL, p. xii.

59 *Clarke* et al., RAND Corporation Workshop – Financial Futures of ISIL, p. xi.

60 *Heißner* et al., Caliphate in Decline, p. 13.

61 *Levallois/Cousseran*, The financing of ISIS, p. 15.

62 http://www.un.org/ga/search/view_doc.asp?symbol=S/2017/97 [last visited 1 January 2019].

63 *Levallois/Cousseran*, The financing of ISIS, p. 14; the same conclusion *Clarke* et al., RAND Corporation Workshop – Financial Futures of ISIL, p. x.

64 *Levallois/Cousseran*, The financing of ISIS, p. 16.

65 *Levallois/Cousseran*, The financing of ISIS, p. 16.

66 *Levallois/Cousseran*, The financing of ISIS, p. 17.

operations against ISIS.[67] In view of this, a discussion of the limits of the Western counterterrorism policy, and the UN sanctions regime as one part of it, seems to be warranted.[68]

One of the remaining important issues in the prevention of ISIS' financing is to ensure that the group is unable to raise money from beyond its territory.[69] To that end, financial sanctions are one possible tool. They can be used not only against international donors but also against ISIS members entering the international financial market or conducting other financial operations abroad; their economic partners can be targeted as well.[70] The objective of sanctions is the financial isolation of ISIS.[71] Moreover, preventing ISIS from access to the international financial market continues to be important as this would open up new possibilities in accessing obscured financial support. Asset freezing can also be a useful tool for targeting charities operating internationally in support of the organization, as the transferred funds are significant and likely to be noticed. In terms of individuals, one option is the listing of wealthy and influential individuals. The overall quantitative value of external donations to ISIS is minimal relative to other revenue sources, but the importance of foreign donor support is expected to increase for ISIS as other sources of revenue diminish. Asset freeze may have a preventive and disruptive effect but what is needed is a comprehensive approach that integrates multilateral strategies with national actions by Member States.[72]

Targeted sanctions fail to address the other problem mentioned above, i.e., terrorist acts committed outside ISIS-held territory. They require a different approach. First, it is questionable whether ISIS has a direct and active influence on the people who commit those acts. Furthermore, the objective of asset freezing has been to target the "big fish" who make substantial contributions to terrorist organizations. Low-cost terrorist attacks present a different challenge in terms of prevention; to prevent those attacks requires other measures than asset freezing. Even if there is a basis for listing the individuals and entities involved in low-cost terrorist attacks because they make a financial contributions to ISIS, they are likely to remain unidentified and will generally fall below a threshold that merits serious investigation.

---

67 *Levallois/Cousseran*, The financing of ISIS, p. 9; *Heißner* et al., Caliphate in Decline, p. 12.

68 *Drezner*, International Studies Review 2003, 107–109; *Elliott*, in: Cortright/Lopez (eds.), Smart Sanctions, p. 171. On counter terrorism law and politics as rooted in predemocratic impulses see *Gearty*, in: English (ed.), Illusions of Terrorism and Counter-Terrorism, pp. 74–93.

69 *Clarke* et al., RAND Corporation Workshop – Financial Futures of ISIL, p. xi.

70 *Clarke* et al., RAND Corporation Workshop – Financial Futures of ISIL, p. xi.

71 *Clarke* et al., RAND Corporation Workshop – Financial Futures of ISIL, pp. xi, xii.

72 Whether more regulations of the financial sector may help solve the problem remains an open question. On regulating the financial sector in order to prevent terrorism and the costs of compliance Barrett, Case W. Res. J. Int'l L. 2009, pp. 17–18; Levi, Brit. J. Criminol. 2010, 650–652.

Unless those individuals have previously been convicted or otherwise come under the radar of law enforcement, they will go unnoticed until they commit a terrorist attack. However, even a decline in ISIS revenues need not necessarily have an immediate impact on terrorist acts carried out outside its territory.[73]

Countering ISIS' financing structure also means dealing with the problem of data reliability. It is simply impossible to provide exact information about ISIS' finances; all that can be provided are estimates.[74] The reports on ISIS' financing quoted in this paper rely mostly on publicly available information, leaked ISIS documents, testimonies, expert interviews, government reports, and media information. The prevention of terrorism financing is largely based on prediction and this should be kept in mind. This also applies to asset freezing. These predictions are based on "suspicious" actions by individuals or entities. The actual connection between these actions and terrorism can be overestimated or underestimated, which assigns counter-terrorist financing in terms of efficiency a modest ranking among counter-terrorist actions in general.[75]

## Bibliography

*Bantekas, Ilias*, Current Developements: The International Law of Terrorist Financing. AJCL 2003, 315–333.

*Barrett, Richard*, Time to Reexamine Regulation Designed to Counter the Financing of Terrorism. Case W. Res. J. Int'l L. 2009, 7–18.

*Beuren, John*, Die Bekämpfung von Al Qaida, dem sog. "Islamischen Staat" und Boko Haram. In: Kerstin Odendahl (ed.), Die Bekämpfung des Terrorismus mit Mitteln des Völker- und Europarechts. Berlin 2017.

*Clarke, Colin P./Jackson, Kimberly/Johnston, Patrick B./Robinson, Eric/Shatz, Howard*, Financial futures of the Islamic State of Iraq and the Levant. Findings from a RAND corporation workshop. Conference proceedings. Santa Monica, CA 2017.

*Drezner, Daniel W.*, How Smart Are Smart Sanctions? International Studies Review 2003, 107–110.

*Elliott, Kimberly A.*, Analyzing the Effects of Targeted Sanctions. In: David Cortright/ George A. Lopez (eds.), Smart Sanctions. Targeting Economic Statecraft. Lanham, MD 2002, pp. 171–182.

Financial Action Task Force (FATF), Financing of the Terrorist Organisation Islamic State in Iraq and the Levant (ISIL). February 2015.

---

73 *Heißner* et al., Caliphate in Decline, p. 13.

74 See *Heißner* et al., Caliphate in Decline, p. 6.

75 *Levi*, Brit. J. Criminol. 2010, 667.

*Gearty, Conor*, No Golden Age: The Deep Origins and Current Utility of Western Counter-Terrorism Policy. In: Richard English (ed.), Illusions of Terrorism and Counter-Terrorism. Oxford 2015, pp. 73–93.

*Ginsborg, Lisa*, The United Nations Security Council's counterterrorism Al-Qaida sanctions regime: Resolution 1267 and the 1267 Committee. In: Ben Saul (ed.), Research handbook on international law and terrorism. Cheltenham 2015, pp. 608–625.

*Heißner, Stefan/Neumann, Peter R./Holland-McCowan, John/Basra, Rajan*, Caliphate in Decline: An Estimate of Islamic State's Financial Fortunes. The International Centre for the Study of Radicalisation and Political Violence. London 2017.

*Levallois, Agnès/Cousseran, Jean-Claude*, The financing of the "Islamic State" in Syria and Iraq (ISIS). In-depth analysis. September 2017. See http://www.europarl.europa.eu/RegData/etudes/IDAN/2017/603835/EXPO_IDA(2017]603835_EN.pdf [last visited 1 January 2019].

*Levi, Michael*, Combating the Financing of Terrorism. A History and Assessment of the Control of Threat Finance. Brit. J. Criminol. 2010, 650–669.

*Levitt, Matthew*, Stemming the Flow of Terrorist Financing: Practical and Conceptual Challenges. Fletcher Forum of World Affairs 2003, 59–70.

*Mimler, Manfred*, Terrorismusbekämpfung bei den Vereinten Nationen. VN, issue 3, 2013, 120–125.

*Rosand, Eric*, The Security Council's Efforts to Monitor the Implementation of Al-Qaeda/Taliban Sanctions. AJIL 2004, 745–763.

*Schmahl, Stefanie*, Maßnahmen der UNO zur Bekämpfung des internationalen Terrorismus: die Rolle des Sicherheutsrats und der Generalversammlung. In: Kerstin Odendahl (ed.), Die Bekämpfung des Terrorismus mit Mitteln des Völker- und Europarechts. Berlin 2017.

*Tehrani, Ramin*, Die "Smart Sanctions" im Kampf gegen den Terrorismus und als Vorbild einer präventiven Vermögensabschöpfung. Berlin et al. 2014.

# The Organised Crime-Terrorism Nexus: How to Address the Issue of ISIS Benefitting from Lucrative Criminal Activities?

*Katalin Ligeti* and *Maxime Lassalle*

## I. Introduction

There are growing concerns about an evolving relationship between terrorism and organised crime, called the "terrorist-criminal nexus" or "crime-terror nexus." This posited nexus is the principal reason for policy-makers' growing calls for the use of measures originally adopted with the aim of combatting organised crime in order to fight terrorism in general and ISIS in particular. Another contributory factor is the alleged inefficiency of the existing legal framework to prevent and suppress terrorism; given the weaknesses of this framework, so the logic goes, the use of instruments originally designed for organised crime in relation to terrorism ought to be encouraged.[1] Both arguments are based on the assumption that the distinction between terrorism and organised crime is blurring and that they can be compared if not assimilated. This contribution chapter shall begin by examining the above assumption and its empirical basis. It shall then demonstrate that the assumption is justified only to a certain extent and will argue that a criminal policy against organised crime ought only to be used indirectly against terrorism through targeted measures in specific domains.

## II. The notion of a new crime-terror nexus

### A. The emergence of networked organisations

The links between terrorism and organised crime in practice have long been recognised by the international community; as early as 2000, the Palermo Convention explicitly "call[ed] upon all States to recognize the links between transnational or-

---

[1] This was proposed for instance in the Conclusions of the second International Conference on Terrorism and Organised Crime, Council of Europe, September 22, 2017. Available online: https://rm.coe.int/conclusions-of-the-2nd-international-conference-on-terrorism-and-organ/168074eeb6 [last visited 1 January 2019].

ganised criminal activities and acts of terrorism [...]."[2] Meanwhile, the literature has often referred to this phenomenon as the terrorism-organised crime "nexus." The term is somewhat misleading, as it could be taken to imply that there is a global alliance between organised crime and terrorist organisations.[3] The main reaction of academics to such a position was to call for (more) evidence of the existence of these links.[4] The resulting empirical studies do not support such a general claim; instead, they show that links between organised crime and terrorism are facilitated by the transformation of both terrorist groups[5] and criminal groups[6] into "networked organisations."[7] There is mounting evidence that terrorists commit offences with the aim of generating profit without, however, being involved in any structured organisation. Characteristic of this transformation is the emergence of networked cells that replace the previously prevalent hierarchical structures and allow for rapid and fluid cooperation between organised criminals and terrorists.[8] Thus, instead of emerging out of a global alliance between organised crime and terrorism, the nexus materialises in local cooperation for profit through criminal activities.

## B. A "business logic" to terrorism

For *Shelley*, whereas terrorists used to be linked to a certain extent to states which provided a reliable source of funding, today's "new nexus"[9] sees them rely more on criminal activities in order to fund terrorist activities[10] and logistical support.[11] This independence vis-à-vis states is revealed by the convergence between transnational organised crime and terrorism that is especially facilitated in situations of weak or failed states[12] and flourishes in conflict areas.[13] Furthermore, the policy targeting terrorist financing has deprived terrorists of most of their funding,

2 General Assembly resolution 55/25, 15 November 2000, Recital 6.

3 See, for example, *Hesterman*, The Terrorist-Criminal Nexus, whose subtitle is "An Alliance of International Drug Cartels, Organized Crime, and Terror Groups", even though this is not justified by the content of the book.

4 *Bovenkerk/Abou Chakra*, 4 Forum sur le crime et la société (2004).

5 *Stohl/Stohl*, 17 Communication Theory (2007).

6 *Williams/Godson*, 37 Crime, Law and Social Change 331–335 (2002).

7 *Dishman*, 28 Studies in Conflict and Terrorism (2005).

8 *Dishman*, 28 Studies in Conflict and Terrorism 246 (2005).

9 *Shelley/Melzer*, 32 International Journal of Comparative and Applied Criminal Justice 43 (2008); *Shelley*, Dirty Entanglements, p. 106; *Shelley*, 6 Georgetown Journal of International Affairs (2005).

10 *Shelley*, Dirty Entanglements, pp. 106–109.

11 *Shelley/Picarelli*, in: Giraldo/Trinkunas (eds.), Terrorism Financing and State Responses: A Comparative Perspective, p. 48.

12 *Makarenko*, 6 Global Crime 138 (2014).

13 *Shelley*, Dirty Entanglements, pp. 100–103.

triggering a "turn to crime":[14] in sum, "since the end of the Cold war and the decline of much state support for terrorism, criminal activity has become the lifeblood of terrorism".[15]

This transformation has led to the emergence of a "business logic to terrorism."[16] Similar to white-collar criminals, terrorists can be considered rational businessmen who want to "maximize their advantages in different environments."[17] Their criminal activities include chiefly trafficking in arms, human trafficking and smuggling of migrants, drug trafficking, trafficking in cultural property, illegal exploitation and trafficking of natural resources, kidnapping for ransom and money laundering.[18]

Notwithstanding this new appetite for crime, links to criminal activities do not necessarily imply links to criminal organisations. The nexus may take different forms: it may be an alliance, where there is a long-term relationship between the two "sides" (terrorism and organised crime), including for example access to specialised knowledge or services, and operational or financial support.[19] The relationship may be one of appropriation/integration where a group from one side integrates with a group from the other in order to acquire tactical capabilities.[20] It may also be a hybridisation when criminal and political motivations converge within one group.[21] Finally, there can be a hybridisation or transformation from one type of group to another[22] – which is extremely rare, if not non-existent, in Europe[23] –, as reported by Europol in 2015:

> In light of the available evidence, convergence between organised crime and terrorism in the EU seems a limited phenomenon. Terrorist and organised crime groups have learned to adapt to changing circumstances such as governmental interventions or changed environments. This makes their structures, activities and methods opportunistic

---

14 U.S. National Council, The threat to U.S. National Security Posed by Transnational Organized Crime, 2011, quoted by *Alda/Sala*, 27 International Journal of Security & Development 3 (2014).

15 *Makarenko*, 6 Global Crime 111 (2014).

16 *Shelley*, Dirty Entanglements, p. 320.

17 *Shelley*, Dirty Entanglements, p. 176.

18 Security Council, Report of the Secretary-General on the threat of terrorists benefiting from transnational organized crime, 21 May 2015.

19 West Sands Advisory LLP, Europe's Crime-Terror Nexus: Links between terrorist and organised crime groups in the European Union, 2012, p. 21. See further for the categories of alliances, operational motivations, convergence and "the black hole" as proposed in *Makarenko*, 6 Global Crime (2014); for coexistence, cooperation and convergence in *Alda/Sala*, 3 International Journal of Security & Development 2 (2014).

20 West Sands Advisory LLP, Europe's Crime-Terror Nexus: Links between terrorist and organised crime groups in the European Union, 2012, p. 30.

21 West Sands Advisory LLP, Europe's Crime-Terror Nexus: Links between terrorist and organised crime groups in the European Union, 2012, p. 36.

22 West Sands Advisory LLP, Europe's Crime-Terror Nexus: Links between terrorist and organised crime groups in the European Union, 2012, p. 38.

23 *Makarenko/Mesquita*, 15 Global Crime (2014).

in nature. The relationship between terrorist and organised crime groups can be characterised as changeable. Based on the cases available in the Europol databases, it can be concluded that convergence in the EU often consists of isolated incidents.[24]

The wording "isolated incidents" is quite restrictive, and tallies with the contention in the U.S. that such relationships are "mostly opportunistic" in that country.[25] Notwithstanding the absence of a precise global assessment, it would appear that in most circumstances in the Western world, terrorists and criminals are not more than "practical partners".[26]

## C. ISIS: crime, terror, or both?

As far as ISIS is concerned, two questions arise. First, what kind of structural nexus, if any, exists between ISIS and organised crime? Second, what is the business logic of ISIS, and what criminal activities does that logic entail?

It has been claimed that ISIS functions exactly like a criminal organisation and that political ideology is only the facade to the criminal activities.[27] According to such views, people do not participate in ISIS for ideological purposes but are attracted for similar reasons (beyond economic gain) as in the case of organised crime: the will to be a member of a group and to be outside society – the idea of "Jihad Cool".[28] For example, third wave jihadism has been described as "a collective solution, devised by young westernised Muslim males to resolve their twin problems of status-frustration and identity-confusion".[29] If the main purpose of ISIS were considered to be criminal as opposed to political, it might be tempting to conclude that the nature of the nexus between ISIS and organised crime is a transformation: ISIS as a criminal organisation *per se*.

However, a recent study suggests another perspective:

> what we have found is not the merging of criminals and terrorists as organisations but of their social networks, environments, or *milieus*. Criminal and terrorist groups have come to recruit from the same pool of people, creating (often unintended) synergies and overlaps that have consequences for how individuals radicalise and operate. This is what we call the *new* crime-terror nexus.[30]

---

[24] Europol, The Nexus Between Organised Crime and Terrorism, July 2015, p. 7.

[25] White House, Strategy to Combat Transnational Organized Crime, Addressing Converging Threats to National Security, July 2011, p. 6.

[26] *Bobic*, 15 Global Crime 254 (2014).

[27] *Roberts*, The Crime-Terror Nexus: Ideology's Misleading Role in Islamist Terrorist Groups, 2016. Available online: http://www.e-ir.info/2016/04/23/the-crime-terror-nexus-ideologys-misleading-role-in-islamist-terrorist-groups/ [last visited 1 January 2019].

[28] *Picart*, 5 Societies (2015).

[29] *Cottee*, 23 Terrorism and Political Violence 738 (2011).

[30] *Basra* et al., Criminal Pasts, Terrorist Futures: European Jihadists and the New Crime-Terror Nexus, p. 11; see also ibid., p. 23: "both criminals and jihadists are recruited from the same demographics – and often in the same places."

Therefore, to reply to the first of the abovementioned questions, it would appear that there is no structured nexus between organised crime and ISIS in Europe. Moreover, the fact that a lot of ISIS members are former criminals is in itself not relevant. Although fight against radicalisation is an important issue,[31] in our view the most important argument to be brought forward for the nexus is its business logic.[32] For this reason, we will focus mainly on this point in the ensuing discussion.

ISIS' business logic is very revealing as to its functioning and its links with crime. An extensive 2015 report from the Financial Action Task Force ("the FATF report") on ISIS' financing concluded that the organisation was using a "new model,"[33] with its sources of revenue "mainly derived from illicit proceeds from its occupation of territory."[34] At the same time, ISIS was also active outside its territory. Accordingly, for *Shelley*, "to understand Islamic State budget flowcharts, it helps to distinguish between big-budget ISIS in the Middle East and low-budget ISIS in Europe."[35] The situation has since evolved in the sense that ISIS has lost exclusive control of the vast majority of "its" territory; in 2018, ISIS is "a global network, with a flat hierarchy and less operational control of its affiliates."[36] Nonetheless, most of the examples used in the following paragraphs relating to ISIS' business logic on the territory it formerly controlled hold true for the numerous territories where the network is still active today.[37]

Turning first to criminal activities carried out by ISIS on the territory it controls, these have included bank looting, extortion and human trafficking, control of oil and gas reservoirs, extorting agriculture, other resource extraction and production facilities, trade in cultural artefacts, illicit taxation of goods and cash that transit territory where ISIS operates as well as salary payments to Iraqi government employees.[38] Moreover, ISIS uses the method of kidnapping for ransom,[39] a way of

---

[31] *Basra* et al., Criminal Pasts, Terrorist Futures: European Jihadists and the New Crime-Terror Nexus.

[32] The linkages between organised crime and terrorism are only developed in relation with financial flows. See Security Council, Resolution 2388, November 21, 2017, para 7 and para 9.

[33] FATF, Financing of the Terrorist Organisation Islamic State in Iraq and the Levant (ISIL) ("FATF report"), April 2015, p. 40.

[34] FATF Report, p. 5.

[35] *Shelley*, How to beat Islamic State? Crack down on cigarette smuggling, The Guardian November 27, 2015.

[36] Security Council, Sixth report of the Secretary General on the threat posed by ISIL (Da'esh) to international peace and security and the range of United Nations efforts in support of Member States in countering the threat, January 31, 2018, p. 2.

[37] The aforementioned Sixth report of the Secretary General is full of such examples, particularly in Iraq, Syria, Yemen, Egypt, Libya, Mali, Niger, Somalia, Afghanistan and Pakistan.

[38] These ways of funding are, however, no longer considered in the Security Council's assessment of ISIS' situation. See Security Council, Fourth report of the Secretary-General on the threat posed by ISIL (Da'esh) to international peace and security and the range of

generating money which is well known to terrorist organisations.[40] On its territory, ISIS clearly qualifies as a criminal organisation. One can say that the nexus, in this case, has led to a transformation. There are, however, no measures of criminal law which can be used in respect of this specific issue considering that such measures would have to be enforced by a state, with the exception of the possibility analysed elsewhere in this book to extend the jurisdiction of the International Criminal Court. Now that ISIS has lost control over virtually all of its former territory, there are calls for ways to hold terrorists accountable, but mainly on the basis of war crimes, crimes against humanity, and genocide.[41]

Moving beyond criminal operations tied to ISIS' own territory, the FATF report insisted on the need to "isolate ISIS from the international financial system";[42] in early 2017, when ISIS was still holding most of its territory, this had not yet been achieved.[43] However, the financial system is not the only route to receive money from the outside world: for example, ISIS conducts human trafficking, including organ harvesting and the selling of women as sex slaves, mostly using business relations with neighbouring countries.[44] The FATF report also highlights links between ISIS and oil smuggling networks.[45] Through intermediaries, the oil is finally sold outside ISIS territory, allowing ISIS to generate revenue from these products. Finally, the same problem applies to the illicit antiquities market. Western countries are market areas for products originating from the numerous cultural sites controlled by ISIS. Even though there is not much evidence that ISIS is directly participating in the illicit antiquities trade, it is most probably benefitting from it.[46] Illicit trade in antiquities can be considered a transnational criminal network in which no hierarchical organisation is in charge but in which a multitude of actors can take part; terrorists do so when the opportunity arises.[47]

---

United Nations efforts in support of Member States in countering the threat, February 2, 2017.

39 FATF report, p. 18.

40 FATF, Organised Maritime Piracy and Related Kidnapping for Ransom, July 2011, p. 24. See also *Dutton*, 53 San Diego Law Review (2016).

41 Security Council, Resolution 2379, September 21, 2017.

42 *Levitt*, Terrorist Financing and the Islamic State. Testimony Submitted to the House Committee on Financial Services.

43 Security Council, Fourth report of the Secretary-General on the threat posed by ISIL (Da'esh) to international peace and security and the range of United Nations efforts in support of Member States in countering the threat, February 2, 2017, pp. 3–4.

44 *Kennedy*, 101 Women Lawyers Journal (2016).

45 FATF report, pp. 13–15.

46 The FATF report, pp. 6–17, single-handedly relies on journalists' reports and concludes that "it might be impossible to show a direct link between the ISIL and the sale of specific artefacts."

47 *Campbell*, 20 International Journal of Cultural Property 128 (2013).

If no measures can be taken within ISIS territory, the activities of these networks might be tackled outside its territory.

Possible solutions to the abovementioned problems include the prosecution of smugglers in neighbouring countries for human trafficking[48] and oil smuggling,[49] and in market countries for antiquities trafficking.[50] These examples are also analysed by *Ana Salinas* in a report on terrorism and transnational organised crime for the Council of Europe. According to this report, terrorism benefits from numerous forms of organised criminal activities and the legal mechanisms to fight these activities should be considerably strengthened.[51] The whole point is to reduce the opportunities[52] for misuse of organised crime activities that are likely to provide sources of terrorist financing and to acknowledge that terrorists benefit mostly indirectly and to a quite limited extent from some types of organised crime.

Finally, even though most terrorist attacks outside ISIS territory are conducted in relation with ISIS members (whether they are directed, enabled or inspired by ISIS)[53] and terrorists seldom act entirely independently from any network,[54] financial relationships between ISIS and Europe have always been much rarer than might be expected. Terrorist cells in Europe do not systematically receive funding from ISIS[55] or from international terrorist organisations[56] and therefore often have to self-fund their activities. Are such funds issued from a nexus with criminal organisations on the territories of western countries? A recent report highlights that in the period 1993–2013 the importance of criminal activities with regard to the funding of terrorist cells in Europe was decreasing.[57] The same report concludes that the way terrorists finance their activities is "remarkably ordinary" in the sense that the funds used are often not related to any criminal activity and can be derived, for instance, from terrorists' legally-earned income.[58]

Nevertheless, it is often claimed that terrorist acts in western countries can be easily funded through petty criminal activities, based on different forms of traffick-

---

48 *Kennedy*, 101 Women Lawyers Journal (2016).

49 *Flinn*, 51 Texas International Law Journal (2016).

50 *Willett*, 58 Arizona Law Review (2016).

51 *Neumann/Salinas*, Report on the Links Between Terrorism and Transnational Organized Crime, pp. 8–11.

52 On the question of opportunities *Mincheva/Gurr*, in: Reuveny/Thompson (eds.), Coping with Terrorism, p. 169.

53 *Callimachi*, Not 'Lone Wolves' After All: How ISIS Guides World's Terror Plots From Afar, New York Times, February 4, 2017.

54 *Burke*, The myth of the 'lone wolf' terrorist, The Guardian, March 30, 2017.

55 *Basra* et al., Criminal Pasts, Terrorist Futures: European Jihadists and the New Crime-Terror Nexus, p. 41.

56 *Oftedal*, The Financing of Jihadi Terrorist Cells in Europe, p. 16.

57 *Oftedal*, The Financing of Jihadi Terrorist Cells in Europe, p. 18.

58 *Oftedal*, The Financing of Jihadi Terrorist Cells in Europe, p. 45.

ing.[59] The point is not so much that petty crime is systematically used for terrorist financing purposes, but that such lucrative criminal activities are easily accessible and not too risky for terrorists.[60] An analysis of the attacks claimed by ISIS confirms this situation to a certain extent.[61] For instance, *Amédy Coulibaly*, who perpetrated the attack against the kosher supermarket following the attack against *Charlie Hebdo*, financed his acts through consumer credit fraud[62] and was known to have been involved in cigarette smuggling.[63] There are, however, other examples where the financing of the operation was based neither on criminal activities in western countries, nor on legal activities, but on direct assistance from ISIS. For instance, the cell responsible for the attacks of 13 November 2015 in Paris was mostly financed by ISIS.[64] Notably, Europol reported that "some of the attackers might have had an active participation in criminal networks, instead of just being their clients",[65] but this assessment is somewhat vague and does not show any significant change since Europol's previous report in 2015 when it was stated that there was no structural nexus between large scale criminal and terrorist organisations. Therefore, concerning the attacks in Europe, one could say that funds can easily be derived from lucrative petty crimes, even though this is not systematically done. This was confirmed by a Europol report in 2017: "these suspects are typically involved at a low level in organised crime and do not fill major roles within organised crime networks."[66]

As regards ISIS and its connections with organised crime, two interim conclusions may be maintained: First, international organised crime networks are involved indirectly and only to a limited extent in the financing of ISIS. Therefore, measures targeting in particular the last stages of the criminal chain,[67] such as the laundering of proceeds of crime and the purchasing of goods originating from territory controlled by ISIS, could work as adequate methods of prevention and sup-

---

59 *Louise Shelley* best represents this position, *Shelley*, Testimony to the Task Force to Investigate Terrorism Financing Entitled "Could America Do More? An Examination of U.S. Efforts to Stop the Financing of Terror," September 9, 2015; *Shelley*, ISIS' Members Depend on Petty Crime to Function in Europe, New York Times, November 20, 2015.

60 *Oftedal*, The Financing of Jihadi Terrorist Cells in Europe, p. 36.

61 *Levitt*, How do ISIS terrorists finance their attacks?, The Hill, November 18, 2015.

62 Centre d'analyse du terrorisme, Le financement des attentats de Paris, October 2016, p. 3.

63 Centre d'analyse du terrorisme, Le financement des attentats de Paris, October 2016, p. 4.

64 Centre d'analyse du terrorisme, Le financement des attentats de Paris, October 2016, p. 1.

65 Europol, Changes in Modus Operandi of Islamic State (IS) Revisited, November 2016, p. 13.

66 Europol, European Union Serious Threat and Organised Crime Threat Assessment, 2017, p. 55.

67 On these stages, see *Campbell*, 20 International Journal of Cultural Property 133 (2013).

pression. Second, terrorists in Europe often rely on lucrative petty crime, which can be, but is not necessarily linked to criminal networks. Therefore, investigations into terrorist financing should target lucrative petty crime irrespective of any link to criminal networks.

In light of these interim conclusions, in the following section we shall analyse if and to which extent the existing legal instruments address the above described problems that transcend terrorism, organised crime and lucrative petty crime.

## III. Alleged weaknesses in the international legal framework

### A. Unclear definition of terrorism leading to fragmentation

How terrorism ought to be defined has been a controversial topic at least since the first proposal was submitted, in 1937, to establish an International Court addressing terrorism, whose main focus was on attacks against state officials and heads of state.[68] Since then, the phenomenon has changed and the focus has moved from state terrorism to terrorist acts as such, but there is still no international definition of terrorism, and no possibility of creating an international offence capable of triggering the jurisdiction of the International Criminal Court. The international legal framework is nevertheless quite developed and has at its disposal nineteen legal instruments adopted to date with the aim of preventing terrorist acts in specific areas, such as civil aviation, the taking of hostages, nuclear material, maritime navigation, and so on.[69]

This framework therefore resembles mostly a patchwork addressing sectoral issues. In the face of this situation, a draft comprehensive convention on international terrorism was proposed in 1996,[70] defining a criminal conduct as terrorist "when the purpose of the conduct, by its nature or context, is to intimidate a population, or to compel a government or an international organization to do or to abstain from doing any act."[71] However, consensus on an international definition has so far proven elusive due to multiple sensitive issues including the extent to which "per-

---

[68] Convention for the Prevention and Punishment of Terrorism, League of Nations, November 16, 1937. See also *Pella*, 44 The American Journal of International Law (1950).

[69] For a list of these legal instruments, see http://www.un.org/en/counterterrorism/legal-instruments.shtml [last visited 1 January 2019]. The scope of these texts varies greatly, as does their ratification; for example, the 2010 Convention on the Suppression of Unlawful Acts Relating to International Civil Aviation still has to be signed by a few countries before it can enter into force.

[70] The draft comprehensive convention on international terrorism was initially discussed at the United Nations General Assembly's Ad Hoc Committee established by Resolution 51/210 of 17 December 1996 on Terrorism.

[71] Art. 2(1) of the draft comprehensive convention.

petrators considered as freedom fighters" should be omitted from its scope, the question how the legitimate right to self-determination should be recognised, the problem of the protection of asylum seekers who see themselves as political opponents but who are considered terrorists in their home countries, and the issue of distinction between terrorist violence and necessary violence during a war.[72]

In general, the extant legal framework does not aim at addressing the crime-terror nexus; most of the criminal activities involved in the nexus as evoked above are not addressed by the sectoral legal instruments. However, and notwithstanding the absence of a common definition of terrorism, the existing legal framework does contain several elements, specified as ancillary acts or preparatory acts of terrorism, which deal indirectly with some manifestations of the nexus. For example, the prohibition of contributing to "nuclear terrorism" under Article 2(4)(c) of the International Convention for the Suppression of Acts of Nuclear Terrorism addresses (albeit indirectly) the fear that criminal networks are involved in the illicit trade in nuclear material.[73] Another document, the International Convention for the Suppression of the Financing of Terrorism, also deals to a certain extent with the profit-oriented activities of terrorists as it prohibits the provision or collection of funds in the knowledge that they will be used for terrorist activities.[74]

The lack of direct attention paid within the international legal framework to the existing and proven facets of the crime-terror nexus was recently criticised by both *Ben Saul*[75] and *Ana Salinas*.[76] In *Salinas'* report, she also argues that international legal instruments in relation to organised crime are not properly implemented in national law, weakening the ability to address the manifestations of the nexus.[77] This means that two different approaches can be followed: can the problem be solved by targeting the links between terrorism and organised crime or by strengthening the fight against organised crime *per se*?

---

72 *Hodgson/Tadros*, 16 New Criminal Law Review (2013). See also *Schmid*, 36 Case Western Journal of International Law (2004).

73 On this fear see *Shelley*, Dirty Entanglements, p. 296.

74 Terrorist activities are defined as namely any "act intended to cause death or serious bodily injury to a civilian, or to any other person not taking an active part in the hostilities in a situation of armed conflict, when the purpose of such act, by its nature or context, is to intimidate a population, or to compel a government or an international organization to do or to abstain from doing any act" in Article 2(1)(b) of the International Convention for the Suppression of the Financing of Terrorism.

75 *Saul*, 3 International Criminal Law Review (2013).

76 *Neumann/Salinas*, Report on the Links Between Terrorism and Transnational Organized Crime, p. 9.

77 *Neumann/Salinas*, Report on the Links Between Terrorism and Transnational Organized Crime, p. 11.

## B. Considering terrorism as a form of organised crime

The situation as regards the treatment of terrorism in international law is in contrast to the comprehensive legal framework on organised crime. According to Article 2(a) of the Palermo Convention,[78] an organised criminal group "shall mean a structured group of three or more persons, existing for a period of time and acting in concert with the aim of committing one or more serious crimes or offences established in accordance with this Convention, in order to obtain, directly or indirectly, a financial or other material benefit." This framework is also supported by some regional instruments,[79] showing that the proposed definition of the phenomenon of organised crime has proven to be more acceptable to the Signatory states than the proposed definitions of terrorism. It has nonetheless been considered that the major success of the Palermo Convention was not the definition of organised crime – which was sufficiently broad and uncontroversial in the eyes of the signatories – but the "tool box" which came with it, especially the "co-operation provisions."[80]

Following the success of the framework related to organised crime and its associated tool box, there are now signs of an extension of the scope of legal instruments addressing organised crime to include terrorism as well; this could give rise to the possibility of the assimilation of terrorism as a sub-category of organised crime. To begin with, the investigative measures used in the fight against organised crime are applied against terrorism. For example in the EU the general approach of the Council on the proposal for a Directive on combating terrorism[81] indicated that the investigative tools available for the fight against organised crime should also be available for investigations in relation to terrorism.[82] This type of assimilation, however, takes place more explicitly at the national level. In France, for example, in 2004 a *dérogatoire* (exceptional) special criminal procedure was adopted that by definition encompasses terrorist acts.[83] This means that in practice, in France terrorist organisations are treated as a specific sub-category of criminal organisations

---

78 United Nations Convention against Transnational Organized Crime, completed by three protocols: the Protocol to Prevent, Suppress and Punish Trafficking in Persons, Especially Women and Children, the Protocol against the Smuggling of Migrants by Land, Sea and Air, and the Protocol against the Illicit Manufacturing of and Trafficking in Firearms, Their Parts and Components and Ammunition.

79 For example for the European Union, see Article 1(1) of the Council framework decision 2008/841/JHA of 24 October 2008 on the fight against organised crime, JO L 300/42, 11 November 2008.

80 *Orlova/Moore*, 27 Houston Journal of International Law 285 (2005).

81 Available online: http://data.consilium.europa.eu/doc/document/ST-6655-2016-INIT/en/pdf [last visited 1 January 2019].

82 See recital 15a and Article 21a of the proposal.

83 Article 706-73 11° of the French Code of Criminal Procedure.

for the purposes of criminal procedure.[84] The creation of a common special regime, considered as being exceptional, to address both terrorism and organised crime has been criticised as constituting an "enemy criminal law".[85] The main point of this criticism is that the French criminal law is moving away from its traditional principles of necessity and proportionality, and tends to be based only on the concept of dangerousness.

The example of the French criminal law shows how tempting it can be for the legislator to "apply [to terrorism] the label that under current conditions provides the most powerful tools for curtailing an organization's activity".[86] Therefore, the suggestion of *Ana Salinas* to address more seriously specific criminal activities which are linked to a certain extent to terrorist activities,[87] carries the risk of labelling all perpetrators involved in those criminal activities as potential terrorists. In reality, however, such activities are linked only to a certain extent to terrorism, and the link is mostly indirect. Therefore, before considering an activity as a whole as terrorism merely on the basis of a nexus, further careful and precise analysis is required.

## IV. Addressing a phenomenon between terrorism, organised crime and lucrative petty crime

### A. Shortcomings of an approach based on the organised crime-terrorism assimilation

> In many respects, terrorism resembles organised crime. For example, several ways to protect from terrorism also protect against organised crime. And yet, in many cases, this is tantamount to confusing a tennis ball and an automobile under the pretext that you can stop both with a brick wall.[88]

The fact that terrorism and organised crime tend to be assimilated is problematic since this is likely to lead to measures which are not proven to be necessary. As a matter of fact, if terrorism is treated as the criminal phenomenon that justifies the least protective criminal procedure – as is often the case when it comes to investi-

---

84 *Massé*, 1 Revue de science criminelle et de droit pénal comparé (2012).

85 On the French system, in relation with the *dérogatoire* procedure used to address both terrorism and organised crime, see for instance *Cahn*, 38 Archives de politique criminelle (2016).

86 *Flanigan*, 24 Terrorism and Political Violence 291 (2012). This article deals with narcoterrorism, which will be addressed further below in this article.

87 *Neumann/Salinas*, Report on the Links Between Terrorism and Transnational Organized Crime, pp. 8–26.

88 Free translation from the French *Leman-Langlois*, in: David/Gagnon (eds.), Repenser le terrorisme, p. 91.

gative powers[89] –, any attempt to link other criminal phenomena to terrorism will necessarily lead to an overall less protective criminal law, even outside the measures that are at the core of the fight against terrorism.[90]

This seems not to be justified, since there is no evidence of a structural nexus between terrorism and organised crime. As has been established above, the nexus finds its roots in the transformation of both terrorist groups and organised crime groups into networked cells facilitating relationships rather than leading to a structural bond.[91] Terrorists often commit crimes without being members of large-scale criminal organisations.[92]

On the other hand, a part of scholarship argues that the nexus contributes to blurring the line between organised crime and terrorism and allows them to be seen as a single combined threat, rather than two distinct phenomena. This view is misleading and pertains to an all-encompassing and ill-defined concept of organised crime. The definition of organised crime has been much contested in the literature[93] and has been heavily criticised for its vagueness and extensive reach.[94] Although it is a "catchy umbrella concept to raise the public's and policy makers' attention", due to its imprecision "it is neither an adequate research nor a policy making concept".[95] As *Levi* rightly points out, the definition of organised crime in the Palermo Convention "can mean anything from major Italian syndicates in sharp suits or Sicilian peasant garb to three very menacing-looking burglars with a window-cleaning business who differentiate their roles by having one act as look-out, another as burglar, and a third as money launderer."[96] For *Paoli*, the broad definition of organised crime tries to put together two different notions, namely the "provision of illegal goods and services" and criminal organisations as such, "understood as a large-scale collectivity primarily engaged in illegal activities with a well-defined collec-

---

89 *Gless*, in: Galli/Weyembergh (eds.), EU counter-terrorism offences: What impact on national legislation and case-law? p. 43: "the importance of anti-terrorist legislation is often not the elements of crime that it defines, but the special investigative methods or other measure provided to deal with it."

90 On the risk of contamination see *Meliá*, 14 New Criminal Law Review 120 (2011).

91 *Neumann/Salinas*, Preliminary Report on Terrorism and Transnational Organized Crime, p. 8.

92 There is more evidence of the appropriation of organised criminal activities by terrorist entities than of a cooperation between terrorist entities and criminal enterprises. See *Williams*, in: Biersteker/Eckert (eds.), Countering the Financing of Terrorism, p. 126.

93 The difficulty to define terrorism will not be addressed in this paper as it is not debatable that ISIS is a terrorist organisation. We focus instead on the nature of the relationship between ISIS and organisations considered as criminal.

94 *Paoli/Fijnaut*, 14 European Journal of Crime, Criminal Law and Criminal Justice 313 (2006); *Calderoni*, 16 European Journal of Crime, Criminal Law and Criminal Justice 272 (2008); *Symeonidou-Kastanidou*, 15 European Journal of Crime, Criminal Law and Criminal Justice 101 (2007).

95 *Paoli*, in: Paoli (ed.), The Oxford Handbook of Organized Crime, p. 14.

96 *Levi*, in: Maguire et al. (eds.), The Oxford Handbook of Criminology, p. 780.

tive identity and subdivision of work among its members",[97] usually referred to as mafia-type organisations.

Terrorists too can engage in activities such as the "provision of illegal goods and services" to finance their activities. Terrorists too can adopt a functioning which is similar to the structure of a criminal organisation.[98] As already mentioned above in relation to the categorisation of the different types of nexus, the existing phenomena manifest themselves neither as a hybridisation nor a transformation of terrorist organisations into criminal organisations, but rather in the form of local and isolated partnerships. Therefore, using *Paoli*'s distinction, one can say that where there is a nexus with organised crime, it is not between large-scale terrorist organisations and large-scale criminal organisations. It is rather an issue of terrorists relying to a certain extent on different criminal activities, including the provision of illegal goods and services.

Therefore, the measures taken to fight ISIS should not be targeted at organised crime in general, but at the specific sub-category constituted by the provision of illegal goods and services, together with all forms of lucrative criminal activities.[99] In other words, a criminal policy intending to address the existing nexus should not target structured criminal organisations or mafia-type organisations, but should rather focus on the perpetrators of lucrative criminal activities.

## B. Towards an adapted criminal policy

The European Parliament emphasised in its 2011 resolution on organised crime that "although there is a risk that criminal organisations may cooperate increasingly frequently with terrorist organisations, organised crime should be treated separately from terrorism."[100] In the same paragraph, the resolution "call[ed] for a specific, horizontal EU Strategy on the issue," in other words: a strategy which addresses only the crime-terror nexus, but which is not only based on criminal law. For this reason, terrorism should not be considered as a specific form of organised crime, but efforts to analyse the specific situations in which terrorism and organised crime can have links would be most welcome. The point is not to study the union of both phenomena, but their intersections. If often "both anti-crime and counterterrorist

---

97 *Paoli*, 37 Crime, Law and Social Change (2002), p. 52. See also *Paoli*, in: Antanopoulos (ed.), Illegal Entrepreneurship, Organized Crime and Social Control, p. 4.

98 *Paoli*, 37 Crime, Law and Social Change 82 (2002).

99 In this sense, see Centre d'analyse du terrorisme, Commerce Illicite et Financement du Terrorisme, December 2016.

100 European Parliament resolution of 25 October 2011 on organised crime in the European Union, § 2.

officers overlook a petty criminal who holds the key to a terrorist cell or plot,"[101] this does not mean that terrorism is systematically linked to organised crime or even to other types of crimes, but that, in practice, an intensified cooperation and exchange of information between investigative authorities would facilitate the detection of such a hitherto unnoticed connection.[102] In the same way, *Louise Shelley* has proposed seven recommendations for a criminal policy that is meant to deal with these intersections,[103] but none of those guidelines implies the extension of the legal framework provided for organised crime to terrorism or an assimilation of both phenomena. Instead of an "umbrella approach" that is based on one single concept with a very large scope and tries to address both issues at the same time on a large scale, a "building block approach"[104] that is based on sectoral legal instruments or policies could be used in order to address specifically those manifestations of the nexus that have been observed in practice.

Attempts at "overlapping counter-terrorist and anti-crime policies"[105] and at addressing specifically the issue of "crime-terrorism partnering activities"[106] can take several forms, but must make sense from a criminological point of view. Let us take for example the offence of narcoterrorism in the U.S., namely, conducting drug activity with the intent to finance terrorism.[107] The purpose of this offence is precisely not to "confuse this [commercial] relationship with a strategic alliance."[108] However, the concept of narcoterrorism is a useful way to legitimise the war on drugs, and the use of the label "terrorism" is to a large extent opportunistic.[109] Using the "terrorist" label can be due to political motivations which are not based on a criminological analysis. The drafting of specific offences is therefore quite sensitive.

---

101 West Sands Advisory LLP, Europe's Crime-Terror Nexus: Links between terrorist and organised crime groups in the European Union, 2012, p. 43.

102 For instance, on the idea to create a "cooperative law enforcement system," *Gonzalez*, Law School Student Scholarship. Paper 227 (2013).

103 *Shelley/Picarelli*, in: Giraldo/Trinkunas (eds.), Terrorism Financing and State Responses: A Comparative Perspective, pp. 54–55.

104 *Orlova/Moore*, 27 Houston Journal of International Law 308 (2005).

105 *Makarenko*, 6 Global Crime 142 (2004).

106 *Rollins/Sun Wyler*, Congressional Research Service 26–27 (2013); *Rollins/Sun Wyler/Rosen*, Congressional Research Service 44–52 (2010).

107 21 U.S.C. § 960a. On this, see *Thomas*, 66 Washington and Lee Law Review (2009), arguing, however, that this offence is also in itself an issue for civil liberties. On the political exploitation of this concept, see *Miller/Damask*, 8 Terrorism and Political Violence (1996).

108 *Villa*, 6 University of Miami National Security & Armed Conflict Law Review 147 (2015–2016).

109 *Leman-Langlois*, in: David/Gagnon (eds.), Repenser le terrorisme, p. 91.

In her report for the Council of Europe, *Salinas* does not explicitly state her position on these specific offences. With regard to the Convention on Offences related to Cultural Property, adopted in 2017, she observes that it:

> has no specific provisions on links between these offences and terrorism as there was no need as far as in the case of trafficking in cultural property […] the sole connection with terrorism is for the purpose of financing, obviously in compulsory cooperation with organized crime groups.[110]

*Salinas* also highlights the neutral nature of international legal instruments regarding the existence of a nexus in the field of drug trafficking.[111] In her third finding she points out that offences taking place within the nexus do not involve heavier penalties.[112]

It appears that the real challenge is not to create new offences or to punish with heavier penalties but to properly fight against terrorist financing based on criminal acitivities.

## C. The specific focus on terrorist financing

Given the importance of lucrative petty crime in the financing of terrorism, focussing on the flows of money is certainly the one specific measure which should result from our analysis of the nexus. This raises the question if it is technically possible to properly monitor the lucrative activities of potential terrorists. The techniques employed tend to be more and more developed, but here again, instead of addressing specifically the issue of individual petty criminals who are suspected of terrorism, the measures are broadly targeted. The current trend is to continue in the direction adopted after 9/11, when the pre-existing preventive system of anti-money laundering was adapted, "refocusing or distorting the concept of money-laundering to include the proceeds from legitimate activities that might support

---

[110] *Neumann/Salinas*, Report on the Links Between Terrorism and Transnational Organized Crime, p. 23.

[111] *Salinas*, Report on Links Between Terrorism and Transnational Organized Crime, p. 4. She notices "a lack of common regulation in times of closer relationship between both types of criminality"; for her "international treaties regulating both phenomena are neutral as far as this interaction is concerned".

[112] *Salinas*, Report on Links Between Terrorism and Transnational Organized Crime, pp. 3–4. "This form of organized crime has ultimately become one of the most important sources of revenue, used by terrorist groups given the fact that it is cheaper and easier to carry out, the absence of any link between the two crimes resulting in lower penalties for those involved." The findings of the report are separated from the report because of the organisation of the research project. In May 2017, the common report with *Neumann* was published without the conclusive findings, and a final conference was organized in September 2017 during which *Salinas* presented these findings. The text of the final conference was published as a report and contains six findings of the project. At the end of the conference, divided in five Sessions, conclusions were adopted.

terrorism."[113] This method of extending a pre-existing regime to a different phenomenon is criticised[114] on the basis of supposedly inherent differences between organised crime and the financing of terrorist groups.[115] Anti-money laundering policy aims to fight against the introduction of money of illicit origin into the financial sector, while a counter terrorist financing policy intends to detect the illegal use of money which can be either of legal or of illegal origin.[116] This difference could imply that the detection of such phenomena requires different procedures – some authors arguethat financial institutions are not able to detect most acts of terrorist financing[117], although this point is controversial.[118] This is only one example of the developing cooperation between investigtors and financial institutions.[119]

The existing regime is therefore applicable both to money laundering and to terrorist financing and is becoming more and more intrusive particularly in response to the attacks directed by ISIS in Europe. To name but two recent examples: the proposed directive amending the fourth anti-money laundering directive[120] would extend the powers of the financial intelligence units in order to facilitate the fight against terrorist financing but without limiting such powers to terrorist financing cases.[121] Similarly, in France new powers have been granted to the financial intelligence unit. This unit is now permitted to request that financial institutions monitor the accounts of individuals who are suspected of terrorism or money laundering[122] and to access financial data even without having received reports of suspicious transactions.[123]

The anti-money laundering system was intended to track criminals' and particularly organised criminals' assets, but the only reason for applying the new investigative powers of the financial intelligence unit in France to cases of money laundering was that the legal frameworks relating to counter terrorist financing and to

113 *Levi*, Controlling the International Money Trail: A Multi-Level Cross-National Public Policy Review, p. 22.

114 *Orlova/Moore*, 27 Houston Journal of International Law 301 (2005).

115 *Schneider*, in: Storti/De Grauwe (eds.), Illicit Trade and the Global Economy, p. 33.

116 It should be noted that even if terrorist financing involves money of illicit origin, evidence shows that the amounts are often modest in comparison to cases of money laundering. See *Wesseling*, The European Fight against terrorism financing: professional fields and new governing practices, p. 206; *Krieger/Meierrieks*, in: Unger/van der Linde (eds.), Research Handbook in Money Laundering, p. 78.

117 *Ibid.*

118 *King/Walker*, 6 New Journal of European Criminal Law 382 (2015); *Gurulé*, Unfunding Terror, p. 376.

119 In general see *Maxwell/Artingstall*, The Role of Financial Information-Sharing Partnerships in the Disruption of Crime.

120 COM(2016) 450 final.

121 *Lassalle*, 4 eucrim 184 (2016).

122 Article L561-29-1 2° of the Code monétaire et financier.

123 Article L561-31 of the Code monétaire et financier.

the fight against money laundering had already been completely merged. The existence of a common regime certainly helps to circumvent the disadvantages of fragmentation[124] and complies with the international framework such as the Warsaw Convention[125] whose explanatory report indicated that the same tools should be used in the fight against terrorist financing as in the fight against money laundering.[126] Yet, this approach overlooks "the possibilities to institute lower standard of rights for terrorists than granted even to organised criminals."[127] As a matter of fact, when there is a common regime, intrusive measures adopted to address terrorist financing will almost automatically be extended to money laundering and this does not take into consideration that the protection of fundamental rights is justifiably different in each case, seeing that a terrorist act is a considerably more serious offence than money laundering. Financial data ought to be protected on the basis of the right to privacy[128] and any interference has to be proportionate to its legitimate aim. Thus, measures that can be proportionate in the fight against terrorist financing may at the same time be disproportionate in the fight against money laundering.

## V. Conclusions

This contribution highlighted that there is no such thing as a large-scale alliance between ISIS and criminal organisations, but there are rather two different kinds of relationships between the Islamic State, lucrative petty crime and criminal networks, justifying the use of measures of criminal law against these criminal activities in order to fight ISIS.

The first kind of relationship arises from the possibility for terrorists in western countries to easily rely on lucrative petty crime to finance their activities. The most important challenge is to acknowledge the importance of petty crime in the financing of terrorism. As suggested by *Louise Shelley*,[129] specific criminal patterns must be identified and receive more attention. This is less a question of which investiga-

---

124 *King/Walker*, 6 New Journal of European Criminal Law (2015).

125 Council of Europe Convention on Laundering, Search, Seizure and Confiscation of the Proceeds from Crime and on the Financing of Terrorism, May 16, 2005.

126 Explanatory Report to the Council of Europe Convention on Laundering, Search, Seizure and Confiscation of the Proceeds from Crime and on the Financing of Terrorism, § 24.

127 *King/Walker*, 6 New Journal of European Criminal Law 395 (2015). The authors criticise fragmentation but bear in mind that the existence of two standards of rights is nevertheless a point to be taken into consideration.

128 ECHR, *Sommer v. Germany*, April 27, 2017, n 73607/13;ECHR, *Brito Ferrinho Bexiga Villa-Nova v. Portugal*, December 1, 2015, n° 69436/10; ECHR, *M.N. and others v. San Marino*, July 7, 2015, n° 28005/12.

129 *Shelley/Picarelli*, in: Giraldo/Trinkunas (eds.), Terrorism Financing and State Responses: A Comparative Perspective, pp. 54–55.

tive tools should be strengthened than one of the organisation of investigative agencies and the cooperation between anti-crime and anti-terror investigations and the private sector. For *Louise Shelley*, the solution is relatively straightforward: "How to beat Islamic State? Crack down on cigarette smuggling."[130] This statement underlines the fact that petty crime and terrorism, which used to be considered as two distinct phenomena, requiring two distinct criminal policies, can to a certain extent be linked or overlapping.

The second kind of relationship is the indirect involvement of some criminal networks in financing ISIS, when they traffic goods that come from ISIS territory while acting outside ISIS territory themselves. The fact that these networks deal with goods originating in ISIS-controlled territory – or rather territories where ISIS is active –, and therefore have financial links with the Islamic State, is the reason why their relationship can be seen as a manifestation of the nexus between terrorism and organised crime. In answer to calls to strengthen the criminal law response to these criminal organisations, our analysis highlighted that this does not mean that these networks are directly involved in terrorist financing or should be considered as terrorist organisations. The point is only to acknowledge the indirect links between both phenomena. This implies for instance, as suggested by *Louise Shelley*, recognising the role of high-status individuals such as bankers, art dealers and accountants in western countries who can to a certain extent be involved in indirect activities of terrorist financing.[131] This means that participating individuals should be held criminally accountable. The ongoing investigation of the French company Lafarge highlights the fact that western companies, even when they do not intend to maintain links with organised crime or terrorism at a large scale, can adopt a reckless behaviour when it is profitable to do so.[132]

Both kinds of relationships, namely a direct relationship with lucrative petty crime and an indirect relationship with criminal networks, are often referred to as a nexus between terrorism and organised crime. Yet, the main conclusion of our analysis is that this relationship exists only between terrorists and the perpetrators of certain forms of criminal activities that fall under the very general label "organised crime." This leads us to question, by way of conclusion, the existing policy on organised crime. As a matter of fact, the prevailing conception of organised crime for instance at the EU level creates some confusion since it embodies a very vague and broad concept[133] which is not based on studies of the harm caused by the phe-

---

130 *Shelley*, How to beat Islamic State? Crack down on cigarette smuggling.

131 *Shelley/Picarelli*, in: Giraldo/Trinkunas (eds.), Terrorism Financing and State Responses: A Comparative Perspective, pp. 54–55.

132 *Seelow*, Financement du terrorisme : le jeu de dupes des dirigeants de Lafarge, Le Monde, January 4, 2018. The investigation is ongoing in February 2018. Apparently the company had financial agreements with ISIS members in order to continue using a plant on ISIS-controlled territory.

133 *Carrera* et al., The Cost of Non-Europe in the Area of Organized Crime, p. 18.

nomenon.[134] Back in 2011, the European Parliament called for a specific strategy on the issue of the crime-terror nexus.[135] One could say that the new evidence of a nexus between ISIS, lucrative criminal activities and some organised crime networks presents an opportunity for the EU to create a precise and relevant strategy which could focus on the specific criminal activities involved directly or indirectly in terrorist financing.

## Bibliography

*Alda, Erik/Sala, Joseph L.*, Links Between Terrorism, Organized Crime and Crime: The Case of the Sahel Region. 3 International Journal of Security & Development 1–9 (2014).

*Basra, Rajan/Neumann, Peter R./Brunner, Claudia*, Criminal Pasts, Terrorist Futures: European Jihadists and the New Crime-Terror Nexus. The International Center for the Study of Radicalisation and Political Violence, 2016.

*Bobic, Marinko*, Transnational Organised Crime and Terrorism: Nexus Needing a Human Security Framework. 15 Global Crime 241–258 (2014).

*Bovenkerk, Frank/Abou Chakra, Bashir*, Terrorisme et Criminalité Organisée. 4 Forum sur le crime et la société 3–17 (2004).

*Burke, Jason*, The myth of the 'lone wolf' terrorist. The Guardian, March 30, 2017.

*Cahn, Olivier*, «Cet ennemi intérieur, nous devons le combattre». Le Dispositif Antiterroriste Français, une Manifestation du Droit Pénal de l'Ennemi. 38 Archives de politique criminelle 89–121 (2016).

*Calderoni, Francesco*, A Definition that Could not Work: the EU Framework Decision on the Fight Against Organised Crime. 16 European Journal of Crime, Criminal Law and Criminal Justice 265–282 (2008).

*Callimachi, Rukmini*, Not 'Lone Wolves' After All: How ISIS Guides World's Terror Plots From Afar. The New York Times, February 4, 2017.

*Campbell, Peter B.*, The Illicit Antiquities Trade as a Transnational Criminal Network: Characterizing and Anticipating Trafficking of Cultural Heritage. 20 International Journal of Cultural Property 113–153 (2013).

*Carrera, Sergio/Guild, Elspeth/Vosyliūtė, Lina/Scherrer, Amandine/Mitsilegas, Valsamis*, The Cost of Non-Europe in the Area of Organized Crime. CEPS Paper in Liberty and Security, 2016.

Centre d'analyse du terrorisme, Commerce Illicite et Financement du Terrorisme, December 2016.

– Le financement des attentats de Paris, October 2016.

---

[134] *Paoli*, 22 European Journal of Crime, Criminal Law and Criminal Justice 5–7 (2014).

[135] European Parliament resolution of 25 October 2011 on organised crime in the European Union, § 2.

*Cottee, Simon*, Jihadism as a Subcultural Response to Social Strain: Extending Marc Sageman's "Bunch of Guys" Thesis. 23 Terrorism and Political Violence 730–751 (2011).

*Dishman, Chris*, The Leaderless Nexus: When Crime and Terror Converge. 28 Studies in Conflict and Terrorism 237–252 (2005).

*Dutton, Yvonne M.*, Funding Terrorism: The Problem of Ransom Payments. 53 San Diego Law Review 335–367 (2016).

Europol, European Union Serious Threat and Organised Crime Threat Assessment, 2017.

– Changes in Modus Operandi of Islamic State (IS) Revisited, November 2016.

– The Nexus Between Organised Crime and Terrorism, July 2015.

FATF, Financing of the Terrorist Organisation Islamic State in Iraq and the Levant (ISIL), April 2015.

– Organised Maritime Piracy and Related Kidnapping for Ransom, July 2011.

*Flanigan, Shawn Teresa*, Terrorists Next Door? A Comparison of Mexican Drug Cartels and Middle Eastern Terrorist Organizations. 24 Terrorism and Political Violence 279–294 (2012).

*Flinn, Crystal M.*, Black Gold in the Black Market: Tackling the Issue of International Oil Smuggling Through Technology, Public Policy, and Internal Corporate Controls. 51 Texas International Law Journal 119–141 (2016).

*Gless, Sabine*, The Two Framework Decisions. In: Francesca Galli and Anne Weyembergh (eds.), EU counter-terrorism offences: What impact on national legislation and case-law? Brussels 2012, pp. 33–46.

*Gonzalez, Elsie*, The Nexus Between Human Trafficking and Terrorism/Organized Crime: Combatting Human Trafficking by Creating a Cooperative Law Enforcement Model. Law School Student Scholarship. Paper 227 (2013).

*Gurulé, Jimmy*, Unfunding Terror. Cheltenham and Northampton 2008.

*Hesterman, Jennifer L.*, The Terrorist-Criminal Nexus. Boca Raton 2013.

*Hodgson, Jacqueline S./Tadros, Victor*, The Impossibility of Defining Terrorism. 16 New Criminal Law Review 494–526 (2013).

*Kennedy, Paloma A.*, Human Trafficking Waivers. 101 Women Lawyers Journal 11–25 (2016).

*King, Colin/Walker, Clive*, Counter Terrorism Financing. A Redundant Fragmentation? 6 New Journal of European Criminal Law 372–395 (2015).

*Krieger, Tim/Meierrieks, Daniel*, Terrorism: Causes, Effects and the Role of Money Laundering. In: Brigitte Unger/Daan van der Linde (eds.), Research Handbook in Money Laundering. Cheltenham and Northampton 2013, pp. 78–92.

*Lassalle, Maxime*, La révision de la quatrième directive anti-blanchiment à la lumière des droits fondamentaux. 4 eucrim 184–188 (2016).

*Leman-Langlois, Stéphane*, Terrorisme et Crime Organisé, Contrastes et Similitudes. In: Charles-Philippe David/Benoît Gagnon (eds.), Repenser le terrorisme. Québec 2007, pp. 91–110.

*Levi, Michael*, Organized Crime and Terrorism. In: Mike Maguire/Rod Morgan/Robert Reiner (eds.), The Oxford Handbook of Criminology. 4th ed. Oxford 2007, pp. 771–809.

– Controlling the International Money Trail: A Multi-Level Cross-National Public Policy Review. Economic and Social Research Council, 2003.

*Levi, Michael/Innes, Martin*, Terrorism and Counter-Terrorism. In: Mike Maguire/Rod Morgan/Robert Reiner (eds.), The Oxford Handbook of Criminology. 4th ed. Oxford 2007, pp. 660–685.

*Levitt, Matthew*, How do ISIS terrorists finance their attacks? The Hill, 18 November 2015.

– Terrorist Financing and the Islamic State. Testimony Submitted to the House Committee on Financial Services, November 13, 2014.

*Makarenko, Tamara*, The Crime-Terror Continuum: Tracing the Interplay between Transnational Organised Crime and Terrorism. 6 Global Crime 142 (2004).

*Makarenko, Tamara/Mesquita, Michael*, Categorising the Crime-Terror Nexus in the European Union. 15 Global Crime 259–274 (2014).

*Massé, Michel*, La Criminalité Terroriste. 1 Revue de science criminelle et de droit pénal comparé 89–130 (2012).

*Maxwell, Nick J./Artingstall, David*, The Role of Financial Information-Sharing Partnerships in the Disruption of Crime. Royal United Services Institute for Defence and Security Studies, 2017.

*Meliá, Manuel Cancio*, Terrorism and Criminal Law: the Dream of Prevention, the Nightmare of the Rule of Law. 14 New Criminal Law Review 108–122 (2011).

*Miller, Abraham/Damask, Nicholas*, The Dual Myths of 'Narco-terrorism': How Myths Drive Policy. 8 Terrorism and Political Violence 114–131 (1996).

*Mincheva, Lyubov G./Gurr, Ted Robert*, Unholy Alliances: How Trans-State Terrorism and International Crime Make Common Cause In: Rafael Reuveny and William R. Thompson (eds.), Coping with Terrorism. Albany 2010, pp. 169–189.

*Neumann, Peter/Salinas, Ana*, Report on the Links Between Terrorism and Transnational Organized Crime, May 10 September 26, 2017.

*Oftedal, Emilie*, The Financing of Jihadi Terrorist Cells in Europe. FFI, January 9, 2015.

*Orlova, Alexandra V./Moore, James W.*, "Umbrellas" or "Building Blocks"? Defining International Terrorism and Transnational Organized Crime in International Law. 27 Houston Journal of International Law 267–310 (2005).

*Paoli, Letizia*, Towards a Theory of Organized Crime: Some Preliminary Reflections. In: Georgios A. Antanopoulos (ed.), Illegal Entrepreneurship, Organized Crime and Social Control. Essays in Honor of Professor Dick Hobbs. New York 2016, pp. 3–17.

– The Oxford Handbook of Organized Crime. New York 2014.

– How to Tackle (Organized) Crime in Europe? The EU Policy Cycle on Serious and Organized Crime and the New Emphasis on Harm. 22 European Journal of Crime, Criminal Law and Criminal Justice 1–12 (2014).

– The Paradoxes of Organized Crime. 37 Crime, Law and Social Change 51–97 (2002).

*Paoli, Letizia/Fijnaut, Cyrille*, Organised Crime and its Control Policies. 14 European Journal of Crime, Criminal Law and Criminal Justice 307–327 (2006).

*Pella, Vespasian V.*, Towards an International Criminal Court. 44 The American Journal of International Law 37–68 (1950).

*Picart, Caroline Joan S.*, "Jihad Cool/Jihad Chic": The Roles of the Internet and Imagined Relations in the Self-Radicalisation of Colleen LaRose (Jihad Jane). 5 Societies 354–383 (2015).

*Roberts, Skye Riddell*, The Crime-Terror Nexus: Ideology's Misleading Role in Islamist Terrorist Groups, 2016. Available online: http://www.e-ir.info/2016/04/23/the-crime-terror-nexus-ideologys-misleading-role-in-islamist-terrorist-groups/ [last visited 1 January 2019].

*Rollins, John/Sun Wyler, Liana*, Terrorism and Transnational Crime: Foreign Policy Issues for Congress. Congressional Research Service, June 11, 2013.

*Rollins, John/Sun Wyler, Liana/Rosen, Seth*, International Terrorism and Transnational Crime: Security Threats, U.S. Policy, and Considerations for Congress. Congressional Research Service, January 5, 2010.

*Saul, Ben*, The Legal Relationship between Terrorism and Transnational Crime. 3 International Criminal Law Review 417-452 (2013).

*Schmid, Alex P.*, Terrorism – The Definitional Problem. 36 Case Western Journal of International Law 375–419 (2004).

*Schneider, Friedrich*, The Hidden Financial Flows of Organized Crime: A Literature Review and Some Preliminary Empirical Results. In: Cláudia Costa Storti/Paul De Grauwe (eds.), Illicit Trade and the Global Economy. Cambridge and London 2012, pp. 31–48.

*Seelow, Soren*, Financement du terrorisme: le jeu de dupes des dirigeants de Lafarge. Le Monde, January 4, 2018.

Security Council, Fourth report of the Secretary-General on the threat posed by ISIL (Da'esh) to international peace and security and the range of United Nations efforts in support of Member States in countering the threat, February 2, 2017.

– Report of the Secretary-General on the threat of terrorists benefiting from transnational organized crime, May 21, 2015.

*Shelley, Louise*, How to beat Islamic State? Crack down on cigarette smuggling. The Guardian, November 27, 2015.

– ISIS' Members Depend on Petty Crime to Function in Europe. The New York Times, November 20, 2015.

– Testimony to the Task Force to Investigate Terrorism Financing Entitled "Could America Do More? An Examination of U.S. Efforts to Stop the Financing of Terror," September 9, 2015.

– Dirty Entanglements. New York 2014.

– Unraveling the New Criminal Nexus. 6 Georgetown Journal of International Affairs 5–13 (2005).

*Shelley, Louise/Melzer, Sharon*, The Nexus of Organized Crime and Terrorism: Two Case Studies in Cigarette Smuggling. 32 International Journal of Comparative and Applied Criminal Justice 43–63 (2008).

*Shelley, Louise/Picarelli, John T.*, Organized crime and terrorism. In: Jeanne K. Giraldo/ Harold A. Trinkunas (eds.), Terrorism Financing and State Responses: A Comparative Perspective. Redwood City 2007, pp. 39–55.

*Stohl, Cynthia/Stohl, Michael*, Networks of Terror: Theoretical Assumptions and Pragmatic Consequences. 17 Communication Theory 93–124 (2007).

*Symeonidou-Kastanidou, Elisabeth*, Towards a New Definition of Organised Crime in the European Union. 15 European Journal of Crime, Criminal Law and Criminal Justice 83–103 (2007).

*Thomas, John E.*, Narco-Terrorism: Could the Legislative and Prosecutorial Responses Threaten Our Civil Liberties? 66 Washington and Lee Law Review 1881–1920 (2009).

U.S. National Council, The threat to U.S. National Security Posed by Transnational Organized Crime, 2011.

*Villa, Andrea*, Combatting Narcoterrorism. 6 U. University of Miami National Security & Armed Conflict Law Review 125–150 (2015–2016).

*Wesseling, Mara*, The European fight against terrorism financing: professional fields and new governing practices. Amsterdam 2013.

West Sands Advisory LLP, Europe's Crime-Terror Nexus: Links between terrorist and organised crime groups in the European Union. Report for the European Parliament, 2012.

White House, Strategy to Combat Transnational Organized Crime, Addressing Converging Threats to National Security, July 2011.

*Willett, Hannah D.*, Ill-Gotten Gains: A Response to the Islamic State's Profits from the Illicit Antiquities Market. 58 Arizona Law Review 831–865 (2016).

*Williams, Phil*, Terrorist financing and organized crime: nexus, appropriation or transformation? In: Thomas J. Biersteker and Sue E. Eckert (eds.), Countering the Financing of Terrorism. London and New York 2008, pp. 126—149.

*Williams, Phil/Godson, Roy*, Anticipating Organized and Transnational Crime. 37 Crime, Law and Social Change 311–355 (2002).

# Together Against ISIS – Police and Justice Cooperation in Europe

*Christophe Paulussen*

## I. Introduction, delimitation, and approach

The title the author of this chapter received from the organizers of the conference on which this book is based is 'Together against ISIS – police and justice cooperation in Europe'. Although clear at first sight, it nonetheless evokes – after further reflection – several questions, which need to be considered first.

To start with, the title assumes that police and justice cooperation in Europe is united and organized ('together') when it comes to countering the threat of ISIS (inspired) terrorism. However, whether that is truly the case remains to be seen. For instance, in the aftermath of the Paris attacks in November 2015, a unified stance seemed far away when France criticized Belgium's police and intelligence service over alleged failures in the run-up to the attacks.[1] This criticism was subsequently rejected by Belgium, which insisted it was not a lawless area.[2] In the following pages, therefore, it will need to be ascertained to what extent one can actually speak of a united and organized approach. In view of the page limit and the impossibility to be comprehensive in scope, this will become quite a challenging if not impossible task. Nonetheless, it is hoped that the following analysis, in combination with conclusions from other studies, may at least provide a provisional answer.

A second point that should be stressed is that the organization ISIS (or ISIL, IS, Da'esh) is a jihadist group particularly active in Syria and Iraq, where the group is waging (and losing) an armed conflict. There are several groups, including the international coalition led by the US, fighting 'together against ISIS', but that fight is of a military nature, taking place in the armed conflict paradigm. By contrast, this chapter will focus on police and justice cooperation in Europe. This 'fight' does not take place in an armed conflict paradigm but in a law enforcement paradigm, which is characterized not by military operations aimed at defeating the ISIS group as such but by intelligence and police investigations, arrests, judicial proceedings, and

---

[1] See 'France and Belgium ease tensions with joint terror talks', The Local/AFP, 1 February 2016, available at https://www.thelocal.fr/20160201/france-and-belgium-to-team-up-to-fight-terror [last visited 1 April 2017].

[2] *Ibid.*

convictions (or acquittals!) of individuals. This means the author will look in this chapter at police and justice operations against (persons related to/involved with/aspiring to be) so-called 'foreign fighters', who could be defined as 'individuals, driven mainly by ideology, religion and/or kinship, who leave their country of origin or their country of habitual residence to join a party engaged in an armed conflict'.[3] In view of the title received (and the general focus of this book), this chapter will focus on foreign fighters who can be linked, in one way or another, to ISIS.

The next section, Section 2, will delve a little deeper into the law enforcement paradigm as such and into the reasons why it is the only appropriate paradigm to fight ISIS-related/inspired terrorism in Europe. After that, the phenomenon of foreign fighters in the EU will be addressed (Section 3), before turning to police and justice cooperation in the EU (Section 4). As has become clear, the focus will be on the EU, although, where appropriate, the European dimension beyond the EU, such as in the context of the Council of Europe, will also be addressed. In the final Section 5, a number of concluding observations will be offered.

## II. The law enforcement paradigm

After terrorist incidents, politicians are often determined to show their constituents that they are not afraid and weak but strong and, in fact, capable of responding to the threat. These kinds of situations tend to elicit flexed muscles, tough language, and war rhetoric. A prime example of this is former US President *Bush's* speech nine days after 9/11, in which he stated that '[o]ur war on terror begins with al Qaeda, but it does not end there. It will not end until every terrorist group of global reach has been found, stopped and defeated.'[4] However, even in France, the country that has often been very critical of *Bush's* foreign policy – remember the French opposition to the 2003 invasion of Iraq, partly engendered by the same 'war on terror' –[5] politicians have used war-like language in announcing their responses

---

3 *de Guttry, A./Capone, F./Paulussen, C.*, Introduction, in: A. de Guttry/F. Capone/C. Paulussen (eds.), Foreign Fighters under International Law and Beyond, T.M.C. Asser Press/Springer Verlag 2016, p. 2.

4 See The White House, 'Address to a Joint Session of Congress and the American People', Office of the Press Secretary, 20 September 2001, available at https://georgewbush-whitehouse.archives.gov/news/releases/2001/09/20010920-8.html [last visited 2 April 2017].

5 See e.g. 'Remarks to the United Nations Security Council', Secretary Colin L. Powell, New York City, 5 February 2003, U.S. Department of State, available at https://2001-2009.state.gov/secretary/former/powell/remarks/2003/17300.htm [last visited 2 April 2017]: "When we confront a regime that harbors ambitions for regional domination, hides weapons of mass destruction, and provides haven and active support for terrorists, we are

to terrorist attacks. For instance, French Prime Minister *Manuel Valls* stated after the January 2015 attacks that '[i]t is a war against terrorism, against jihadism, against radical Islam, against everything that is aimed at breaking fraternity, freedom, solidarity',[6] and similar statements were made after the November 2015[7] and July 2016[8] attacks.

Whereas this is to some extent understandable from a political point of view, and whereas this does not exclude the possibility of actually being engaged, as a country, in an armed conflict with groups such as ISIS,[9] the language is arguably dangerous. It is dangerous because it leads to a political climate in which it is increasingly accepted that society *at home* is finding itself in a war-like situation, in which civil liberties and legal safeguards are increasingly pushed to the background, following *Cicero's* famous phrase *silent enim leges inter arma* (for in times of war, the laws are silent). Indeed, the author of this chapter already overheard the remark in the counter-terrorism community that we may need to move from peacetime human rights observance to a tougher regime based on the laws of war. Obviously, a statement like this cannot be refuted strongly enough. To be very clear: even though France is indeed involved in an armed conflict and thus 'at war', no war is being waged on French territory, no matter how many heavily-guarded soldiers are patrolling the streets of Paris or Nice. In Europe, there is no armed conflict, which means that the fight on the repression side can be fought only in one way, via the law enforcement paradigm, and hence via intelligence, police work, and prosecutions.[10] This has been eloquently explained by the EU Counter-Terrorism Coordi-

---

not confronting the past; we are confronting the present. And unless we act, we are confronting an even more frightening future."

6 *Bilefsky, D./de la Baume M.*, French Premier Declares 'War' on Radical Islam as Paris Girds for Rally, The New York Times, 10 January 2015, available at https://www.nytimes.com/2015/01/11/world/europe/paris-terrorist-attacks.html?_r=0 [last visited 2 April 2017].

7 'France 'at war' with Daesh, says PM Manuel Valls', Euronews, 14 November 2015, available at http://www.euronews.com/2015/11/14/france-at-war-with-daesh-says-pm-manuel-valls [last visited 2 April 2017].

8 *Breeden A./Morenne, B.*, Prime Minister Says France is at 'War', The New York Times, 15 July 2016, available at https://www.nytimes.com/live/truck-plows-into-crowd-in-nice-france/french-pri/ [last visited 2 April 2017].

9 See the description of France in the useful Geneva Academy of International Humanitarian Law and Human Rights' RULAC (Rule of Law in Armed Conflicts) project, available at http://www.rulac.org/browse/countries/france [last visited 2 April 2017]: "France is involved in the non-international armed conflicts against the Islamic State group by undertaking airstrikes in Iraq and Syria as part of the international coalition led by the United States."

10 Cf. *MacDonald, K.*, Security and Rights. Speech to the UK Criminal Bar Association, 23 January 2007, available at http://www.cps.gov.uk/news/articles/security_rights/ [last visited 2 April 2017]: "London is not a battlefield. Those innocents who were murdered on 7 July 2005 were not victims of war. And the men who killed them were not, as in their vanity they claimed on their ludicrous videos, 'soldiers'. They were deluded, narcissistic inadequates. They were criminals. They were fantasists. We need to be very clear about this. On the streets of London, there is no such thing as a 'war on terror', just as there can

nator (EU CTC) *Gilles De Kerchove* and his advisor *Christiane Höhn*, with whom the author fully agrees:

> Terrorism is a crime that needs to be investigated and prosecuted. Treating terrorism as the crime that it is de-glorifies terrorists and shows them as the criminals they are (they would rather be seen as combatants and martyrs). It also avoids terrorist groups using counter-terrorism measures as propaganda tools leading to radicalization and recruitment to terrorism—as for example President Obama has said happens with Guantánamo. (Perceived) double standards pose the risk of feeding into the terrorist narrative. A criminal justice response, which provides the terrorist suspects with full respect of human rights, rule of law and fundamental freedoms, defends our Western values and does not change who we are as societies because of the terrorist threat. The terrorists want us to change and provoke us to betray our values in the response. Maintaining the traditional criminal justice paradigm and using regular criminal courts to try terrorists does not give the terrorist groups this victory. Criminal trials are also important for the victims.[11]

## III. The foreign fighters phenomenon in the EU

Now that it has been argued that the law enforcement paradigm is the only correct way to respond[12] to ISIS-related/inspired terrorism *in Europe*, let us take a closer look at the object of police and justice cooperation. As explained before, this chapter will examine police and justice cooperation against (people related to/involved with/aspiring to be) so-called 'foreign fighters', with a focus on foreign fighters who can be linked, in one way or another, to ISIS.

Although the phenomenon of foreign fighters is not new (in the late 1930s for instance, *George Orwell* went to Spain to fight the troops of Franco), what is new these days is the scale of the phenomenon and of its potential threat. *Edwin Bakker* and *Mark Singleton*, using the then latest estimates published in early 2015, arrived at 'a total number of more than 30,000 foreign fighters of all sorts for the entire

---

be no such thing as a 'war on drugs'. The fight against terrorism on the streets of Britain is not a war. It is the prevention of crime, the enforcement of our laws and the winning of justice for those damaged by their infringement. Acts of unlawful violence are proscribed by the criminal law. They are criminal offences. We should hold it as an article of faith that crimes of terrorism are dealt with by criminal justice."

11 *De Kerchove, G./Höhn, C.*, Counter-Terrorism and International Law Since 9/11, Including in the EU-US Context, in: T.D. Gill et al. (eds.), Yearbook of International Humanitarian Law, Vol. 16 (2013), T.M.C. Asser Press/Springer Verlag 2015, p. 271.

12 In view of the offered title, this chapter will look at the repressive and not preventive dimension, although the author of this chapter has stressed before that prevention should have priority in states' counter-terrorism measures, as only these tackle the underlying causes, rather than fight the symptoms. See *Paulussen, C.*, Repressing the Foreign Fighters Phenomenon and Terrorism in Western Europe: Towards an Effective Response Based on Human Rights, ICCT Research Paper, November 2016, available at https://icct.nl/wp-content/uploads/2016/11/ICCT-Paulussen-Rule-of-Law-Nov2016-1.pdf [last visited 2 April 2017] (hereinafter: *Paulussen* 2016), pp. 4–5.

conflict in Syria and Iraq since 2011'[13] – far exceeding the number of 20,000 foreign fighters attracted by the Afghanistan conflict in the 1980s.[14] This number has been confirmed by the UN Security Council,[15] although the Council uses the more restricted definition of foreign *terrorist* fighters.[16]

How many of these foreign fighters originate from the EU? In Europol's EU Terrorism Situation and Trend Report (TE-SAT) 2016, it was noted that '[a]t the end of 2015, it was estimated that over 5,000 Europeans had travelled to Syria and Iraq.'[17] A lower (but still high) estimate can be found in the 2016 ICCT report 'The Foreign Fighters Phenomenon in the European Union. Profiles, Threats & Policies' (hereinafter: ICCT Foreign Fighters Report 2016), to which the author of this chapter contributed as well.[18] It is interesting to note that twenty-three of the twenty-eight EU Member States delivered input for this latter report,[19] which arguably shows the willingness of states to cooperate on and disclose information about a phenomenon that does indeed require an international response. In this report, the researchers concluded that the EU-wide estimate is between 3,922 and 4,294 (hence an average of 4,108) foreign fighters.[20] Before delving into the European context in more detail, it should be underlined that even though these numbers pose serious problems for (especially Western) European authorities, it is important to see matters in perspective. For instance, the number of foreign fighters from countries in the Middle East and North Africa (MENA) region is much more troublesome; in a publication finalized in the autumn of 2015 and published in the beginning of 2016, *Daveed Gartenstein-Ross* and *Bridget Moreng* concluded that more than 11,000 people from the MENA region had joined Sunni militant organizations

---

[13] *Bakker, E./Singleton, M.*, Foreign Fighters in the Syria and Iraq Conflict: Statistics and Characteristics of a Rapidly Growing Phenomenon, in: A. de Guttry/F. Capone/C. Paulussen (eds.), Foreign Fighters under International Law and Beyond, T.M.C. Asser Press/Springer Verlag 2016, p. 23.

[14] *Neumann, P.R.*, Foreign fighter total in Syria/Iraq now exceeds 20,000; surpasses Afghanistan conflict in the 1980s'. ICSR, 26 January 2015, available at http://icsr.info/2015/01/foreign-fighter-total-syriairaq-now-exceeds-20000-surpasses-afghanistan-conflict-1980s/ [last visited 2 April 2017].

[15] See UN Security Council Counter-Terrorism Committee, Foreign terrorist fighters, undated, available at https://www.un.org/sc/ctc/focus-areas/foreign-terrorist-fighters/ [last visited 2 April 2017].

[16] For this difference, see *Paulussen* 2016, pp. 3–4.

[17] Europol, European Union Terrorism Situation and Trend Report 2016, available at https://www.europol.europa.eu/sites/default/files/documents/europol_tesat_2016.pdf [last visited 2 April 2017], p. 27.

[18] *Van Ginkel, B./Entenmann, E.* (eds.), The Foreign Fighters Phenomenon in the European Union. Profiles, Threats & Policies. ICCT Research Paper, April 2016, available at https://www.icct.nl/wp-content/uploads/2016/03/ICCT-Report_Foreign-Fighters-Phenomenon-in-the-EU_1-April-2016_including-AnnexesLinks.pdf [last visited 1 April 2017] (hereinafter: ICCT Foreign Fighters Report 2016).

[19] *Ibid.*, p. 71.

[20] *Ibid.*, p. 3.

in Syria and Iraq,[21] and in December 2015, The Soufan Group noted that 18,240 people from the Middle East (8,240) and the Maghreb (8,000) regions had travelled to Syria and Iraq to join the Islamic State and other violent extremist groups.[22] Particularly worrying is the number of foreign fighters from Tunisia, a country of almost 11 million people. In June 2014, The Soufan Group published a number of 'about 3,000' (an official figure from April 2014) for this North African country,[23] whereas in the December 2015 update, this high number had even risen to a staggering 6,000 (official count) to 7,000 (non-official count),[24] far exceeding the total number of foreign fighters for the entire EU (a territory inhabited by about 510 million people).

Turning back to Europe and the numbers from the ICCT Foreign Fighters Report 2016, a majority of around 2,838 foreign fighters come from just four countries: Belgium (420–516), France (more than 900), Germany (720–760), and the UK (700–760),[25] and when looking at numbers relative to population size, Belgium clearly jumps out with 41 foreign fighters per million inhabitants, followed by Austria (31), and Sweden (28).[26] The report also concluded that 47 % of foreign fighters are still abroad, 14 % are confirmed dead, the whereabouts of 9 % are not clear, and some 30 % have already returned to their home countries – which, at 1,232 individuals, is quite a large number.[27] But even though it is important to have a clear idea of the scope of the problem, numbers are not everything either. After all, it takes only one (or a few) foreign fighter(s) to stage an attack.[28] In fact, a number

---

21 *Gartenstein-Ross, D./Moreng, B.*, MENA Countries' Responses to the Foreign Fighter Phenomenon, in: A. de Guttry/F. Capone/C. Paulussen (eds.), Foreign Fighters under International Law and Beyond, T.M.C. Asser Press/Springer Verlag 2016, pp. 446–447.

22 The Soufan Group, Foreign Fighters. An Updated Assessment of the Flow of Foreign Fighters into Syria and Iraq, December 2015, available at http://soufangroup.com/wp-content/uploads/2015/12/TSG_ForeignFightersUpdate3.pdf [last visited 2 April 2016), p. 5.

23 *Barrett, R.*, Foreign Fighters in Syria, The Soufan Group, June 2014, available at http://soufangroup.com/wp-content/uploads/2014/06/TSG-Foreign-Fighters-in-Syria.pdf [last visited 2 April 2017], p. 13.

24 The Soufan Group, Foreign Fighters. An Updated Assessment of the Flow of Foreign Fighters into Syria and Iraq, December 2015, available at http://soufangroup.com/wp-content/uploads/2015/12/TSG_ForeignFightersUpdate3.pdf [last visited 2 April 2016), p. 9.

25 ICCT Foreign Fighters Report 2016, pp. 3 and 50.

26 *Ibid.*, pp. 50-51.

27 *Ibid.*, p. 49.

28 See e.g. the attack perpetrated by Mehdi Nemmouche in Brussels in 2014. This case also shows the need for proper cooperation and information exchange in Europe, with its open borders and free movement of people. Nemmouche is a French national, who returned from Syria, entered the EU in Germany, and allegedly committed the attack in Belgium. See *De Kerchove G./Höhn, C.*, The Regional Answers and Governance Structure for Dealing with Foreign Fighters: The Case of the EU, in: A. de Guttry/F. Capone/C. Paulussen

of recent terrorist attacks were not even committed by people who had left for Syria and Iraq themselves but who may have been inspired by the jihad in the Levant and then decided to take up arms at home themselves.[29]

Finally, the researchers of the ICCT Foreign Fighters Report 2016 noted that while there is no clear-cut profile of a European foreign fighter, a majority originates from metropolitan areas, with many coming from the same neighbourhoods, an average of 17 % is female, and the percentage of converts among foreign fighters ranges from 6 % to 23 %.[30] Finally, it was stated that the radicalization process of foreign fighters is reported to be short and often involves circles of friends radicalizing as a group and deciding to leave jointly for Syria and Iraq.[31] As explained above, this chapter addresses the repressive dimension and does not focus on the preventive side and the root causes of radicalization;[32] still, it should be noted that the reasons *why* people radicalize and may ultimately decide to join a fight in a distant land they may never have heard of before should inform the responses in the repression domain. For instance, recent research from the Netherlands, in which mental health care providers were involved, has shown that 'approximately (but probably more than) 60 % of suspected jihadi radicals … had a history of mental health issues, … rang[ing] from psycho-social problems to psychiatric disorders [original footnotes omitted]',[33] a percentage 'clearly disproportionate to the number in the general population where some 25 % suffers from such mental health problems'.[34] If the authorities know that a potential or returned foreign fighter is suffering from serious mental health problems, the question might be raised whether his or her case should be handled by police and justice officers (alone) and not (also) by doctors. To conclude this section, it can be stated that the foreign fighters phenomenon is vast, extremely complex, and will stay with us for many years to come. And again: in view of the phenomenon's international character, police and justice cooperation is of the utmost importance.

---

(eds.), Foreign Fighters under International Law and Beyond. T.M.C. Asser Press/Springer Verlag 2016 (hereinafter: *De Kerchove* and *Höhn* 2016), p. 301.

29 See e.g. the attack perpetrated by Omar Abdel Hamid El-Hussein in Copenhagen in 2015 or the attack perpetrated by Anis Amri in Berlin in 2016. Both of them reportedly pledged allegiance to ISIS leader Abu Bakr al-Baghdadi.

30 ICCT Foreign Fighters Report 2016, p. 4.

31 *Ibid.*

32 See n. 12.

33 *Paulussen, C./Nijman, J./Lismont, K.,* Mental Health and the Foreign Fighter Phenomenon: A Case Study from the Netherlands. ICCT Report, March 2017, available at https://icct.nl/wp-content/uploads/2017/03/ICCT-Paulussen-Nijman-Lismont-Mental-Health-and-the-Foreign-Fighter-Phenomenon-March-2017.pdf [last visited 11 April 2017], p. 7.

34 *Ibid.*

## IV. Police and justice cooperation at the EU level

This section will – at least initially – take a step away from the specific foreign fighters topic and look into the general counter-terrorism landscape in Europe to see how police and justice cooperation is organized in this regard. Moreover, and while the title of this chapter refers to Europe more generally, the focus will be on the EU area, and, subsequently, also on a selection of important institutions, mechanisms, and instruments at the (supra-national) EU level. This latter qualification was made fully aware of the fact that cooperation at the inter-state level, between individual states within the EU, is also possible. In fact, the Member States of the EU are the key actors when it comes to countering terrorism – the EU itself is only playing a supporting role.[35] For instance, since 2013 a group of Member States most affected by the foreign fighters phenomenon has been meeting on a regular basis 'to exchange information on the threat, compare notes on policy measures and discuss areas where intensified cooperation is needed.'[36] According to the EU CTC, '[t]he work of this group has paved the way for progress at the EU level.'[37] Another example are bilateral requests of cooperation, such as the arrest by the Dutch authorities of a terrorism suspect in Rotterdam at the request of the French authorities in March 2016.[38] However, having said that, this chapter will focus on cooperation at the supra-national EU level. Again, it should be stressed that the following section cannot be comprehensive in scope. For a more elaborate study on EU police and justice cooperation in the field of counter-terrorism, the reader is referred to the 2017 study 'The European Union's Policies on Counter-Terrorism. Relevance, Coherence and Effectiveness'[39] (hereinafter: EU CT Study 2017], to which this author contributed and which will be referred to in the following pages as well.

A selection of important institutions, mechanisms, and instruments at the EU level in the context of countering terrorism cannot but start with Council Framework Decision of 13 June 2002 on combating terrorism, adopted after 9/11.[40] It has

35 *De Kerchove* and *Höhn* 2016, p. 301.

36 *Ibid.*

37 *Ibid.*

38 Dutch anti-terrorism police arrest suspect at France's request. Reuters, 27 March 2016, available at http://www.reuters.com/article/us-rotterdam-dutch-france-idUSKCN0WT0MT [last visited 11 April 2017].

39 European Parliament, Directorate-General for Internal Policies, Policy Department C: Citizens' Rights and Constitutional Affairs, 'The European Union's Policies on Counter-Terrorism. Relevance, Coherence and Effectiveness', Study for the LIBE Committee, PE 583.124, European Union, 2017, available at http://www.europarl.europa.eu/RegData/etudes/STUD/2017/583124/IPOL_STU(2017]583124_EN.pdf [last visited 11 April 2017] (hereinafter: EU CT Study 2017].

40 Council Framework Decision of 13 June 2002 on combating terrorism (2002/475/JHA), available at http://eur-lex.europa.eu/legal-content/DA/TXT/?uri=uriserv: OJ.L_.2002.164.01.0003.01.ENG [last visited 12 April 2017].

been termed 'the basis of the counter-terrorist policy of the European Union'[41] and 'the cornerstone of the Member States' criminal justice response to counter terrorism'.[42] This framework decision, as well as its amending decision of 2008,[43] define terrorist offences[44] and related offences, including public provocation, recruitment, and training for terrorism,[45] and require EU Member States to align their legislation.

On the same day, 13 June 2002, another important instrument was adopted, namely Council Framework Decision of 13 June 2002 on the European arrest warrant and the surrender procedures between Member States.[46] The European Arrest Warrant replaced the system of (lengthy) extradition procedures by simplifying judicial surrender procedures, among other things for the purpose of conducting a criminal prosecution, including for terrorism-related charges. The European Arrest Warrant came into force in January 2004 and was also the basis for the surrender of persons such as Salah Abdeslam, suspect of the November 2015 Paris attacks, from Belgium to France.[47]

And as if this was not already enough, the Council *also* adopted that day, besides the substantive and procedural instruments described above, a more institutional instrument, namely Council Framework Decision of 13 June 2002 on joint investigation teams (JITs).[48] Pursuant to Article 1 of this Framework Decision, the com-

---

41 Council Framework Decision 2008/919/JHA of 28 November 2008 amending Framework Decision 2002/475/JHA on combating terrorism, available at http://eur-lex.europa.eu/legal-content/en/TXT/?uri=CELEX:32008F0919 [last visited 12 April 2017], preambular para. 2.

42 Directive (EU) 2017/541 of the European Parliament and of the Council of 15 March 2017 on combating terrorism and replacing Council Framework Decision 2002/475/JHA and amending Council Decision 2005/671/JHA, available at http://eur-lex.europa.eu/legal-content/EN/TXT/?uri=CELEX:32017L0541 [last visited 12 April 2017], preambular para. 3.

43 Council Framework Decision 2008/919/JHA of 28 November 2008 amending Framework Decision 2002/475/JHA on combating terrorism, available at http://eur-lex.europa.eu/legal-content/en/TXT/?uri=CELEX:32008F0919 [last visited 12 April 2017].

44 Council Framework Decision of 13 June 2002 on combating terrorism (2002/475/JHA), available at http://eur-lex.europa.eu/legal-content/DA/TXT/?uri=uriserv:OJ.L_.2002.164.01.0003.01.ENG [last visited 12 April 2017], art. 1, para. 1.

45 Council Framework Decision 2008/919/JHA of 28 November 2008 amending Framework Decision 2002/475/JHA on combating terrorism, available at http://eur-lex.europa.eu/legal-content/en/TXT/?uri=CELEX:32008F0919 [last visited 12 April 2017], art. 1.

46 Council Framework Decision of 13 June 2002 on the European arrest warrant and the surrender procedures between Member States (2002/584/JHA), available at http://eur-lex.europa.eu/legal-content/EN/ALL/?uri=celex:32002F0584 [last visited 12 April 2017].

47 Paris attacks suspect Salah Abdeslam extradited to France. BBC News, 27 April 2016, available at http://www.bbc.com/news/world-europe-36147575 [last visited 12 April 2017].

48 Council Framework Decision of 13 June 2002 on joint investigation teams (2002/465/JHA), available at http://eur-lex.europa.eu/legal-content/EN/ALL/?uri=CELEX:32002F0465 [last visited 12 April 2017]. Note that establishing a JIT was already possible pursuant to art. 13 of Council Act of 29 May 2000 establishing in accordance with Article

petent authorities of two or more Member States may set up a JIT for a specific purpose and a limited period, to carry out criminal investigations in one or more of the Member States setting up the team. At that time, the Council considered 'that such teams should be set up, as a matter of priority, to combat offences committed by terrorists'.[49] In view of their supporting and coordinating role in the field of cross-border police and justice work, it is only natural that JITs have also been supported by Europol,[50] the EU's law enforcement agency since 2010, and Eurojust,[51] the EU's judicial cooperation unit since 2002. For instance, in 2011, both agencies produced a JITs Manual, whose main goal 'is to inform practitioners about the legal basis and requirements for setting up a JIT and to provide advice on when a JIT can be usefully employed',[52] and, in 2017, both agencies were involved in the development of the JITs Practical Guide, which, among other things, enhances the previous JITs Manual, taking into account acquired practical experience.[53] JITs have also been set up in the context of the foreign fighter phenomenon. One example is JIT 'Vendredi 13', established in the aftermath of the November 2015 Paris attacks.[54]

In March 2004, the world and Europe in particular were shocked by the terrorist attacks in Madrid, after which the EU established the position of the already-mentioned EU CTC,[55] who is in charge of, among other things, coordinating the work of the Council in combating terrorism, presenting policy recommendations

---

34 of the Treaty on European Union the Convention on Mutual Assistance in Criminal Matters between the Member States of the European Union (2000/C 197/01), but slow progress in the ratification of this convention led to the adoption of this specific framework decision.

49 Council Framework Decision of 13 June 2002 on joint investigation teams (2002/465/JHA), available at http://eur-lex.europa.eu/legal-content/EN/ALL/?uri=CELEX: 32002F0465 [last visited 12 April 2017], preambular para. 7.

50 See Europol, Joint Investigation Teams – JITs, available at https://www.europol.europa.eu/activities-services/services-support/joint-investigation-teams [last visited 12 April 2017].

51 See Eurojust, Joint Investigation Teams (JITs), available at http://eurojust.europa.eu/Practitioners/JITs/Pages/historical-background.aspx [last visited 12 April 2017].

52 European Council, Joint Investigation Teams Manual, 15790/11, 4 November 2011, available at https://www.europol.europa.eu/sites/default/files/documents/st15790-re01.en11.pdf [last visited 12 April 2017], p. 2.

53 Council of the European Union, Joint Investigation Teams Practical Guide, 6128/1/17, 14 February 2017, available at http://www.eurojust.europa.eu/doclibrary/JITs/JITs%20framework/JITs%20Practical%20Guide/JIT-GUIDE-2017-EN.pdf [last visited 12 April 2017].

54 See Council of the European Union, Implementation of the counter-terrorism agenda set by the European Council, 13627/16, 4 November 2016, available at http://www.statewatch.org/news/2016/nov/eu-council-CTC-implementation-a-t-strategy-13627-%20ADD-1-16.pdf [last visited 12 April 2017], p. 4.

55 European Council, Declaration on combating terrorism, 7906/04, 29 March 2004, available at http://data.consilium.europa.eu/doc/document/ST-7906-2004-INIT/en/pdf [last visited 12 April 2017], para. 14.

and proposing priority areas for action to the Council, and monitoring the implementation of the EU Counter-Terrorism Strategy.[56]

This EU Counter-Terrorism Strategy should be addressed here as well. It was adopted by the European Council in 2005 in the aftermath of the London bombings[57] and consists of four main pillars, namely Prevent, Protect, Pursue, and Respond. When it comes to police and justice cooperation, the Pursue pillar is especially relevant. Here, the focus is '[t]o pursue and investigate terrorists across our borders and globally; to impede planning, travel, and communications; to disrupt support networks; to cut off funding and access to attack materials, and bring terrorists to justice'.[58]

Zooming in again on the specific issue of foreign fighters, the EU started working on this topic in January 2013, when the EU CTC warned 'about young Europeans going to Syria to get trained and join the jihad with terrorist groups such as Jabhat-al-Nusra and Da'esh'.[59] The EU CTC then proposed 22 measures, which were subsequently endorsed by the Justice and Home Affairs (JHA) Council in June 2013.[60] In August 2014, the European Council called for

> the accelerated implementation of the package of EU measures in support of Member States efforts, as agreed by the Council since June 2013, in particular to prevent radicalisation and extremism, share information more effectively - including with relevant third countries, dissuade, detect and disrupt suspicious travel and investigate and prosecute foreign fighters.[61]

As will become clear from the following pages, manifestations of police and justice cooperation can be connected to all these four priority areas in the context of countering the foreign fighters phenomenon.

As regards the first area (prevention), it is clear that social media is playing an increasingly important role in recruitment efforts of organizations like ISIS. Therefore, efforts have been made to detect and remove extremist social media content.[62] In July 2015 Europol set up its EU Internet Referral Unit (EU IRU), which 'will

---

56 European Council, Counter-Terrorism Coordinator, available at http://www.consilium.europa.eu/en/policies/fight-against-terrorism/counter-terrorism-coordinator/ [last visited 12 April 2017].

57 European Council, The European Union Counter-Terrorism Strategy, 14469/4/05, 30 November 2005, available at http://register.consilium.europa.eu/doc/srv?l=EN&f=ST%2014469%202005%20REV%204 [last visited 12 April 2017].

58 *Ibid.*, p. 3.

59 *De Kerchove* and *Höhn* 2016, p. 300.

60 Council of the European Union, Report on the implementation of the EU Counter-Terrorism Strategy, 15799/14, 24 November 2014, available at http://data.consilium.europa.eu/doc/document/ST-15799-2014-INIT/en/pdf [last visited 12 April 2017], p. 6.

61 European Council, Special meeting of the European Council (30 August 2014) – Conclusions, EUCO 163/14, 30 August 2014, available at https://www.consilium.europa.eu/uedocs/cms_data/docs/pressdata/en/ec/144538.pdf [last visited 12 April 2017], p. 6.

62 ICCT Foreign Fighters Report 2016, p. 5.

identify and refer relevant online content towards concerned internet service providers and support Member States with operational and strategic analysis'.[63] The linkage with the private sector is noteworthy, showing that all societal actors can be involved in countering terrorism.

With respect to the second area (information sharing), the establishment of Europol's European Counter Terrorism Centre (ECTC) in The Hague in January 2016 must be mentioned. Europol Director *Rob Wainwright* stated that their 'ambition is for the ECTC to become a central information hub in the fight against terrorism in the EU, providing analysis for ongoing investigations and contributing to a coordinated reaction in the event of major terrorist attacks'.[64] More concretely, the ECTC 'will focus on tackling foreign fighters, sharing intelligence and expertise on terrorism financing ..., online terrorist propaganda and extremism ([the just-explained] Internet Referral Unit), illegal arms trafficking and international cooperation to increase effectiveness and prevention [original footnote omitted]'.[65] After the Paris attacks in November 2015, Europol established Taskforce Fraternité, in which 60 officers were assigned to support the French and Belgian investigations and which resulted in 800 intelligence leads and more than 1,600 leads on suspicious financial transactions.[66] This Taskforce, which must be distinguished from the above mentioned French-Belgian JIT established after the Paris attacks,[67] began operating on 7 December 2015,[68] before the formal launch of the ECTC to the general public (end of January 2016); however, the ECTC also got involved in the Taskforce after it had been established.[69]

Europol's Focal Point Travellers is noteworthy as to the third priority area (travel). This Focal Point 'coordinates investigations into, and data analysis on, foreign terrorist fighters, and supports law enforcement efforts to counter foreign fighters

63 Europol, Europol's Internet Referral Unit to combat terrorist and violent extremist propaganda. Press release, 1 July 2015, available at https://www.europol.europa.eu/newsroom/news/europol%E2%80%99s-internet-referral-unit-to-combat-terrorist-and-violent-extremist-propaganda [last visited 12 April 2017].

64 Europol, Europol's European Counter Terrorism Centre strengthens the EU's response to terror. Press release, 25 January 2016, available at https://www.europol.europa.eu/newsroom/news/europol%E2%80%99s-european-counter-terrorism-centre-strengthens-eu%E2%80%99s-response-to-terror [last visited 12 April 2017].

65 *Ibid.*

66 *Ibid.*

67 See Council of the European Union, Implementation of the counter-terrorism agenda set by the European Council, 13627/16, 4 November 2016, available at http://www.statewatch.org/news/2016/nov/eu-council-CTC-implementation-a-t-strategy-13627-%20ADD-1-16.pdf [last visited 12 April 2017], p. 4.

68 *Ibid.*

69 See Europol, ECTC – European Counter Terrorism Centre – Infographic, available at https://www.europol.europa.eu/publications-documents/ectc-european-counter-terrorism-centre-infographic [last visited 12 April 2017].

when they return to Europe or the US from i.e. [*sic*] Syria or Iraq'.[70] Moreover, the new EU Passenger Name Record (PNR) Directive cannot go undiscussed. This Directive[71] obliges air carriers operating flights between a third country and the territory of at least one EU Member State to transfer their PNR data to the so-called PIU (Passenger Information Unit) of the Member State in which the international flight arrives or from which it departs, with the aim of assisting authorities to better fight terrorism and serious crime.[72] In view of the obvious human rights implications of such a directive, the European Parliament's Committee on Civil Liberties, Justice and Home Affairs (LIBE) rejected the initial (2011) proposal in 2013, but after revisions had been made and also in view of the subsequent terrorist attacks and the phenomenon of foreign fighters (and the resulting political pressure), the European Parliament decided to agree on 14 April 2016 on a revised text, which was adopted by the Council one week later.[73] The adoption was heavily criticized by human rights groups, such as the European Association for the Defence of Human Rights (AEDH), which noted that '[t]he current security context together with the emotional reactions following the recent terrorist attacks pushed the European Parliament to abandon its opposition to this directive.'[74]

The prime example of the fourth priority area (investigation and prosecution) is the new (2017] EU Directive on Combating Terrorism, which has replaced the earlier-discussed Framework Decisions of 2002 and 2008.[75] The directive, engendered by the phenomenon of foreign terrorist fighters, including people inspired by the jihad abroad, and in consideration of the obligations arising from UN Security Council Resolution 2178 of September 2014 and the adoption, in 2015, of the Additional Protocol to the Council of Europe Convention on the Prevention of Terrorism that try to stem this phenomenon,[76] aims to strengthen these framework decisions and crimi-

---

[70] Europol, Europol Focal Points, available at https://www.europol.europa.eu/crime-areas-trends/europol-focal-points [last visited 13 April 2017].

[71] Directive (EU) 2016/681 of the European Parliament and of the Council of 27 April 2016 on the use of passenger name record (PNR) data for the prevention, detection, investigation and prosecution of terrorist offences and serious crime, available at http://eur-lex.europa.eu/eli/dir/2016/681/oj [last visited 13 April 2017].

[72] European Parliament, EU Passenger Name Record (PNR) directive: an overview. 1 June 2016, available at http://www.europarl.europa.eu/news/en/news-room/20150123 BKG12902/eu-passenger-name-record-(pnr)-directive-an-overview [last visited 13 April 2017].

[73] *Ibid.*

[74] AEDH, PNR: the European Parliament adopts a controversial text. 26 April 2016, available at http://www.aedh.eu/PNR-the-European-Parliament-adopts.html [last visited 13 April 2017].

[75] Directive (EU) 2017/541 of the European Parliament and of the Council of 15 March 2017 on combating terrorism and replacing Council Framework Decision 2002/475/JHA and amending Council Decision 2005/671/JHA, available at http://eur-lex.europa.eu/legal-content/EN/TXT/?uri=CELEX:32017L0541 [last visited 13 April 2017].

[76] *Ibid.*, preambular paras. 4–6.

nalizes conduct such as receiving training for terrorism (Article 8), travelling for the purpose of terrorism (Article 9),[77] and organizing or otherwise facilitating travelling for the purpose of terrorism (Article 10). The proposal, which in the end led to the directive and was exceptionally presented without an impact assessment (even though such an assessment was promised back in April 2015),[78] was also heavily criticized by several (human rights) groups. Their criticism was directed not only at this lack of an impact assessment but also at, among other things, the proposal's unclear definitions, the criminalization of conduct without any direct link to specific terrorist offences and resulting human rights ramifications, and the fact that civil society organizations had not been properly heard in the design process.[79]

## V. Conclusion

This chapter has argued in favor of the law enforcement paradigm for the repression of terrorism in European countries, has clarified the scope of the phenomenon of foreign fighters in the EU, and has presented a selection of important institutions, mechanisms, and instruments at the EU level in the context of police and justice cooperation that try to counter these phenomena.

Arguably, the previous section has shown that there is no lack of political will at the EU level to be active in the fight against terrorism. Among other things because of terrorist attacks in Europe and beyond, the EU has witnessed the creation of various valuable institutions/mechanisms (e.g. Eurojust, Europol, JITs, EU CTC, ECTC) and instruments (e.g. the two framework decisions and the European Arrest Warrant). But one may wonder whether the EU legislator is currently not becoming a little *overenthusiastic* in the effort to protect Europeans from the scourge of terrorism. For instance, aspects of the last two examples mentioned above, the EU PNR Directive and the new EU Directive on Combating Terrorism, have been severely criticized by various (human rights) groups. Concerns were raised about the fact that the instruments were pushed through because of the political climate (the so-called 'window of opportunity'),[80] about the necessity (no proper evaluation and

---

77 *Ibid.*, art. 9.

78 European Commission, Communication from the Commission to the European Parliament, the Council, the European Economic and Social Committee and the Committee of the Regions. The European Agenda on Security, Strasbourg, 28 April 2015, COM(2015) 185 final, available at https://www.cepol.europa.eu/sites/default/files/european-agenda-security.pdf [last visited 13 April 2017], p. 14.

79 See *Paulussen* 2016, pp. 21–23 and *Voronova, S.*, Combating terrorism. Briefing, EU Legislation in Progress, February 2017, available at http://www.europarl.europa.eu/RegData/etudes/BRIE/2017/599269/EPRS_BRI(2017]599269_EN.pdf [last visited 13 April 2017], pp. 9–10.

80 See also the EU CT Study 2017, p. 66.

assessment of the inadequacy of the old situation) and proportionality (no sufficient safeguards in place in view of the potential for human rights infringements) of the instruments, as well as about the fact that relevant stakeholders were not adequately heard in the design process.[81]

Although a quick adoption of certain instruments may lead to a short-term victory for the legislators, to become *truly* effective, to make sure that we are all – 'together' – united in the fight against terrorism and ISIS in the long run, instruments such as these arguably need the backing of a much larger group of societal actors, such as the Member States, that need to implement the directives, the practitioners on the ground who need to work with the new laws once implemented, civil society organizations that will critically follow the (human rights) effects of the instruments in future practice, and, finally, the public at large. It is essential that all these actors have trust[82] in the new instruments. But the fact that various stakeholders were not adequately heard in the design process or that (because of this?) the instruments' potential for human rights violations has been criticized has already – and unnecessarily – weakened the legitimacy of and trust in these instruments.[83]

Trust is also of vital importance in making sure the newly established institutions/mechanisms will work as planned: the databases of Europol, for instance, will only operate efficiently if enough Member States are confident that the national information fed into these systems is sufficiently protected and thus that they are willing to share this information with third parties.[84] In that sense, the EU and its Member States are well advised to focus more on creating a culture of trust in which the existing information is better shared, in full conformity with human rights, rather than trying to obtain as much information as possible,[85] which may not only lead to the obvious human rights infringements but also, incidentally, to operational problems (data overkill).

Moving from the level of the EU to the inter-state level: here, trust is just as essential in ensuring an increase in cooperation. This can be achieved especially by strengthening the *informal* channels of cooperation, as recommended in the EU CT Study 2017:

> The EU is recommended to invest in informal channels of cooperation (personal contacts/networking) between practitioners in the criminal justice sector in a multidisciplinary way. One could think of the setting up of a network comparable to the European Judicial Network specifically focused on countering terrorism, in which context prosecutors, judges, defence lawyers, prison wards and parole officers can organise, in an informal but structured manner, conferences, workshops and expert meetings on topical

---

[81] See the earlier references mentioned above, as well as *Paulussen* 2016, p. 23 and the EU CT Study 2017, pp. 19, 56, 65, 73 and 83.

[82] See generally *Paulussen* 2016, pp. 28–29.

[83] See also the EU CT Study 2017, pp. 17 and 81.

[84] See also *ibid.*, p. 76.

[85] See also *ibid.*, pp. 19 and 80.

counter-terrorism issues and can share experiences and good (and bad) practices, for instance in the context of the gathering and use of (digital/cyber) evidence, or the assessment of rehabilitation needs. This will enhance intra-EU trust, and will lead to more cooperation and information exchange.[86]

Moreover, and following up on the two levels just discussed, a point that should also be mentioned but could not be discussed here due to the page limit is the fact that there is still a world to win when it comes to the complex interaction and division of power among the EU agencies and between the EU level and the national level in the field of counter-terrorism. Again, as noted in the EU CT Study 2017:

> Currently, too many actors are involved in the design and implementation of this policy area, the tasks of the individual actors at times overlap. This is notably the case when it concerns strategies that can be issued by the European Council, the Council of the EU and by the Commission, making it unclear who is in the lead. The recently appointed Commissioner for the Security Union and the delimitation of his competences vis-à-vis the EU Counter-Terrorism Coordinator furthermore complicates the questions concerning coordination. Certainly not helpful to this situation is the lack of clarity on the scope of the term 'internal security', and the extent to which Member States are willing to call on that exceptional clause in order to give priority to their national competences. This seems to be at odds with the otherwise regularly expressed conviction that the nature of the threat of terrorism has a cross-border character, and therefore merely a sum of national actions would fall short to address the true nature of the threat.[87]

Hence, it can be concluded that there is no lack of European ideas in countering ISIS in the field of criminal and justice cooperation; still, the manner in which these ideas are implemented *at the national level*, how many obstacles the implementation will encounter, and how many friends or enemies will be made in the process will, to a large extent, determine whether one can add an exclamation or a question mark after the first part of this chapter's title.

## Bibliography

AEDH, PNR: the European Parliament adopts a controversial text, 26 April 2016, available at http://www.aedh.eu/PNR-the-European-Parliament-adopts.html [last visited 13 April 2017].

*Bakker, E./Singleton, M.*, Foreign Fighters in the Syria and Iraq Conflict: Statistics and Characteristics of a Rapidly Growing Phenomenon, in: A. de Guttry/F. Capone/C. Paulussen (eds.), Foreign Fighters under International Law and Beyond. T.M.C. Asser Press/Springer Verlag: 2016, pp. 9–25.

---

86 *Ibid.*, p. 82. See also *ibid.*, p. 55. In that sense, it is good to note that investments are being made in trust and more informal networks, see Eurojust, Foreign terrorist fighters remain high on Eurojust agenda, Press release, 24 June 2016, available at http://eurojust.europa.eu/press/PressReleases/Pages/2016/2016-06-24.aspx [last visited 20 April 2017].

87 EU CT Study 2017, p. 16.

*Barrett, R.*, Foreign Fighters in Syria, *The Soufan Group*, June 2014, available at http://soufangroup.com/wp-content/uploads/2014/06/TSG-Foreign-Fighters-in-Syria.pdf [last visited 2 April 2017].

*Bilefsky, D./de la Baume, M.*, French Premier Declares 'War' on Radical Islam as Paris Girds for Rally. The New York Times, 10 January 2015, available at https://www.nytimes.com/2015/01/11/world/europe/paris-terrorist-attacks.html?_r=0 [last visited 2 April 2017].

*Breeden, A./Morenne, B.*, Prime Minister Says France is at 'War'. The New York Times, 15 July 2016, available at https://www.nytimes.com/live/truck-plows-into-crowd-in-nice-france/french-pri/ [last visited 2 April 2017].

Council Framework Decision 2008/919/JHA of 28 November 2008 amending Framework Decision 2002/475/JHA on combating terrorism, available at http://eur-lex.europa.eu/legal-content/en/TXT/?uri=CELEX:32008F0919 [last visited 12 April 2017].

Council Framework Decision of 13 June 2002 on combating terrorism (2002/475/JHA), available at http://eur-lex.europa.eu/legal-content/DA/TXT/?uri=uriserv:OJ.L_.2002.164.01. 0003.01.ENG [last visited 12 April 2017].

Council Framework Decision of 13 June 2002 on joint investigation teams (2002/465/JHA), available at http://eur-lex.europa.eu/legal-content/EN/ALL/?uri=CELEX: 32002F0465 [last visited 12 April 2017].

Council Framework Decision of 13 June 2002 on the European arrest warrant and the surrender procedures between Member States (2002/584/JHA), available at http://eur-lex.europa.eu/legal-content/EN/ALL/?uri=celex:32002F0584 [last visited 12 April 2017].

Council of the European Union, Implementation of the counter-terrorism agenda set by the European Council, 13627/16, 4 November 2016, available at http://www.statewatch.org/news/2016/nov/eu-council-CTC-implementation-a-t-strategy-13627-%20ADD-1-16.pdf [last visited 12 April 2017].

Council of the European Union, Joint Investigation Teams Practical Guide, 6128/1/17, 14 February 2017, available at http://www.eurojust.europa.eu/doclibrary/JITs/JITs%20framework/JITs%20Practical%20Guide/JIT-GUIDE-2017-EN.pdf [last visited 12 April 2017].

Council of the European Union, Report on the implementation of the EU Counter-Terrorism Strategy, 15799/14, 24 November 2014, available at http://data.consilium.europa.eu/doc/document/ST-15799-2014-INIT/en/pdf [last visited 12 April 2017].

*De Guttry, A./Capone, F./Paulussen, C.*, Introduction, in: A. de Guttry/F. Capone/C. Paulussen (eds.), Foreign Fighters under International Law and Beyond. T.M.C. Asser Press/Springer Verlag 2016, pp. 1–5.

*De Kerchove, G./Höhn, C.*, Counter-Terrorism and International Law Since 9/11, Including in the EU-US Context, in: T.D. Gill/T. McCormack/R. Geiss/R. Heinsch/C. Paulussen/J. Dorsey (eds.), Yearbook of International Humanitarian Law, Vol. 16 (2013). T.M.C. Asser Press/Springer Verlag 2015, pp. 267–295.

– The Regional Answers and Governance Structure for Dealing with Foreign Fighters: The Case of the EU, in: A. de Guttry/F. Capone/C. Paulussen (eds.), Foreign Fighters under International Law and Beyond. T.M.C. Asser Press/Springer Verlag 2016, pp. 299–331.

Directive (EU) 2016/681 of the European Parliament and of the Council of 27 April 2016 on the use of passenger name record (PNR) data for the prevention, detection, investigation and prosecution of terrorist offences and serious crime, available at http://eur-lex.europa.eu/eli/dir/2016/681/oj [last visited 13 April 2017].

Directive (EU) 2017/541 of the European Parliament and of the Council of 15 March 2017 on combating terrorism and replacing Council Framework Decision 2002/475/JHA and amending Council Decision 2005/671/JHA, available at http://eur-lex.europa.eu/legal-content/EN/TXT/?uri=CELEX:32017L0541 [last visited 12 April 2017].

Dutch anti-terrorism police arrest suspect at France's request. Reuters, 27 March 2016, available at http://www.reuters.com/article/us-rotterdam-dutch-france-idUSKCN0WT0MT [last visited 11 April 2017].

Eurojust, Foreign terrorist fighters remain high on Eurojust agenda. Press release, 24 June 2016, available at http://eurojust.europa.eu/press/PressReleases/Pages/2016/2016-06-24.aspx [last visited 20 April 2017].

Eurojust, Joint Investigation Teams (JITs), available at http://eurojust.europa.eu/Practitioners/JITs/Pages/historical-background.aspx [last visited 12 April 2017].

European Commission, Communication from the Commission to the European Parliament, the Council, the European Economic and Social Committee and the Committee of the Regions. The European Agenda on Security, Strasbourg, 28 April 2015, COM(2015) 185 final, available at https://www.cepol.europa.eu/sites/default/files/european-agenda-security.pdf [last visited 13 April 2017].

European Council, Counter-Terrorism Coordinator, available at http://www.consilium.europa.eu/en/policies/fight-against-terrorism/counter-terrorism-coordinator/ [last visited 12 April 2017].

European Council, Declaration on combating terrorism, 7906/04, 29 March 2004, available at http://data.consilium.europa.eu/doc/document/ST-7906-2004-INIT/en/pdf [last visited 12 April 2017].

European Council, Joint Investigation Teams Manual, 15790/11, 4 November 2011, available at https://www.europol.europa.eu/sites/default/files/documents/st15790-re01.en11.pdf [last visited 12 April 2017].

European Council, Special meeting of the European Council (30 August 2014) – Conclusions. EUCO 163/14, 30 August 2014, available at https://www.consilium.europa.eu/uedocs/cms_data/docs/pressdata/en/ec/144538.pdf [last visited 12 April 2017].

European Council, The European Union Counter-Terrorism Strategy, 14469/4/05, 30 November 2005, available at http://register.consilium.europa.eu/doc/srv?l=EN&f=ST%2014469%202005%20REV%204 [last visited 12 April 2017].

European Parliament, Directorate-General for Internal Policies, Policy Department C: Citizens' Rights and Constitutional Affairs, 'The European Union's Policies on Counter-Terrorism. Relevance, Coherence and Effectiveness'. Study for the LIBE Committee, PE 583.124, European Union, 2017, available at http://www.europarl.europa.eu/RegData/etudes/STUD/2017/583124/IPOL_STU(2017]583124_EN.pdf [last visited 11 April 2017].

European Parliament, EU Passenger Name Record (PNR) directive: an overview. 1 June 2016, available at http://www.europarl.europa.eu/news/en/news-room/20150123BKG 12902/eu-passenger-name-record-(pnr)-directive-an-overview [last visited 13 April 2017].

Europol, ECTC – European Counter Terrorism Centre – Infographic, available at https:// www.europol.europa.eu/publications-documents/ectc-european-counter-terrorism-centre-infographic [last visited 12 April 2017].

Europol, European Union Terrorism Situation and Trend Report 2016, available at https://www.europol.europa.eu/sites/default/files/documents/europol_tesat_2016.pdf [last visited 2 April 2017].

Europol, Europol Focal Points, available at https://www.europol.europa.eu/crime-areas-trends/europol-focal-points [last visited 13 April 2017].

Europol, Europol's European Counter Terrorism Centre strengthens the EU's response to terror. Press release, 25 January 2016, available at https://www.europol.europa.eu/news room/news/europol%E2%80%99s-european-counter-terrorism-centre-strengthens-eu%E 2%80%99s-response-to-terror [last visited 12 April 2017].

Europol, Europol's Internet Referral Unit to combat terrorist and violent extremist propaganda. Press release, 1 July 2015, available at https://www.europol.europa.eu/news room/news/europol%E2%80%99s-internet-referral-unit-to-combat-terrorist-and-violent-extremist-propaganda [last visited 12 April 2017].

Europol, Joint Investigation Teams – JITs, available at https://www.europol.europa.eu/acti vities-services/services-support/joint-investigation-teams [last visited 12 April 2017].

France and Belgium ease tensions with joint terror talks. The Local/AFP, 1 February 2016, available at https://www.thelocal.fr/20160201/france-and-belgium-to-team-up-to-fight-terror [last visited 1 April 2017].

France 'at war' with Daesh, says PM Manuel Valls. Euronews, 14 November 2015, available at http://www.euronews.com/2015/11/14/france-at-war-with-daesh-says-pm-manuel-valls [last visited 2 April 2017].

*Gartenstein-Ross, D./Moreng, B.*, MENA Countries' Responses to the Foreign Fighter Phenomenon, in: A. de Guttry/F. Capone/C. Paulussen (eds.), Foreign Fighters under International Law and Beyond. T.M.C. Asser Press/Springer Verlag 2016, pp. 445–468.

Geneva Academy of International Humanitarian Law and Human Rights' RULAC (Rule of Law in Armed Conflicts) project, available at http://www.rulac.org/browse/countries/ france [last visited 2 April 2017].

*MacDonald, K.*, Security and Rights. Speech to the UK Criminal Bar Association, 23 January 2007, available at http://www.cps.gov.uk/news/articles/security_rights/ [last visited 2 April 2017].

*Neumann, P.R.*, Foreign fighter total in Syria/Iraq now exceeds 20,000; surpasses Afghanistan conflict in the 1980s. ICSR, 26 January 2015, available at http://icsr.info/2015/01/ foreign-fighter-total-syriairaq-now-exceeds-20000-surpasses-afghanistan-conflict-1980s/ [last visited 2 April 2017].

Paris attacks suspect Salah Abdeslam extradited to France. BBC News, 27 April 2016, available at http://www.bbc.com/news/world-europe-36147575 [last visited 12 April 2017].

*Paulussen, C.*, Repressing the Foreign Fighters Phenomenon and Terrorism in Western Europe: Towards an Effective Response Based on Human Rights. ICCT Research Paper, November 2016, available at https://icct.nl/wp-content/uploads/2016/11/ICCT-Paulussen-Rule-of-Law-Nov2016-1.pdf [last visited 2 April 2017].

*Paulussen, C./Nijman, J./Lismont, K.*, Mental Health and the Foreign Fighter Phenomenon: A Case Study from the Netherlands. ICCT Report, March 2017, available at https://icct.nl/wp-content/uploads/2017/03/ICCT-Paulussen-Nijman-Lismont-Mental-Health-and-the-Foreign-Fighter-Phenomenon-March-2017.pdf [last visited 11 April 2017].

Remarks to the United Nations Security Council. Secretary Colin L. Powell, New York City, 5 February 2003, U.S. Department of State, available at https://2001-2009.state.gov/secretary/former/powell/remarks/2003/17300.htm [last visited 2 April 2017].

The Soufan Group, Foreign Fighters. An Updated Assessment of the Flow of Foreign Fighters into Syria and Iraq, December 2015, available at http://soufangroup.com/wp-content/uploads/2015/12/TSG_ForeignFightersUpdate3.pdf [last visited 2 April 2016].

The White House, Address to a Joint Session of Congress and the American People. Office of the Press Secretary, 20 September 2001, available at https://georgewbush-whitehouse.archives.gov/news/releases/2001/09/20010920-8.html [last visited 2 April 2017].

UN Security Council Counter-Terrorism Committee, Foreign terrorist fighters, undated, available at https://www.un.org/sc/ctc/focus-areas/foreign-terrorist-fighters/ [last visited 2 April 2017].

*Van Ginkel, B./Entenmann, E.* (eds.), The Foreign Fighters Phenomenon in the European Union. Profiles, Threats & Policies. ICCT Research Paper, April 2016, available at https://www.icct.nl/wp-content/uploads/2016/03/ICCT-Report_Foreign-Fighters-Pheno menon-in-the-EU_1-April-2016_including-AnnexesLinks.pdf [last visited 1 April 2017].

*Voronova, S.*, Combating terrorism, Briefing, EU Legislation in Progress, February 2017, available at http://www.europarl.europa.eu/RegData/etudes/BRIE/2017/599269/EPRS_BRI(2017]599269_EN.pdf [last visited 13 April 2017].

# Funding Conflict Through Cultural Property: The Destruction and Trafficking of Cultural Heritage by Islamic State

*Peter B. Campbell* and *Katie A. Paul*

Islamic State exploits cultural heritage for purposes of funding, propaganda, recruitment, and state-building. Evidence from Islamic State and Al Qaeda affiliates suggests that antiquities are a revenue source, while destruction of cultural monuments frequently appear in propaganda material. This chapter examines the trafficking networks that connect Syria and Iraq, and other areas under Islamic State control such as Libya, to outside markets, how terror organizations profit from antiquities, and the role of attacks on culture in recruitment and propaganda.

## I. Introduction

Cultural heritage is frequently a target during conflict, and Islamic State (IS) has exploited the history of Iraq and Syria, as well as other areas under their control such as Libya and Yemen, to loot or destroy cultural sites. Due to the ongoing conflict, estimates for the scale of looting and profits by Islamic State are problematic. Further information is becoming available as IS loses territory and records are captured, so while the scale of the activity is unknown, it is clear that cultural heritage is used by IS for profit and propaganda.

This chapter explores the evidence of Islamic State's exploitation of cultural heritage and the strategy behind their actions, before examining the legal instruments for prosecuting the looting and destruction of cultural heritage. Specifically, the authors discuss the destruction of *cultural heritage* and theft or looting of *cultural property*. Cultural property is the term preferred by lawyers and refers to the portable antiquities often trafficked across borders, such as works of art, ancient coins, or statuaries.[1] Cultural heritage is the term preferred by archaeologists as it encompasses not only portable antiquities, but landscapes, ecofacts, and the immobile

---

[1] *Merryman*, 80 American Journal of International Law (1986), 831–832.

aspects of ancient sites that are destroyed by looting.[2] Islamic State frequently profits from cultural property, while threatening to destroy cultural heritage.

*Figure 1*. Photograph of an artifact found on *Abu Sayyaf*'s computer following the US Special Forces raid (US Department of State)

Destruction of cultural heritage serves several purposes. Since the rise of Islamic State in Iraq and Syria, the group has carried out a series of performative destruction tactics deliberately targeting archaeological sites and historic structures.[3] Although past groups have targeted cultural sites, such as the Taliban's destruction of the Bamiyan Buddha, the strategy of wholesale deliberate destruction or erasure of cultural heritage has not been witnessed on a similar scale to Islamic State; the strategy has been deemed "cultural cleansing" by UNESCO Director-General *Irina Bokova*.[4] The destruction of cultural heritage has been argued to be a war crime and crime against humanity.[5] The Hague prosecuted Yugoslav leaders for actions against culture during the 1990s and Ansar Dine for destruction in Mali, and there

---

2 Article 1 (a) of the 1954 Hague Convention for the Protection of Cultural Property in Armed Conflict defines cultural property as, "movable or immovable property of great importance to the cultural heritage of every people, such as monuments of architecture, art or history, whether religious or secular; archaeological sites; groups of buildings which, as a whole, are of historical or artistic interest; works of art; manuscripts, books and other objects of artistic, historical or archaeological interest; as well as scientific collections and important collections or books or archives or of reproductions of [such] property."

3 *Harmanşah*, 78 Near Eastern Archaeology (2015), 170–177.

4 UNESCO, UNESCO News Centre (2015).

5 *Daniels*, Apollo Magazine (2016).

is evidence to suggest that the International Criminal Court may pursue a similar charge against Islamic State.[6]

The trafficking of cultural property is one of Islamic State's revenue sources, though the scope of this revenue is unclear with the limited public evidence available at present. Portable cultural property is looted by impoverished local residents and sold to traffickers who pay a tax to Islamic State. Traffickers pass the antiquities along smuggling routes to reach transit and market countries where the artifacts can be laundered into the legal market.[7] The effect of theft from cultural sites and looting of archaeological sites has negative impacts on local communities, both socio-culturally and economically. As regions emerge from Islamic State control, the widespread looting and destruction of cultural sites will have an effect on tourism.[8]

## II. Context

Like other black markets, the scale and scope of the illicit antiquities trade is difficult to estimate. The legal market was estimated by UNESCO to be USD 2.2 billion annually,[9] a significant percentage of the market appears to be laundered goods. The legal market can only be composed of artifacts in collections dating prior to the 1970 UNESCO Convention protecting artifacts excavated since 1970 from trafficking.[10] However, the growth of the market does not match the growth based solely on the resale of previously known antiquities. In fact, the appearance of artifacts covered in dirt indicating recent looting,[11] law enforcement raids,[12] personal accounts by former dealers and museum collectors,[13] and recent court cases demonstrate that a significant percentage of the legal market must be composed of laundered artifacts.[14]

In fact, there is growing evidence of the sophistication of trafficking networks that supply the global antiquities market. The trafficked cultural property includes stolen artifacts from museums or cultural sites and looted artifacts, illegally exca-

---

6 ICC-01/12-01/15.

7 *Campbell*, 20 International Journal of Cultural Property (2013), 122–123.

8 *Klamer*, 13 Public Archaeology (2014), 60–68.

9 UNESCO, International Flows, p. 37.

10 Convention on the Means of Prohibiting and Preventing the Illicit Import, Export and Transfer of Ownership of Cultural Property 1970, http://www.unesco.org/new/en/culture/themes/illicit-trafficking-of-cultural-property/1970-convention/text-of-the-convention/ [last visited 12 November 2018].

11 *Brems/van den Eynde*, Blood Antiquities (2009).

12 EUROPOL, EUROPOL Newsroom (2015).

13 *Hoving*, Making, pp. 103, 217; *McNall/D'Antonio*, Fun, p. 65; *van Rijn*, Hot Art, p. 31.

14 *Mashberg/Bearak*, New York Times (2015).

vated from buried or sunken archaeological deposits. The former can generally be repatriated due to evidence or documentation of the item's ownership history, while the latter represent a significant legal challenge due to their lack of records.

The antiquities trade is characterized by artifacts being trafficked from "source" countries to collections in "market" countries, typically via transit countries.[15] Source countries generally have significant archaeological deposits (e.g., Iraq, Italy, Cambodia), but high rates of unemployment and poor authority to control theft and looting. Looters are typically "subsistence diggers" in countries with unemployment over 10 % (e.g., Iraq and Afghanistan), which are unskilled laborers seeking any income source to survive. In countries with unemployment below 10 % (e.g., Italy and Peru), looters are often more specialized individuals seeking to supplement their regular income.[16] Transit countries have free trade agreements with source countries, lenient import laws, or corrupt border security that allows illicit goods to enter (e.g., Switzerland and United Arab Emirates). Once in a transit country, the artifacts are more easily transferred to market countries or laundered into the legal market.[17] Market countries have middle or upper classes with disposable income and social status conferred by wealth or connoisseurship (e.g., United States, United Kingdom, Japan).[18] Demand in market countries drives looting in source countries, which is why archaeologist Ricardo Elia argues that collectors are the real force behind the illicit trade.[19] Trafficking networks connect looters in source countries to collectors in the market countries.

## III. Trafficking networks

Illicit antiquities networks are organized similar to other trafficking networks, characterized by loosely connected and interchangeable participants.[20] Today, most criminal groups are characterized by "fluid network structures rather than more formal hierarchies," an organizational structure that is particularly well suited for trafficking.[21] These networks are opportunistic and participants are not typically career criminals. Instead, they are rational thinking individuals who see

---

15 *Merryman*, 80 American Journal of International Law (1986), 832.

16 *Campbell*, 20 International Journal of Cultural Property (2013), 135.

17 For example, looted Bulgarian artifacts were trafficked via Germany en route to Canada and the United States, as German imports were viewed less scrupulously than Bulgarian imports. Switzerland is a transit country because of its freeport policy. *Shentov*, Organized Crime, p. 186; *Watson/Todeschini*, Medici Conspiracy, pp. 25–26.

18 *Campbell*, 20 International Journal of Cultural Property (2013), 117.

19 *Elia*, Seductive, pp. 54–61.

20 *Coluccello/Massey*, 10 Trends in Organized Crime (2007), 86; *Williams*, Networks, Markets, and Hierarchies, p. 62; *Williams*, Transnational Criminal Networks, pp. 61–97.

21 *Williams/Godson*, 37 Crime, Law & Social Change (2002), 333.

an opportunity and exploit it to supplement their income.[22] These networks of everyday people – where participants might be farmers, customs agents, or university trained art specialists – lack the hierarchy of centralized criminal organizations such as the mafia.

Fluid networks with constantly changing participants create challenges for legal instruments that were written to prosecute hierarchal, mafia-like, criminal organizations. One law enforcement officer described the frustration of viewing the network but failing to be able to pin single participants by stating the network is like a, "plate of spaghetti [where] every piece seems to touch each other, but you are never sure where it all leads."[23] The benefits of fluid networks to participants stem from each interaction being personal and without an obligation to others in the network. Profit is not divided upon final sale; instead, money is exchanged at the point of interaction along the network.[24] Individual risk is reduced since further interaction past the point of sale is not necessary, limiting the amount of direct contact. Examples show participants with diverse backgrounds, some of which only participate in a single transaction, while others participate in many.[25]

Fluid networks have the appearance of complexity, which has led some to categorize them as "disorganized crime."[26] In reality, fluid networks are sophisticated. Participants are guided by an underlying structure that is based on a socio-political landscape of law enforcement, legal instruments, and cultural values. A change in this landscape causes networks to reorganize. New legal instruments targeting trafficking networks will reduce not only antiquities trafficking but also human, arms, and narcotics trafficking, among others.[27]

Antiquities trafficking is unique in so far as most antiquities need to be laundered onto the legal art market for sale, whereas other forms of trafficking – humans, arms, and narcotics – remain on the black market from source to market. Due to this need to launder the artifacts, there is an underlying structure to the trade that is composed of four observable stages.[28] While each artifact passes through these four stages, the number of participants in each stage may differ and the amount of time spent in each stage changes on a case-to-case basis.

The first stage is where the artifact is looted or stolen, either taken from an archaeological deposit or a cultural site such as a museum. Looters are often local

---

22 *Felson*, Ecosystem, p. 7.

23 *Green*, The Smugglers, p. 9.

24 *Campbell*, 20 International Journal of Cultural Property (2013), 118.

25 *Drake*, Art Newspaper (2008), 11.

26 *Williams*, Networks, Markets, and Hierarchies, p. 73.

27 *Campbell*, 20 International Journal of Cultural Property (2013), 135.

28 *Bator*, 34 Stanford Law Review (1982), 292: *Campbell*, 20 International Journal of Cultural Property (2013), 116.

individuals that are impoverished or opportunistic.[29] They use local information to find sites and exploit the lack of authority and protection. Since these participants are impoverished or exploiting an authority vacuum, arresting and prosecuting these individuals rarely has a sustained impact, as there are typically many participants to replace them.[30] Long term disruption of this stage is possible only through strong governmental authority and local community protection.

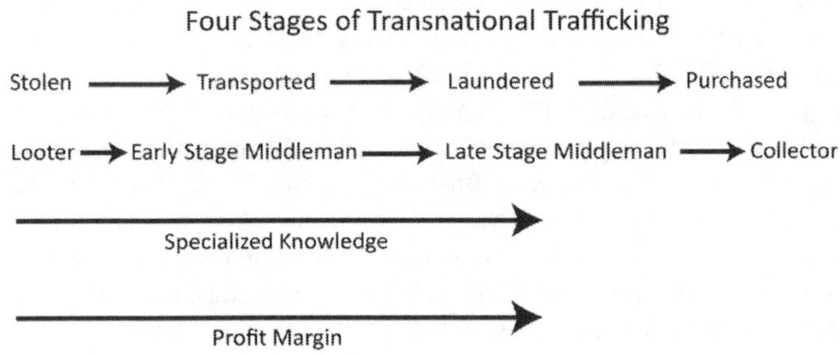


*Figure 2.* Diagram of the stages artifacts pass through when being trafficked, including the specialized knowledge and profit margin of participants in each stage (Authors)

The second stage consists in trafficking the artifact from its origin to the market country. This typically involves the looter selling the artifact to a trafficker, since most looters lack mobility or do not possess the finances for international travel and the knowledge of how to smuggle objects across borders. Most second stage middlemen are general traffickers who transport a number of illicit goods.[31] They understand the local security conditions and have connections to transport goods to transit or market countries. For this reason, most criminal organizations within the trade are found in this stage.[32]

The third stage consists in laundering the artifact onto the legal market. This requires a "grey" market individual, a participant with specialized art history knowledge and a legitimate storefront.[33] This group is the smallest but the most specialized population in the network and receives the highest percentage of the value.[34] As the smallest population, and being tied to physical locations such as

29 *Atwood*, Stealing History, p. 5.

30 *Bator*, 34 Stanford Law Review (1982), 292.

31 *Campbell*, 20 International Journal of Cultural Property (2013), 132–134.

32 *Campbell*, 20 International Journal of Cultural Property (2013), 132.

33 *Bowman*, 24 Journal of Contemporary Criminal Justice (2008), 225–228.

34 *Brodie*, 3 Culture Without Context (1998), 7–9.

galleries or auction houses, this stage is the most prone to disruption through law enforcement, regulation, and prosecution.

The fourth stage consists in the collector, either a private individual or a museum. In many cases, the collector may not know that the artifact has been laundered onto the market, but in other cases – even with museums – the collector is knowledgeable or complicit in the laundering, perhaps even knowing the location that the artifact was looted from.[35]

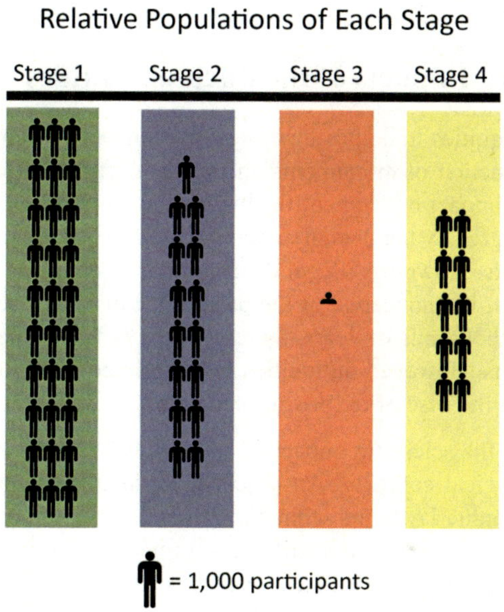


*Figure 3.* The relative populations of participants in each stage of the antiquities trafficking network (Authors)

While each stage describes the transfer of artifacts, the number of participants in each stage varies. In Afghanistan, local diggers provide artifacts to businessmen who traffic them to Pakistan through smuggling routes organized by the Haqqani Network and under the authority of the Taliban, after which they are sold on to dealers in market countries.[36] In Italy, *Giacomo Medici* bought artifacts from loosely affiliated looters who sold to several traffickers. *Medici* would traffic and store artifacts in Swiss freeports, before selling them to dealer *Robert Hecht*, who bought antiquities from several early stage middlemen similar to Medici. *Hecht* laundered the artifacts onto the legal market and sold them to collections such as the J. Paul Getty Museum, Boston Museum of Fine Arts, and the Metropolitan Museum in

35 *Slayman*, Archaeology (2006); *Hersher*, NPR (2016).

36 *Peters*, Crime and Insurgency, p. 36.

New York.[37] The participants in the first stage likely never meet those in the third or fourth stages or know of them. While this is quite different from hierarchical organized crime, the network is nevertheless organized and it is criminal throughout.[38] Opportunistic individuals may only participate in the network once, in contrast to the career criminals that the public imagines. Disrupting the network therefore does not involve arresting a kingpin but in disrupting the second and third stages that connect looters to collectors.

## IV. Impacts of the illicit antiquities trade

The illicit antiquities trade has three negative impacts: scientific, economic, and social. The destruction of monuments and theft of artifacts from museums has the most immediate impact both scientifically and economically, but their loss is mitigated to some degree by the documentation that exists for previously excavated and registered artifacts. However, illegal digging at archaeological sites creates an immeasurable deficit in knowledge of the past. Since these artifacts have been buried for hundreds or thousands of years, there is no record for either scientific study or repatriation claims. However, antiquities from both theft and looting pose a national security risk in the case of terrorism financing.

To understand the scientific impact of antiquities, it is important to take into account "archaeological context." An object in context has links to other artifacts, ecofacts, stratigraphic layers of sediment, structures, and other archaeological features. For this reason, an artifact is different from a work of art; an artifact has links to production, habitation, or burial areas. Alone, an object's story is superficial, capable of providing information only on its material (e.g., stone, wood, paint, writing, etc.). Within a context, an object can tell a more meaningful story of spatial patterning, economy, behaviors, and social changes (e.g., age and status of associated skeleton, import or export production, religious or habitation area). Once an artifact is removed, context is difficult – often impossible – to recreate. Therefore, a trafficked artifact represents not only a stolen object but a significant scientific loss as well. For example, Cycladic figurines are popular among collectors for their modernist depiction of the human body, but collectors' demand for the figurines led to such widespread looting that we do not know why these figures were created or what they were used for. Unfortunately, due to the widespread destruction of the archaeological sites that contained the figurines, it may now be impossible to ever learn what these object meant to the ancient people who created them.[39]

---

37 *Watson/Todeschini*, Medici Conspiracy, pp. 166–168.

38 *Mackenzie*, Identifying and Preventing, p. 41.

39 *Gill/Chippindale*, 97 American Journal of Archaeology (1993), 602–673.

The economic impact of the antiquities trade is difficult to measure, since quantifying the economic influence of cultural sites is a challenge to assess (e.g., Paris' Eiffel Tower, London's Westminster Abbey, or Barcelona's Sagrada Familia do not contribute directly to the economy of their communities but are foci of economic and social activities).[40] Economist *Arjo Klamer* has written a number of articles on measuring the economic contribution of culture,[41] the most direct attribution is tourism which provides significant percentages of the GDP in many countries. Looting is a destructive process and heavily damaged sites are not attractive venues for generating or maintaining tourism. In addition, many of the extremist or mafia groups that traffic on an industrial scale are armed and operate in large numbers. In Egypt, guards at archaeological sites have been shot,[42] had limbs broken,[43] and killed[44] in their efforts to stop violent gangs from looting sites and storage facilities since the 2011 Arab Spring. Egypt's economy has suffered significantly as a result, losing billions of USD in potential revenue from tourism at archaeological sites.[45] This revenue would have served as the source of funding to protect sites, creating a vicious cycle of looting and loss that impacts both the nation's heritage and economy.

The socio-cultural impact of antiquities trafficking and attacks on cultural heritage is difficult to quantify, but it represents one of the most significant impacts of the illicit trade. Cultural heritage serves as physical evidence of the historical narratives that provide social cohesion and cultural legitimacy. Removing the objects and monuments that reinforce cultural memory is a means to threaten the foundation of a group's identity.[46] This has been a tactic in the most destructive wars, where one group does not simply wish to defeat or conquer but eliminate a cultural narrative and identity entirely. Targeting historical narratives has been termed "symbolic domination" or "symbolic annihilation,"[47] and examples include the Nazis during World War II, the Khmer Rouge during the Cambodian civil war, and the attacks on the ancient bridge at Mostar and the historic city of Dubrovnik during the Balkan Wars.[48]

Beyond cultural identity, the socio-cultural impact of antiquities trafficking includes national security risks in the case of terrorism financing.[49] Antiquities can

---

40 *Klamer*, 13 Public Archaeology (2014), 69.

41 *Klamer*, 13 Public Archaeology (2014), 60–68.

42 *Marei*, The Art Newspaper (2011).

43 *El-Aref*, 1125 Al Ahram Weekly (2012).

44 *Sutton*, Hyperallergic (2016).

45 *Hassan*, Al Monitor (2016).

46 *Bell*, 54 British Journal of Sociology (2003), 67–69; *Anderson*, Imagined, pp. 182–184.

47 *Eichstedt/Small*, Representations; *Alderman/Campbell*, 48 Southeastern Geographer (2008), 338.

48 *Petrovic*, Old Bridge, pp. 39–43.

49 *Fitzpatrick/Lynch*, Stopping Terror, p. 3.

directly fund terror groups, such as was reported by German law enforcement to Der Spiegel revealing that September 11, 2001 attacker *Mohammed Atta* attempted to sell artifacts to a university professor to raise money.[50] In Afghanistan, the Haqqani Network paid the Taliban a tax for permission to traffic antiquities out of the country.[51] Antiquities can also facilitate criminal activity, such as laundering large sums of money.[52] Small artifacts, such as coins or cylinder seals, are portable and easily carried across borders, but can be worth thousands of USD.

While cultural heritage plays a significant role in our lives as humans and in regional and national economies, regulation of the antiquities trade is weak. Antiquities researcher *Samuel Hardy* made the observation that ancient artifacts are less regulated than eggs.[53] While any egg in an EU supermarket has records of its origin, most antiquities – even those valued at hundreds of thousands of euros – often have few records upon sale.[54] In addition, records that accompany artifacts can be manufactured or provide false provenience trails.[55] It was common practice in the 1990s for dealers to sell their artifacts back and forth to each other, creating a fake chain of records.[56] Poor regulation could be tied to antiquities lobbyists who have fought regulation measures. For example, the American Council for Cultural Policy lobbied the Bush Administration to relax import laws for Iraqi antiquities two months prior to the United States' invasion of Iraq in 2003.[57] Poor regulation has the unfortunate consequence of allowing black market artifacts to be laundered, as well as enabling the proliferation of forgeries, on the licit market.[58]

## V. Destruction of cultural heritage for propaganda and recruitment

The destruction of cultural heritage by Islamic State as well as other Al Qaeda affiliates became an important propaganda strategy in 2014. Destruction, rather than profit through looting and sale, has two purposes: to remove evidence of cultural history different from the Caliphate – part of the state-building process – and as a recruitment and propaganda tool. Sites targeted for destruction are generally monuments, which are immobile and have importance to the community. These are

---

50 Der Spiegel, Kunst, 1.

51 *Peters*, Crime and Insurgency, p. 36.

52 *St. Hilaire*, $2 Billion, p. 1.

53 *Ahmed*, Think Progress (2016).

54 *Chippindale/Gill*, 104 American Journal of Archaeology (2000), 494–499.

55 *Merryman/Elsen/Urice*, Law, pp. 289–291.

56 *Watson/Todeschini*, Medici Conspiracy, p. 139.

57 *Johnson*, The Smash of Civilizations (2005).

58 *Stanish,* Forging Ahead (2009).

often large and visible symbols, which create a spectacle for the local audience as well as an international audience through social media.

The targeting of cultural heritage sites by Islamic State appears to have its origins in the 2006 destruction of the al-Askari Mosque, also known as the Golden Dome Mosque, in Samarra by Al Qaeda in Iraq. The mosque was built in 944 AD and is revered as one of the most holy sites in Shi'ite Islam.[59] As the prophesized location of the reappearance of the Hidden Imam, al-Askari is closely tied to the future of Shi'ite identity. The decision to bomb the site was made by Sunni Al Qaeda leader *Abu Musab al-Zarqawi* as a strategy to spread sectarian discord and increase Sunni recruitment numbers. The attack succeeded in splitting Iraq along sectarian lines and drew a large number of unemployed Sunni soldiers to *Zarqawi*.[60] Islamic State succeeded Al Qaeda in Iraq, and *Abu Bakr al-Baghdadi* succeeded *Zarqawi*, who learned the impact of targeting culture from the Samarra attack.

Monuments anchor cultural memory, playing a significant role in the cohesion in social groups, Shi'ite Islam in the case of Samarra.[61] A witness told the International Criminal Court that the destruction of the monuments at Timbuktu was justified by Al Qaeda affiliates because, "The best way to tear someone down is to tear down their culture, tear down everything that is important to them."[62] This view is the basis for the current destruction in Syria, Iraq, and elsewhere across the Middle East and North Africa. Destruction of large cultural monuments, which includes ancient sites like Palmyra and religious sites like Samarra or the Tomb of Jonah, removes evidence of cultural identities that differ from the extremist Sunni Islamic State ideology.

IS destroyed the Tomb of Jonah, also known as the mosque of Nabi Yunus, in 2014. The same Jonah of Biblical and Qur'an renown, the goal of the destruction was to inflict a psychological blow and reinforce Islamic State's ideology. IS actively kept worshipers, both Muslim and Christian, away from the site while it was stripped of its valuable relics and movable pieces, down to the air conditioner.[63] The site was then lined with explosives and members of IS removed neighboring residents from their homes to force them to watch the explosion. Even after the destruction, armed guards kept devotees away from the site.

Since 2014, Islamic State has produced professional quality videos of destruction targeting world-famous sites, including those on the UNESCO World Heritage List. Islamic State's widely used and masterfully implemented tactics of performa-

---

[59] *Crowley*, Time (2014).

[60] *Crowley*, Time (2014).

[61] *Kane*, The Politics, pp. 1–10.

[62] *William/Paterson*, World Post (2016).

[63] AFP, The Telegraph (2014).

tive destruction occur at some of the world's most important archaeological sites in the "Cradle of Civilization." This created a propaganda machine that has been nearly unstoppable in the era of social media and broad global internet access. Journalist *Rukmini Callimachi* documented Islamic State's propaganda campaigns and her insights provide context for how the destruction of cultural heritage fits their media strategy. She describes how the videos fit their recruitment strategy, noting:

> You have to think that for every one of these beheading videos … especially the ones that are well crafted, they sat around and the thought about every single aspect of it. They think about the lighting, they think about the quote that they are going to take from scripture, they have thought about what they allow the victim to say, and with all of that they are trying to communicate something to us and also something to potential recruits.[64]

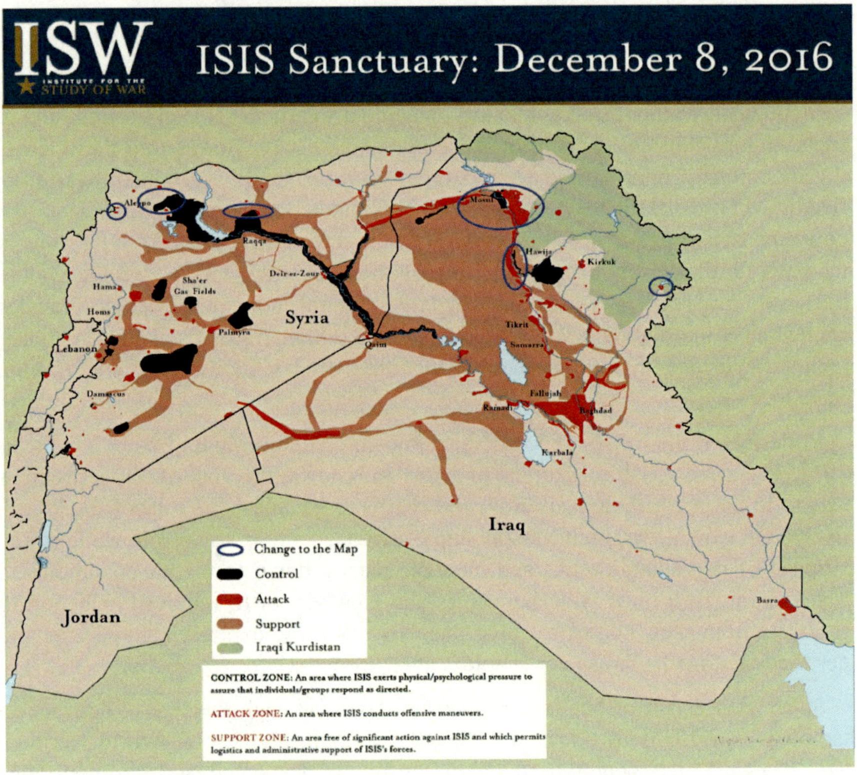


*Figure 4.* Map of the IS control areas in Syria and Iraq in 2016
(Institute for the Study of War)

Early news coverage of Islamic State drew widespread international attention due to their extreme barbarity, notably beheadings. However, the large volume of

64 *Callimachi*, Longform (2015).

continual beheadings – new beheading videos are released every few days – led to a decrease in media attention due to normalization and oversaturation of the violence.[65] As the global media shared less of the violent propaganda videos, including the US media's policy against airing murders, the media's willingness to share or reproduce videos of cultural destruction provided a continued platform to amplify IS recruitment.

A progression can be seen in how Islamic State used the international media through the destruction of cultural sites from Samarra in 2006 through Palmyra in 2016. Initially, destruction was for local impact and reported to the media later, such as Samarra and other shrines in Iraq.[66] A second phase began with the Tomb of Jonah, where IS appears to have leaked false stories of its destruction, causing world-wide media attention. Once attention was focused on the mosque, the destruction was carried out in front of cameras, which maximized media coverage. This was followed by announcements of attacks to be carried out at Nimrud, Nineveh, and Hatra, which led to the release of a lengthy video documenting the destruction following international uproar.[67] It was at this time that IS leaders in Syria were initially against the destruction of cultural heritage in Palmyra.[68] However, their position changed in May 2015, and the destruction of monuments at sites such as Palmyra have come to epitomize the targeting of cultural heritage in war. This represents the third phase, where Islamic State combined staged destruction and execution spectacles that would maximize media impact. Elements of Palmyra were destroyed at regular intervals to keep public attention on Islamic State.[69] Frequent beheadings and murders occurred in the ancient theater and other monuments, including the execution of *Khaled Al-Assaad*, an archaeologist who directed research at the ancient site for many years and who may have been hiding the locations of antiquities from Islamic State.[70] While the beheadings that had captured media attention during the rise of Islamic State led to oversaturation and decreased coverage, the choreographed attacks on cultural sites, including those combined with executions, were covered by the media as they occurred. The result was increased recruitment by those who engaged with the extremist ideology and constant propaganda communicated to those who opposed Islamic State.

---

65 *Callimachi*, Longform (2015).
66 *Crowley*, Time (2014).
67 *Shaheen*, Guardian (2015).
68 *Hall*, Daily Mail (2015).
69 *Jefferies*, Guardian (2015).
70 *Shaheen/Black*, Guardian (2015).

## VI. Legal and ideological challengers to cultural cleansing

While many believe this tactic is the product of an extremist attempt to eliminate "idolatry," which is considered *haram* in Islam, some of Sunni Islam's highest clerics have condemned the practice as un-Islamic. Al Azhar Mosque and University, as well as the educational institute of Dar al Ifta in Egypt – considered two of the foremost authorities on Sunni Islam in the Muslim world – have both voiced opposition to the deliberate destruction of cultural heritage sites. Following the Islamic State bulldozing of the ancient site of Nimrud, Iraq in March 2015, the Grand Mufti of Al Azhar issued a *fatwa*[71] condemning the destruction of ancient sites and artifacts. The official statement from Al Azhar notes, "These artefacts have important cultural and historical significance, they are an important part of our collective legacy that must not be harmed."[72]

Recently, the legal implications for the destruction of cultural heritage have increased with the conviction of *Ahmad Al Faqi Al Mahdi* for the destruction of ancient shrines in Timbuktu, Mali. The International Criminal Court pursued attacks on culture as crimes against humanity.[73] *Mahdi* oversaw the destruction while affiliated with the Movement for Oneness and Jihad in West Africa (MOJWA) and Ansar Dine.[74] Of particular note to Islamic State, the chief prosecutor in the case against Mahdi specifically mentioned the destruction of Aleppo and Palmyra to the International Criminal Court,[75] suggesting that cases may be brought against Islamic State leadership and other groups in the future.

## VII. Terror financing through the looting of cultural property

While monuments, which are largely immobile, are destroyed for propaganda and recruitment, portable cultural heritage such as coins, pottery, and statues are stolen from museums, storage facilities, and religious centers, or looted from the ground at archaeological sites to fund the Islamic State's activities. It is important to note that Islamic State is not the only group profiting from the looting of antiquities in Iraq and Syria. There is evidence that both *Bashar al-Assad*'s government forces and the Free Syrian Army are selling antiquities to purchase arms and pro-

71 A *fatwa* is a legal interpretation or ruling point of Islamic law (also known as Sharia Law) that is issued by one of the high-ranking muftis, a jurist or learned individual who is part of an authority and who has studied and been charged with the legal interpretation of Islamic law.

72 TNN, Al Azhar Observer (2015).

73 ICC-01/12-01/15.

74 ICC-01/12-01/15.

75 *Simons*, New York Times (2016).

long the conflict.[76] Within the region, there are likely non-affiliated individuals, from criminal organizations to regular citizens, likewise profiting from antiquities. While the focus of this chapter is on IS, the reality on the ground is complex.

The nature of the antiquities trade under IS was made clear during a US Special Forces raid in May 2015 on the stronghold of IS financial leader *Abu Sayyaf* in eastern Syria. According to *Andrew Keller* from the U.S. Department of State,

> Between October 2014 and April of 2015, *Abu Sayyaf* signed eight 'Antiquities Division' memoranda, which authorize certain individuals to excavate and supervise the excavation of artifacts in ISIL-controlled territory, and in some cases to detain anyone searching for artifacts without the prior approval of the Diwan of Natural Resources.[77]

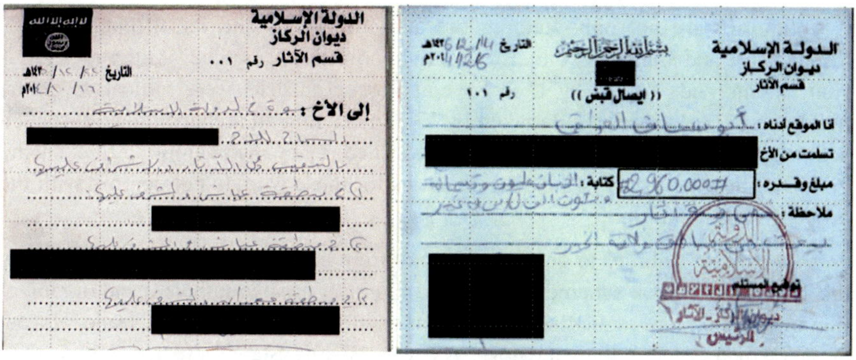


*Figure 5.* IS antiquities permit and receipt for *khums* tax found during the US raid (US Department of State)

The documents detailed an antiquities bureaucracy that included a central authority, eastern and western governorate offices, and permits and paperwork for various activities.[78] The result is highly controlled exploitation of cultural resources within IS territory, maximizing the profits from antiquities.

Among the materials recovered from the IS leader's compound were antiquities intended for sale, computers with images of artifacts that appeared to be looted, and receipts for taxation and permits. The receipts seized by U.S. Special Forces including eleven covering a three month period for *khums* tax, a 20 % "war booty" placed on antiquities among other items, amounting to over USD 267,000, accord-

76 The ancient sites of Dura Europos and Apamea were looted while under control of Assad's forces or the Free Syrian Army. *Giglio/al-Awad*, Buzzfeed (2015); *Taylor*, Washington Post (2015); *Hardy*, Conflict Antiquities (2015); *Baker/Anjar*, Time (2012).

77 *Keller*, U.S. Department of State (2015).

78 *Keller*, U.S. Department of State (2015).

ing to the U.S. Department of State, the receipts "suggest total sales transactions worth more than USD 1.25 million" from December 2014 to March 2015.[79]

The evidence of terrorists using antiquities as a source of funding extends beyond Syria alone. In May 2016, the head of Libya's Department of Antiquities revealed that artifacts were found by authorities when examining the recaptured home of an IS commander in Benghazi.[80] Even with increased international and political attention on antiquities trafficking issues, IS has continued to seek antiquities as a resource. The connections between antiquities trafficking and the Islamic State continued into January 2017, when authorities in Iraq seized more than 100 ancient artifacts from an IS safe house in Mosul.[81]

Antiquities are not only funding the activities of IS and its affiliated groups through sale and *khums* tax but also through permitting fees. The "Antiquities Division" memoranda seized by U.S. Special Forces in 2015 were indicative of the highly organized process undertaken by IS in managing all archaeologically-related activities within their territory. Permits are issued to anyone attempting to excavate within IS-held territory;[82] IS exacts penalties for those who do not comply with the proper documentation.

Islamic State's ability to generate revenue from antiquities is therefore similar to the Taliban's taxation scheme.[83] However, IS exerts greater authority and organization over the region, regulating both the first and second stages of the trade, at least until traffickers leave their territory. As with Islamic State's other finances, they keep meticulous records and appear to consult archaeological texts to identify artifacts and estimate their value.[84] While the final sale price is unknowable to IS since it occurs in market countries, IS ensures a larger percentage than most second stage middlemen through its authority over the first stage and awareness of market value. Islamic State's highly organized profit system includes several tiers, whereby looters have three to five weeks to find a buyer and split the profit 80–20 % with IS, then IS would claim it and try to find a buyer for 4–5 weeks with a 40–60 % split, and, finally, if there is no buyer after this period, then IS sells the artifact at auction in Raqqa with a 20–80 % split.[85] This creates more profit than other known second stage middlemen. The Financial Action Task Force report released in 2015 by the Global Coalition to Counter ISIL noted that "ISIL's ability to earn revenue from the illicit sale of antiquities is contingent upon the presence of antiquities within

79 *Keller*, Bureau of Educational and Cultural Affairs (2016).

80 *Lewis*, Reuters (2016).

81 *Untalan*, International Business Times (2017].

82 *Al Azm*, Middle East Institute (2015).

83 *Campbell*, 20 International Journal of Cultural Property (2013), 128.

84 Financial Action Task Force, Global Coalition, pp. 29–31.

85 *Paul*, Antiquities Coalition (2016).

territory where ISIL operates, knowledge of their existence, ability to recognize materials as artefacts and develop some estimation of their value."[86]

The stockpiling of antiquities as well as the highly organized taxation and permitting scheme makes clear that it is not sales alone that make cultural property a source of financing for terrorist groups. Market regulations to combat illicit material must be applied vigilantly to have enough impact on demand of conflict antiquities in order to deter the base level financing schemes of the Islamic State's antiquities network. Terrorist groups are expending significant resources in manpower, equipment, and organizational hierarchy to this trade. These resources would not be utilized without the guarantee of a significant reward.

Trafficking of the artifacts from Islamic State appears to follow established smuggling routes, either through Turkey or Lebanon and on to transit and market countries.[87] Smugglers may not necessarily be IS affiliated, as it appears that many are opportunistic given the current conflict.[88] Much like the looters, these opportunists appear to operate whether IS, the Free Syrian Army, or Assad's forces control a region.

High ticket items go into storage such as freeports – untaxed and unregistered – to accrue value as investments;[89] the Geneva freeport holds as much as GBP 80 billion in goods, and antiquities are a significant proportion of the warehouse spaces, with known traffickers and dealers such as *Giacomo Medici* and *Robin Symes* having facilities there.[90] Antiquities from Palmyra have been found in Swiss freeports, though imported in 2009–2010.[91] Due to the safety of freeports and other storage facilities, the amount of time that it may take for IS looted antiquities to appear on the market is uncertain. *Medici*'s Italian antiquities took several years to reach the market, so artifacts from the IS region may not appear for a while.

From transit countries, the antiquities enter arterial trafficking routes to market countries. At this point, antiquities from IS are transported and join galleries or collections alongside artifacts from other areas. Recently, two Spanish dealers were arrested with antiquities believe to be smuggled by IS as part of counter-trafficking raid; the pieces were mixed in among with their other items.[92] While the early stages of the network are tailored to the local circumstances in the market country, the last two stages are reoccurring along arterial routes. Low ticket antiquities are difficult to distinguish from those originating in Greece, Italy, Bulgaria, or elsewhere,

---

86 Financial Action Task Force, Global Coalition, p. 16.

87 *Naharnet,* Report (2015); *Parkinson/Albayrak/Mavin*, Wall Street Journal (2015).

88 *Baker/Anjar*, Time (2012).

89 UNESCO, Intergovernmental Committee, p. 2.

90 *Milmo*, iNews (2016).

91 *McGivern*, Art Newspaper (2016); *Roberts*, Daily Mail (2016).

92 *Barker*, ABC News (2018).

and may enter the market sooner. eBay has had large-scale sales of looted antiquities in the past.[93] The large amount of looting that has been observed through satellite images and on the ground reports is likely at various stages within the network, and the antiquities will likely continue to appear on the market for many years.[94]

## VIII. Legal instruments

Trafficking thrives where there are gaps between national and international laws, or where communication between countries is poor or lacking. National legislation differs considerably depending on the legal histories of nations. Italy prosecuted *Giacomo Medici* under laws designating a mafia definition of organized crime – the case pended on the use of the term *cordata* by a looter during a wiretap – which was successful for the prosecution but did not accurately describe the trafficking network.[95] While it was successful in the *Medici* case, it may lead to acquittals in other cases. Legislators with an understanding of human trafficking and antiquities networks would be wise to revise the definition of organized crime to suit modern network structures. A recent example of this is the 2016 United States Protect and Preserve International Cultural Property Act.[96] This legislation increases interagency cooperation to prevent importation of cultural property from conflict zones, specifically targeting Syrian cultural property. Following the passage of the Act, the US Attorney's Office filed a civil complaint against cultural property used for terror financing, citing four artifacts in *Abu Sayyaf* possession, an action that would allow the United States to seize foreign cultural property assets belonging to IS and allow the FBI to investigate.[97]

It is international legal instruments that are most pertinent to antiquities trafficking by Islamic State. The key pieces are the 1970 UNESCO Convention on the Means of Prohibiting and Preventing the Illicit Import, Export and Transfer of Ownership of Cultural Property, 1995 UNIDROIT Convention,[98] UNESCO 1999 Second Protocol to the 1954 Convention on the Protection of Cultural Property in

---

93 *Campbell*, 20 International Journal of Cultural Property (2013), 124.

94 *Parkinson/Albayrak/Mavin*, Wall Street Journal (2015); UNESCO, Satellite-Based, pp. 4–6, 9–14.

95 *Watson/Todeschini*, Medici Conspiracy, pp. 17, 79.

96 H.R. 1493 Protect and Preserve International Cultural Property Act. Became Public Law No. 114–151.

97 U.S. Attorney's Office, Department of Justice (2016).

98 1995 UNIDROIT Convention on Stolen or Illegally Exported Cultural Objects, http://www.unidroit.org/english/conventions/1995culturalproperty/1995culturalproperty-e.pdf [last visited 12 November 2018].

the Event of Armed Conflict,[99] and United Nations Resolution 2199. UN Resolution 2199 forbids direct or indirect commerce with Islamic State and Al Qaeda affiliates for a number of commodities including cultural property.[100] The UN tasked UNESCO with determining how to implement the cultural property section, with the participation of other UN offices including the UNODC, which has played a significant role in preventing cultural property trafficking.[101]

## IX. Discussion

Antiquities trafficking networks present a challenge to legal experts. Fluid networks have not traditionally been the subject of legislation, as most laws were written for hierarchical mafia-type organizations. The *Giacomo Medici* and *Subhash Kapoor* cases, and the current case against Islamic State by the US Attorney's Office demonstrate how laws can challenge networks, but future legislation will hopefully specifically target fluid networks.

Transnational trafficking occurs where countries have poor cooperation and legal differences. International cooperation is necessary to stem trafficking. Recently, the Organization for Security and Cooperation in Europe (OSCE), INTERPOL, EUROPOL, UNODC, and other organizations have been proactive in specifically targeting antiquities trafficking. A network of cooperation is being built to diminish or prevent trafficking from source to transit and market countries, though increased participation is needed from key states. Legal experts are helping to create memoranda of understanding between source and market countries to increase protection of cultural heritage and encourage repatriation.[102] INTERPOL has created a cultural property database accessible to all member states, which is particularly useful for stolen cultural property with records. Border security should create a record of suspicious artifacts, even if the objects are allowed to pass the border, so the records can be accessed for future reference or court cases. This is especially important for looted artifacts that have no previous records. Importantly, trafficking that is disrupted, whether it is antiquities, arms, or others, also prevents other forms of trafficking. Prosecuting traffickers for antiquities may prevent them from human, arms, or narcotics smuggling.[103] While the current focus is on diminishing income

99 UNESCO, http://www.unesco.org/new/en/culture/themes/armed-conflict-and-heritage/convention-and-protocols/1999-second-protocol/text/ [last visited 12 November 2018].

100 UN Resolution 2199 (2015), https://www.un.org/press/en/2015/sc11775.doc.htm [last visited 12 November 2018].

101 UNODC, UNODC (2017].

102 US Department of State, Press Release (2016).

103 *Campbell*, 20 International Journal of Cultural Property (2013), 134–135.

for Islamic State, actions and legislation should be broadened to all conflict zones to prevent similar situations in the future.

## X. Conclusion

Islamic State is currently the largest organization funding terror through the sale of antiquities, but the looting and trafficking of cultural property is a significant – and overlooked – issue in every conflict and economically depressed region. While the threat of Islamic State may pass in the next few years, the trafficking of cultural property will continue long into the future. It is through legislators, law enforcement, and legal experts that cultural trafficking from conflict regions will be limited.

## Bibliography

AFP, Iraq jihadists blow up 'Jonah's tomb' in Mosul. The Telegraph, 25 July 2014, http://www.telegraph.co.uk/news/worldnews/middleeast/iraq/10989959/Iraq-jihadists-blow-up-Jonahs-tomb-in-Mosul.html (last visited 12 November 2018).

*Ahmed, Beenish*, Experts Believe Hobby Lobby Stole Biblical Antiquities from Iraq. ThinkProgress, 4 November 2015, https://thinkprogress.org/experts-believe-hobby-lobby-stole-biblical-antiquities-from-iraq-heres-why (last visited 12 November 2018).

*Al Azm, Amr,* The Pillaging of Syria's Cultural Heritage. Middle East Institute, 22 May 2015, http://www.mei.edu/content/at/pillaging-syrias-cultural-heritage (last visited 12 November 2018).

*Alderman, Derek/Campbell, Rachel*, Symbolic Excavation and the Artifact Politics of Remembering Slavery in the American South: Observations from Walterboro, South Carolina. 48 Southeastern Geographer 338–355 (2008).

*Anderson, Benedict,* Imagined Communities: Reflections on the Origin and Spread of Nationalism. London 2006.

*Baker, Anne,* Tracking the smugglers' trail of priceless Islamic State loot to art markets in the West. ABC News 6 June 2018, https://www.abc.net.au/news/2018-06-06/priceless-antiques-looted-by-is-smuggled-into-western-markets/9833554 (last visited 12 November 2018).

*Baker, Aryn/Anjar, Majdal*, Syria's Looted Past: How Ancient Artifacts Are Being Traded for Guns. TIME World, 12 September 2012, http://world.time.com/2012/09/12/syrias-looted-past-how-ancient-artifacts-are-being-traded-for-guns (last visited 12 November 2018).

*Bell, Duncan S. A.*, Mythscapes: Memory, Mythology, and National Identity. 54 British Journal of Sociology 63–81 (2003).

*Bowman, Blythe*, Transnational Crimes Against Culture: Looting at Archaeological Sites and the "Grey" Market in Antiquities. 24 Journal of Contemporary Criminal Justice 225–242 (2008).

*Brems, Peter/Van den Eynde, Wim*, Blood Antiquities. Journeyman Pictures. Surrey 2009.

*Brodie, Neil*, Pity the Poor Middlemen. 3 Culture Without Context 7–9 (1998).

*Callimachi, Rukmini*, #129: Rukmini Callimachi. Longform, 18 February 2015, https://longform.org/posts/longform-podcast-129-rukmini-callimachi-part-1 (last visited 12 November 2018).

*Campbell, Peter*, The Illicit Antiquities Trade as a Transnational Criminal Network: Characterizing and Anticipating Trafficking of Cultural Heritage. 20 International Journal of Cultural Property 113–153 (2013).

*Chalmers Johnson*, The Smash of Civilizations. Asia Times, 9 July 2005, http://www.atimes. com/atimes/Middle_East/GG09Ak01.html (last visited 12 November 2018).

*Chippindale, Christopher/Gill, David W.J.*, Material Consequences of Contemporary Classical Collecting. 104 American Journal of Archaeology 463–511 (2000).

*Coluccello, Salvatore/Massey, Simon*, Out of Africa: The Human Trade Between Libya and Lampedusa. 10 Trends in Organized Crime 77–90 (2007).

*Crowley, Michael*, How the Fate of One Holy Site Could Plunge Iraq into Civil War. Time, 26 June 2014, http://time.com/2920692/iraq-isis-samarra-al-askari-mosque/ (last visited 12 November 2018).

*Daniels, Brian*, Is the destruction of cultural property a war crime? Apollo Magazine, 28 November 2016, https://www.apollo-magazine.com/is-the-destruction-of-cultural-property-a-war-crime/ (last visited 12 November 2018).

Der Spiegel, Kunst als Terrorfinanzierung? 18 July 2005, http://www.spiegel.de/spiegel/print/d-41106138.html (last visited 12 November 2018).

*Drake, Cathryn*, Italy Awaits Biggest Ever Trial of Tomb Robbers. 187 The Art Newspaper 11 (2008).

*Eichstedt, Jennifer L./Small, Stephen*, Representations of Slavery: Race and Ideology in Southern Plantation Museums. Washington, D.C. and London 2002.

*El-Aref, Nevine*, No longer a sacred site. Al Ahram Weekly 12 December 2012. http://weekly.ahram.org.eg/News/1061.aspx (last visited 12 November 2018).

*Elia, Ricardo*, A Seductive and Troubling Work. In: Karen Vitelli (ed.), Archaeological Ethics. Walnut Creek, CA 1996, pp. 54–61.

EUROPOL, European Police Arrest 35 and Recover Thousands of Stolen Cultural Artefacts. EUROPOL News Room, 28 January 2015, https://www.europol. europa.eu/newsroom/news/european-police-arrest-35-and-recover-thousands-of-stolen-cultural-artefacts (last visited 12 November 2018).

*Felson, Marcus*, Crime and Nature. London 2006.

– The Ecosystem for Organized Crime. HEUNI Paper no. 26. Helsinki 2006.

*Felson, Marcus/Boba, Rachel*, Crime and Everyday Life. London 2010.

Financial Action Task Force, Financing of the Terrorist Organisation Islamic State in Iraq and the Levant (ISIL). Global Coalition to Counter ISIL, February 2015, http://www.fatf-gafi.org/media/fatf/documents/reports/Financing-of-the-terrorist-organisation-ISIL.pdf (last visited 12 November 2018).

*Fitzpatrick, Michael/Lynch, Stephen F.*, Stopping Terror Finance: Securing The U.S. Financial Sector. Report prepared by the Staff of the Task Force to Investigate Terror Financing, Committee on Financial Service, U.S. House of Representatives. Washington, DC 2015.

*Giglio, Mike/al-Awad, Munzer*, Inside the Underground Trade to Sell off Syria's History. Buzzfeed, 30 July 2015, https://www.buzzfeed.com/mikegiglio/the-trade-in-stolen-syrian-artifacts (last visited 12 November 2018).

*Gill, David W. J./Chippindale, Christopher*, Material and Intellectual Consequences of Esteem for Cycladic Figures. 97 American Journal of Archaeology 602–673 (1993).

*Green, Timothy*, The Smugglers. New York 1969.

House of Representatives, Protect and Preserve International Cultural Property Act, H.R. 1493, 114th Cong. (2016) (enacted). Congress.gov, 5 September 2016, https://www.congress.gov/bill/114th-congress/house-bill/1493 (last visited 12 November 2018).

*Hall, Jon*, ISIS 'destroys' famous lion god statue in captured Syrian city of Palmyra. Daily Mail, 28 May 2015, http://www.dailymail.co.uk/news/article-3101031/ISIS-destroys-famous-lion-god-statue-captured-Syrian-city-just-days-promising-locals-not-obliterate-Palmyra-s-ancient-monuments.html (last visited 12 November 2018).

*Hardy, Samuel*, Was most of the looting at the most extensively looted site in Syria conducted under the Islamic State or the Free Syrian Army? Conflict Antiquities, 12 March 2015, https://conflictantiquities.wordpress.com/2015/03/12/syria-islamic-state-free-syrian-army-paramilitary-funding-dura-europos/ (last visited 12 November 2018).

*Harmanşah, Omur*, Heritage, and the Spectacles of Destruction in the Global Media. 78 Near Eastern Archaeology 170–177 (2015).

*Hassan, Khalid*, How Egypt's antiquities minister plans to lure back tourists. Al Monitor 31 August 2016, http://www.al-monitor.com/pulse/originals/2016/08/egypt-antiquities-minister-tourism-decline-plan-pyramids.html (last visited 12 November 2018).

*Hersher, Rebecca*, New York Gallery Owner Arrested, Accused of Trafficking Stolen Antiquities. NPR, 22 December 2016, http://www.npr.org/sections/thetwo-way/2016/12/22/506615096/gallery-owner-arrested-for-trafficking-stolen-antiquities-worth-millions-of-doll (last visited 12 November 2018).

*Hoving, Thomas*, Making the Mummies Dance: Inside the Metropolitan Museum of Art. New York 1993.

*Jeffries, Stuart*, Isis's destruction of Palmyra. The Guardian, 2 September 2015, https://www.theguardian.com/world/2015/sep/02/isis-destruction-of-palmyra-syria-heart-been-ripped-out-of-the-city (last visited 12 November 2018).

*Kane, Susan*, The Politics of Archaeology and Identity in a Global Context. In: Susan Kane (ed.), The Politics of Archaeology and Identity in a Global Context. Boston 2003, pp. 1–10.

*Keller, Andrew*, Documenting ISIL's Antiquities Trafficking: The Looting and Destruction of Iraqi and Syrian Cultural Heritage: What We Know and What Can Be Done. U.S. Department of State, 2015, https://www.state.gov/e/eb/rls/rm/2015/247610.htm (last visited 12 November 2018).

– Conflict Antiquities. Bureau of Educational and Cultural Affairs, 18 July 2016, https://eca.state.gov/video/conflict-antiquities-panel-1-video/transcript (last visited 12 November 2018).

*Klamer, Arjo*, The Values of Archaeological and Heritage Sites. 13 Public Archaeology 59–70 (2014).

*Lewis, Allen*, Libya's ancient sites not exposed to same risk as in Syria, Iraq: experts. Reuters, 11 May 2016, http://www.reuters.com/article/us-libya-security-culture-idUSKCN0Y22G3 (last visited 12 November 2018).

*Mackenzie, Simon R.M.*, Identifying and Preventing Opportunities for Organized Crime in the International Antiquities Market. In: Stefano Manacorda (ed.), Organised Crime in Art and Antiquities. Milan 2009, pp. 41–62.

*Marei, Sarah*, Tales from the Egyptian revolution. The Art Newspaper, 24 March 2011, http://www.theartnewspaper.com/articles/Tales+from+the+Egyptian+revolution/23394 (last visited 12 November 2018).

*Mashberg, Tom/Bearak, Max*, The Ultimate Temple Raider? Inside an Antiquities-Smuggling Operation. New York Times, 23 July 2015, https://www.nytimes.com/2015/07/26/arts/design/the-ultimate-temple-raider-inside-an-antiquities-smuggling-operation.html (last visited 12 November 2018).

*McGivern, Hannah*, Palmyra antiquities seized at Geneva Free Port. The Art Newspaper, 5 December 2016, http://theartnewspaper.com/news/news/palmyra-antiquities-seized-at-geneva-free-port-/ (last visited 12 November 2018).

*McNall, Bruce/D'Antonio Michael*, Fun While It Lasted: My Rise and Fall in the Land of Fame and Fortune. New York 2003.

*Merryman, John Henry*, Two Ways of Thinking About Cultural Property. 80 American Journal of International Law 831–853 (1986).

*Merryman, John Henry/Elsen, Albert Edward/Urice, Stephen K.*, Law, Ethics, and the Visual Arts. Frederick 2007.

*Milmo, Cahal*, Treasures 'hidden' in free ports at risk of being used to fund ISIS. iNews, 13 November 2016, https://inews.co.uk/essentials/news/treasures-worth-billions-hidden-free-ports-fund-isis/ (last visited 12 November 2018).

*Naharnet,* Report: IS Smuggling Syrian Artifacts Through Lebanon. Naharnet, 23 December 2015, http://www.naharnet.com/stories/en/197773-report-is-smuggling-syrian-artifacts-through-lebanon (last visited 12 November 2018).

*Parkinson, Joe/Albayrak, Ayla/Mavin, Duncan*, Syrian 'Monuments Men' Race to Protect Antiquities as Looting Bankrolls Terror. Wall Street Journal, 10 February 2015, https://www.wsj.com/articles/syrian-monuments-men-race-to-protect-antiquities-as-looting-bankrolls-terror-1423615241 (last visited 12 November 2018).

*Paul, Katie A.,* How Daesh Turns Illicit Digs into Dollars. Antiquities Coalition, https://theantiquitiescoalition.org/blog-posts/how-daesh-turns-illicit-digs-into-dollars/ (last visited 12 November 2018).

*Peters, Gretchen*, Crime and Insurgency in the Tribal Areas of Afghanistan and Pakistan. New York 2010.

– Seeds of Terror: How Drugs, Thugs, and Crime Are Reshaping the Afghan War. New York 2010.

*Petrovic, Jadranka*, The Old Bridge of Mostar and Increasing Respect for Cultural Property in Armed Conflict. Leiden 2013.

*Roberts, Hannah*, Hundreds of looted antiquities including mosaics from Pompeii and ancient sarcophagi are uncovered in Switzerland. Daily Mail, 5 February 2016, http://www.dailymail.co.uk/news/article-3427051/Hundreds-looted-antiquities-including-mosaics-Pompeii-ancient-sarcophagi-uncovered-Switzerland.html (last visited 12 November 2018).

*Sedra, Mark*, Introduction. In: Mark Sedra (ed.), Confronting Afghanistan's Security Dilemma: Reforming the Security Sector. Bonn 2003, pp. 8–16.

*Simons, Marlise*, Prosecutors Lay out Case Against Suspect in Destruction of Mali Shrines. New York Times, 1 March 2016, https://www.nytimes.com/2016/03/02/world/europe/prosecutors-lay-out-case-against-suspect-in-destruction-of-mali-shrines.html (last visited 12 November 2018).

*Shaheen, Kareem*, ISIS Video Confirms Destruction at UNESCO World Heritage Site in Hatra. Guardian, 5 April 2015, https://www.theguardian.com/world/2015/apr/05/isis-video-confirms-destruction-at-unesco-world-heritage-site-on-hatra (last visited 12 November 2018).

*Shaheen, Kareem/Black, Ian*, Beheaded Syrian Scholar Refused to Lead ISIS to Hidden Palmyra Antiquities. Guardian, 19 August 2015, https://www.theguardian.com/world/2015/aug/18/isis-beheads-archaeologist-syria (last visited 12 November 2018).

*Slayman, Andrew*, The Trial in Rome. Archaeology, 6 February 2006, http://archive.archaeology.org/online/features/italytrial/ (last visited 12 November 2018).

*St. Hilaire, Rick*, $2 Billion Missing in U.S.-U.K Art and Antiquities Trade. Trade Based Money Laundering or Some Other Explanation? Cultural Heritage Lawyer, 23 April 2014, http://culturalheritagelawyer.blogspot.co.uk/2014/04/2-billion-missing-in-us-uk-art-and.html (last visited 12 November 2018).

*Stanish, Charles*, Forging Ahead: Or, How I Learned to Stop Worrying and Love eBay. Archaeology May 2009, http://archive.archaeology.org/0905/etc/insider.html (last visited 12 November 2018).

*Sutton, Benjamin*, Looters Kill Two Guards at Ancient Egyptian Necropolis. Hyperallergic, 22 February 2016, http://hyperallergic.com/277551/looters-kill-two-guards-at-ancient-egyptian-necropolis/ (last visited 12 November 2018).

*Taylor, Adam,* The Islamic State isn't the only group looting Syrian archaeological sites. The Washington Post, 21 October 2015, https://www.washingtonpost.com/news/worldviews/wp/2015/10/21/the-islamic-state-isnt-the-only-group-looting-syrian-archaeolo gical-sites/?utm_term=.8b43e575ee30 (last visited 12 November 2018).

TNN, Al-Azhar releases fatwa forbidding the destruction of artefacts. Al Azhar Observer 6 March 2015, http://www.azhar.eg/observer-en/details/ArtMID/1153/ArticleID/2059/Al-Azhar-releases-fatwa-forbidding-the-destruction-of-artefacts (last visited 12 November 2018).

UNESCO, Institute for Statistics, International Flows of Selected Cultural Goods and Services, 1994–2003: Defining and Capturing the Flows of Global Cultural Trade. Montreal 2005.

UNESCO, UNESCO deplores 'cultural cleansing' of Iraq as armed extremists ransack Mosul libraries. UNESCO News Centre, 3 February 2015, http://www.un.org/apps/news/story.asp?NewsID=49982#.WJpNfxIrKRs (last visited 12 November 2018).

UNESCO, Satellite-Based Damage Assessment of Cultural Heritage Sites. UNESCO, June 2016, http://en.unesco.org/system/files/full-chs-report_28062016_final.pdf (last visited 12 November 2018).

U.S. Attorney's Office, United States Files Complaint Seeking Forfeiture of Antiquities Associated with the Islamic State of Iraq and the Levant (ISIL). Department of Justice, 15 December 2016, https://www.justice.gov/usao-dc/pr/united-states-files-complaint-seeking-forfeiture-antiquities-associated-islamic-state (last visited 12 November 2018).

U.S. Department of State, Secretary Kerry Signs Cultural Property Protection Agreement With Egypt, US Department of State, 29 November 2016, https://2009–2017.state.gov/r/pa/prs/ps/2016/11/264632.htm (last visited 12 November 2018).

UNODC, UNODC mandates on trafficking in cultural property. http://www.unodc.org/unodc/en/organized-crime/trafficking-in-cultural-property-mandate.html (last visited 12 November 2018).

*Untalan, Frenalyn*, Iraqi authorities discovered Assyrian artefacts in IS home. International Business Times, 27 January 2017, http://www.ibtimes.com.au/iraqi-authorities-discovered-assyrian-artefacts-home-1541484 (last visited 12 November 2018).

*van Rijn, Michel*, Hot Art, Cold Cash. London 1993.

*Watson, Peter*, Sotheby's: The Inside Story. New York 1997.

*Watson, Peter/Todeschini, Cecilia*, The Medici Conspiracy: The Illicit Journey of Looted Antiquities from Italy's Tomb Raiders to the World's Greatest Museums. New York 2007.

*Williams, Paul/Paterson, C. Danae*, Tear It All Down: The Significance of the al-Mahdi Case and the War Crime of Destruction of Cultural Heritage. Huffington Post, 26 September 2016, http://www.huffingtonpost.com/entry/tear-it-all-down-the-significance-of-the-al-mahdi_us_57e93786e4b09f67131e4b52 (last visited 12 November 2018).

*Williams, Phil*, Networks, Markets, and Hierarchies. In: Phil Williams/Dimitri Vlassis (eds.), Combating Transnational Crime: Concepts, Activities, and Responses. London 2001, pp. 57–87.

– Transnational Criminal Networks. In: John Arquilla/David Ronfeldt (eds.), Networks and Netwars: The Future of Terror, Crime, and Militancy. Santa Monica 2001, pp. 61–97.

*Williams, Phil/Godson, Roy*, Anticipating Organized and Transnational Crime. 37 Crime, Law & Social Change 311–355 (2002).

# Part 2
# National Legal Answers to Terrorism and Recruitment

# Surveying German Security Jurisprudence

*Russell A. Miller**

In the last decade the German Federal Constitutional Court has issued a number of major judgments that have decisively shaped German security policy. This jurisprudence consists in constitutional commitments as disparate as the enforcement of the absolute protection owed to the "core-area of privacy," on the one hand, and the pragmatic balancing of security and limitable liberty interests through the application of the proportionality principle, on the other hand. In both modes the Court demands extremely detailed corrections to the relevant enabling statutes. In the former case as a prophylactic to ensure respect for an absolute right and in the latter case as a means of ensuring the fullest possible – but proportionate – enjoyment of competing limitable constitutional rights.

## I. Introduction

The German Federal Constitutional Court *(Bundesverfassungsgericht)* has been deeply and decisively involved in shaping Germany's post-9/11 security and counter-terrorism policy. This is not surprising. The Court is a colossus in the German polity. Still, it would have been reasonable for the uninitiated to wonder if security policy is an exception to the Court's ubiquity. After all, as Germans have latterly learned, these literally are questions of life and death that touch the core of the logic of the state.[1] If any issue should be reserved for the democratic will, then it might be the question of national security. At least that's the way American law sees it. In a number of ways American jurisprudence keeps security matters in the hands of the more representative branches. American courts strictly enforce justiciability requirements to avoid hearing the cases.[2] And national security exceptions disable

* J.B. Stombock, Professor of Law, Washington & Lee University School of Law.

1 See, e.g., *Liam Stack*, Deadly Berlin Christmas Market Episode Is Latest in Europe, NY Times (Dec. 19, 2016), available at https://www.nytimes.com/2016/12/19/world/europe/europe-terror-attacks-2016.html.

2 See, e.g., *Clapper v. Amnesty International*, 133 S.Ct.1138 (2013).

constitutional claims in this area even if a case is found to be justiciable.[3] But the German Federal Constitutional Court cannot be bothered with "passive virtues," not even in an area so fraught as security policy.[4] In fact, in a way that would be unimaginable in the American context, it is possible to map Germany's recent security policy by reference to nothing but the string of major decisions issued by the Constitutional Court in the last decade.

That is the aim of this article. Beginning with the groundbreaking *Acoustical Surveillance Case* from 2004 and ending with the seminal *BKA-Act Case* from 2016, I summarize the Court's rulings in eight recent, major security cases. I hope this will make the German Court's jurisprudence in this area accessible to scholars and policymakers interested in comparative reflection on the well-worn struggle to balance security and liberty in constitutional democracies. My survey highlights two fundamental features in the distinctly German resolution of that tension. Naturally, no legal institution characterizes this (or any) area of the law more than the Court's inexhaustible and highly-formalized application of the proportionality principle.[5] If German security policy is a judicial matter, then German security policy primarily should be understood as a matter of proportionality and balancing. But these cases also highlight a more absolutist feature of German constitutional law, as the Court has sought to develop a framework of rules that will ensure the inviolability of the "core-area of privacy," which is a liberty interest derived from the intersection of various privacy rights and the categorical protection given to human dignity.

## A. The German Constitutional Court's recent security jurisprudence

### 1. Fundamentals of German security jurisprudence

The following survey of the Constitutional Court's recent security cases, largely arising out of challenges to new counter-terrorism policies, reveals the fundamental contours of the Court's jurisprudence in this area. This involves two general features: proportionality review, on the one hand, and the enforcement of the absolute protection owed to the "core-area of privacy," on the other hand.

---

[3] See, e.g., *Atkinson*, 66 Vanderbilt Law Review 1343 (2013).

[4] See, e.g., *Bickel*, 75 Harvard Law Review 40 (1961-1962).

[5] See, e.g., *Schlink*, 22 Duke Journal of Comparative and International Law 291 (2012); *Jackson*, 124 Yale Law Journal 2680 (2014-2015); *Barak*, Proportionality, passim.

## 2. Proportionality review

One common feature of the Court's security jurisprudence involves the application of the proportionality principle in several distinct and formalized steps.[6] The result of this analysis, almost unfailingly, is that the challenged policy is allowed to go forward following the implementation of a number of detailed, Court-imposed refinements. In the first step the Court acknowledges the state's strong interest in providing security. In fact, the Court views this as the state's constitutional duty, a duty that derives from basic rights *(Grundrechte)* – such as the right to life – that are enjoyed by individuals.[7] In the second step the Court identifies the individual liberty interests implicated by the challenged policy. In the security context these typically include privacy rights: the inviolable right to human dignity;[8] the right to privacy as secured by the right to freely develop one's personality;[9] the privacy of correspondence, posts, and telecommunications;[10] and the inviolability of the home.[11] The Court usually finds that the scope of these rights extends to the state's challenged conduct. But it also concludes that the state's conduct constitutes a severe infringement of the implicated basic rights. In the third step the Court determines that the infringement is justified, either by a simple act of parliament or by an act of parliament helping to actualize a countervailing constitutional interest. In the fourth step, sometimes referred to as "proportionality in the narrower sense" *(Verhältnismäßigkeit im engeren Sinne)*,[12] the Court assesses whether the challenged policy maintains the necessary constitutional balance between conflicting interests. At this stage the Court invariably finds the balance improperly tilting toward security and orders nuanced changes to the policy to ensure fuller respect for the infringed individual liberties. The refinements include a number of stock limitations: adequately weighty security interests as a justification for counter-terrorism or law enforcement measures; a high degree of certainty or specificity regarding a threat and a suspect's connection to it as a justification for counter-terrorism or law enforcement measures; unambiguous statutory terms outlining the scope of and limits on counter-terrorism or law enforcement measures (including the use and storage of the resulting information gathered by the state); a range of general procedural protections to limit counter-terrorism or law enforcement measures and to protect individual liberty; and parliamentary reporting and oversight obligations. Derived from the non-textual constitutional commitment to proportionality, these

---

6 See, e.g., *Hailbronner*, Traditions and Transformations, pp. 117–121; *Stone Sweet/Mathews*, 47 Columbia Journal of Transnational Law 72 (2008).

7 Article 2(2) GG.

8 Article 1(1) GG.

9 Article 2(1) GG.

10 Article 10(1) GG.

11 Article 13(1) GG.

12 See, e.g., *Alexy*, in: Augsberg/Unger (eds.), Basis Texte, pp. 267–296.

limits must do the work of the Basic Law's explicit liberty protections, many of which are limitable.

### 3. Absolute protection for the "core-area of privacy"

Another common feature of the Court's security and privacy jurisprudence involves the Court's efforts to give absolute protection to what is known as the "core-area for the private arrangement of one's life" *(Kernbereich privater Lebensgestaltung)*.[13] Considering the German Court's well-known, widely-respected, and intensively-studied balancing jurisprudence, its practice regarding this absolute constitutional protection is less well understood outside Germany.

The Constitutional Court's privacy jurisprudence (under Articles 2(1) and 1(1) of the Basic Law) has involved a varying standard of review depending on the intensity of the intrusion and the intimacy of the exposed conduct.[14] To help systematize its assessment of the latter of these two factors, the Court developed the so-called "spheres of privacy theory" *(Sphärentheorie)*, pursuant to which the Court has assigned absolute and inviolable protection to a "core-area for the private arrangement of one's life." This sphere is owed heightened protection because of its intersection with human dignity.[15] The Constitutional Court explained in the *Elfes Case* that the Basic Law *(Grundgesetz)* recognizes "a last inviolable sphere of human freedom that is securely removed from the effects of all state power" and it concluded that "a law that intrudes on that sphere never could be compatible with the constitutional order and must, therefore, be declared void."[16] In the first of the cases to be examined in this survey the Court explained that the "core-area of privacy" consists in the protected opportunity "to express inner processes of the most personal nature such as feelings and reflections, as well as views and experiences."[17] Examples of the "core-area of privacy" include the inner thoughts one records in a diary[18] or expressions of sexuality.[19]

The absolute protection owed to the "core-area of privacy" led the Court to give the concept a narrow scope that excludes many intimate issues, such as a person's

---

13 See *Poscher*, JuristenZeitung 2009, 269, 269–270.

14 *Di Fabio*, in: Maunz/Dürig, Grundgesetz, Art. 2 Rn. 1.

15 *Di Fabio*, in: Maunz/Dürig, Grundgesetz, Art. 2 Rn. 1. The "Spheres of Privacy Theory" has private law origins. See *Geis*, JuristenZeitung 1991, 112, 112. But some recognize, in the work of *Otto von Gierke*, an early connection with public law as well. See *Baldus*, JuristenZeitung 2008, 218, 218. See also *Kutscha*, Neue Juristische Wochenschrift 2005, 20.

16 BVerfGE 6, 32, 41 – Elfes – (author's translation).

17 BVerfGE 109, 279, 313 – Acoustical Surveillance Case –.

18 See BVerfGE 80, 367 – Diary Case –.

19 See BVerfGE 109, 279, 313-314 – Acoustical Surveillance Case –.

health conditions, marital relations, or business discussions.[20] These interests belong to a second sphere of privacy known as the "intimate sphere," into which a person must be able to retreat in a way that is largely free of state interference.[21] The "intimate sphere of privacy" *(Intimsphäre)* is closely related to the "core-area of privacy" and is given heightened protection, chiefly through the stringent application of the proportionality principle. Still, the "intimate sphere of privacy" is not an absolute liberty interest. The Court justified this distinction by reasoning that, "as socially-oriented and socially-bound citizens, all must accept that some state actions (particularly those overwhelmingly serving the public interest) have to be tolerated within the parameters allowed by a strict application of the proportionality principle so long as they do not interfere with the inviolable realm needed for the private arrangement of one's life."[22] Two other, less protected spheres of privacy have been identified, including the "private or secret sphere" and the "public sphere."[23]

*Table 1:* German spheres of privacy

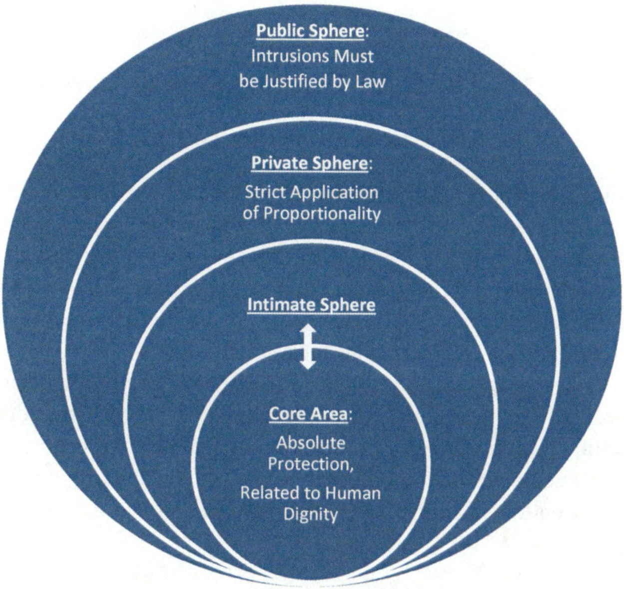


[20] *Di Fabio*, in: Maunz/Dürig, Grundgesetz, Art. 2 Rn. 1.

[21] *Di Fabio*, in: Maunz/Dürig, Grundgesetz, Art. 2 Rn. 1.

[22] BVerfGE 27, 344, 351 – Divorce Records Case – (author's translation).

[23] BVerfGE 27, 344, 351 – Divorce Records Case – (author's translation). See *Poscher*, JuristenZeitung 2009, 271.

My survey of the Court's recent security cases reveals that the Court increasingly is willing to find that the state's counter-terrorism or law enforcement measures implicate the "core-area of privacy." This is the most recent development in the Court's pioneering concern for the highly intrusive potential of information technology.[24] Out of respect for those concerns the Court has used its recent security cases to insist on a number of finely-calibrated legislative refinements. It is tempting to see these in the same light as the detailed legislative corrections the Court demands to render counter-terrorism or law enforcement measures proportionate. But that is not their role in relation to the "core-area of privacy." Instead, the Court insists on these provisions to preemptively ensure the inviolable protection of the "core-area of privacy." These refinements often include: rules explicitly prohibiting intrusions upon the "core-area of privacy"; rules requiring the use of automated investigative measures if there is a risk that there may be an intrusion upon the "core-area of privacy"; rules clearly requiring state agents to immediately cease surveillance or investigations that, despite all precautions, nevertheless intrude upon the "core-area of privacy"; and rules requiring the immediate deletion of any information obtained through an intrusion upon the "core-area of privacy."

## II. The Court's recent security cases

### A. Acoustical Surveillance Case (2004)

The Court's recent privacy and security cases involve some policy changes that predated the 11 September 2001 terrorist attacks in the United States. The first of these cases, although it was decided by the Court several years after the attacks, involved challenges to a 1998 amendment of the Basic Law.[25] The amendments qualified the basic right to the inviolability of the home to permit acoustical surveillance of residences if "particular facts justify the suspicion that any person has committed an especially serious crime" or in order to "avert acute dangers to public safety, especially dangers to life or to the public."[26] The constitutional amendment served as the basis for changes to the Code of Criminal Procedure that authorized acoustical surveillance of the home as a way of developing evidence to support criminal prosecutions.[27] In the *Acoustical Surveillance Case*, the Court's First Sen-

---

24 BVerfGE 65, 1 – Census Act Case –.

25 Gesetz zur Änderung des Grundgesetzes (Artikel 13) [Act to Amend the Constitution (Article 13)], 26 March 1998, BGBl. I at 610. See Art. 13 GG.

26 § 1(1) Gesetz zur Änderung des Grundgesetzes (Artikel 13) [Act to Amend the Constitution (Article 13)], 26 March 1998, BGBl. I at 610 (author's translation).

27 See § 2 Gesetz zur Verbesserung der Bekämpfung der Organisierten Kriminalität [Act to Improve the Fight against Organized Crime], 4 May 1998, BGBl. I at 845. See also

ate upheld the challenged constitutional amendment but found many of the new implementing provisions in the Code of Criminal Procedure to be unconstitutional.[28]

Beginning with this case it is possible to see the broad contours of the Court's approach to this area of the law. Above all, this involves a proportionality balancing analysis that, on the one hand, considers the significance of the relevant basic right and, on the other hand, calls for a range of substantive and procedural parameters that minimize the impact of any intrusion upon the right. More sensationally, however, in the *Acoustical Surveillance Case* the Court insisted on the immense importance of the right to privacy in one's home and concluded that retreat to this space is part of the Basic Law's absolute and inviolable protection of the "core-area of privacy."[29]

The Court emphasized the link between the "core-area of privacy" and human dignity, which is the constitution's highest value.[30] To preserve these high-ranking liberty interests, the Court insisted that the scope of surveillance of the home be proportionate, and it insisted on a number of limitations that were not adequately reflected in the challenged amendments to the Code of Criminal Procedure. First, the home surveillance measures should be deployed only in relation to serious crimes.[31] Second, the home surveillance measures should be limited to efforts to record conversations that law enforcement knows, in advance, to be directly linked to criminality.[32] The Court explained that these are the only kinds of conversations that are not owed absolute protection within the home.[33] Furthermore, extreme care must be taken to ensure that conversations with innocent intimates are not swept up by the surveillance, largely because the Court establishes a presumption of the confidentiality owed to communications with family members and close acquaintances in the home.[34] These limitations, the Court demanded, also must preserve the absolute inviolability of the "core-area of privacy" and should include explicit legislative provisions that require the following protections: the immediate termination of any surveillance that crosses this sacrosanct privacy threshold; if necessary, a resort to automatic surveillance systems that can filter out information that is owed abso-

§ 100c Strafprozessordnung [StPO] [Federal Code of Criminal Procedure], 7 April 1987, BGBl. I at 1074, 1319), last amended by Gesetz, 4 May 1998, BGBl. I at 845.

28 See BVerfGE 109, 279 – Acoustical Surveillance Case –.

29 See BVerfGE 109, 279, 313-324 – Acoustical Surveillance Case –.

30 BVerfGE 109, 279, 311-313 – Acoustical Surveillance Case –. The Court's conclusion in the *Acoustical Surveillance Case* that the "core-area of privacy" has a fundamental nexus with human dignity led several commentators to conclude that the case was one of the Court's most significant decisions. See *Baldus*, JuristenZeitung 2008, 218, 219 (citing *Wesel*, Gang nach Karlsruhe, p. 346).

31 BVerfGE 109, 279, 315–316 – Acoustical Surveillance Case –.

32 BVerfGE 109, 279, 320 – Acoustical Surveillance Case –.

33 BVerfGE 109, 279, 320 – Acoustical Surveillance Case –.

34 BVerfGE 109, 279, 321–322 – Acoustical Surveillance Case –.

lute protection; the immediate deletion of any information improperly acquired from the "core-area of privacy"; and the prohibition on the use of any measures of acoustical surveillance of the home that exceed the narrow, permissible exception to this sphere's inviolability.[35] Finally, the Court concluded that the amended Code of Criminal Procedure provisions did not provide for the necessary general procedural protections, including the necessity of a detailed judicial order authorizing the surveillance measures,[36] requiring the law enforcement authorities to inform (at a reasonable time) the targets that they had been the objects of surveillance measures,[37] and imposing on law enforcement authorities the twin responsibilities of retaining collected information in a way that would permit *ex post* judicial review of the measures and timely deleting the information.[38]

### 2. GPS Case (2005)

A year later, in the *GPS Case*, the Court had the occasion to grapple with other doctrinal elements that have become central to its security jurisprudence.[39] The case involved a convicted criminal's constitutional complaint challenging the prosecution's reliance on evidence acquired from the use of a GPS tracking device. The device had been secretly attached to the complainant's car, allowing the police to comprehensively monitor his movements for nearly three months.[40] The Second Senate rejected the complaint but used the occasion to identify general constitutional limits on law enforcement's use of rapidly evolving and developing technologies for investigative purposes.[41] Again, the aim of these limitations is to ensure that the use of these technologies remains proportional. First, referring to the "specificity requirement," the Court insisted that empowering legislation must clearly and concretely identify the technology that can be used as part of intrusive investigative measures.[42] Still, the Court found that the provision of the Code of Criminal Procedure implicated by the GPS Case was "adequately specific." The Court explained that legislation satisfying that standard does not have to anticipate and name every possible newly emerging technology. The necessary specificity, the Court reasoned, can be secured through an interpretation of the relevant statutory

35 BVerfGE 109, 279, 327 – Acoustical Surveillance Case –.
36 BVerfGE 109, 279, 357–361 – Acoustical Surveillance Case –.
37 BVerfGE 109, 279, 375–380 – Acoustical Surveillance Case –.
38 BVerfGE 109, 279, 380–381 – Acoustical Surveillance Case –.
39 BVerfGE 112, 304 – GPS Case –.
40 BVerfGE 112, 304, 308–314 – GPS Case –.
41 BVerfGE 112, 304, 315–321 – GPS Case –.
42 BVerfGE 112, 304, 316–317 – GPS Case –.

provision (permitting "observation by special means")[43] that brings it into conformity with the constitution.[44] Second, the Court cautioned against the risk to the "core-area privacy" posed by the state's use of intensely intrusive technology, even as a supplement to the physical observation of suspects (such as trailing a suspect or maintaining a stake-out).[45] To limit the worrisome effects of these new technologies, the Court insisted that a judge must authorize long-term observation measures (lasting more than one month).[46] The Court's concern was a nod to emerging "mosaic" or "additive" theories of privacy, and it anticipated the constitutional problems associated with mass-surveillance and data-collecting measures that would emerge as a major theme in later security cases.[47] In this respect the Court unequivocally excluded total surveillance measures that would allow law enforcement authorities to develop complete personality profiles.[48]

### 3. Preventive Telecommunications Surveillance Case (2005)

Legislative specificity and proportionality formed the analytical framework for the Court's decision in another security case decided in 2005. The year's second such case is also relevant to a general understanding of the Court's recent privacy and security jurisprudence because it involved a challenge to a state law (Lower Saxony's Law for Public Security and Order *[Gesetz über die öffentliche Sicherheit und Ordnung]*) as opposed to federal policy.[49] This is an important reminder that in Germany law enforcement authority (and the Court's assessment of law enforcement excesses) largely is a concern of federal states *(Länder)*. The case also is distinguished from the previous two decisions by the fact that it involved security reform enacted after the 11 September 2001 terrorist attacks in the United States. For this reason the *Preventive Telecommunications Surveillance Case* also gives us the chance to judge the Constitutional Court's response to the dramatic geopolitical circumstances of the so-called "war on terror" and the law-and-order policies being implemented by the federal states in response to the changed nature of threats to

---

43 BVerfGE 112, 304, 317 – GPS Case –. See § 100c (1)[1] Strafprozessordnung [StPO] [Federal Code of Criminal Procedure], 7 April 1987, BGBl. I at 1074, 1319), last amended by Gesetz, 4 May 1998, BGBl. I at 845.

44 BVerfGE 112, 304, 316–317 – GPS Case –.

45 BVerfGE 112, 304, 318 – GPS Case –.

46 BVerfGE 112, 304, 318–319 – GPS Case –.

47 BVerfGE 112, 304, 319–320 – GPS Case –. See, e.g., *Kerr*, 111 Michigan Law Review 311 (2012); *United States v. Jones*, 132 S.Ct. 945, 954–957 (2012) (Sotomayor, J., concurring).

48 BVerfGE 112, 304, 319 – GPS Case –.

49 See, e.g., Niedersächsisches Gesetz über die öffentliche Sicherheit und Ordnung [Nds. SOG; Lower Saxony Act Concerning Public Safety and Order], 19 Jan. 2005, Nds. GVBl. at 9.

Germany's security.[50] The First Senate concluded that the challenged provisions of the Lower Saxony law, which authorized telecommunications surveillance for the prevention and prosecution of criminal acts, were unconstitutional and void.[51] The law was not adequately specific, the Court explained, because it authorized police to conduct telecommunications surveillance on the basis of nothing more than "facts that justify the assumption that someone will commit a crime of considerable gravity in the future."[52] The Court was troubled by the fact that the challenged provisions neither called for concrete preliminary actions nor limited the surveillance measures to circumstances involving specific factual indications.[53] Not even the provisions' reference to "crimes of considerable gravity" was specific enough to redeem the law.[54] At the same time the Court found that the provisions were disproportionate. The surveillance authorized by the law, the Court reasoned, amounted to a weighty intrusion on telecommunications privacy.[55] This could be justified only by the state's interest in protecting an important public interest against a serious threat.[56] The Court concluded that the provisions' ambiguous terms would not limit the state's use of these preventive surveillance measures to such concrete and grave circumstances. Finally, the Court found the Lower Saxony law unconstitutional because it did not provide adequate precautions to avoid intrusions on the inviolable "core-area of privacy."[57]

### 4. Data Mining Case (2006)

The Court was confronted by another post-9/11 state police policy in the *Data Mining Case* from 2006.[58] The basic right involved in the case – the right to informational self-determination *(Recht auf informationelle Selbstbestimmung)* – was not central to the previous cases discussed in this survey.[59] This right, first articulated by the Federal Constitutional Court in 1983 as an implication of the Basic Law's liberty (Article 2) and dignity (Article 1) clauses, secures protection of personally revealing data in an age of increasing technological exposure.[60] Still, the

---

[50] BVerfGE 113, 348 – Preventive Telecommunications Surveillance Case –.

[51] BVerfGE 113, 348, 349 – Preventive Telecommunications Surveillance Case –.

[52] BVerfGE 113, 348, 350–351, 354 – Preventive Telecommunications Surveillance Case –.

[53] BVerfGE 113, 348, 378 – Preventive Telecommunications Surveillance Case –.

[54] BVerfGE 113, 348, 379 – Preventive Telecommunications Surveillance Case –.

[55] BVerfGE 113, 348, 382 – Preventive Telecommunications Surveillance Case –.

[56] BVerfGE 113, 348, 386–387 – Preventive Telecommunications Surveillance Case –.

[57] BVerfGE 113, 348, 390–392 – Preventive Telecommunications Surveillance Case –.

[58] BVerfGE 115, 320 – Data Mining Case –.

[59] Article 2(1) GG.

[60] See BVerfGE 65, 1 – Census Act Case –; BVerfGE 115, 320, 335 – Data Mining Case –.

*Data Mining Case* was decided on the same proportionality analysis that framed its decisions in the previously discussed cases. North Rhine-Westphalia's data mining law (operating in tandem with other states and with the support of the BKA) called for the collection of public records that would be mined in an attempt to uncover "sleeper" terrorist cells similar to those of the 9/11 terrorists in Hamburg.[61] The data was to be scoured for records pointing to young, male, Muslim university students from particular countries.[62] The data mining law survived constitutional scrutiny, but only because the First Senate gave it a strict interpretation. The Court found that the data mining measures constituted a very severe intrusion on the right to informational self-determination.[63] This, the Court explained, could only be justified if the measures were undertaken in response to an adequately concrete threat to legal interests of a very high rank, such as preserving the foundations or survival of the state, or the life, limbs, or freedom of an individual.[64]

### 5. Online Search Case (2008)

The Constitutional Court used its 2008 decision in a set of challenges to North Rhine-Westphalia's Act for the Protection of the Constitution *(Verfassungsschutzgesetz)* to announce a completely new constitutional privacy protection.[65]

Before I summarize that development, however, it may be useful to offer a few words about the concept of constitutional protection *(Verfassungsschutz)*.[66] The Offices for the Protection of the Constitution *(Verfassungsschutzämter)* are domestic intelligence agencies operating in each of the states (*Landesbehörden für Verfassungsschutz* – LfV) and on behalf of the federation (*Bundesamt für Verfassungsschutz* – BfV).[67] They are to be distinguished from the country's chief foreign intelligence-gathering agency, the Federal Intelligence Service (*Bundesnachrichtendienst* – BND). Drawing on the theory of "militant democracy" *(streitbare Demokratie)* conceptualized and formalized by *Karl Löwenstein*,[68] the Offices for

61 BVerfGE 115, 320, 323 – Data Mining Case –.

62 BVerfGE 115, 320, 324-326 – Data Mining Case –.

63 BVerfGE 115, 320, 368 – Data Mining Case –.

64 BVerfGE 115, 320, 368 – Data Mining Case –.

65 See Gesetz zur Änderung des Gesetzes über den Verfassungsschutz in Nordrhein-Westfalen [Act to Amend the Law Concerning Constitutional Protection in North Rhine-Westphalia], 20 Dec. 2006, GV.NW at 620.

66 See generally *Andreas Noll/Mirjam Klaussner*, Germany's Domestic Security Services Explained, Deutsche Welle (4 July 2012), available at http://www.dw.com/en/germanys-domestic-security-services-explained/a-16070984.

67 The Offices for the Protection of the Constitution, and the federation's role in this respect, have a constitutional basis. See Article 73(1)[10]{b} GG.

68 See generally *Loewenstein*, 31 American Political Science Review 417 (1937); *Loewenstein*, 31 American Political Science Review 638 (1937); *Sajó* (ed.), Militant Democ-

the Protection of the Constitution are charged with the collection and analysis of information about domestic threats to the free basic democratic order.[69] This contrasts with the BND's statutory mandate, which calls on the agency to collect and analyze the foreign information needed by Germany's federal authorities.[70] The distinction between the American FBI and CIA would be an inapposite parallel, however, because the Offices for the Protection of the Constitution are strictly intelligence-gathering agencies and do not have the FBI's law enforcement competences.[71] The work of the Federal Office for the Protection of the Constitution is concentrated on four categories of threat: right-wing extremism and terror; defense against espionage, other secret activities, and the protection of economic interests; foreign threats and left-wing extremism; and Islamism and Islamic terrorism.[72] The Federal Office claims that most of the information it collects is drawn from public observation and the careful scrutiny of publicly available sources.[73] Nevertheless, the federal enabling act authorizes the agencies, among other measures, to electronically collect personally revealing information and to deploy both undercover agents and informants.[74] In 2006 the state of North Rhine-Westphalia granted the State Office for the Protection of the Constitution new authority to secretly intrude on suspects' information-technology systems.[75] These "online searches," facilitated by Trojan or malware technology,[76] were the basis of the Constitutional Court's pioneering 2008 decision in the *Online Search Case*.[77]

---

racy, passim. *Miller*, in: Miller (ed.), US National Security, Intelligence and Democracy, p. 229.

69 § 3 Bundesverfassungsschutzgesetz [Act for the Protection of the Constitution], 20 Dec. 1990, BGBl. I at 2954, last amended by Article 4 of Gesetz, 17 Nov. 2015, BGBl. I at 1938.

70 See Bundesnachrichtendienstgesetz [Law on the Federal Intelligence Service], 20 Dec. 1990, BGBl. I at 2954, 2979, last amended by Article 1 of Gesetz, 23 Dec. 2016, BGBl. I at 3346.

71 § 8(3) Bundesverfassungsschutzgesetz [Act for the Protection of the Constitution], 20 Dec. 1990, BGBl. I at 2954, last amended by Article 4 of Gesetz, 17 Nov. 2015, BGBl. I at 1938.

72 Bundesamt für Verfassungsschutz, Die Organisation des Amtes ist kein Geheimnis, available at https://www.verfassungsschutz.de/de/das-bfv/aufgaben/die-organisation-des-amtes-ist-kein-geheimnis.

73 Bundesamt für Verfassungsschutz, Was genau macht der Verfassungsschutz?, available at https://www.verfassungsschutz.de/de/das-bfv/aufgaben/was-genau-macht-der-verfassungsschutz.

74 §§ 8, 8a, 8b, 8c, 8d, 9, 9a, 9b, 10 Bundesverfassungsschutzgesetz [Act for the Protection of the Constitution], 20 Dec. 1990, BGBl. I at 2954, last amended by Article 4 of Gesetz, 17 Nov. 2015, BGBl. I at 1938.

75 § 5 Gesetz zur Änderung des Gesetzes über den Verfassungsschutz in Nordrhein-Westfalen [Act to Amend the Law Concerning Constitutional Protection in North Rhine-Westphalia], 20 Dec. 2006, GV.NW at 620.

76 See generally *Reißmann*, Spähsoftware – Berlin schafft umstrittenen Staatstrojaner an, Der Spiegel (27 Jan. 2012), available at http://www.spiegel.de/netzwelt/netzpolitik/spaehsoftware-berlin-schafft-umstrittenen-staatstrojaner-an-a-811723.html; *Lischka*, Online-

In the *Online Search Case* the Court's First Senate found that the new authority to conduct online searches violated the constitution and it declared the law void.[78] The Court's innovation was to identify a new constitutional right, derived from the Basic Law's dignity and personality protections.[79] The new right guarantees the confidentiality and integrity of information technology systems *(Grundrecht auf Gewährleistung der Vertraulichkeit und Integrität informationstechnischer Systeme).*[80]

To justify the new protection, the Court pointed to two factors. First, the Court acknowledged the central and deepening (and deeply personal) nature of most people's use of technology and warned against the new threats to privacy this development poses.[81] Showing an ever more sophisticated concern for mosaic or additive theories of privacy, the Court stressed that the information catalogued by or saved on these ubiquitous technologies can be used to develop penetrating and revealing personal profiles.[82] Second, the Court wanted to fill a seeming gap in the Basic Law's protective framework that left precisely these privacy concerns unaddressed. Regarding this second factor, the Court raised two points. On the one hand, the Court explained that Article 10 of the Basic Law extends telecommunications privacy to ongoing telecommunications activities, even those taking place via the Internet.[83] But the Court worried that the text of Article 10 might not protect the digital residue of these activities (including content or metadata) once the act of communication is concluded. Yet, the Court acknowledged that these revealing forms of information frequently are stored by information technology systems and they can be retrieved or reconstructed by the online searches authorized under the new North Rhine-Westphalia law.[84] On the other hand, the Court doubted the applicability of Article 13 of the Basic Law (inviolability of the home) to these circumstances because the information technology systems in question often are used outside the home.[85] The Court also noted that the state's intrusion on this sphere

Durchsuchung – BKA suchte Trojaner-Nachhilfe im Ausland, Der Spiegel (14 March 2012), available at http://www.spiegel.de/netzwelt/netzpolitik/bka-staatstrojaner-a-821153.html.

77 BVerfGE 120, 274 – Online Search Case –.

78 BVerfGE 120, 274, 275 – Online Search Case –.

79 BVerfGE 120, 274, 302–303 – Online Search Case –.

80 BVerfGE 120, 274, 302–303 – Online Search Case –.

81 BVerfGE 120, 274, 303 – Online Search Case –.

82 BVerfGE 120, 274, 306 – Online Search Case –.

83 BVerfGE 120, 274, 306-307 – Online Search Case –.

84 § 5 Gesetz zur Änderung des Gesetzes über den Verfassungsschutz in Nordrhein-Westfalen [Act to Amend the Law Concerning Constitutional Protection in North Rhine-Westphalia], 20 Dec. 2006, GV.NW at 620.

85 BVerfGE 120, 274, 309-310 – Online Search Case –.

would likely take place via technological systems operated far from the target's home.[86]

For these reasons the Court articulated a new right that "applies when intrusive technology can capture personally revealing information in such a degree of scope and diversity – either on their own or in their connection with networked information – that they permit a glimpse into fundamental parts of the private arrangement of one's life *(wesentliche Teile der Lebensgestaltung einer Person)* or the development of a revealing portrait."[87]

Having in mind the way in which online searches would deeply intrude upon the newly articulated right, the Court found that North Rhine-Westphalia's law was disproportionate, largely because it lacked the necessary limitations. It did not restrict the use of online searches to cases involving "factual indications of a concrete threat to preeminently important legal interest."[88] The Court explained that such an especially weighty interest could consist in the "life, limbs, or freedom of an individual" or "public goods, which, if threatened, implicate either the foundations or survival of the state or the foundations of human existence."[89] As with any application of proportionality in such cases, however, the Court noted that the necessary degree of certainty regarding the threat recedes as the suspected threat becomes graver or more imminent.[90] North Rhine-Westphalia's law also did not provide the required procedural protections, including judicial authorization.[91] Finally, the Court found that the law did not provide special precautions to ensure that online search measures would not violate the absolute protection owed the "core-area of privacy."[92]

### 6. Data Retention Case (2010)

The 2010 *Data Retention Case* introduced yet another central feature of the Court's recent privacy and security jurisprudence, namely, the direct and indirect role played by European law and institutions in these fields.[93] The constitutional complaints challenged the changes made to German law – especially the Telecommunications Act *(Telekommunikationsgesetz)* and the Code of Criminal Procedure – which sought to implement the European Union's Data Retention Directive

---

86 BVerfGE 120, 274, 309–311 – Online Search Case –.

87 BVerfGE 120, 274, 314 – Online Search Case –.

88 BVerfGE 120, 274, 342–343 – Online Search Case –.

89 BVerfGE 120, 274, 328 – Online Search Case –.

90 BVerfGE 120, 274, 328 – Online Search Case –.

91 BVerfGE 120, 274, 340–342 – Online Search Case –.

92 BVerfGE 120, 274, 343 – Online Search Case –.

93 BVerfGE 125, 260 – Data Retention Case –.

2006/24/EC.[94] The European Directive, partly a response to the terrorist bombings in Madrid and London, "sought to harmonize legal arrangements for retention of data generated or processed by publicly available electronic communications services and public communications networks across Europe. The Directive was intended to ensure that this data was available to help prevent, detect, investigate, and prosecute serious crime, particularly organized crime and terrorism, by obliging E.U. member states to ensure that providers of publically available electronic communications services and networks retained metadata."[95] The indiscriminately collected telecommunications data were to be stored for a minimum of six months and a maximum of two years.[96] The Directive itself deferred to the Member States' domestic data-protection regimes for the supervision of and limits on the use of the stored data. Avoiding direct engagement with the EU legal regime, the Constitutional Court scrutinized the German implementing provisions for their conformity with Article 10(1) of the Basic Law, which provides for "the privacy of correspondence, posts, and telecommunications."[97] The Court concluded that the mandated data retention, although conceivably permissible, was disproportionate as implemented by the challenged norms. The familiar proportionality analysis began with the Court's insistence that the required storage of telecommunications data constitutes a new and serious intrusion on telecommunications privacy because that metadata, especially when combined, allows the state to draw accurate conclusions about the content of telecommunications exchanges and to cobble together particularly revealing personality profiles.[98] The Court also emphasized the passive harm that results from the awareness that all of one's telecommunications metadata are being indiscriminately collected and stored. The Court described this "chilling effect" as the "diffuse, threatening feeling of being watched, which can impair free exercise of fundamental rights in many areas."[99]

To be proportional, the Court explained, the great harm done by data retention must be limited by a range of conditions that were either missing altogether or inadequately developed in the German implementing laws. First, the Court demanded provisions that ensure a high-level of security for the retained data.[100] Second, the Court insisted that the stored data be used only for the protection of paramount le-

---

[94] Directive 2006/24/EC of the European Parliament and of the Council of 15 March 2006 on the Retention of Data Generated or Processed in Connection with the Provision of Publicly Available Electronic Communications Services or of Public Communications Networks and Amending Directive 2002/58/EC, 2006 O.J. (L 105) 54 [hereinafter Data Retention Directive].

[95] *Zedner*, in: Miller (ed.), Privacy and Power, p. 564.

[96] See BVerfGE 125, 260, 277 – Data Retention Case –.

[97] BVerfGE 125, 260, 309–310 – Data Retention Case –.

[98] BVerfGE 125, 260, 319 – Data Retention Case –.

[99] BVerfGE 125, 260, 320 – Data Retention Case –.

[100] BVerfGE 125, 260, 325–327 – Data Retention Case –.

gal interests.[101] In the law enforcement context this would require an exhaustive list of the relevant, serious crimes.[102] In the threat prevention context, use of the stored data would be limited to instances involving the "life, limbs, or freedom of an individual" or "public goods, which, if imperiled, implicate either the foundations or survival of the state or the foundations of human existence."[103] In both cases use of the stored data would have to be limited to specific circumstances involving the existence of concrete factual indications justifying suspicion of criminal activity or the existence of a paramount threat.[104] Third, the Court demanded greater transparency regarding the storage and use of the data in a form that would ease the regime's potential chilling effects.[105]

The Constitutional Court's ruling was just one in a series of decisions from the Member States' courts that either burdened the domestic implementation of the Directive or cast its substance – under EU law – into doubt.[106] Eventually, the European Court of Justice would invalidate the Directive, ruling that the Directive's disregard for European fundamental rights meant that it lacked legal force from the time of its enactment.[107] These events represent a form of inductive signaling from the Member States that eventually has an impact at the European level.[108] But the European authorities, especially including the Court of Justice of the European Union, also have been extremely active in the area of privacy and data-protection (as the 2006 Data Retention Directive suggests). This means that European law, in turn, has come to influence Member States' domestic constitutional privacy and security jurisprudence, including Germany's.

### 7. Counter-terrorism Database Case (2013)

The *Counter-terrorism Database Case* involved constitutional complaints challenging the 2006 legislation that established the joint Counter-terrorism Database (*Antiterrordatei* –ATD).[109] The ATD is a joint, standardized, and centralized, coun-

---

101 BVerfGE 125, 260, 327–328 – Data Retention Case –.

102 BVerfGE 125, 260, 328–329 – Data Retention Case –.

103 BVerfGE 125, 260, 330–331 – Data Retention Case –.

104 BVerfGE 125, 260, 330–331 – Data Retention Case –.

105 BVerfGE 125, 260, 334–340 – Data Retention Case –.

106 See *Fabbrini*, 28 Harvard Human Rights Journal 65, 74 (2015); *Jones*, National Legal Challenges to Data Retention Directive, EU Law Analysis (8 April 2014), available at http://eulawanalysis.blogspot.com/2014/04/national-legal-challenges-to-data.html; *Vainio/Miettinen*, 23 Int'l J.L. & Info. Tech. 290 (2015).

107 See *Zedner*, in: Miller (ed.), Privacy and Power, p. 564.

108 See Joined Cases C-293/12 & C-594/12, *Digital Rights Ir. Ltd. v. Minister for Commc'n*, 2014 E.C.R. 1-238. See also *Fabbrini*, 28 Harvard Human Rights Journal 65, 74 (2015); *Krotoszynski*, 56 Wm. & Mary L. Rev. 1279 (2014-2015).

109 Antiterrordateigesetz [Counter-terrorism Database Act], 22 Dec. 2006, BGBl. I at 3409 (original version). See *Hellmuth,* Counterterrorism, 104-107.

ter-terrorism database that contains a comprehensive catalogue of information about individuals linked (in stronger or weaker ways) to terrorism activities. This information is assigned to different categories with different thresholds for access. On the one hand, the participating agencies would have ready access to *basic information* (name, aliases, date of birth, gender, nationality, residence, physical traits).[110] On the other hand, access to a long list of *extended information* (communications data, banking practices, transport and weapons certifications, contact persons, and religious affiliations) would be harder to justify.[111] All of Germany's federal and state law enforcement and intelligence agencies contribute to the database and, in return, have access to the information under the conditions framed by the law.[112]

In the *Counter-terrorism Database Case* from 2013 the Constitutional Court ruled that the basic structure of the database was compatible with the Basic Law.[113] But the First Senate objected, once again as a result of a proportionality analysis, to a number of the ATD program's details.[114]

First, the Court concluded that the collection of data in the ATD constituted a significant intrusion on the right to informational self-determination, which derives from the Basic Law's protection of personality and human dignity.[115] This was particularly true, the Court explained, because the ATD brings together information originating in the law enforcement and intelligence-gathering contexts, thereby jeopardizing the fundamental duty that these distinct forms of investigative information be kept strictly separate *(informationelles Trennungsprinzip)*.[116] The Court conceded, however, that the gravity of the intrusion is mitigated by the fact that the information brought together in the ATD database was already held by state authorities. The ATD only combined and collected these pre-existing data and largely submitted any transfers of the data across the newly created platform to the same discrete rules that governed such exchanges before the creation of the ATD.[117] Despite the qualified nature of the intrusion, the Court concluded that the ATD regime would be constitutionally permissible only in exceptional cases and only in the service of a paramount public interest.[118]

110 § 3(1)[1]{a} Counter-terrorism Database Act (original version).

111 § 3(1)[1]{b} Counter-terrorism Database Act (original version).

112 §§ 1 and 5 Counter-terrorism Database Act (original version).

113 BVerfGE, 133, 277 – Counter-terrorism Database Case –. See Articles 2(1) and 1(1) GG.

114 BVerfGE, 133, 277–279 – Counter-terrorism Database Case –.

115 BVerfGE, 133, 316–317 – Counter-terrorism Database Case –.

116 BVerfGE, 133, 329–331 – Counter-terrorism Database Case –.

117 BVerfGE, 133, 329–331 – Counter-terrorism Database Case –.

118 BVerfGE, 133, 329 – Counter-terrorism Database Case –.

In the second step of its analysis the Court acknowledged that the state's efforts to combat terrorism satisfy this standard because terrorism aims directly at the foundational pillars of the constitutional order and society as such.[119] On this point, however, the Court offered *obiter dicta*, insisting that the terrorist threat was not the equivalent of a state of war or a state of emergency that might justify derogations from constitutional protections.[120] Instead, the Court urged that the state confront terrorism as a matter of criminal law within the ordinary constitutional framework.[121] Third, the Court found that the ATD law did not adequately ensure the strict separation of information according to the justification for its original collection: law enforcement or threat assessment. The shortcomings again involved the law's substantive and procedural contours. With respect to the former, the Court held that the law was neither specific nor clear enough.[122] The Court also ruled that some of the ATD provisions were over-inclusive (thereby violating another component of constitutional proportionality referred to as the *Übermaßverbot*).[123] The Court objected to the fact that the law anticipated the inclusion in the ATD database of information concerning mere supporters of terrorist groups,[124] or information concerning individuals in close contact with the terrorist scene,[125] or information concerning individuals who are merely in contact with terrorist ringleaders.[126] With regard to the latter, the Court held that the ATD did not impose adequate procedural protections, such as the duty to document and publish its internal interpretations of the law's more ambiguous terms,[127] or limitations on the kind of information produced as a result of inverted or key-term searches of the ATD database (as opposed to searches targeting specific individuals),[128] or the imposition of adequate transparency and control (including a duty to report and oversight from data-protection authorities),[129] or limitations on the transfer and further use of the data.[130]

---

119 BVerfGE, 133, 333–334 – Counter-terrorism Database Case –.

120 BVerfGE, 133, 334 – Counter-terrorism Database Case –.

121 BVerfGE, 133, 334 – Counter-terrorism Database Case –.

122 BVerfGE, 133, 338–339 – Counter-terrorism Database Case –.

123 BVerfGE, 133, 339 – Counter-terrorism Database Case –.

124 BVerfGE, 133, 341–343 – Counter-terrorism Database Case –.

125 BVerfGE, 133, 342–343 – Counter-terrorism Database Case –.

126 BVerfGE, 133, 340–350 – Counter-terrorism Database Case –.

127 BVerfGE, 133, 351 – Counter-terrorism Database Case –.

128 BVerfGE, 133, 354 – Counter-terrorism Database Case –.

129 BVerfGE, 133, 357 – Counter-terrorism Database Case –.

130 BVerfGE, 133, 358–359 – Counter-terrorism Database Case –.

## 8. BKA-Act Case

The Court used the *BKA-Act Case* from 2016 to consolidate and codify its security jurisprudence from the last decade.[131] This was possible because the law challenged before the Court granted sweeping investigative powers to federal police authorities, including many of the counter-terrorism and law enforcement investigative measures the federal states had been developing in the years following the 11 September 2001, terrorist attacks in the United States.[132] Those state-level security policies had been challenged and assessed by the Court in some of the cases discussed earlier in this survey, including the *GPS Case*, the *Preventive Telecommunications Surveillance Case*, the *Data Mining Case*, and the *Online Search Case*. The scope of the *BKA-Act Case* led one commentator to describe the decision as "a compendium of the checks and balances in security law."[133] For this reason the *BKA-Act Case* provides clear examples of both fundamental features of the German constitutional security jurisprudence: proportionality and the absolute protection owed to the "core-area of privacy." The case offers an especially insightful outline of the prophylactic limitations the Court requires as a way of ensuring the absolute protection of the "core-area of privacy." The *BKA-Act Case* also is noteworthy because the Court used its judgment to articulate the constitutional parameters governing Germany's transfer of counter-terrorism and law enforcement information to foreign security partners.

### *a) Background to the BKA-Act*

The BKA-Act of 2008, in one sweeping gesture, granted to the Federal Criminal Police Office (*Bundeskriminalamt* – BKA) many of the investigative and surveillance powers Germany's other law enforcement and intelligence services had been accumulating – sometimes in piecemeal reforms – over decades.[134] The new investigative measures included: special measures to collect information, such as the use of informants; technological surveillance inside/outside the home; data mining;

---

131 BVerfGE 141, 220 – BKA-Act Case –.

132 See, e.g., *Hellmuth*, Counterterrorism, at 78–127.

133 *Geuther*, Ein Meilenstein des Datenschutzes, Deutschlandfunk (20 April 2016), available at http://www.deutschlandfunk.de/urteil-zum-bka-gesetz-ein-meilenstein-des-datenschutzes.720.de.html?dram:article_id=351945 (author's translation).

134 Gesetz zur Abwehr von Gefahren des internationalen Terrorismus durch das Bundeskriminalamt [The Act for the Federal Criminal Police Office's Role in the Defense against the Threat of International Terrorism], 25 Dec. 2008, BGBl. I at 3083. This law was amended and integrated into the pre-existing BKA-Act. Bundeskriminalamtgesetz [Federal Criminal Police Office Act], 7 July 1997, BGBl. I. at 1650, as amended by Gesetz, Art. 7, 26 July 2016, BGBl. I at 1818 (hereinafter "BKA-Act").

Trojan/malware surveillance; telecommunications surveillance; and the collection of telecommunications metadata.[135]

The BKA-Act significantly empowered the Federal Criminal Police Office, particularly in the struggle against terrorism. But the law was by no means an unchecked "*wünsch mir was*" for the BKA. Instead, it sought to frame the BKA's immense new powers within a large number of substantive and procedural limits imposed by the basic rights as they had been interpreted by the Constitutional Court over the years, especially in the cases described earlier in this survey. The result was a terrible mess of a statute that struggled, in long and detailed provisions, to find a functional compromise between the conflicting demands of security and liberty.

### *b) Proportionality in the BKA-Act Case*

Characteristically, the Court found that the vast majority of the BKA-Act's provisions succeeded in striking the proper balance between an increasing need for security and the constitution's liberty protections. Still, the Court ordered the parliament to implement a number of detailed modifications and to reissue the law to ensure the proportionality of the federation's new investigative powers. These corrections were similar to those the Court had been refining in its previous security cases. The law was not specific enough at some points. The law had not always demanded the most reliable form of suspicion as the basis for undertaking surveillance. The law did not limit the exercise of the new investigative measures to crimes or threats of the gravest character. Sometimes the law did not draw the scope of permissible surveillance narrowly enough. Many of the procedures established to assure that the BKA would not abuse its new powers were inadequate, including: rules regarding independent authorization for investigative measures; rules regarding notice to those being investigated; rules regarding the documentation of investigative measures; rules regarding the deletion of investigative protocols as well as the information collected; and rules establishing oversight and reporting measures.

### *c) Protection of the "Core-Area of Privacy" in the BKA-Act Case*

Perhaps a more important achievement of the *BKA-Act Case* involved the Court's conclusion that the BKA-Act too often failed to show the required respect for the sacrosanct "core-area of privacy." In response to this shortcoming, which implicated several of the BKA-Act's provisions, the Court concluded that the law required a number of intricate modifications. One of many examples can be found in the Court's assessment of the "Special Technical Investigative Measures Inside

---

135 §§20(b)–(m) BKA-Act.

or Outside the Home" permitted by § 20h(5) of the BKA-Act. This provision permitted intrusions into the private sanctum of the home, where the federal police would be allowed to conduct audio and video surveillance. The Court found that the deeply intrusive character of these surveillance measures implicated the human dignity elements of the constitutional right to privacy in the home.[136] For this reason the Court insisted on the strictest safeguards in order to protect the "core-area of privacy."[137] The Court ruled that § 20h(5) failed to meet this high standard with respect to the *collection* as well as the *analysis and use* of information collected through surveillance in the home.[138]

With respect to the *collection* of information, the Court found that § 20h(5) should have clearly established a presumption against surveillance involving conversations between especially trusted confidants or intimates *(Personen des höchstpersönlichen Vertrauens)* that often take place in the home.[139] The Court explained that this circle of people includes marital or life partners, siblings and direct relatives – especially when they are living in the same home – some professional service providers (such as criminal defense lawyers or doctors), and very close friends.[140] The privacy of conversations with these people in one's home must be preserved, the Court noted, as a way of satisfying the deeply human need to express one's dreams, sensitivities, feelings, and thoughts.[141] The presumption against surveillance of these conversations, the Court ruled, can be overcome only if concrete evidence suggests that, with respect to a discrete conversation, criminal matters will be discussed.[142] In these exceptional circumstances surveillance should proceed only for short periods of time and only with the use of automatic recording technology.[143]

The Court was mollified, however, by the fact that § 20h(5) required judicial approval for the implementation of these surveillance measures. The judiciary's role also properly extended to decisions concerning the *analysis and use* of automatically recorded surveillance content, a practice the statute required if there was any uncertainty regarding possible exposure of the "core-area of privacy."[144] But the Court found that this arrangement improperly limited the role of independent review. It was not enough, the Court explained, that independent approval is neces-

---

136 BVerfGE 141, 220 Rn. 196 – BKA-Act Case –.

137 BVerfGE 141, 220 Rn. 197 – BKA-Act Case –.

138 BVerfGE 141, 220 Rn. 196 – BKA-Act Case –.

139 BVerfGE 141, 220 Rn. 198 – BKA-Act Case –.

140 BVerfGE 141, 220 Rn. 121 – BKA-Act Case – (citing BVerfGE 109, 279, 321 – Acoustical Surveillance Case –).

141 BVerfGE 141, 220 Rn. 121 – BKA-Act Case –.

142 BVerfGE 141, 220 Rn. 122 – BKA-Act Case –.

143 BVerfGE 141, 220 Rn. 199 – BKA-Act Case –.

144 § 20h(5)[4] BKA-Act.

sary for the initial authorization of surveillance in the home, on the one hand, and with respect to the analysis and use of this surveillance when the information is gathered through automatic means, on the other hand.[145] The supervision of an independent authority also is required for the *analysis and use* of all information drawn from home surveillance that risks intrusions on the "core-area of privacy."[146] It was an infinitely small gap seemingly left open by the legislature's belief that it would be adequate to have judicial involvement in deciding whether to proceed with surveillance in the first instance. Instead, the Court insisted that, in order to give the "core-area of privacy" the absolute protection demanded by the Basic Law, independent review also was necessary concerning information that might slip through at the time of its collection and then become relevant at the time the agency sought to *analyze or use* the information.

### *d) Foreign transfers of information*

The BKA-Act also authorized the Federal Criminal Police Office to transfer to foreign security entities the information it might collect pursuant to its new investigative powers. By the time of the Court's consideration of the challenge to the BKA-Act these had become some of the new law's most sensational and intensely disputed provisions. That is because Edward Snowden's leaks and the resulting NSA-Affair had cast Germany's international security and intelligence cooperation

---

145 BVerfGE 141, 220 Rn. 204 – BKA-Act Case –.

146 BVerfGE 141, 220 Rn. 204 – BKA-Act Case –. It is interesting to note that, throughout this part of the decision, the Court took care to use the phrases "unabhängige Sichtung" (independent examination) and "unabhängige Kontrolle" (independent oversight) despite the fact that § 20h(5)[4] refers explicitly to a "Gericht" (court). It seems possible that the Court could accept a role here for a non-judicial entity, such as the G10 Commission (which controls the Federal Intelligence Service's intelligence-gathering operations) or the Office of the Federal Commissioner for Data Protection and Freedom of Information *(Bundesbeauftragte für den Datenschutz und die Informationsfreiheit)*. The Federal Data Protection Commissioner is charged with monitoring public entities' compliance with the Federal Data Protection Act and "other data protection provisions." See §§ 22–26 Bundesdatenschutzgesetz [Federal Data Protection Act], 14 Jan. 2003, BGBl. I at 66, last amended by Gesetz, 25 Feb. 2015, BGBl. I at 162. In conjunction with changes made to the BKA-Act after the Court's decision, § 24 of the Federal Data Protection Act would be an adequate statutory basis for a role of the Commissioner in supervising the investigative operations of the BKA, id. at § 24(1). The Federal Data Protection Commissioner already plays an oversight role in the security sector, with six staff members in "Department V" monitoring data protection obligations in the police and intelligence services. *Niederer*, The German Federal Data Protection Authority – The BfDI (Conference PowerPoint), The Federal Commissioner for Data Protection and Freedom of Information 4 (2014), available at http://profiling-project.eu/wp-content/uploads/2014/10/The-German-Federal-Data-Protection-Authority.pdf. See generally *Lang*, Juristische Arbeitsblätter 2006, 395, 398; *Simitis*, in: Simitis (ed.), Bundesdatenschutzgesetz Kommentar, § 4f, in 579–638; *Zell*, 15 German Law Journal 461, 461 (2014).

into harsh, critical light.[147] The NSA-Affair is never mentioned in the *BKA-Act Case*. Still, it is difficult not to read the Court's judgment, and especially its assessment of the provisions permitting foreign transfers of information, in the light of the Snowden scandal.[148]

The Court treated the foreign transfer of information as a "new use" and applied the "hypothetical data collection" standard and a number of other parameters to ensure that foreign transfers conform to constitutional safeguards.

The Court explained that "new uses" of information must satisfy the "hypothetical data collection" *(hypothetische Datenerhebung)* standard.[149] This is more demanding than the standard applied to additional uses of information that serve the

---

147 A parliamentary committee of inquiry exposed the breadth and troubling character of the German intelligence services' cooperation with (some might prefer the term "subservience to") America's intelligence agencies, including the NSA. See *Borene*, in: Miller (ed.), Privacy and Power, p. 257; *Zedner*, in: Miller (ed.), Privacy and Power, p. 564; *Wittes, B.*, in: Miller (ed.), Privacy and Power, p. 180; *Kirschbaum*, Merkel Defends German Intelligence Cooperation with NSA, Reuters (4 May 2015), available at http://www.reuters.com/article/us-germany-spying-merkel-idUSKBN0NP13620150504; Spying Together: Germany's Deep Cooperation with the NSA, Spiegel Online (18 June 2014), available at http://www.spiegel.de/international/germany/the-german-bnd-and-american-nsa-cooperate-more-closely-than-thought-a-975445.html.

148 See generally Merkel to Testify Before German Parliament Panel Probing NSA, N.Y. Times (10 Feb. 2017), available at https://www.nytimes.com/aponline/2017/02/10/world/europe/ap-eu-germany-us-eavesdropping.html?_r=0; *Cottrell*, German Spy Agency Systematically Broke the Law: Report, Deutsche Welle (1 Sept. 2016), available at http://www.dw.com/en/german-spy-agency-systematically-broke-the-law-report/a-19521787; America's Willing Helper: Intelligence Scandal Puts Merkel in Tight, Spiegel Online (4 May 2015), available at http://www.spiegel.de/international/germany/bnd-intelligence-scandal-puts-merkel-in-tight-place-a-1031944.html; *Oltermann*, Germany Blocks Edward Snowden from Testifying in Person in NSA Inquiry, The Guardian (1 May 2014), available at https://www.theguardian.com/world/2014/may/01/germany-edward-snowden-nsa-inquiry; *Medick/Meiritz*, NSA Scandal: Parliamentary Spying Inquiry Poses Challenges, Spiegel Online (29 Oct. 2013), available at http://www.spiegel.de/international/world/germany-faces-challenges-in-investigating-nsa-spying-a-930639.html. See also Deutscher Bundestag, 1. Untersuchungsausschuss ("NSA"), https://www.bundestag.de/ausschuesse18/ua/1untersuchungsausschuss (last visited 14 Feb. 2017).

Green Party Parliamentarian Renate Künast made the link between the Court's decision and the NSA-Affair explicit, praising the Court for drawing a sharp contrast with what she believes to be the lawless regime under which the American Intelligence Community operates. "The Constitutional Court has in mind a model other than the NSA," Künast crowed. "It attends to the protection of the core of basic rights and has even demanded independent oversight." *Böhm/Gruber*, Urteil zum BKA-Gesetz, Spiegel Online (20 April 2016), available at http://www.spiegel.de/netzwelt/netzpolitik/bka-gesetz-was-das-urteil-fuer-computer nutzer-bedeutet-a-1088215.html. The German Pirate Party's Representative for Data-Protection called the decision "Karlsruhe's answer to the NSA." *Breyer*, Piraten: Bundesverfassungsgericht Bremst Internationale Datenwäsche durch BKA und BND, Presse-Service der Piratenpartei Deutschland (April 20, 2016), available at https://www.piratenpartei.de/2016/04/20/piraten-bundesverfassungsgericht-bremst-internationale-datenwaesche-durch-bka-und-bnd/.

149 BVerfGE 141, 220 Rn. 287 – BKA-Act Case –.

same objectives that originally justified its collection. The standard of a "hypothetical data collection" will be satisfied, the Court explained, only if the information could have been collected in the first instance by the BKA, using the same intrusive measures, for the wholly new objectives.[150] That is, the new use of the information is to be treated as a new (hypothetical) search in its own right. The point of this standard is clear: subsequent use of information is not to serve as a backdoor around constitutional safeguards thereby permitting the analysis and use of information for purposes that would not justify its collection.

The Court also discussed a number of other constitutional parameters related to the foreign transfer of information. First, the Court found that the Basic Law does not fundamentally preclude foreign security cooperation of this sort, even when the receiving state's legal system does not conform to the high level of rights protection secured by the Basic Law.[151] To the contrary, the Court found that transfers may be part of the Basic Law's command that Germany participate in systems of international cooperation.[152] Second, the Court nevertheless insisted that the legislature ensure, to the degree possible, the enjoyment of constitutional protections on both sides of the transfer. To achieve this, the Court found that the law authorizing foreign, non-E.U. transfers of information would have to have two features. The law must carefully limit transfers due to concerns for privacy.[153] If a transfer is allowed, the law also must limit the ways in which the receiving state may use the information.[154] In both respects – transfer and the receiving state's use of the information – the Court emphasized that the law must be guided by the interest in promoting human rights. Third, and most important, the Court insisted that the BKA's transfer of information to foreign security entities must not contribute to human rights violations.[155] The Court explained that the legislature can navigate the potentially competing demands of international security cooperation and respect for human rights by enacting the following principles in clear and specific terms: (1) limiting the transfer of personally revealing information to circumstances involving adequately weighty objectives that would satisfy the "hypothetical data collection" standard; and (2) requiring assurances that the receiving state's use of transferred information – formally and practically – will respect the rule of law.[156]

150 BVerfGE 141, 220 Rn. 287 – BKA-Act Case –.

151 BVerfGE 141, 220 Rn. 325 – BKA-Act Case –.

152 See, e.g., Articles 1(2), 9(2), 16(2), 23-26, 59(2) GG. See also BVerfGE 141, 220 Rn. 325 – BKA-Act Case – (citing BVerfGE 63, 343, 370 – Legal Help Contract Case –; BVerfGE 111, 307, 318 – Görgülü –; BVerfGE 112, 1, 25-27 – Land Reform III Case –).

153 BVerfGE 141, 220 Rn. 325 – BKA-Act Case –.

154 BVerfGE 141, 220 Rn. 325 – BKA-Act Case –.

155 BVerfGE 141, 220 Rn. 328 – BKA-Act Case –.

156 BVerfGE 141, 220 Rn. 328 – BKA-Act Case –.

The first of these demands has familiar parallels in the proportionality analysis the Court has applied in other security cases. In this context it seems likely that it will be achieved through the application of the "hypothetical data collection" standard that is to be applied to all transfers of information to foreign security entities.

The second demand is unique to the context of international transfers. The Court explained that the requisite assurance that a foreign legal system will respect the rule of law does not mean that the foreign legal system must be identical to Germany's.[157] Instead, the Court insisted that "it can be expected that the receiving state's handling of the transferred information will adequately observe the rule of law."[158] The receiving state cannot subvert the human rights protection owed to personally revealing information.[159] To the contrary, its legal regime must guarantee "a measured, material data-protection standard that is applicable in the receiving state" and that accounts for the following essential privacy safeguards: linking the use of surveillance information to the objectives for which it is gathered, a duty to eventually delete the information, and fundamental arrangements for oversight and data security.[160] The Court emphasized that the receiving state's legal regime, in order to meet this standard, must make particular guarantees that the transferred information is not used for political persecution and does not contribute to inhumane or degrading treatment.[161] A receiving state's satisfaction of this standard, the Court explained, should be determined by reference to the local law and the receiving state's international law commitments – both in formal and practical terms.[162] But this determination need not be made on a case-by-case basis. The law could permit the BKA to make a general assessment of conditions in specific states, with such a general assessment continuing in force as long as it is not called into question by developments in specific circumstances.[163] In reaching a conclusion about the integrity of a receiving state's legal system, however, the Court concluded that the BKA's assessment is not merely a political question. Instead, it must be a substantive legal decision based on regularly updated information.[164] Finally, the Court required that the BKA thoroughly document its decision about a foreign, non-E.U. state's fitness to receive transferred information so that it can be subject to review

---

157 BVerfGE 141, 220 Rn. 335 – BKA-Act Case –.

158 BVerfGE 141, 220 Rn. 335 – BKA-Act Case – (author's translation).

159 BVerfGE 141, 220 Rn. 335 – BKA-Act Case –.

160 BVerfGE 141, 220 Rn. 335 – BKA-Act Case –.

161 BVerfGE 141, 220 Rn. 335 – BKA-Act Case –.

162 BVerfGE 141, 220 Rn. 335 – BKA-Act Case – (citing Case C-362/14, *Maximillian Schrems v. Data Protection Commissioner*, 2015 E.C.R. 615, http://curia.europa.eu/juris/document/document.jsf?docid=169195&doclang=EN).

163 BVerfGE 141, 220 Rn. 338–339 – BKA-Act Case –.

164 BVerfGE 141, 220 Rn. 338–339 – BKA-Act Case –.

by data-protection and judicial authorities.[165] This regime has obvious debts to the Court of Justice of the European Union and the European Court of Human Rights.[166]

The Constitutional Court applied this nuanced regime to the BKA-Act and concluded that the law's provisions for international transfers of information were unconstitutional.[167] First, the Court found that the law did not ensure that transfers would satisfy the "hypothetical data collection" standard. The relevant provisions of the BKA-Act, the Court reasoned, authorized foreign transfers for the most general of purposes: the fulfillment of the BKA's responsibilities or, in discrete cases, to promote public security in the face of a serious threat.[168] These vague objectives, the Court worried, might involve aims that fall short of those that originally justified the surveillance measures.[169] For example, the Court found that the authority to transfer information for the general aim of promoting public security in the face of a serious threat did not adequately limit the transfer of information taken from home surveillance. The Court insisted that information gathered pursuant to this extreme intrusion could be transferred only in response to the most imminent and grave threats.[170] Second, the Court ruled that the law did not limit the transfer of information to circumstances in which evidence established an adequately concrete suspicion of a security threat or crime.[171] Finally, the Court found these provisions of the law unconstitutional because they did not provide adequate oversight and reporting requirements, including the duty to thoroughly document the transfer of information.[172]

## B. Conclusion

It is possible to divine a settled framework from the Federal Constitutional Court's frequent forays into the security area. The contours of that framework are shaped by the Court's interpretation of a number of basic rights secured by the constitution: Article 10 (telecommunications privacy), Article 13 (inviolability of the home), and Article 2(1) (right to freely develop one's personality). The last of these

---

165 BVerfGE 141, 220 Rn. 339 – BKA-Act Case –.

166 See Case C-362/14, *Maximillian Schrems v. Data Protection Commissioner*, 2015 E.C.R. 615, http://curia.europa.eu/juris/document/document.jsf?docid=169195&doclang=EN (hereinafter "Schrems Case"); *Zakharov v. Russia*, App. No. 47143/06, Eur. Ct. H.R., 233 (4 Dec. 2015), http://hudoc.echr.coe.int/eng?i-001-159324 (hereinafter "Zakharov Case"). See *Woods*, 55 International Legal Materials 207 (2016).

167 BVerfGE 141, 220 Rn. 335 – BKA-Act Case –.

168 See § 14(1)[1]{1} and {3} BKA-Act.

169 BVerfGE 141, 220 Rn. 343–345 – BKA-Act Case –.

170 BVerfGE 141, 220 Rn. 345 – BKA-Act Case –.

171 BVerfGE 141, 220 Rn. 345 – BKA-Act Case –.

172 BVerfGE 141, 220 Rn. 345 – BKA-Act Case –.

textual provisions has served as the basis for judicially articulated *lex specialis*, including the venerable "right to informational self-determination" and the novel "right to the confidentiality and integrity of information-technology systems." In nearly every case, however, the Court has applied the proportionality principle to its assessment of legislation or law enforcement actions that intrude upon these guarantees. Only the "core-area," as the most intimate sphere of privacy, has been given something like absolute protection by the Constitutional Court.

When applying the proportionality principle to limitable privacy rights, the Court has drawn a distinction between, on the one hand, law enforcement investigations into criminal activity, and, on the other hand, law enforcement and intelligence service investigations into security threats. The Court has given the latter circumstances greater scrutiny and demanded more rigorous safeguards. For example, the distinction matters as regards the nature of the requisite threat. In all cases the Court has demanded concrete evidence of serious crimes or threats that have been clearly and specifically identified in the empowering statute. But in the law enforcement context the Court has insisted that the privacy-infringing measures be employed only in response to serious crimes. In the context of security threats, however, the Court has found that there must be a grave danger to an individual (implicating his/her life, limbs, or freedom) or to the community (implicating the foundation or survival of the state). The Court has drawn other distinctions to help refine the constitution's demands in the security context. It has recognized, for example, that the suspicion justifying surveillance measures might be less concrete or less directly linked to the suspected threat in the event of an imminent, extremely serious security danger. Finally, the Court has found that a number of general procedures are necessary to rendering intrusive surveillance proportionate. These procedures include a judicial role in authorizing the surveillance, an obligation to inform subjects of the surveillance, precise duties regarding the storage and deletion of the information, limits on using the information for new purposes, and a duty to rigorously document all actions related to personally revealing information as a way of facilitating *ex post* judicial review.

The Court has imposed a categorical prohibition on surveillance measures that intrude upon the "core-area of privacy." To be sure that this unique form of privacy is protected, the Court has demanded a number of measures. First, an empowering statute must require the immediate termination of any surveillance measure that comes to implicate this sphere. Second, if it would be too difficult to manually assess ongoing surveillance in order to determine when it must be terminated for violating the "core-area of privacy," then the empowering statute must require that the investigating authority employ automatic collection and recording technology that will more effectively allow for this assessment after the fact. Third, in the event that information from the "core-area of privacy" is nonetheless acquired, the empowering statute must require its immediate deletion and prohibit any use of the information.

The Court enforces this framework – both the proportionality analysis applied to limitable rights and the absolute protection owed to the "core-area of privacy" – by demanding specific, finely-calibrated corrections of the challenged security policies. This suggests another fundamental element of Germany's constitutional framework for the security area. It is clear from the Court's readiness to review these cases and from the invasive and detailed nature of its judgments that security law in Germany is as much a judicial matter as it is a concern of the more representative authorities in the executive and legislative branches. The Court's judicialization of security policy has attracted repeated dissenting opinions from Justices Schluckebier and Eichberger who have written to express their concerns about the comprehensive and duteous nature of the Court's decisions in the *Data Retention Case* and *BKA-Act Case*. In a tone that will seem familiar to those who are aware of criticism of judicial activism in the American constitutional law debate, Justice Schluckebier complained that the majority's decision in the *Data Retention Case* "completely restricts the legislature's latitude for assessment and drafting, which would permit it to pass appropriate and reasonable provisions in the field of the investigation of crimes and the warding off of danger for the protection of the population."[173]

More than anything else, Germany's security policy is distinguished by the Constitutional Court's decisive role.

## Bibliography

*Alexy, Robert*, Die Struktur der Grundrechtsnormen. In: Ino Augsberg/Sebastian Unger (eds.), Basis Texte: Grundrechtstheorie. Baden-Baden 2012, pp. 267–296.

*Atkinson, L. Rush*, The Fourth Amendment's National Security Exception: Its History and Limits. 66 Vanderbilt Law Review 1343–1406 (2013).

*Baldus. Manfred*, Der Kernbereich privater Lebensgestaltung. Absolut geschützt, aber abwägungsoffen. JuristenZeitung (63) 2008, 218–227.

*Barak, Aharon*, Proportionality: Constitutional Rights and their Limitations. Cambridge et al. 2012.

*Bickel, Alexander M.*, Foreword: The Passive Virtues. 75 Harvard Law Review 40–79 (1961-1962).

*Borene, Andrew*, "We're in This Together": Reframing E.U. Responses to Criminal Unauthorized Disclosures of U.S. Intelligence Activities. In: Russell A. Miller (ed.), Privacy and Power: A Transatlantic Dialogue in the Shadow of the NSA-Affair. Cambridge et al. 2017, pp. 257–281.

---

[173] BVerfGE 125, 260, 373 – Data Retention Case –.

*Fabbrini, Federico*, Human Rights in the Digital Age. The European Court of Justice Ruling in the Data Retention Case and Its Lessons for Privacy and Surveillance in the United States. 28 Harvard Human Rights Journal, 65–96 (2015).

*Geis Max-Emanuel*, Der Kernbereich des Persönlichkeitsrechts. Ein Plädoyer für die „Sphärentheorie". JuristenZeitung (46) 1991, 112–117.

*Hailbronner, Michaela*, Traditions and Transformations: The Rise of German Constitutionalism. Oxford et al. 2015.

*Hellmuth, Dorle*, Counterterrorism and the State. Western Responses to 9/11. Philadelphia, PA 2015.

*Jackson, Vicki C.*, Constitutional Law in an Age of Proportionality. 124 Yale Law Journal 3094–3197 (2014-2015).

*Kerr, Orin S.*, The Mosaic Theory of the Fourth Amendment. 111 Michigan Law Review 311–354 (2012).

*Krotoszynski, Ronald J. Jr.*, Reconciling Privacy and Speech in the Era of Big Data. A Comparative Legal Analysis. 56 William & Mary Law Review 1279–1338 (2014-2015).

*Kutscha, Martin*, Verfassungsrechtlicher Schutz des Kernbereichs privater Lebensgestaltung. Nichts Neues aus Karlsruhe? Neue Juristische Wochenschrift (58) 2005, 20–22.

*Lang, Andrea*, Einführung in das Datenschutzrecht. Juristische Arbeitsblätter (38) 2006, 395–399.

*Loewenstein, Karl*, Militant Democracy and Fundamental Rights – Part I. 31 American Political Science Review 417–432 (1937).

– Militant Democracy and Fundamental Rights – Part II. 31 American Political Science Review 638–658 (1937).

*Maunz, Theodor/Dürig, Günter* (eds.), Kommentar zum Grundgesetz. 76th ed. München 2015.

*Miller, Russell A.*, Comparative Law and Germany's Militant Democracy. In: Russell A. Miller (ed.), US National Security, Intelligence and Democracy. From the Church Committee to the War on Terror. New York 2009, pp. 229–251.

*Poscher, Ralf*, Menschenwürde und Kernbereichsschutz: Von den Gefahren einer Verräumlichung des Grundrechtsdenkens. JuristenZeitung (64) 2009, 269–277.

*Sajó, András* (ed.), Militant Democracy. Utrecht 2004.

*Schlink, Bernhard*, Proportionality in Constitutional Law: Why Everywhere but Here? 22 Duke Journal of Comparative and International Law 291–302 (2012).

*Simitis, Spiros* (ed.), Bundesdatenschutzgesetz Kommentar. 8th ed. München 2014.

*Stone Sweet, Alec/Mathews, Jud*, Proportionality Balancing and Global Constitutionalism. 47 Columbia Journal of Transnational Law 72–164 (2008).

*Vainio, Niklas/Miettinen, Samuli*, Telecommunications Data Retention after Digital Rights Ireland: Legislative and Judicial Reactions in the Member States. 23 International Journal of Law and Information Technology 290–309 (2015).

*Wesel, Uwe*, Der Gang nach Karlsruhe. Das Bundesverfassungsgericht in der Geschichte der Bundesrepublik. München 2004.

*Wittes, Benjamin*, Privacy, Hypocrisy, and a Defense of Surveillance. In: Russell A. Miller (ed.), Privacy and Power: A Transatlantic Dialogue in the Shadow of the NSA-Affair. Cambridge et al. 2017, pp. 180–198.

*Woods, Lorna*, Zakharov V. Russia (Eur. CT. H.R.). 55 International Legal Materials 207–266 (2016).

*Zedner, Lucia*, Why Blanket Surveillance Is No Security Blanket: Data Retention in the UK after the European Data Retention Directive. In: Russell A. Miller (ed.), Privacy and Power: A Transatlantic Dialogue in the Shadow of the NSA-Affair. Cambridge et al. 2017, pp. 564–585.

*Zell, Anne-Marie*, Data Protection in the Federal Republic of Germany and the European Union. An Unequal Playing Field. 15 German Law Journal 461–494 (2014).

# Terrorism and Anticipative Criminalization. Ius poenale sine limite?

*John A.E. Vervaele**

## I. Introduction

Until the 1980s, terrorists were still largely considered political offenders, enjoying the privilege of being shielded from political prosecution and punishment under the liberal state concept. Meanwhile the counterterrorism narrative has completely changed, certainly regarding persons and organizations that pretend to act in the name of Islam, are of Arabic origin, and refer to their duty to fight enemies as part of their jihad.[1] Violent attacks in the name of jihad are not only executed in Muslim conflict areas such as Syria, Iraq, Yemen, Libya, and Afghanistan but on an international and global scale. Organizations such as ISIS have made their brand with the internationalization, globalization, and digitalization of their holy war. The terrorist attacks in France and Belgium are evidence of their more recent and visible expansion. Moreover, the ISIS fighters have linked these terrorist attacks to the development of a proper territory and state structure (ISIS caliphate).

With the aim of countering terrorism and investigating and punishing the responsible perpetrators, the international community and domestic legislators have considerably increased their legislative and operational activities. There is clearly a trend to criminalize the anticipative field or sphere (acts even prior to the commission of preparatory offenses) and to decrease the protection of human rights. Potential perpetrators or potential members of terrorist groups are being criminalized for their radical ideas and their sympathies with certain movements or Islamist tendencies. Having been labeled political enemies of the Western political legal order and values, they turn into mere political offenders. Instead of receiving protection against political prosecution and punishment, they have become the scapegoats of repressive state action. The association between Muslim foreign fighters[2] and radi-

* Professor in Economic and European Criminal Law, Utrecht Law School, Professor in European Criminal Law, College of Europe/Bruges, and President of the AIDP.

[1] Jihad means the duty for Muslims to maintain and spread Islam as a belief. Obviously, this needs to be distinguished from what is called violent Jihad.

[2] *De Guttry, A./Capone, F./Paulussen, C.* (eds.), Foreign Fighters under International Law and Beyond. Asser Press, The Hague 2016, p. 533 and *Malet, D.*, Foreign Fighters: transnational identity in civil conflicts, Oxford University Press, 2013, p. 256.

calized Arab youths in Western Europe risks to criminalize whole neighborhoods, like Molenbeek in Brussels.

In this paper, we first need to assess the extent to which the internationalization of the criminal response is new and transforms the concepts and principles of our criminal justice systems. In a second step we can then assess the extent to which the content of the specific criminal counterterrorism response is new and transforms the concepts and principles of our criminal justice systems. Ultimately, the main question is whether the criminal justice systems can face these challenges without turning their criminal law into security law altogether.

## II. Internationalization/globalization/integration and criminal justice in the post-industrial information society

The internationalization of criminal justice is not new, in particular where internationalization is defined as a process of increasing cooperation between states and where states are influenced or controlled by international organizations. International public law conventions that prescribe binding rules of substantive criminal law have been in existence for a century by now, but their number and impact have significantly increased in recent years, mainly because of the following two reasons: First, in the field of criminal justice, international organizations such as the UN, the Council of Europe, the Organisation for Economic Co-operation and Development (OECD), and the Financial Action Task Force (FATF) are monitoring compliance with international obligations, mostly through very detailed and politically binding evaluation mechanisms. We can find clear examples in the areas of money laundering, corruption, and terrorism. Second, the UN Security Council is imposing international obligations upon Member States in criminal matters without any specific conventional source and is thereby bypassing the signature and ratification process. In the aftermath of 9/11, the Security Council made the conventional UN *acquis* in terrorism matters binding, independent of the signature or ratification by Party States. Through resolutions based on Chapter VII of the Charter, the Security Council has closely linked global security with the anti-terrorist criminal response and has called on states to criminalize conduct such as traveling abroad, facilitating traveling, or offering or receiving training, etc., provided these acts are committed for terrorist purposes.[3] By 2015, the FATF adopted Recommendation 5[4] on terrorist financing, including obligations under the UN resolution and extending the scope of terrorist financing to the financing of terrorist travel.

---

3 Resolution 2178 (UNSCR 2178) of 2014 is a good example.

4 http://www.fatf-gafi.org/media/fatf/documents/recommendations/pdfs/FATF_Recom mendations.pdf.

These processes of internationalization, globalization, and integration evolved in the past decades hand in hand with the transformation of our societies into post-industrial information societies. The e-society or online society has completely reshaped social behavior and social structure. But there is no single agreed understanding of the concept of information society. Scientists are struggling with concept-related definitions and values, focusing on economic, technical, sociological, and cultural patterns. Postmodern society is often characterized as "information society" because of the widespread availability and use of information and communications technology (ICT). In fact, the most common definition of information society emphasizes technological innovation. Information processing, storage, and transmission have led to the application of ICT and related biotechnology and nanotechnology in virtually all corners of society. The information society is a post-industrial society in which information and knowledge are key resources and play a pivotal role.[5] However, information societies are not solely defined by the technological infrastructure in place but are multidimensional phenomena. Any information society is a complex web, consisting not only of a technological infrastructure but also an economic structure, a pattern of social relations, organizational patterns, and other facets of social organization. This is why it is important to focus not only on the technological aspect but also on the social attributes of the information society, including the social impact of the information revolution on social organizations such as the criminal justice system. Moreover, the postmodern age of information technology is transforming the content, accessibility, and utilization of information and knowledge in social organizations, including the criminal justice system. The relationship between knowledge and order has fundamentally changed. The transformation of communications into instantaneous information-making technology has altered the way society values knowledge. In today's rapidly changing age, the structure of traditional authority is being undermined and replaced by an alternative method of societal control. The emergence of a new technological paradigm based on ICT has resulted in a network society,[6] in which the key social structures and activities are organized around electronically processed information networks. There is an even deeper transformation of political institutions in the network society: the rise of a new form of state (network state) that is gradually replacing the nation-states of the industrial era. In these times of rapid change, the structure of traditional authority is being undermined and replaced by an alternative method of societal control (surveillance society).

The phenomenon of radical and terrorist jihadism,[7] especially in its latest manifestation in the Islamic State in Iraq and Syria (ISIS), would be unthinkable without

---

5 *Bell, D.*, The Coming of Post-Industrial Society. Basic Books, New York 1976.

6 *Castells, M.*, The Rise of the Network Society. The Information Age: Economy, Society and Culture, vol. 1. 2nd ed. Blackwell Publishing Ltd. 2000.

7 *Kepel, G.*, Jihad: The Trail of Political Islam. I.B. Tauris, London 2004.

the information society. For ISIS, social media are the perfect instrument for propaganda and recruitment.[8] It is interesting to note that ISIS combines classic notions of state and territory (caliphate) with a very advanced system of "network governance." As the information society turns the globe into a global city, ISIS is becoming a global player, and its actions qualify as global terrorism that threatens global security.

## III. Internationalization and transformation of the criminal justice system

What is the impact of these developments on the domestic criminal justice system? Clearly, the domestic criminal justice system has not been replaced by a global one, in the global city. Social globalization does not automatically lead to legal globalization or globalization of criminal justice, and not even to globalization of political authority with regard to criminal justice. The birth of resolutions of international criminal law in the UN Security Council is the exception and the result of a process that has been developing for a century. Even at the implementation stage, this new justice system is still creating its own concepts of criminal law and criminal procedure. However, the impact of this process of internationalization and globalization, both offline and online, on the domestic criminal justice system is substantial. Domestic criminal justice is faced with societal changes where the crime, the perpetrators, and, *inter alia*, the evidence, are not always linked with the territory of the nation-state. As a consequence of the increasing mobility of persons, goods, services, and capital, domestic criminal justice systems have to protect new legal interests *(Rechtsgüter)*, usually with a strong transnational background (for example, protection against hate speech and xenophobia, protection against child pornography, or protection against securities fraud or against ID theft). The domestic criminal justice system is internationalizing in a process of top-down and bottom-up internationalization.[9] International and regional organizations are imposing new substantive and procedural obligations on domestic criminal justice systems; at the same time, the domestic criminal justice systems are expanding their jurisdiction in order to deal with criminality in a globalizing society on an international level. This means that the domestic criminal justice system is both on the user and the supply side of this process. However, this renewal is not limited to a few updates to offense definitions based on new or renewed protected legal interests nor limited to an increase in mutual legal assistance. In fact, the classical

[8] *Viganò, F.*, Sul contrasto al terrorismo di matrice islamica tramite il sistema penale tra 'diritto penale del nemico' e legittimi bilanciamenti. Studi Urbinati, Scienze giuridiche, politiche ed economiche. 19 Jan. 2014; 58(4), pp. 329–348.

[9] *Vervaele, J.A.E.*, Internacionalización del derecho penal procesal penal. Necesidades y desafíos, Lima 2015, p. 403.

rationale for the use of criminal justice (starting with the primary criminalization by the definition of offences), based upon *ultimum remedium*, strict conditions of harmful conduct that violates legally protected interests and concepts derived from the Enlightenment and Kantian philosophy, has been replaced in the past decades by a globalizing criminal policy concept, translated into criminal policy paradigms: combat/ war against drugs, combat/war against organized crime, combat/war against terrorism. I call them paradigms, because they function as a frame of reference for the perception of reality and thus for the definition of social constructs as crime, danger, risk and insecurity.[10] These criminal policy paradigms have been used both at the domestic and at the international level in order to justify substantial changes in the relation between state-society and criminal justice and within the criminal justice system itself.

Modern criminal justice, with its roots in the Enlightenment, provides for an integrated system by offering *protection* to individuals (not only to suspects) (the shield dimension), *instruments* for the law enforcement community made up of the police, the Public Prosecutor's Office, and the judiciary (the sword dimension), and *checks and balances/trias politica* (the constitutional dimension). The abovementioned three paradigms, the combat/war on drugs, the combat/war on organized crime, and the combat/war on terrorism swept like a tidal wave through the criminal justice system. All three dimensions of the criminal justice system have been affected by these three waves. These paradigms completely transformed our criminal justice systems, affecting general criminal law, special criminal law, criminal procedure, and international criminal law. There is no doubt that substantial and far-reaching changes have also occurred during the last decade. The new security paradigm and counterterrorism policy resulted in transformations that go far beyond the field of terrorist offenses. International pressure for a common approach to the investigation, prosecution, and judgment of terrorism cases has been intense. An impressive set of international and regional conventions on organized crime and counterterrorism have been elaborated both at the UN and the Council of Europe. After 9/11, the UN paved the way with Security Council resolutions and the establishment of a Counter-Terrorism Committee to supervise the implementation of the resolutions, including the substance of the conventions.[11] Even though the counterterrorism paradigm evolved before the events of 9/11 and those in Madrid and London, these terrorist attacks have certainly intensified it. Counterterrorism is definitely the criminal policy area where the transformation of the criminal justice systems is most visible and justified under the banner of security.

---

[10] *Zaffaroni, E. Raúl*, El enemigo en el derecho penal. Dykinson, Madrid 2006, p. 225.

[11] See http://www.un.org/sc/ctc/countryreports/reportA.shtml for the comprehensive national reports.

# IV. Criminal justice and terrorism

## A. Historical and international approach

Violent attacks for political purposes are obviously not the monopoly of contemporary terrorism. The end of the nineteenth century, for example, was characterized by violent rebellions of the popular classes and brutal acts of anarchist movements. At that time, these acts were not defined as acts of terrorism but rather as subversion or crimes against the security of the state. In view of the atrocities committed during the First World War, the League of Nations and the Association Internationale de Droit Pénal (AIDP; congress in 1925) discussed a new legal regime on the criminal responsibility of the state for crimes against other states or collectivities. It was V. Pella who, in 1925, in a report on war crimes, talked of war of aggression as state crime. He also elaborated the basic notions of his "Code of Nations," based on the limitation of the absolute independence of states and their external sovereignty in order to protect international order and justice. The establishment of a new international criminal justice system failed in the inter-war period. However, following the violent deaths of the King of Yugoslavia and the French Minister of Justice at the hands of Croatian terrorists in Marseille, states were ready to agree on the 1937 Convention for the Prevention of Terrorism and a related Convention for the Creation of An International Criminal Court in the League of Nations, based in The Hague, to prosecute terrorist offenses.[12] Even at that time, the doctrine criticized the entire configuration of the Convention on Terrorism for lacking legal certainty owing to vague offense definitions and very extensive preparatory acts. The Conventions never entered into force due to the Second World War.

Since the 1960s, in response to the first acts of air piracy, the international community – both at global and regional levels – has been developing international conventions to prevent and punish acts of terrorist violence. Under the auspices of the UN and the International Atomic Energy Agency, the international community has created 19 conventions (so-called "suppression conventions") to prevent and criminalize terrorist acts. Some conventions are directly related to civil aviation, such as the Convention on Offenses and Certain Other Acts Committed on Board Aircraft (1963) or the Convention for the Suppression of Unlawful Acts Relating to International Civil Aviation (2010). Others relate to the protection of international personnel, such as the International Convention against the Taking of Hostages (1979), or to a specific modus operandi, such as the International Convention for the Suppression of Terrorist Bombings (1997) and the International Convention for the Suppression of the Financing of Terrorism (1999).

---

12 Documents can be found in the International Review of Penal law of the AIDP, volume on Historic Documentation of the Association (1926-2014), 2015/3-4, pp. 851–914.

Since 1996,[13] a Comprehensive Convention on International Terrorism has been negotiated at the UN with the aim of criminalizing all forms of terrorism, including funding and other preparatory acts or acts of material support. The negotiations, which took place in the Ad Hoc Committee on International Terrorism and the 6th Legal Committee, have been stalled since 2013. The main problem is the definition of terrorism. What is the difference between a terrorist group and a rebel group or national liberation front? Are terrorist acts committed by armies or by states excluded from the definition?

After the Arab Spring, the rise of violent conflicts in Iraq, Afghanistan, Syria, and Yemen, and especially after the exodus of young Arabs and converts to conflict zones, especially Syria, the international community has increasingly focused on counterterrorism. The threat of the Taliban, ISIS, the Al Nusra Front, etc. justified an even wider criminal response. The UN Security Council in 2014 unanimously endorsed, based on Chapter VII of the Charter, Resolution 2178, which deals *inter alia* with the threat by foreign terrorist fighters, namely, individuals traveling to a state other than their state of residence or nationality for the purpose of committing, planning, or preparing terrorist acts or participating in them, or providing or receiving training for purposes of terrorism, including in connection with armed conflict. The resolution, binding on all States Parties to the UN, clearly imposes an even broader expansion of criminal law:

> 5. [The Security Council] [d]ecides that Member States shall, consistent with international human rights law, international refugee law, and international humanitarian law, prevent and suppress the recruiting, organizing, transporting or equipping of individuals who travel to a State other than their States of residence or nationality for the purpose of the perpetration, planning, or preparation of, or participation in, terrorist acts or the providing or receiving of terrorist training, and the financing of their travel and of their activities;
>
> 6. Recalls its decision, in resolution 1373 (2001), that all Member States shall ensure that any person who participates in the financing, planning, preparation or perpetration of terrorist acts or in supporting terrorist acts is brought to justice, and decides that all States shall ensure that their domestic laws and regulations establish serious criminal offenses sufficient to provide the ability to prosecute and to penalize in a manner duly reflecting the seriousness of the offense:
>
> (a) their nationals who travel or attempt to travel to a State other than their States of residence or nationality, and other individuals who travel or attempt to travel from their territories to a State other than their States of residence or nationality, for the purpose of the perpetration, planning, or preparation of, or participation in, terrorist acts, or the providing or receiving of terrorist training;
>
> (b) the willful provision or collection, by any means, directly or indirectly, of funds by their nationals or in their territories with the intention that the funds should be used, or in the knowledge that they are to be used, in order to finance the travel of individuals who travel to a State other than their States of residence or nationality for the purpose of

[13] Established by Resolution 51/210, 17 Dec. 1996, with reference to Resolution 49/60 of 9 Dec. 1994 and Resolution 50/53 of 11 Dec. 1995 that call for measures to eliminate international terrorism.

the perpetration, planning, or preparation of, or participation in, terrorist acts or the providing or receiving of terrorist training; and,
(c) the willful organization, or other facilitation, including acts of recruitment, by their nationals or in their territories, of the travel of individuals who travel to a State other than their States of residence or nationality for the purpose of the perpetration, planning, or preparation of, or participation in, terrorist acts or the providing or receiving of terrorist training.

Despite the lack of unanimity in the international community on the role of criminal law in countering terrorism, there is clearly an expansion of criminal law in all 19 international conventions and UN resolutions. Not only do they oblige states to incriminate violent and harmful conduct but also to increasingly incriminate preparatory and anticipative acts that consist of abstract or concrete endangerment, such as certain acts of glorification or financing.[14]

The lack of unanimity at the international level has not prevented major progress at the regional level, for example on the European continent.

## B. The European approach

The phenomena of terrorism and criminal anti-terrorist legislation are deeply rooted in some European countries, mainly due to the problem of domestic terrorism, such as ETA/GRAPO in Spain, IRA in England, Brigate Rosse in Italy, RAF in Germany, Action directe in France, etc. However, most countries in the Council of Europe and in the EU did not have specific criminal offenses in their criminal legislation to counter terrorism. Nor did the Convention for the Suppression of Terrorism of 1977,[15] negotiated in the Council of Europe, require their introduction. The Convention limited itself mainly to not recognizing acts of terrorism as political offenses in light of the extradition treaties, based on what was called the climate of mutual trust between the Council of Europe states.

The political and legal landscape changed with the attacks of 11 September 2001 in the United States. The EU wanted to demonstrate solidarity with the United States. The 2002 Framework Decision[16] was adopted in accordance with the conclusions of the 1999 Tampere European Council, which identified terrorism as one of the most serious violations of fundamental freedoms and human rights principles, and following the action plan adopted by the extraordinary meeting of the

14 The International Convention for the Suppression of the Financing of Terrorism (1999) is a good example.

15 Explanatory Report to the European Convention on the Suppression of Terrorism, Strasbourg, 27 Jan. 1977.

16 Council Framework Decision on combating terrorism, 13 June 2002, OJ L 164, 22 June 2002.

European Council on 21 September 2001. The 2002 Framework Decision[17] and the amending Framework Decision 2008[18] define terrorist offenses as well as offenses relating to terrorist groups or to terrorist activities. The 2002 Framework Decision introduces a criminal definition of terrorism – clearly inspired by US counter-terrorist legislation[19] – by combining objective elements (murder, bodily injury, hostage-taking, extortion, committing assaults, threatening to commit any of the previous acts, etc.) with the subjective element of intention but with a specific purpose: acts committed with the aim of seriously intimidating a population, destabilizing or destroying the structures of a country or an international organization, or compelling public authorities to abstain from performing an act. The Framework Decisions of 2002 and 2008 require Member States to incriminate the establishment of terrorist groups and the management of and participation in them. These groups are defined as structured organizations of two or more persons, established over a period of time, acting in concert with a view to committing terrorist offenses. In addition, EU countries were required to criminalize certain preparatory or anticipatory acts (public provocation, recruitment and training of terrorists, extortion or counterfeiting in order to commit a terrorist offense) as terrorist activities if committed with a terrorist aim.

The Council of Europe also clearly took the attacks of 11 September 2001 as a starting point for a reorientation of criminal legislation. The protocol of amendment to the Convention of 1977 represented only the first phase. The new 2005 Warsaw Convention on the Prevention of Terrorism was more important.[20] This Convention increased incriminations in the anticipative field, especially in relation to public provocation (Art. 5), recruitment (Art. 6), and training (Art. 7). Art. 8 stipulates that these incriminations must be autonomous and not dependent upon any result in the form of the commission of a terrorist act. In addition, Art. 9 requires the incrimination of participating in these autonomous crimes in the form of establishing and/or directing groups. In other words, the terrorist group concept also applies to these pre-emptive offenses. In accordance with Art. 5, provocation refers to "the distribution, or otherwise making available, of a message to the public, with the intent to incite the commission of a terrorist offence, where such conduct, whether or not directly advocating terrorist offences, causes a danger that one or more such offences may be committed." An indirect and temporary causal link (*ex ante* or *ex*

---

[17] For more information, see Commission Reports on combating terrorism, COM (2004) 409 final, 9 June 2004; COM (2007) 681 final, 6 Nov. 2007; and COM (2014) 554 final, 5 Sept. 2014.

[18] Council Framework Decision on combating terrorism, 28 Nov 2008, OJ L 330, 9 Dec. 2008.

[19] *Vervaele, J.A.E.*, The Anti-terrorist Legislation in the US: Criminal Law for the Enemies?, European Journal of Law Reform, 2007, vol. 08, no. 1, 137–171.

[20] Explanatory Report to the Council of Europe Convention on the Prevention of Terrorism, Warsaw, 16 May 2005.

*post*) with the perpetration of a terrorist act is sufficient or the fact that the conduct could create a danger that a terrorist act might be committed. In order to assess the danger, one must take into account the actor's profile, the content of the message, and the context in which it is expressed. Recruitment under Art. 6 may occur physically or digitally and refers only to active recruitment by the person. It is not necessary for the recruiter to participate in a terrorist act as a result of it. An effective solicitation with the aim of committing, participating, or contributing to a terrorist act is sufficient. Art. 7 incriminates training insofar as it is the transfer of know-how to persons with the purpose of committing or contributing to the commission of terrorist acts. The subjective element is limited to knowing that this training can be used for the commission of or as a contribution to these acts. The incrimination does not include receiving training. The fact that it is a pre-emptive offense is clearly recognized in the Explanatory Report, which refers to "establishing as criminal offenses certain acts that may lead to the commission of terrorist offenses."[21] Again, reference is made to the mutual trust among states to advance in this new area of criminalization.

The response to the implementation of UN Resolution 2178 in Europe was two-fold. On the one hand, the Council of Europe adopted in 2015 the Additional Riga Protocol[22] to the Warsaw Convention of 2005, adding new offenses, especially regarding foreign terrorist fighters and their passive training, their travel to areas of conflict, and the funding and material support for these trips. Passive training (Art. 3) may also consist in attending a training camp online, for example by participating in online interactive training sessions. Traveling to conflict zones (Art. 4) as such is not a criminal act but must be incriminated when undertaken with the intent to commit or engage in terrorist acts or to receive or offer training. The financing and material support for such travel (Art. 5) is criminalized when there is awareness that these funds or aids are collected, completely or partially, with the aforementioned objective. Point 29 of the Explanatory Report clearly states that "Parties shall take into account that Articles 2 to 6 criminalise behaviour at a stage preceding the actual commission of a terrorist offence but already having the potential to lead to the commission of such acts."[23] Article 2 of the Protocol also requires that acts such as passive training and travel to or from a conflict zone may qualify as acts of participation in a terrorist group or association. Under point 35, it is stated that "participation in the activities of an association or group for the purpose of terrorism may be the result of contacts established via the Internet, including social media, or through other IT-based platforms."[24] In point 22, the authors of the Ex-

21 Explanatory Report, point 26.

22 CETS No. 217. Although signed by many states, it did not yet enter into force for lack of a sufficient number of ratifications.

23 Explanatory Report to the Additional Protocol to the Council of Europe Convention on the Prevention of Terrorism, https://rm.coe.int/168047c5ec.

24 Explanatory Report to the Additional Protocol to the Council of Europe Convention on the Prevention of Terrorism, point 35.

planatory Report[25] indicate that these new types are acts of a serious nature simply because they have the potential to become terrorist acts. However, it is not necessary for the terrorist act to be consummated in order to be incriminated and prosecuted.

The second European initiative is even more recent, was launched by the EU, and reflects the wave of cruel attacks in France and Belgium. I am referring to Directive 2017/541[26] replacing Framework Decision 2002/2008. Recital 9 refers to the fact that crimes related to terrorist activities are extremely serious, as they may lead to the commission of terrorist offenses and allow terrorists and terrorist groups to continue to carry out their criminal activities, which justifies the criminalization of such conduct. The proposal distinguishes between terrorist offenses and offenses related to a terrorist group (Title II) and offenses related to terrorist activities (Title III). The first category (in Title II) comprises terrorist offenses (Art. 3) and the direction of or participation in a terrorist group (Art. 4), already incriminated in the Framework Decision of 2002. Interference in computer systems or data banks has been added as one of the acts that can qualify. The second category (in Title III) comprises the anticipative acts and related terrorist activities. There are no fewer than 12 different subcategories, such as public provocation to commit a terrorist offense (Art. 5), recruitment for terrorism (Art. 6), providing training for terrorism (Art. 7), receiving training for terrorism (Art. 8), traveling for the purpose of terrorism (Art. 9), organizing or facilitating such travel (Art. 10), terrorist financing (Art. 11), and other offenses related to terrorist activities such as theft or drawing up or using false administrative documents (Art. 12). The phenomenon of foreign terrorist fighters is at the center of the new criminal intervention, since it is not only a matter of traveling for terrorist purposes (including receiving training) but also involves the financing, organization, and facilitation of such travel, including logistical and material support, accommodation, means of transport, services, goods, and merchandise.

## V. Criminal justice and terrorism: The paradigm of risk and security

### A. Criminal justice and paradigm change

The classic criminal law, based on the ideas of the Enlightenment and further elaborated in the general part of criminal codification and in dogmatic doctrine, aims both at justifying criminal intervention but also at limiting it to the protection of legal interests in the event of related harmful conduct.

---

25 Explanatory Report to the Additional Protocol to the Council of Europe Convention on the Prevention of Terrorism, point 22.

26 Directive 2017/541 on combating terrorism, OJ L 88/6, 31 March 2017.

Since the 1980s societies have recognized and justified a growing need for criminal intervention, even if no criminal offense was committed and no harm was caused. Paradigms of criminal policy to counter drug trafficking and therefore to suppress organized crime and terrorism justified an anticipative and pre-emptive criminal law, that is, a law that sanctions acts prior to the commission of a concrete and harmful act that violates the legally protected interest. In reality, the three aforementioned paradigm shifts resulted in an expansion of criminal law at different stages. The first stage was the introduction of new types of criminal associations. The types of "bande de malfaiteurs" or "conspiracy" already existed, but the scope of incrimination of criminal organizations and terrorist organizations has gone much further. In fact, a specific commission of crime is not required, but only the formation of a group for the purpose of committing a crime. In a second phase and associated with the first, preparatory acts (inchoate offenses), unrelated to attempt, were expanded. In a third step, acts of financial or material support or simple possession were defined. Many of these acts are legal in and of themselves but become unlawful if associated with a terrorism-related purpose because of their aim (for example, to establish a criminal group or to commit acts of terrorism).

## B. Terrorism: expansion and anticipation of the criminal intervention

Anticipating the threshold of punishability of human behavior based on associative acts and/or preparatory acts and/or related acts is justified by the need to punish behavior prior to the execution of violent acts. The big problem, obviously, is that in the absence of offensiveness criteria, the prevention of danger becomes the purpose of incrimination.[27] How to define criteria of dangerousness corresponding to the necessity of the rate of criminal intervention in a way that avoids incriminating conduct that is based on personal freedoms, thus avoiding political-ideological persecutions? It is obviously not sufficient for an association to have an organizational structure with features of stability and permanence and which is configured to a degree of effectiveness that makes the execution of a plan feasible. What is required is a serious, concrete, and current criminal plan that is more than an exchange of ideas or ideologies and reflects the objective, the purpose of committing violent acts of terrorism.

The expansion of terrorist offenses is exacerbated when preparatory or related offenses are not aimed at committing terrorist offenses but merely at the creation of a terrorist association or the preparation of related offenses. The anticipation of the criminal intervention is not limited only to constructs such as the crime of belonging to a terrorist organization or the crime of collaborating with a terrorist organiza-

---

27 *Hassemer, W.*, Sicherheit durch Strafrecht, StV 2006, 321–332; *Weisser, B.*, Über den Umgang des Strafrechts mit terroristischen Bedrohungslagen, ZStW 121 (2009), 131–161.

tion. We can observe constructions in European legislation and their implementation in criminal justice practice in which acts related to terrorist offenses may constitute a terrorist association as such if they are carried out in a group. At this point it may be useful to draw on an example to illustrate the unlimited expansion of the intervention. Three young friends of Arab origin living in Holland are collecting information, online and through social media, on techniques necessary for a smooth trip to Syria, among them how to fake passports and how to pass security checks without seeming nervous. They also collect information on survival methods in the desert. Satisfied with what they have gathered, they regularly exchange electronic messages between the three of them. In some of these messages, they glorify the courage of some of their friends who went to Syria as combatants. These three young men were prosecuted in Holland for passive training and forming a terrorist association, despite the fact that they did not communicate any of this information to the outside world and in the absence of any other factor indicating their terrorist aims or their intention to prepare a trip to Syria as fighters (terrorist purpose). What is at stake here is an expansion of the membership in a terrorist group in a way that violates the principles of legality and proportionality, since there is no specific purpose of committing terrorist acts. Legal constructs of this type come close to an actor criminal law, being limited to the actor's thought and freedom to inform him- or herself.[28] We can also verify that in our information society the definitional elements of a terrorist group are changing from those of a stable and permanent structure to online communication.

A second problem is obviously linked to the latest wave of incriminations in relation to mere acts related to terrorism or those acts which the EU calls crimes related to terrorist activities. It is mostly legal behavior that becomes a criminal offense because of its terrorist purpose. In the US, which has been incriminating this conduct in its anti-terrorist legislation, this last wave has been conceptualized as "terrorist precursor crimes." Precursors are usually substances needed to produce pharmaceuticals or drugs. Here, they are basic products and services to enable terrorist activity and/or to establish terrorist groups. The Congressional Research Service defines "precursor" like this: "Irrespective of ideology or strategic goals, all terrorist groups have several basic needs in common: funding, security, operatives/support, propaganda, and means and/or appearance of force. In order to meet these needs, terrorists engage in a series of activities, some of which are legal, many of which are not, including various fraud schemes, petty crime, identity and immigration crimes, the counterfeit of goods, narcotics trade, and illegal weapons

---

[28] *Asúa Batarrita, A.*, Apología del terrorismo y colaboración con banda armada: delimitación de los respectivos ámbitos típicos (comentario a la sentencia de 29 de noviembre de 1997 de la Sala Penal del Tribunal Supremo), La Ley, no. 3, 1998, pp. 1639 et seq. and *Cancio Meliá, M./Petzsche, A.*, Terrorism as a criminal offence, in: A. Masferrer/C. Walker (eds.), Counter-Terrorism, Human Rights and the Rule of Law: Crossing Legal Boundaries in Defence of the State. Edward Elgar Publishing, Cheltenham 2013, pp. 87–105.

procurement, amongst others. *Terrorist precursor crimes can be defined as unlawful acts undertaken to facilitate a terrorist attack or to support a terrorist campaign.*"[29]

Taking this approach, any act or conduct may easily qualify as a precursor offense. It comes therefore as no surprise that the same document qualifies acts of setting up front businesses and charities, food stamp fraud, passive training, etc. as precursor offenses. In other words, all acts that can be linked to terrorist groups and/or preparatory acts and related acts could qualify as "terrorist predicate crimes," in the same vein as predicate offenses for money laundering. To qualify as a predicate offense for money laundering requires the prior commission of a criminal act of a certain gravity. In the case of terrorism, however, it is a process of the threshold of incrimination rising to the crime of terrorism. As it is rising, the underlying or reference crime has not yet been committed, nor is it being prepared yet. It is an autonomous pre-emptive incrimination. The underlying offense is not limited to violent terrorist acts such as the attacks in France or Belgium but may only consist of the formation of a terrorist group or of preparatory acts.

Again, a couple of practical judicial examples from Holland may serve to illustrate the problem. A young Arab visits different websites in order to find out how to obtain a visa for Turkey and how to travel to Syria. He also asks some questions online about detonators. Finally, he watches ISIS propaganda on YouTube, especially decapitation images, and stores some of them on his computer. He was prosecuted for obtaining information and knowledge skills, constituting passive training (article 134[a] Dutch Penal Code), in order to prepare and facilitate terrorist acts. His sentence of 15 months of imprisonment was confirmed by the Dutch Supreme Court.[30] In this case, ideological thinking is penalized as such. No act is unlawful in itself, there are no specific indications of preparatory acts, nor is there a specific *mens rea* that should characterize the conduct and should constitute an external projection of this purpose.

In another case two boys of Arab origin collect money in Holland to start a transport company in Syria. The Rotterdam court[31] in the Netherlands sentenced them to three and a half years of imprisonment, absent any proof that they were combatants or that they had participated in terrorist acts. Supporting the ISIS organization in the caliphate, whether in the form of transport or as a cook, is a type of facilitation that qualifies as participation in the terrorist organization ISIS. Traveling to the caliphate almost automatically becomes a crime, unless the person joins "friendly" organizations fighting the "enemy", i.e. ISIS. This means that anyone

29 *O'Neil, S.*, CRS Report for Congress, Terrorist Precursor Crimes: Issues and Options for Congress, 24 May 2007, Introduction, p. 1 [Italics not in original but provided by the author].

30 Hoge Raad, 31-05-2016, ECLI:NL:HR:2016: 1011.

31 ECLI:NL:RBROT:2016:1264.

who travels to Syria, including the caliphate, to participate in the fighting on the side of the Kurdish Peshmerga could be considered a hero. Thus, whether conduct is considered a criminal act or an act of liberation depends on the political definition of "enemy." That is exactly how criminal justice should not be working.

## VI. Conclusion

Our analysis shows how the anti-terrorist paradigm is turning criminal law into a mere instrument of security and risk control policy. Through resolutions based on Chapter VII of the Charter, the Security Council established a close link between global security and the anti-terrorist criminal response. As the information society turns the globe into a global city, groups like ISIS are positioned as global actors and their actions qualify as global terrorism that threatens global security. Although there is no international definition of terrorism, the international community labels enemies *ad-hoc* to combat. The most visible aspect of this mechanism is the listing of terrorist groups, individuals, and entities by the UN, the EU, and some states, resulting in the imposition of "smart sanctions" (freezing of bank accounts, visa prohibitions, etc.).[32]

This paradigmatic change has very important consequences for the legislative policy in criminal matters and in the construction of criminal offenses. The focus on prevention and anticipative criminalization made it necessary to treat the establishment of a terrorist group as a criminal offense, without any direct link to terrorist acts. The group's purpose becomes the distinguishing criterion between a lawful and a terrorist association. The problem is that there are cases where this purpose is limited to the thinking of the people active in the group. In addition, the group can be formed online, without a stable and permanent structure. As a result, we end up with completely open offenses consisting in the criminalization of a person's thought instead of his or her harmful conduct. When the actor is penalized solely for his or her way of thinking, he or she has become a pure enemy.

Curiously enough, this expansive criminalization is the result of a dialectic interaction between international, European, and national law. They all preach the same standards, but the states often provide the most open and vague offenses in their legislation and/or criminal jurisprudence. Only in a minority of states, such as Italy, are offenses restricted by the supreme court and/or the constitutional court through the application of general principles (principle of legality, principle of proportionality, etc.). In international law, a consensus definition of terrorism remains elusive whereas the definition used in the EU is of a political nature as it refers to the purpose of terrorism in political terms.

---

[32] *Cameron, I.* (ed.), EU Sanctions: Law and Policy Issues concerning restrictive measures. Intersentia, Cambridge 2013.

The counterterrorism paradigm has resulted in a vast array of anticipated and associative offenses, reflecting an expansionist punitivism, whereby the goal of criminal justice has shifted from the punishment of perpetrators (for purposes of general and special prevention, including rehabilitation) to a wider field of social control of danger and risk. As a result, the commission of a criminal act by a suspect is no longer the threshold that triggers the state's *ius puniendi*. The focus on security in criminal law has led to an expansion of substantive criminal law (general and special part) beyond the traditional borders and boundaries defined in the Enlightenment era. By redefining the objective of criminal justice, its nature has also been redefined. The higher the risk or the danger, which is based on a social construction and certainly not on empirical facts, the lower the threshold for the use of *ius puniendi*, which means that criminal law becomes security law. Security law is based less on a legal definition of suspects and criminal conduct linked to serious harm to protected legal interests than on a pre-established definition of an enemy[33] that is associated with risk, danger, and insecurity. The widening net of incriminations led to a function creep and dehumanization of the criminal law,[34] combined with a political instrumentalization and mediation of crime, and the fear of crime.[35] As a result, the state's *ius puniendi* (being one of the most repressive interferences in freedom) is being instrumentalized and put at the service of danger and risk management. When the prevention of danger becomes the triggering mechanism for criminal punishment, the criminal justice system is at risk of becoming a security system, with an increasing interference in the freedom of all citizens. The main targets of the security criminal law are, however, enemies pre-defined on the basis of political criteria, i.e. persons/groups that could potentially undermine our political order. By means of the anticipative offenses they become political offenders. For instance, foreign fighters are prosecuted based on their nationality and on the group they have been active for in the conflict.[36] Criminal law is used as an instrument for the defense of the state,[37] subject to the political definition of endangerment.

The expansion of criminal justice also goes hand in hand with the erosion of the basic principles of modern criminal justice, as elaborated in the Enlightenment (*nullum crimen sine iniuria*, *nulla poena sine culpa*, *ultimum remedium*, fair trial, etc.).[38] At the same time, criminal repression becomes a *passe partout* formula for

33 *Jakobs, G.*, Bürgerstrafrecht und Feindstrafrecht, HRRS 3/2004, pp. 88–95.

34 See *Arroyo, L./Delmas-Marty, M.* (eds.), Securitarismo y Derecho Penal, Ediciones de la Universidad de Castilla-La Mancha, Cuenca 2013.

35 *Simon, J.,* Governing through Crime. Oxford University Press 2007.

36 *Sciso, E.*, Foreign Terrorist Fighters e legge antiterrorismo, Rivista di diritto internazionale, vol. 98, no. E3, 2015, 881–887.

37 See *Masferrer, A./Walker, C.* (eds.), Counter-Terrorism, Human Rights and the Rule of Law: Crossing Legal Boundaries in Defence of the State. Edward Elgar Publishing, Cheltenham 2013.

38 *Ferrajoli, L.*, Diritto e Ragione. Teoria del garantismo penale. Laterza 2011.

solving social problems. Expectations regarding the ability of criminal justice to solve problems are, however, in sharp contrast to the actual performance. The expansion of criminal justice is very real in terms of social control, but it is very symbolic in terms of solving social problems.

Finally, criminal offense definitions to counter terrorism require high conceptual rigor and an interpretation that ensures that the basic principles of modern criminal justice, also recognized as fundamental rights and/or human rights, are not undermined by the counterterrorism policy itself. We have to avoid triggering a state response that ends up affecting what the state seeks to defend: human rights, democracy, and ultimately, the fundamental legal values of a society. They are the foundations and limits of *ius puniendi* and the basis of a humanistic criminal law. A criminal law without limits becomes an instrument of social control by the state that undermines not only the mere essence of criminal law but also the legitimacy of the punitive power of the state. This is why it is important to redefine and limit the role of criminal law in countering terrorism and to reinforce the human rights approach in this area.[39]

[39] See Special Rapporteur on the promotion and protection of human rights and fundamental freedoms while countering terrorism, Human Rights Council, 22 February 2016.

# Legislating Non-Violent Extremism in Prevent Strategies: The Example of the UK

*David Lowe*

## I. Introduction

Following terrorist attacks in the US in 2001 as well as Madrid in 2004 and London in 2005, a number of states introduced Prevent strategies aimed at preventing people being drawn into terrorism. As it is the only nation state that introduced statutory obligations linked to its Prevent strategy in addition to proposing to introduce legislation related to extremism, the main focus of this chapter is on the UK. This study examines how by focusing on violent extremism linked to the Islamist ideology, a number of states' Prevent strategies have been divisive in society by alienating Muslim communities.

One of the problems associated with Prevent strategies has been how they have defined extremism. Since 2011 the UK's definition has applied to all forms of extremism, be they violent or non-violent. This has taken on greater importance as the UK has now placed a statutory obligation on staff in public bodies to prevent people from being drawn into terrorist activity and it proposes to introduce a Counter-Extremism and Safeguarding Bill containing wider powers to disrupt all forms of extremist activity. By examining the UK's current definition of extremism, the chapter reveals problems associated with the definition, which, if left uncorrected, will only further enhance the divisiveness currently existing with Prevent strategies. As the definition is subjective, it is also problematic as it raises the potential for thought being policed and criminalized, something that runs counter to both the European Convention on Human Rights and the European Union's Charter of Fundamental Rights and Freedoms.

## II. The introduction of prevent/resilience strategies

The Madrid bombing and the killing of the Dutch filmmaker *Theo van Gogh* in 2004 along with the London bombing in 2005 were watershed moments for a number of European states in revaluating their counterterrorism policies (*Briggs* 2010, p. 972, *Vidino* and *Brandon* 2012, pp. 163–164, *O'Toole, DeHanas*, and *Modood*

2012, p. 373, *Staniforth* 2014 p. 167). As a result, the Prevent strand of the UK's terrorism policy CONTEST was implemented. Prevent is aimed at deterring the vulnerable from being drawn into terrorism and became a much stronger element as part of the measures to tackle the 'home grown' terrorist (*Rogers* 2008, pp. 44–46). Along with the UK, the Netherlands, Denmark, and Norway introduced a comprehensive national strategy to prevent the radicalization of those more vulnerable to being drawn into terrorism, with other European states developing a less comprehensive programme led at local level (*Vidino* and *Brandon* 2012, p. 164). One example of the strategy being led at local level is Germany, where Berlin authorities adopted an institutionalized format and created the Islam Forum Berlin (*Vermeulen* 2014, p. 297). Similar government responses to the radicalizing processes were also considered in other states. Following the 2003 Bali bombing by Al Qaeda that resulted in the deaths of many Australian tourists, the Australian government developed its Resilience strategy. Resilience is designed to prevent the growth of home-grown terrorism with programmes and activities focusing largely on social harmony, the promotion of Australian democratic values, and the integration of 'suspect' communities into broader Australian society (*Aly, Balbi*, and *Jacques* 2015, p. 8). The European Union (EU) also examined methods of adopting prevent strategies in countering terrorism. The EU was concerned over the diverse approaches to integration, in particular Muslim communities, among its Member States. Examples of the lack of uniformity in approaches by Member States ranged from the UK embracing multiculturalism, to Germany and Spain doing little to integrate their Muslim communities, to France eschewing multiculturalism and offering citizenship to Muslims only if they embraced the French language and French norms (*Gallis* et al. 2005, p. 2). In September 2005 the EU Commission issued a document to be considered by EU leaders in formulating their Prevent-style strategies. It is explicit that extremism is not just religious extremism:

> The ideologies and propaganda have varied and included extremism of different types – whether from the extreme left or right, anarchist and religious or in many cases nationalist. All of these groups have tried to terrorise democratic states to concede political transformations by non-democratic means. … The Commission believes that there is no such thing as 'Islamic terrorism', nor 'catholic' nor 'red' terrorism. None of the religions or democratic political choices of European citizens tolerates, let alone justifies, terrorism. *The fact that some individuals unscrupulously attempt to justify their crimes in the name of a religion or an ideology cannot be allowed in any way and to any extent whatsoever to cast a shadow upon such a religion or ideology*. (Commission of the European Communities 2005, p. 11) [my emphasis]

As its Member States introduced Prevent strategies focused solely on violent extremism linked to Islam, the EU's wide definition of extremism got lost, resulting in the opposite effect they were intended to have. Having such a narrow focus not only alienated Muslim communities; inspired by their narrative, these strategies resulted in many Muslims joining Islamist terrorist groups (*Malik* 2008, pp. 97–100, *Duffy* 2009, p. 138).

## III. Radicalized, alienated, or marginalized towards violent extremism: it's a Muslim thing

As early Prevent strategies were introduced four or five years following the Al Qaeda attacks on the US in September 2001 (more commonly referred to as 9/11) and within a couple of years of the Al Qaeda-inspired bombings in Madrid in 2004 and London in 2005, this could explain why the early Prevent strategies ignored other forms of extremism and focused on Islamist extremism. With the US response to 9/11 being a declaration of war on terror, these three tragic events were all perceived as part of this ongoing war. As a result, this phrase (the War on Terror) constructed in the public imagination a cultural clash between the progressive West and a culturally resistant Islam (*Aly* et al 2015, p. 6). This concept was not just present in the public imagination; it was also present in government departments responsible for drafting early Prevent strategies as many initial prevent strategies singled out Muslim communities as being vulnerable to radicalization and susceptible to isolation and marginalization (*Aly* 2013, p. 10). By implicitly focusing on reforming the values and attitudes of British Muslims, the UK's initial Prevent strategy launched in June 2008 (*Briggs* 2010, p. 975) alienated many Muslims who objected to the stigmatizing effects of this focus. They saw Prevent demonizing them and holding all Muslims responsible for terrorism (*O'Toole* et al 2012, p. 377). This was evident in the well-meaning but misguided strategy document issued by the UK's Department for Communities and Local Government on preventing violent extremism where the aim was to win 'hearts and minds' (Communities and Local Government 2007). The document states that the challenge in tackling the threat posed by Islamist groups is not about a clash of civilizations or a struggle between Islam and 'the West' (Communities and Local Government 2007, p. 4). Following this claim, the rest of the document covers the potential threat emanating from the Muslim community. This is evident in the priorities it set in broadening the provision of citizenship education in supplementary schools and madrassahs (Communities and Local Government 2007, p. 5). This move to promote faith in the education system was necessary as violent extremists have exploited the lack of understanding of Islam with the aim of recruiting people to their cause. While this may be true in relation to Islamist groups, one can understand the concerns of the Muslim community in being singled out as there is no mention of other forms of extremist activity that poses a threat. As a result, by creating a distinct other, this strategy did not conclusively treat the problem of detachment of state from non-state (*Duffy* 2009, p. 139).

Between 2005–2010 Prevent and Resilience strategies' main focus was on countering the radicalizing of Muslims to Islamist causes. The 2006 UK Government's strategy document on countering international terrorism was clear that the principal threat it faced came from radicalized individuals using a distorted and unrepresentative interpretation of Islam to justify violence (HM Government 2006, p. 6). As a result, the whole document focuses on Islam and the role of Muslim communities in the UK. While this is only recent history, context has to be considered when looking at the official documentation during this period. The UK was not alone in only identifying the Islamist threat and discounting other forms of extremism that pose a potential threat. The US' 2003 strategy for combating terrorism has a goal of diminishing conditions terrorists seek to exploit. The strategy recognizes that factors such as poverty, deprivation, social disenfranchisement, and unresolved political disputes can result in individuals being vulnerable to being radicalized to terrorist causes. However, the US does not look internally how it can combat this threat, it looks externally through its foreign policy such as the US-Middle East partnerships as to how it can diminish these factors (US Government 2003, pp. 22–24). Another example is the Dutch 2007 Action plan on preventing the radicalization of people at risk of slipping away from Dutch society and democratic legal order and is not really generic in relation to extremism; its main focus is on young Dutch Muslims concerned about their identity as they look for guidance in what it is to be a Muslim in today's world (*Vidino* and *Brandon* 2012, p. 165). Taking such positions only serves to reinforce the Islamist extremist threat Western states faced at that time. This is due to Al Qaeda-inspired attacks carried out in Western states from 2001–2005, attacks carried out without warning and targeting civilians that resulted in high death rates.

## IV. Problems associated with radicalization and alienation

There are problems associated with states' defining radicalization. The UK government's 2006 strategy saw radicalization as:

> a process whereby certain experiences and events in a person's life cause them to become radicalised, to the extent of turning to violence to resolve perceived grievances, are critical to understanding how terrorist groups recruit new members and sustain support for their activities. (HM Government 2006, p. 9)

*Edwards* sees this definition as incoherent as to be radicalized is to both undergo a kind of influence and to be influenced to the point of turning to violence, adding that the majority of people that hold radical views are not involved in terrorism (*Edwards* 2016, p. 299). This is the problem with associating radicalization directly with violent extremism and discounting non-violent extremism. During the 1968–1997 Irish Troubles the UK sustained violent terrorist activity carried out by loyalist groups such as the Ulster Volunteer Force and republican groups such as the Provisional IRA that included attacks on hard and soft targets ranging from bombing 10 Downing Street, the British military, and civilians on both sides of the Irish Sea (*Omand* 2010, pp. 67–80). In both official government documents and academic literature on political violence and terrorism covering the Irish Troubles there is hardly any reference to radicalization (*Richards* 2011, p. 144).

*Richards* raises a valid point in relation to radicalization, asking whether the radicalized are only those who engage in violent extremism or whether it includes those who support violent extremism or understand why people become violent, or even those who disapprove of violence but have sympathy with various groups' causes or feel these groups have legitimate grievances (*Richards* 2011, p. 144). While these may be radical thoughts, it would be dangerous legal ground to assume that those who have sympathy for or feel that certain groups have legitimate grievances are violent extremists. *Edwards*' study shows that the majority of those who hold radical views are not involved in terrorism (*Edwards* 2016, p. 299). A 2010 Demos Report recommended that governments should distinguish between radicalization that leads to violence and radicalization that does not. The Report states that it is possible for people to read radical texts opposed to Western foreign policy or to support the principle of Islamist groups fighting in conflict zones in the Middle East while being vocal in denouncing Islamist inspired terrorism in Western countries. The Report adds that, provided their message does not involve intolerance or a threat to the democratic order, such individuals can become important allies if it leads to them becoming engaged in political and community activity (*Bartlett*, *Birdwell*, and *King* 2010, p. 38). As *Richards*' research found, such radicals have come into contact with individuals contemplating violent acts and successfully dissuaded them (*Richards* 2011, p. 148).

In identifying those vulnerable to being drawn into terrorism, the early Prevent strategies' first area of action to counter radicalization was in addressing structural problems with a firm emphasis on tackling disadvantage and inequalities, improving the educational performance, employment prospects, and housing conditions of Muslims (*Richards* 2011, p. 146). This is to help prevent individuals from being alienated. An alienated individual is one isolated from the machinations of civil society and can become subject to an extremist view whereby both the individual and the wider social structure come to see each other as a threat (*Duffy* 2009, p. 129). This process of alienation is compounded when the individual has an inability to interact with the social sphere, thereby seeing him- or herself as an 'island', separated from his or her fellows, unattached to them, having few bonds or ties of any enduring nature (*Duffy* 2009, p. 131). As a result, alienated individuals are more likely to engage with radical groups when they perceive themselves to be isolated from and not represented by social constructs of the broader community (*Aly* 2013, p. 5). State responses to alienation have been in promoting greater integration to deradicalize extremist religious groups. It is important to distinguish between extremist religio-political groups from religious groups who choose to separate themselves because they are orthodox. In some cases, religious groups may be illiberal and inward-looking as they try to sustain a way of life for their own members and to reproduce that culture or faith for future generations. For *Malik*, some of these orthodox groups may not adhere to the norms of a liberal democracy as they may choose to segregate themselves from mainstream society, and yet:

> A liberal democracy, as a matter of principle, has to respect the rights of individuals who choose to isolate themselves from mainstream society, but who respect the limits of law (*Malik* 2008, p. 89).

If a liberal democratic state denies isolated but law-abiding religious groups their way of life, rather than starting out with any political goals or interest in joining the liberal public sphere, they will then become politically active, posing an extremist threat (*Vermeulen* 2014, p. 290). As highlighted in this section, the problem with early Prevent/Resilience strategies was the main focus being on deradicalizing extremists within the Muslim community and not taking on the EU's 2005 recommendation of considering all forms of extremism. As a result, these early strategies led to a 'them and us' position of the Muslim community within wider society. Seeing how one of the watershed moments in the development of Prevent strategies encouraging greater integration was the 2005 London 7/7 bombing, the paradox is that the 7/7 bombers were UK born citizens who were socialized and schooled in the UK, and relatively highly educated (*Vermeulen* 2014, p. 290).

## V. The divisiveness of early prevent/resilience strategies related to identifying extremism: the example of the UK

*Gallis* et al.'s 2005 study into integration policies in Europe identified that government policies can have the opposite impact of what they are trying to achieve by actually contributing to alienation. The UK's battle for Muslim hearts and minds resulted in Muslims believing such policies were unfair against the Muslim community (*Gallis* et al. 2005, pp. 20–21). As the early Prevent strategies were mainly implicitly, but sometimes explicitly, focused on reforming the values and attitudes of British Muslims as a whole, they alienated many UK Muslims who objected to the stigmatization of these early strategies (*O'Toole, Nilsson*, and *Modood* 2012, p. 377). *Kundnani*'s 2009 empirical study on the impact of the UK's Prevent strategy reveals scathing views and responses from various members of the UK's Muslim community, resulting in a fairly overwhelming rejection of Prevent. What stands out in this study regarding the impact of the early Prevent strategies is the divisiveness it created. This ranged from where some mosques took advantage of Prevent money to resource their libraries, but once their members found how the library was financed, they did not get involved (*Kundnani* 2009, p. 25). Perhaps more disturbing in *Kundnani*'s report is the response to Prevent by younger Muslims. A manager in the voluntary sector said that his organization became opposed to dealing with Prevent as the young people it dealt with were not 'buying' into Muslims working against Muslims, with the worker saying:

> This will only lead to more extremism. [Prevent] has created mistrust and organisations like ours are consequently devalued. Our organisation is now under scrutiny because we are opposed to getting involved with the Prevent agenda (*Kundnani* 2009, p. 26).

A manager of a youth project that worked with Prevent said that young Muslims have a large degree of animosity towards the strategy and that there is a stigma attached to those who accept Prevent funding, seeing it as 'dirty money' (*Kundnani* 2009, p. 26).

While there is evidence revealing that one mistake with the UK's early Prevent strategies was in focusing on Muslim communities and the Islamic connection with terrorism, another mistake was in how it was policed. The main concern centres on allegations that Prevent is another method open to the police for intelligence gathering. *Kundnani*'s Report claims Prevent projects were being used to 'trawl for intelligence' and that many intelligence analysts were in place to do so. His research suggests a major objective of Prevent is to foster close relations between counterterrorism policing and non-policing local providers to facilitate information on individuals whose opinions are considered as extreme and on the local Muslim population in general, adding:

> The elaborate 'mapping' of Muslim communities is then used not just for the investigations of criminal activity but also to identify areas, groups and individuals that are 'are risk' of extremism (*Kundnani* 2009, p. 28).

Included in the examples he provides in support is UK Security Service (MI5) officers harassing Muslim youth workers to become informants and, in another project, Prevent funding that included free IT facilities at a youth centre to enable the police to monitor the websites people were visiting (*Kundnani* 2009, p. 29). Another incident that damaged the role of the police involvement in Prevent was the evidence presented to the House of Commons Communities and Local Government Committee's inquiry into preventing violent extremism that a West Midlands Counter-Terrorism Unit officer (who are normally working in the Pursue strand of the UK's CONTEST programmes that is involved in investigation and arrest of terrorist suspects) was permanently seconded to manage Prevent work in the Birmingham area, raising further suspicions about surveillance, transparency, accountability, and local democracy (House of Commons 2010, p. 12). This led to a Birmingham community activist to comment that this appointment was controversial, leading to the suspicion that his involvement in Prevent projects was security led as well as being intelligence led (*O'Toole* et al. 2012, p. 378). In response to this allegation, Birmingham City Council rejected any notions of secrecy in its approach. The Council said that West Midlands Police Security and Partnership officers work within communities as part of the Counter-Terrorism Unit to assist in delivering the Prevent Agenda to provide an overt, visible, and accessible link between covert counterterrorism function, the police, communities, and partners (House of Commons 2010, p. 12).

In 2009 media reporting brought these suspicions of the role of the police in Prevent into the public arena. The BBC's *Panorama* programme reported intelligence gathering was being carried out by the police in Prevent (*Kundnani* 2009, p. 28), and the newspaper *The Guardian* made claims that intelligence was being gathered as part of the Prevent programme, saying:

> Serious concerns that the Prevent programme is being used at least in part to 'spy' on Muslims have been voiced not just by Islamic groups, but youth workers, teachers and others. Some involved in the programme have told *The Guardian* of their fears that they are being co-opted into spying (*Dodd* 2009).

The direct involvement of the police in core services delivered by local authorities, the police role in funding decisions, and the key Prevent function of mapping Muslim communities muddied perceptions about neighbourhood policing. This led to questions being asked if Prevent was directly tied to background intelligence gathering. This suspicion by the wider community was damaging the police role in Prevent. As *Birt* observed:

> It has raised questions about how to preserve relationships of trust, confidentiality and professional integrity for those working with disadvantaged communities, and particularly with young Muslim people. … [I]t has raised questions of police interference in the political relationships between local authorities and Muslim communities (*Birt* 2009, p. 56).

While the police response to the negative media reporting on Prevent was that it was not a 'Trojan Horse' dedicated to intelligence gathering but rather a strategy aimed at blocking radicalization and reducing the supply of terror recruits (BBC 2009), the damage to and suspicion of the police's role in Prevent had been done. The residue of this damage has not disappeared with the recently revised Prevent strategy. In 2015 a report in *The Guardian* had a former senior Metropolitan Police senior officer claiming that Prevent is a 'toxic brand' that is 'widely mistrusted' (*Halliday* and *Dodd* 2015). Although this claim was denied by the president of the National Association of Muslim Police, these suspicions remain and appear to be deepening. As the UK Government has revised the Prevent, placed a duty on staff in public bodies to report those they feel are vulnerable to being drawn into terrorism on a statutory footing under section 26 of the Counter-Terrorism and Security Act 2015, and is proposing to introduce a Counter-Extremism and Safeguarding Bill, the role of the police is key in ensuring Prevent is successful. It is now not simply a case for damage limitation; rather, this myth and damaging suspicion must be dispelled and clarity given regarding the role of the police in Prevent.

## VI. Current prevent/resilience strategies

In 2011 the UK Government revised the Prevent strategy with three main objectives:

1. Respond to the ideological challenge of terrorism and the threat faced by those who promote it;
2. Prevent people from being drawn into terrorism and ensure that they are given appropriate advice and support;

3. Work with sectors and institutions where there are risks of radicalisation that need to be addressed (HM Government 2011, p. 7).

Compared to the 2007 version, there were key changes in the 2011 Prevent strategy. The term 'violent extremism' was abandoned with the focus on radicalization being defined as the process by which a person comes to support terrorism and forms of extremism leading to terrorism (*Edwards* 2016, pp. 302–303, HM Government 2011, p. 107). To assist in assessing radicalization, the 2011 Prevent strategy provides a definition of extremism, which is discussed in more details below. Regarding the accusations that Prevent funding was 'dirty money', the 2011 Prevent strategy is clear it will not fund or support organizations that hold extremist views or support terrorist-related activity. As a result, there is an obligation on local authorities and other public bodies to publish details of expenditure in order to introduce greater levels of transparency (HM Government 2011 p. 35). While the UK 2011 strategy looks at the wider aspects of extremism, Australia's 2010 Resilience strategy still focused on resisting the development of any form of violent extremism (Commonwealth of Australia 2010, p. 65). This position had not changed in 2015, where the Australian government's document on strengthening Resilience states that Australia's task is to limit the spread and influence of violent extremist idea (Commonwealth of Australia 2015, p. 7). There are similarities in the developments of the strategy in Australia and the UK, such as having an emphasis on identifying and diverting at-risk individuals, and government agencies and communities working to reduce the driver of radicalization (Commonwealth of Australia 2015, p. 10).

The UK's 2011 Prevent strategy addresses the issues related to the connection between the police and intelligence gathering. Acknowledging that the police collection of information for community mapping was confused with covert operation activity that led to allegations based on a misunderstanding about the process for supporting vulnerable people (HM Government 2011, p. 31), the strategy document clearly states:

> we emphasise that it must be a guiding principle of prevent that the programme is not used as a means for covert spying on people or communities. We do not believe that has been the case. It must not be. Data collected about people for the purposes of Prevent must be necessary and proportionate (HM Government 2011, p. 32).

This point is reinforced in the 2011 CONTEST document that states the relationship between Prevent and Pursue (work to investigate and disrupt terrorist activity) must be carefully managed as Prevent is not a means for spying or for other covert activity (HM Government 2011a, p. 63). Unfortunately, this message is still not being believed. The suspicion that Prevent is another method of intelligence gathering for counterterrorism agencies with the programme targeting black and Asian communities has increased with the UK government's placing on specified authorities (local government, prisons, education, health and social care, and, the police)[1] the obligation to prevent people being drawn into terrorism on a statutory footing.

## VII. Placing the UK's Prevent strategy on statutory footing: The impact of section 26 Counter-Terrorism and Security Act 2015

Causing great consternation with many of the specified authorities listed in Schedule 6 of the Counter-Terrorism and Security Act 2015, especially among staff employed in education, is determining what the parameters are under their section 26 obligation. This has led to uncertainty as to what the level of behaviour or words expressed has to be before determining if it should be reported to their local Prevent team. In addition to this, staff employed in the specified authorities appear to have a degree of consternation regarding their section 26 obligation. An example of this is due to teachers' fear of falling foul of section 26, which has led to some referrals, resulting in sensationalist coverage in national media, giving a negative image of the role and work carried out by Prevent teams. Recent examples include an incident in December 2015 when a ten-year-old boy from Lancashire wrote in school that he lived in a 'terrorist house' (BBC 2016), a four-year-old boy from Luton who mispronounced 'cucumber' saying 'cooker-bomb' and drawing a man cutting something with a knife (BBC 2016a), and an eight-year-old boy who said he wanted to fight terrorists after learning of the plight of Syrian refugees (*Williams* 2016). Negative media headlines like these and those related to the counter-radicalization strategy in general damage the good work carried out by Prevent teams and those they work with. The accelerant resulting in strident opinions decrying Prevent has been the section 26 requirement that authorities take preventative action. As a result, the education sector has witnessed the formation of pressure groups and movements such as 'students not suspects' (*McVeigh* 2015), 'Educators not Informants', and 'Education not Surveillance' (Institute of Race Relations 2015). All of these groups were formed with the aim to lobby for the repeal of the section 26 requirement placed on education establishments. Concerns related to section 26 are the degree of uncertainty as to what factors need to be present to ascertain if words or action amount to extremism and a misunderstanding by many staff members of authorities as to their obligation and the primary purpose under Prevent.

---

[1] These are the specified authorities listed in Schedule 6 Counter-Terrorism and Security Act 2015.

## VIII. Home Office policy: October 2015 Counter-Extremism Strategy

In October 2015 the UK Government published its latest Counter-Extremism Strategy that along with outlining the Government's approach to countering extremist ideology, building partnerships with those opposed to extremism, and building cohesive communities, the document provides a definition of non-violent extremism. The document mentions how non-violent extremism is an active [act of] opposition to British values. In itself, the term 'British values' is not a term which helps staff in the authorities to determine if behaviour is extremist. However, in the Strategy document it has been defined as behaviour which is vocal or active opposition to:

> our fundamental values, including democracy, the rule of law, individual liberty and the mutual respect and tolerance of different faiths and beliefs. We also include in our definition of extremism calls for the death of members of our armed forces, whether in this country or overseas (HM Government 2015, p. 9).

The document discusses hate crime and issues around radicalizing processes and, while stressing that the strategy is not aimed solely at extreme Islamist ideology, the group Islamic State is mentioned referring to the group as a

> grotesque manifestation of an extreme Islamist narrative which seeks to impose a new Islamic State governed by a harsh interpretation of Shari'a as state law and totally rejects liberal values such as democracy, the rule of law and quality (HM Government 2015, p. 22).

While making the point that the current Prevent strategy addresses all forms of terrorism and non-violent extremism, the House of Commons February 2016 overview of the UK's counter-extremism policy reinforces the UK Government's definition of non-violent extremism as that defined above, only changing the first part to it being opposition to 'fundamental British values' (*Dawson* 2016, p. 9). It is debatable if this definition provides sufficient guidance to the authorities the section 26 obligation applies to. There are three parts to this definition that potentially can cause uncertainty, resulting in anxiety with individuals as to when action should be taken to report events to Prevent teams. They are 'fundamental British values', 'democracy', and 'rule of law'.

This leads to the question: what are fundamental British values? Not only does this phrase immediately discount one of the states that make up the UK, Northern Ireland, it is [also] purely a subjective term. Due to the diversity of the UK population, what amounts to British values will vary from person to person based on factors such as their geographical location or the community and socio-economic conditions they live in. As stated in the Counter-Extremism Strategy, Britain has been built on a successful multi-racial, multi-faith democracy that is open, diverse, and welcoming (HM Government 2015, p. 9). With such diversity in its population, there will be a diversity of opinions as to what constitutes British values. Another problem is where terrorist ideologies go uncontested and are not exposed to free, open, and balanced debate and challenge, it positions these ideologies as inferior and lacking when confronted by 'British values' (*Martin* 2014, p. 71). Should a person be highly critical of the UK's foreign policy towards Muslim states in the Middle East, the conflict in Syria, or legislation and policies related to targeting certain groups or communities in the UK, this could be perceived as challenging British values. As such, just this phrase can be divisive as such views could potentially be seen as a disassociation from Britishness and, as *Martin* states, come 'to be understood as representing a potential problem for the future' (*Martin* 2014, p. 68). The group Cage that supports those detained under terrorism legislation sees using terms like 'British values' as an Orwellian concept that attacks basic rights, saying in relation to the definition of extremism:

> 'Our values' and 'our way of life' is the language of alienation, designed to marginalise particular communities. The [UK] government is perpetuating the very same 'us v them' narrative it denounces in its Prevent strategy (*Cage* 2016).

Emphasizing 'British values' can be counter-productive, as *Sedgwick* points out, where attempts at cohesion will fail if cohesion is underpinned by integration that includes a neo-nationalist cultural agenda as this may increase support for messages that are radical in security terms (*Sedgwick* 2010, p. 490). Just this one phrase in the definition has the potential to undo both the Prevent and the Counter-Extremism Strategy's primary objective.

Regarding democracy and rule of law, while not wanting to delve too deep into a constitutional debate, it is worth noting that these terms are not as axiomatic as one may first think. For *Elliott* and *Thomas*, the rule of law is one of the most elusive of constitutional principles where most people agree that it is a good thing while disagreeing as to what it means (*Elliott* and *Thomas* 2015, p. 63). They add that

> the rule of law is little more than a rhetorical device: someone might seek to add gravitas to their support for or criticism of a given legal provision by saying that it does or does not comply with the rule of law, but that is as far as it goes (*Elliott* and *Thomas* 2015, p. 50).

For *Loveland*, the rule of law has no single meaning and it is not a legal rule but a moral principle, which means different things to different people (*Loveland* 2012, p. 50). For *Tomkins* it is only in legal philosophy that confusion arises over rule of law. However, in public law the rule of law has a clear meaning as it governs not just citizens, but the executive as the rule of law provides that the executive cannot do anything without there being a legal authority permitting its actions (*Tomkins* 2008, p. 78).

This leads to another contentious issue in the UK's democracy where the executive is supreme (except in matters of EU law) (*Kaczorowska* 2011, pp. 341–342). Democracy is a taken-for-granted element of the UK constitution, and it has no single meaning (*Loveland* 2012, p. 50) as there are differing conclusions about how democratic the UK actually is (*Loveland* 2012, pp. 4–5). This debate has led to calls for changes to democratic processes in the UK, including the call for a written constitution that would achieve a special place in the legal system where any changes would be constitutional [and] not political issues, thereby making it more difficult to alter it (*Brazier* 2008, p. 161). With these debates resulting in a divergence of legal and political reasoning as to what amounts to democracy and the rule of law, it makes it harder for those employed in [the] authorities to determine if what they are witnessing amounts to extremism at a level where they feel they should take action and report it to Prevent teams. It is submitted that to aid those operating under section 26 (1) of the Counter-Terrorism and Security Act 2015, they need a statutory definition of extremism with possibly an accompanying Codes of Practice like that seen with the Police and Criminal Evidence Act 1984 and the Regulation of Investigatory Powers Act 2000 to assist them in this task.

## IX. UK's Counter-Extremism and Safeguarding Bill

In an attempt to address this issue, the UK Government released in 2015 that during the 2015/16 parliamentary session they would be introducing a Counter-Extremism Bill, which would have introduced new powers to ban extremist organizations that promote hatred and draw people into extremism (HM Government 2015, p. 34).

Following the UK-EU referendum result in June 2016 where the electorate voted by small majority to leave the EU, the subsequent Brexit negotiations has resulted in reducing Parliamentary time to introduce a number of Bills. As the UK Parliament Report in July 2016 states, the Counter-Extremism and Safeguarding Bill has become a victim with the Bill being stalled for the moment. The Report adds that current UK legislation including the Public Order Act 1986 and the Terrorism Act 2000 (as amended) forms a sufficient legal framework for, '...dealing with people who promote violence' (UK Parliament 2016). The only UK proposal related to terrorism is the Counter-Terrorism and Border Security Bill introduced in 2018. This Bill proposes among other areas to introduce offences related to supporting proscribed groups, publication of terrorist related images and obtaining or viewing internet images and documents related to extremism and terrorism, the Bill does not really deal with extremism per se and how to support those who are vulnerable to being drawn towards terrorism. No doubt the terrorist attacks in the UK and the rest of Europe in 2017 was instrumental in the UK feeling the requirement to introduce this Bill. As the UK Government has attempted to introduce a Counter-Extremism Bill maybe when Parliamentary time allows, such a Bill will contain those in the 2015 Bill and will be expected to include:

1. Banning orders for extremist organizations which seek to undermine democracy or use hate speech in public places;
2. Disruption orders to restrict people who seek to radicalize young people;
3. Powers to close premises where extremists seek to influence others (Gov UK 2015).

Crucial to this legislation being successful in countering non-violent extremism will be the legal definition of what actions amount to extremism. The UK government's press release in May 2015 only indicated that it will be based on British values (Gov UK) which, as discussed above, is problematic as this is a very subjective term that lacks any legal certainty. When examining other Westerns states' legislation there appears to be no comparator from which to draft a legal definition of non-violent extremism due to the fact that many states have no legal definition, be it in the US (US Homeland Security 2016), Canada (Canadian Security Intelligence Service 2016), or Australia (Australian Government Attorney-General's Department 2016). One of the few states that has legislated in this area and possesses a legal definition of extremism is the Russian Federation. According to Russian Federal Law, non-violent extremism is defined as

> the will to forcibly change the constitutional system; incitement to social, racial, national or religious discord; propaganda of racial inferiority of a nation and superiority of another; encouragement and justification of terrorist activities and participation therein; preventing people from the realization of their rights; calls for extremist acts; circulation of extremist materials; as well as their storage and production with a view of such dissemination; financing of such actions and any contribution thereto (Russian Federal law).[2]

In 2006 amendments to this definition were introduced to include into the law activities taken for political and ideological hatred.[3] This is quite a comprehensive definition and one that provides a high degree of legal certainty that not only the courts can apply in their interpretation of the statute to cases heard before them but that can be easily understood and applied by citizens. It is not argued that the UK incorporates the Russian definition verbatim into the Counter-Extremism and Safeguarding Bill, rather it introduces a more workable definition that contains minimal subjective or disputed terminology such as 'British values', 'democracy', or 'rule of law'. As seen in the Russian definition it refers to the constitutional system rather than democracy and covers a broad spectrum of activities, including the prevention of people realizing their rights. While the current UK definition contained in the Prevent strategy mentions opposition to mutual respect and tolerance of different faiths, the Russian definition covers storage and circulation of extremist materials. While the UK currently covers these activities within both the 2006 Terrorism Act and sections 57 and 58 of the Terrorism Act 2000, these statutory provisions are more in line with the work carried out by staff involved in Pursue rather than Prevent.

In his 2015 report, the Independent Reviewer of Terrorism Legislation in the UK, *David Anderson* QC, raises concerns regarding the Bill. While he covers a number of issues related to the civil orders the UK Government has indicated will be contained in the Bill, *Anderson* also has concerns related to the definition of

---

[2] No. 114 (25 July 2002).

[3] Article 24 Federal Law No.35-FZ of 6 March 2006 on Counteraction of Terrorism.

non-violent extremism, in particular the range of political and religious views, and whether it includes views critical of the government, adding that the definition must be intelligible, clear, and predictable, and that its objectives are consistent with the European Convention on Human Rights (ECHR). One concern in introducing legislation related to extremism is the impact it will have on the right to freedom of expression[4] and right to freedom of thought, conscience, and religion.[5] As *Anderson* states, legislation must be compatible with the ECHR, but it needs to go further than that. It is of supreme importance that any legislation be compatible with the European Union's Charter of Fundamental Rights and Freedoms (CFRF). The UK has signed in both of these instruments to protect these rights so it is important when drafting the Counter-Extremism and Safeguarding Bill that it complies especially under the CFRF. The UK and other EU Member States and EU bodies themselves have found through decisions of the European Court of Justice (ECJ), in particular the *Digital Rights* case,[6] that legislation can be struck down where it violates among other legal instruments the CFRF. It is important that freedom of expression is kept inviolate as this is a British value contained in the Counter-Extremism Strategy provided it is non-violent. This principle is one that the UK courts will defend as seen in the Court of Appeal decision in *Redmond-Bate v DPP*[7] where it was held that freedom only to speak inoffensively is not worth having. In addition to the Bill there should be an accompanying Codes of Practice to assist staff in the relevant authorities under the section 26 Counter-Terrorism and Security Act 2015 obligation in applying the legislation to behaviour they suspect to be extremist.

## X. Conclusion

As stated in the overview of the counter-extremism policy:

> Prevent needs to deal with extremism where terrorism draws on extremist ideas: and where people who are extremists are being drawn to terrorist activity (*Dawson* 2016, p. 7).

Prevent has received a number of negative comments ranging from the media, including media outlets not normally associated with critiquing action taken to deal with extremism (*Johnston* 2015), lobby groups (*Qureshi* 2015), even the independent reviewer of terrorism legislation. In January 2016 *Anderson* submitted written and oral evidence to the Home Office Select Committee where he mentions there

---

4 Article 10 European Convention on Human Rights, article 11 EU's Charter of Fundamental Rights and Freedoms.

5 Article 9 European Convention on Human Rights, article 10 EU's Charter of Fundamental Rights and Freedoms.

6 [2014] EUECJ C-293/12, [2014] 3 WLR 1607.

7 [1999] EWHC Admin 732.

being a lack of confidence in Prevent. He says the programme is suffering from a widespread problem of perception, particularly in relation to the statutory duty on schools in relation to non-violent extremism where aspects of the programme are ineffective or are being applied in an insensitive or discriminatory manner (*Anderson* 2016). Yet the main function of Prevent is to prevent people from being drawn into terrorism and ensure they are given the appropriate advice and support. This entails various agencies from the criminal justice system, education, and health and faith organizations working together when the needs of radicalization need to be addressed. To aid this work it is important that it is carried out within a legislative framework such as the Counter-Extremism and Safeguarding Bill. Vitally important is that the definition of non-violent extremism is carefully drafted to enable the work of Prevent to be applied in a non-discriminatory and effective manner. To sum up, the main aim of Prevent is not what many pressure groups like the Northern Police Monitoring Project espouse, that of criminalizing blacks and Asians in UK society (The Northern Police Mentoring Project 2016). The aim of Prevent is to protect all in society from terrorism as well as individuals who are susceptible to being drawn into the terrorists' extremist narrative.

## Bibliography

*Aly, A.* (2013) The policy response to home-grown terrorism: reconceptualising Prevent and Resilience as collective resistance. Journal of Policing, Intelligence and Counter Terrorism 8(1) 2–18.

*Aly, A./Balbi, A./Jacques, C.* (2015) Rethinking countering violent extremism: implanting the role of civil society. Journal of Policing, Intelligence and Counter Terrorism 10(1) 3–13.

*Anderson, D.* (2016) Supplementary written evidence submitted by David Anderson QC (Independent Reviewer of Terrorism Legislation) retrieved from http://data.parliament.uk/writtenevidence/committeeevidence.svc/evidencedocument/home-affairs-committee/countering-extremism/written/27920.pdf [last visited 1 January 2019].

*Bartlett, J./Birdwell, J./King, M.* (2010) The edge of violence: a radical approach to extremism. London: Demos retrieved from http://www.demos.co.uk/files/Edge_of_Violence_-_web.pdf [last visited 1 January 2019].

BBC (2009) UK to shift anti-terror strategy. BBC News, 16 February 2009, retrieved from http://news.bbc.co.uk/1/hi/uk/7889631.stm [last visited 1 January 2019].

– (2016) Lancashire 'terrorist house' row 'not a spelling mistake'. BBC News 20th January 2016 retrieved from http://www.bbc.co.uk/news/uk-england-lancashire-35354061 [last visited 1 January 2019].

– (2016a) Radicalisation fear over cucumber drawing boy, 4. BBC News 11 March 2016 retrieved from http://www.bbc.co.uk/news/uk-england-beds-bucks-herts-35783659 [last visited 1 January 2019].

*Birt, Y.* (2009) Promoting Virulent Envy? The RUSI Journal, 154(4) 52–58.

*Brazier, R.* (2008) Constitutional Reform: reshaping the British Political System Oxford. Oxford University Press.

*Briggs, R.* (2010) Community engagement for counterterrorism: lessons for the United Kingdom. International Affairs 86(4) 971–981.

*Cage* (2016) Cage's response to Counter-Extremism and Safeguarding Bill. Cage Blog 19th May 2016 available at http://www.cageuk.org/article/cages-response-to-counter-extremism-and-safeguarding-bill/ [last visited 1 January 2019].

Commission of the European Communities (2005) Terrorist recruitment: addressing the factors contributing to violent radicalisation, Brussels 21 September 2005, COM(2005) 313 final retrieved from http://eur-lex.europa.eu/legal-content/EN/TXT/PDF/?uri=CELEX:52005DC0313&from=EN [last visited 1 January 2019].

Commonwealth of Australia (2010) Counter-Terrorism White Paper: Securing Australia – protecting our Community, Canberra: Department of the Prime Minister and the Cabinet retrieved from https://www.asio.gov.au/img/files/counter-terrorism_white_paper.pdf [last visited 1 January 2019].

– (2015) Australia's Counter-Terrorism Strategy: Strengthening our Resilience, retrieved from https://www.nationalsecurity.gov.au/Media-and-publications/Publications/Documents/Australias-Counter-Terrorism-Strategy-2015.pdf [last visited 1 January 2019].

Communities and Local Government (2007) 'Preventing violent extremism – winning hearts and minds' London: Department for Communities and Local Government retrieved from http://resources.cohesioninstitute.org.uk/Publications/Documents/Document/DownloadDocumentsFile.aspx?recordId=133&file=PDFversion [last visited 1 January 2019].

*Dawson, J.* (2016) Counter-Extremism policy: an overview. Briefing paper 7738, 5th February 2016 retrieved from http://researchbriefings.files.parliament.uk/documents/CBP-7238/CBP-7238.pdf [last visited 1 January 2019].

*Dodd, V.* (2009) Government anti-terrorism strategy 'spies' on innocent: data on politics, sexual activity and religion gathered by government. The Guardian 16th October 2009, retrieved from http://www.theguardian.com/uk/2009/oct/16/anti-terrorism-strategy-spies-innocents [last visited 1 January 2019].

*Duffy, D.* (2009) Alienated radicals and detached deviants: what do the lessons of the 1970 Falls Curfew and the alienation-radicalisation hypothesis mean for current British approaches to counter-terrorism? Policy Studies 30(2), 127–142.

*Edwards, P.* (2016) Closure through Resilience: the Case of Prevent. Studies in Conflict & Terrorism 39(4), 292–307.

*Elliott, M./Thomas, R.* (2015) Public Law. 2d edition. Oxford: Oxford University Press.

*Gallis, P.* et al. (2005) Muslims in Europe: Integration Polices in Selected Countries, 18th November 2005 Congressional Research Service. The Library of Congress retrieved from http://www.investigativeproject.org/documents/testimony/332.pdf [last visited 1 January 2019].

*Halliday, J./Dodd, V.* (2015) UK anti-radicalisation Prevent strategy a 'toxic brand'. The Guardian, 9th March 2015, retrieved from http://www.theguardian.com/uk-news/2015/mar/09/anti-radicalisation-prevent-strategy-a-toxic-brand [last visited 1 January 2019].

HM Government (2011) Prevent Strategy, Cm 8092, London: The Stationary Office.

– (2011a) CONTEST: The United Kingdom's Strategy for Countering Terrorism, London: The Stationary Office.

– (2015) Counter-Extremism Strategy Cm9148, retrieved from https://www.gov.uk/government/publications/counter-extremism-strategy [last visited 1 January 2019].

House of Commons (2010) Preventing Violent Extremism – Sixth Report of Session 2009–10 HC 65, London: Stationary Office Limited retrieved from http://www.publications.parliament.uk/pa/cm200910/cmselect/cmcomloc/65/65.pdf [last visited 1 January 2019].

Institute of Race Relations (2015) Education not Surveillance. 22 October 2015 retrieved from http://www.irr.org.uk/news/education-not-surveillance/ [last visited 1 January 2019].

*Johnston, P.* (2015) Laws against 'extremism' risk criminalising us all. Daily Telegraph 28th September 2015 retrieved from http://www.telegraph.co.uk/news/uknews/law-and-order/11897355/Laws-against-extremism-risk-criminalising-us-all.html [last visited 1 January 2019].

*Klausen, K.* (2015) Tweeting the Jihad: Social Media Networks of Western Foreign Fighters in Syria and Iraq. Studies in Conflict & Terrorism 38(1), 1–22, DOI: 10.1080/1057610X.2014.974948.

*Kundnani, A.* (2009) Spooked! How not to prevent violent extremism, London: Institute of race relations retrieved from http://www.irr.org.uk/pdf2/spooked.pdf [last visited 1 January 2019].

*Kaczorowska, A.* (2011) European Law. 2nd edition. London: Routledge.

*Loveland, I.* (2012) Constitutional law, Administrative Law and Human Rights: A critical introduction. 6th edition. Oxford: Oxford University Press.

*Malik, M.* (2008) Engaging with Extremists. International Review 22(1), 85–104.

*Martin, T.* (2014) Governing an unknowable future: the politics of Britain's Prevent policy. Critical Studies on Terrorism 7(1) 62–78.

*McVeigh, K.* (2015) NUS fights back against government's 'chilling' counter-radicalisation strategy. The Guardian, retrieved from http://www.theguardian.com/education/2015/sep/02/nus-fights-back-against-governments-chilling-counter-radicalisation-strategy [last visited 1 January 2019].

*Omand, D.* (2012) Securing the State. Oxford: Oxford University Press.

*O'Toole, T./DeHanas, D./Modood, T.* (2012) Balancing tolerance, security and Muslim engagement in the United Kingdom: the impact of the 'Prevent' agenda. Critical Studies on Terrorism 5(3), 373–389.

*Qureshi, A.* (2015) Responding to David Cameron's 'clash of civilisation' speech. 22 July 2015 retrieved from http://www.cageuk.org/article/responding-david-cameron%E2%80%99s-%E2%80%98clash-civilisations%E2%80%99-speech [last visited 1 January 2019].

*Richards, A.* (2011) The problem with 'radicalization': the remit of 'Prevent' and the need to refocus on terrorism in the UK. International Affairs 86(4), 143–152.

*Rogers, P.* (2008) Contesting and preventing terrorism: On the development of the UK strategic policy on radicalisation and community resilience. Journal of Policing, Intelligence and Counter Terrorism 3(2), 38–61.

*Sedgwick, M.* (2010) The Concept of Radicalisation as a Source of Confusion Terrorism and Political Violence 22(4) 479–494.

*Staniforth, A.* (2014) Preventing Terrorism and Violent Extremism. Oxford: Oxford University Press.

*Tomkins, A.* (2003) Public Law. Oxford: Oxford University Press.

UK Parliament (2016) Counter-extremism summary, 21st July 2016, retrieved from https://publications.parliament.uk/pa/jt201617/jtselect/jtrights/105/10503.htm [last visited 1 January 2019].

US Government (2003) National Strategy For Combating Terrorism, retrieved from https://www.cia.gov/news-information/cia-the-war-on-terrorism/Counter_Terrorism_Strategy.pdf [last visited 1 January 2019].

US Homeland Security (2015) website retrieved from https://www.dhs.gov/topic/countering-violent-extremism [last visited 1 January 2019].

*Vermeulen, F.* (2014) Suspect Communities – Targeting Violent Extremism at the Local Level: Polices of Engagement in Amsterdam, Berlin, and London. Terrorism and Political Violence 26(3), 286–306.

*Vidino, L./Brandon, J.* (2012) Europe's experience in countering radicalisation: approaches and challenges. Journal of Policing, Intelligence and Counter Terrorism 7(2) 163–179.

*Williams, A.* (2016) Father's fury at school who called in social services because son, eight, said he wanted to 'fight terrorist' after seeing Syrian refugees on the news. Daily Mail 2 March 2016 retrieved from http://www.dailymail.co.uk/news/article-3472655/Father-s-fury-school-calls-social-services-son-8-told-teachers-wanted-fight-terrorists-watching-news-report-Syrian-refugee-crisis.html [last visited 1 January 2019].

# Transition to Terrorism: Developments in U.S. Terrorism Legislation from Law Enforcement to Intelligence Gathering

## The lasting impact of shifting paradigms on the criminal justice system

*Steven W. Becker**

This article will provide an overview of the development of terrorism legislation in the United States from a traditional law enforcement approach to an intelligence-gathering model, briefly summarize the scope of such legislation, and address the permanent impact that this paradigmatic change has had upon the criminal justice system, as well as upon surveillance methods in anticipation thereof. To set the stage for this discussion, a real-life case exemplar will be provided as an introduction to demonstrate the real-life effects of such a shift in strategy from a practitioner's perspective.

# I. Introduction

Not long after the September 11, 2001 terrorist attacks in the United States, the author initiated a lawsuit under the federal Privacy Act[1] against the Federal Bureau of Investigation (FBI) on behalf of one of the world's most-renowned Arab-American legal scholars, *M. Cherif Bassiouni*, a Nobel Peace Prize-nominated law professor who was an expert in both international criminal law and human rights law.[2] Just months before the attacks, the professor learned that the FBI had maintained a secret dossier on him for over 30 years.[3] The file, which was retrievable by his name, contained excerpts from a speech the professor gave to an Arab organization in the United States in 1973 as well as several FBI memoranda pertaining to his lawful, constitutionally protected First Amendment activities.[4]

---

* Founding Member, Law Office of Steven W. Becker LLC, Chicago, Illinois USA; Deputy Secretary General, International Association of Penal Law (France).

1 5 U.S.C. § 552a (2012 & Supp. II 2014).

2 See *Bassiouni v. FBI*, 436 F.3d 712, 714, 718 (7th Cir. 2006).

3 *Ibid.* at 718.

4 *Id.* at 718–719.

More significantly, however, the dossier contained documents describing certain "terrorist" organizations, one of which was listed among the U.S. State Department's list of designated Foreign Terrorist Organizations.[5] These records pertaining to the terrorist organizations, however, contained no reference whatsoever to the professor. Rather, by inclusion in his personal file, the documents wrongfully implied that the professor associated with such organizations. In this regard, the appellate court pointed out that

> [n]one of the record memoranda concluded that Mr. *Bassiouni* was a member of a terrorist organization. Mr. *Bassiouni* denies any such membership, and the FBI concedes that it does not suspect him of ties to terrorist groups.[6]

The purpose of the lawsuit was to expunge the offending records from the FBI's files and to enjoin the FBI from continuing to maintain such prejudicial records in a name-retrievable file pursuant to the Privacy Act's "law enforcement activity exception," which provides that an agency that maintains a system of records

> shall … maintain no record describing how any individual exercises rights guaranteed by the First Amendment … unless pertinent to and within the scope of an authorized law enforcement activity.[7]

As detailed below, the professor's case vividly highlights in fluorescent hues the seismic changes wrought by the September 11th attacks in three critical areas of the law: (1) predictability, (2) substantive law, and (3) procedural law. The professor's case is unique because the records upon which the case was based pre-dated the attacks by decades, but the case was, unfortunately for the professor, litigated in the immediate wake of the tragic events that unfolded in 2001 in an atmosphere thick with the heightened fear of terrorism and concerns over national security. As one commentator remarked,

> It is worth noting that while Bassiouni was decided post-9/11, the case began before the attacks, and the records in question related to activities which took place long before 9/11. It is hardly a stretch to believe courts would be at least as deferential, if not more so, in cases involving national security related information post-9/11.[8]

The statutory intricacies of the case are not relevant to the present discussion; however, let it suffice to say that the federal district court eventually ruled in favor of the FBI, and the case was appealed to the Seventh Circuit Court of Appeals in Chicago.

First of all, one of the great hallmarks of the law should be consistency, whereby the outcome of a case should be reasonably predictable based on legal precedent. Prior to the professor's case and before the September 11th attacks, the Seventh Circuit decided another case under the Privacy Act's law enforcement activity ex-

---

[5] *Id.* at 719.

[6] *Id.*

[7] 5 U.S.C. § 552a(e)(7) (2012). For an in-depth analysis of the law enforcement activity exception, see *Becker*, 50 DePaul L. Rev. 675–736 (2000).

[8] *Sherman*, 19 St. Thomas L. Rev. 286 (2006).

ception on virtually identical grounds in favor of the plaintiffs.[9] Therein, an executive agency maintained prejudicial records in the name-retrievable files of three brothers, although the agency's investigation had been terminated.[10] The records, various newspaper articles and a book advertisement, made no mention of the brothers but implied that the brothers associated with the individuals mentioned in the records.[11] The Seventh Circuit ordered that the records be expunged from the brothers' files because they implicated the brothers' First Amendment rights of association.[12]

Yet, in deciding the professor's case, the Seventh Circuit simply cast aside its prior precedent, instead relying on the FBI's assertion that

> [b]ecause of the nature of [the FBI's] investigative activities [concerning terrorism], and because of the breadth of Mr. Bassiouni's contacts with the Middle East, the FBI anticipates that it will continue to receive information about Mr. Bassiouni in the future, [and] [t]he Bureau's file on Mr. Bassiouni will provide context for evaluating that new information.[13]

This, of course, is the very retention of records unrelated to a current law enforcement investigation that the Privacy Act was enacted to prevent. Thus, the advent of the FBI's shift from a law enforcement agency to an anti-terrorism organization engaged in the collection of intelligence data dramatically altered the attitude of the courts and, accordingly, the predictability as to the outcome of such cases.

Secondly, the fundamental alteration in the nature of the FBI's function in the fight against terrorism resulted in a clear change in the substantive law, at least in so far as it is interpreted by the courts. For example, prior to the professor's case, the law was clearly established that an agency could not maintain First Amendment records on a citizen unless it was currently involved in a law enforcement investigation vis-à-vis the litigant;[14] otherwise, the file could be utilized as a political, religious, or ideological dossier for future harassment or scrutiny by the government. Yet, as a result of the FBI's role change in terrorism investigations, the Seventh Circuit suddenly granted the agency extreme deference based upon its newfound national security status:

> We note at the outset that the realm of national security belongs to the executive branch, and we owe considerable deference to that branch's assessment in matters of national security.[15]

---

[9] *Becker v. IRS*, 34 F.3d 398, 409 (7th Cir. 1994) (involving the author and his two brothers).

[10] *Id.* at 408.

[11] *Id.*

[12] *Id.* at 409.

[13] *Bassiouni*, 436 F.3d at 724.

[14] *Becker*, 34 F.3d at 409.

[15] *Bassiouni*, 436 F.3d at 724.

The court further justified the maintenance of these records in the professor's file based upon the FBI's claim that "the records are important for evaluating the continued reliability of its intelligence sources."[16] As such, the substantive law in such records cases was consciously altered to accommodate the FBI's transition from a law enforcement agency to an intelligence-gathering entity, a point emphasized in the FBI's own submissions in the case: "[T]he FBI has amended its investigative priorities, naming as its number one priority to 'protect the United States from terrorist attack.'"[17]

In reaction to the appellate court's decision denying the professor relief under the Privacy Act, one writer remarked upon the negative impact on the substantive law as follows:

> [T]he courts have signaled a clear willingness to grant the government a fair amount of flexibility in national security cases. As a result, [records] suits may turn out differently than they would have in the absence of the attacks on the World Trade Center and the Pentagon.[18]

Thirdly, the professor's case signals a radical departure in the area of procedural law. During oral argument in front of the Seventh Circuit, the attorney for the FBI repeatedly requested that the panel consider *ex parte* a classified declaration by an FBI supervisor, although the declaration was not reviewed by the lower court judge and was never made part of the record on appeal, contending that the secret declaration would explain to the judges why the agency needed to maintain the records in the professor's file.[19] The professor's counsel strenuously objected at the argument and subsequently in writing; however, the panel reviewed the declaration *in camera* and then relied upon the declaration in ruling against the professor, despite the fact that neither the professor's counsel nor the professor ever saw the declaration or had the opportunity to challenge the validity of its claims.[20] The panel's review of the classified declaration violated an explicit rule of appellate procedure,[21] which prohibits the use of documents on appeal that were not considered by the district court; however, the panel – although conceding its departure from ordinary procedure – then attempted to justify its use of the secret document in the professor's case on the grounds that "we do not believe that the evidentiary submission can be considered 'ordinary'"[22] – thus admittedly transgressing well-established procedure to accommodate the war against terror.

---

16 *Id.*

17 *Id.*

18 *Sherman*, 19 St. Thomas L. Rev. 286–287 (2006).

19 *Bassiouni*, 436 F.3d at 722 n.7.

20 *Becker*, in: Becker/Derenčinović (eds.), International Terrorism (2008), p. 15.

21 Fed. R. App. P. 10.

22 *Bassiouni*, 436 F.3d at 722 n.7.

In sum, the professor's case illustrates, in a microcosm, the shift from law enforcement to intelligence gathering in the fight against terrorism and demonstrates the substantial impact that such a fundamental change has had upon the courts, substantive and procedural law, and the very constancy of the law itself.

## II. Developments toward an intelligence-gathering approach

To understand the significance of the transition from a law enforcement strategy to an intelligence-gathering approach, it is important to define the marked differences between these two diverse traditions.[23] Law enforcement agencies are generally involved in the investigation of crime and the collection of evidence with a view toward prosecution. Such agencies are required to follow the parameters of the law, and their conduct is subject to judicial scrutiny. In addition, after the exhaustion of appeals, the information collected is of little value. On the other hand, intelligence agencies are involved in the aggressive collection of data for the purposes of foreign policy and the prevention of threats to national security. Intelligence operations are conducted in secret, and the methods employed are often illegal. The greatest priority is given to the protection of sources and methods because exposure could risk not only a source's usefulness but efforts to recruit other sources. Moreover, unlike law enforcement, intelligence organizations actively seek gossip and hearsay, which fulfills a need for a continuous stream of data by which they can attempt to create a mosaic of world events.

Following revelations that, during the late 1960s and early 1970s, there was an unprecedented amount of intelligence gathering activity in the United States directed at innocent citizens and domestic organizations by the FBI, the Central Intelligence Agency (CIA), and the United States military, there was a significant effort in the United States "to create a wall between law enforcement agencies and to eject the CIA from domestic activities."[24] This "wall" was particularly evident in the distinct provisions that governed wiretapping and eavesdropping for law enforcement and intelligence,[25] viz., Title III, which regulates wiretapping and eavesdropping during criminal investigations,[26] and the 1978 Foreign Intelligence Surveillance Act (FISA),[27] which governs the electronic surveillance of "agents of a foreign power inside the United States for the purpose of gathering foreign intelligence."[28]

---

23 Portions of this section are excerpted from *Becker*, in: Bassiouni (ed.), 2 International Criminal Law (2008), pp. 71–75; *Becker*, 76 RIDP 60–66 (2005).

24 *Martin*, 29 Human Rights 6 (2002).

25 *Id.*

26 18 U.S.C. §§ 2510–2522 (2000).

27 50 U.S.C. §§ 1801–1862 (West 1991 & Supp. 2002).

28 *Martin*, 29 Hum. Rights 5 (2002).

The separation between law enforcement and intelligence was also clearly delineated in the two sets of guidelines, first prepared by the Attorney General in 1976, that established rules to regulate the FBI's bifurcated duties: (1) The Attorney General's Guidelines on General Crimes, Racketeering Enterprise and Domestic Security/Terrorism Investigations, and (2) The Attorney General Guidelines for FBI Foreign Intelligence Collection and Foreign Counterintelligence Investigations.[29] These guidelines provided "one set of rules for criminal investigations and another for gathering foreign intelligence relating to espionage or international terrorism inside the United States."[30]

Yet, following the events of September 11th, the wall separating law enforcement and intelligence was quickly dismantled. With little or no deliberation, the United States Congress passed the "Uniting and Strengthening America by Providing Appropriate Tools Required to Intercept and Obstruct Terrorism Act of 2001" (USA Patriot Act or Act),[31] which President Bush signed into law slightly more than one month after the attacks.

Several provisions of the USA Patriot Act directly affected the sharing of information between law enforcement and intelligence organizations. For example, section 203 of the Act provided that

> it shall be lawful for foreign intelligence or counterintelligence … or foreign intelligence information obtained as part of a criminal investigation to be disclosed to any Federal law enforcement, intelligence … or national security official in order to assist the official receiving that information in the performance of his official duties.[32]

Similarly, section 905 of the Act provided, in pertinent part, that

> the Attorney General, or the head of any other department or agency of the Federal Government with law enforcement responsibilities, shall expeditiously disclose to the Director of Central Intelligence … foreign intelligence acquired by an element of the Department of Justice or an element of such department or agency, as the case may be, in the course of a criminal investigation.[33]

In addition, section 218 of the Act lowered the standard by which foreign intelligence information could be gathered for use as evidence in criminal cases. Prior to passage of the USA Patriot Act, the FBI was authorized under FISA to conduct electronic surveillance and to carry out physical searches without satisfying the probable cause standard required in criminal cases.[34] FISA mandated only that the government applicant had probable cause to believe that the target was "an agent of

---

29 Various archived versions of these documents are available at www.cnss.org/data/files/Surveillance/fbi_guidelines_Resources.doc (last visited Sept. 15, 2016).

30 *Martin*, 29 Hum. Rights 5 (2002).

31 Pub. L. No. 107-56, 115 Stat. 272 (2001) [hereinafter USA Patriot Act].

32 USA Patriot Act § 203(d)(1), 115 Stat. at 281.

33 *Id.* § 905(a)(2), 115 Stat. at 388–389.

34 *Dempsey*, 29 Hum. Rights 10 (2002).

a foreign power."[35] Yet, because of the extraordinary nature of wiretaps and searches under FISA (the target "is never notified of the intrusion"), the use of such methods was permitted only on the understanding that such surveillance techniques would not be utilized for investigating crimes.[36] Congress, however, recognized that, during the process of gathering foreign intelligence information, evidence of crimes, such as espionage, might be collected.[37] Thus, Congress allowed the use of material collected under FISA to be used as evidence in criminal cases, but only in circumstances where "the purpose" of the investigation was the gathering of foreign intelligence.[38] Otherwise, FISA would provide the government with a loophole by which to bypass the traditional probable cause requirement mandated for searches and seizures in criminal cases.[39] Section 218 of the Act, however, amended FISA to allow wiretaps and searches as long as a "significant purpose" of the surveillance was the gathering of foreign intelligence information.[40] To date, none of the constitutional challenges to FISA's denuding of the traditional requirement of probable cause in criminal cases has been successful.[41]

To reflect the legislative changes enacted by means of the USA Patriot Act,[42] the Attorney General issued a new set of guidelines on May 30, 2002, which announced that the FBI's "highest priority is to protect the security of the nation and the safety of the American people against the depredations of terrorists and foreign aggressors."[43] The revised guidelines provided that,

> [f]or the purpose of detecting or preventing terrorist activities, the FBI is authorized to visit any place and attend any event that is open to the public, on the same terms and conditions as members of the public generally.[44]

This authorization eliminated the decades-old restriction that prevented the FBI from spying on lawful activities, including political gatherings and religious services, absent some indication of a potential federal crime.[45]

Thus, the transition of the FBI from a traditional law enforcement agency to an intelligence gathering entity engaged in the fight against terrorism can only be de-

---

35 50 U.S.C. §§ 1805(a)(3)(A), 1824(a)(3)(A) (2000).

36 *Dempsey*, 29 Hum. Rights 10 (2002).

37 *Id.*

38 *Id.* See 50 U.S.C. §§ 1804(a)(7)(B), 1823(a)(7)(B) (2000).

39 *Dempsey*, 29 Hum. Rights 10 (2002).

40 USA Patriot Act § 218, 115 Stat. at 291. See *Dempsey*, 29 Hum. Rights 10 (2002).

41 *United States v. Duka*, 671 F.3d 329, 338–345 (3d Cir. 2011) (collecting cases).

42 For an overview of various controversial provisions of the USA Patriot Act, see *Becker*, 37 Valparaiso Univ. L. Rev. 592–611 (2003).

43 The Attorney General's Guidelines on General Crimes, Racketeering Enterprise and Terrorism Enterprise Investigations, at ii (issued May 30, 2002), available at https://epic.org/privacy/fbi/FBI-2002-Guidelines.pdf (last visited Sept. 15, 2016).

44 *Id.* at 22.

45 *Cole*, Chicago Daily Law Bull. 24 (June 5, 2002).

scribed as meteoric. Yet, as reflected in recent controversies surrounding the FBI's demand for access to private cell phone data stemming from the terrorist attacks in San Bernardino, California, it is clear that the agency is still trying to find ways to fulfill its weighty mandate and, at the same time, navigate the realities of the 21st century and confront the perceptions of the past.

## III. Expanding scope of U.S. terrorism legislation

One of the prime examples of the expanding scope of terrorism legislation, which has likewise seen an exponential increase in the number of criminal prosecutions since September 11th, relates to the area of providing "material support" to designated foreign terrorist organizations (FTOs). By repeatedly narrowing the type of support or resources that one may provide to such an organization and thereby widening the net of criminal culpability for those who may attempt to provide such support, Congress has created a criminal statute that, in its current form, can only be described as Draconian, as it verges on a strict liability statute in which one's intent to aid in terror-related activities is legally irrelevant and even humanitarian support, with very limited exceptions, is criminalized. In its present form, the material support statute provides that

> [w]hoever knowingly provides material support or resources to a foreign terrorist organization, or attempts or conspires to do so, shall be fined under this title or imprisoned not more than 20 years, or both, and, if the death of any person results, shall be imprisoned for any term of years or for life. To violate this paragraph, a person must have knowledge that the organization is a designated terrorist organization …, that the organization has engaged or engages in terrorist activity …, or that the organization has engaged or engages in terrorism… .[46]

Prior to September 11th, the material support statute

> was only invoked three times for criminal prosecutions. However, since 9/11 it has become the most-commonly used statute by the government in conducting terrorism-related prosecutions.[47]

On account of continuous legal challenges to the definition of "material support or resources" on vagueness and First Amendment grounds, as well as resulting court rulings favorable to the plaintiffs, Congress amended the statute on various occasions.[48] First, in 2001, the legislature expanded the scope of the statutory prohibitions by adding "expert advice or assistance" to the definition of "material support or resources."[49] Then, in 2004, Congress again amended the statutory definition to include "service" and provided specific definitions to the terms "training,"

[46] 18 U.S.C. § 2339B(a)(1) (2012) (internal statutory references omitted).

[47] *Tunis*, 49 Am. Crim. L. Rev. 269–270 (2012).

[48] *Id.* at 283–286.

[49] *Holder v. Humanitarian Law Project*, 561 U.S. 1, 11–12 (2010).

"expert advice and assistance," and "personnel."[50] Thus, currently, the term "material support or resources" means

> any property, tangible or intangible, or service, including currency or monetary instruments or financial securities, financial services, lodging, training, expert advice or assistance, safehouses, false documentation or identification, communications equipment, facilities, weapons, lethal substances, explosives, personnel (1 or more individuals who may be or include oneself), and transportation, except medicine or religious materials.[51]

As one commentator noted with respect to the impact of the aforementioned amendments, the statute "banned virtually all forms of advocacy and association with an FTO in an effort to prevent national security threats."[52]

An accused charged with violating the material support statute finds himself in an unenviable position, with a defense that is virtually non-existent. First of all, he is forbidden by statute from challenging the Secretary of State's FTO designation of the organization:

> [A] defendant in a criminal action or an alien in a removal proceeding shall not be permitted to raise any question concerning the validity of the issuance of such designation as a defense or an objection at any trial or hearing.[53]

Secondly, the mental element is not defined by specific intent or even a general criminal intent to commit an offense or to otherwise further illegal terrorist activities. Instead, one "knowingly" commits a federal crime simply by being aware of the organization's FTO designation or its engagement in terrorist activity or terrorism.[54] As the United States Supreme Court explained with respect to this aspect of the material support statute:

> Congress plainly spoke to the necessary mental element for a violation of [the statute], and it chose knowledge about that organization's connection to terrorism, not specific intent to further the organization's terrorist activities.[55]

Thus, a peaceful, purely humanitarian motivation[56] is wholly irrelevant in determining *mens rea* under the statute:

> [I]n preventing terrorism, it was necessary to prohibit providing material support in the form of training, expert advice, personnel, and services to foreign terrorist groups, even if the supporters meant to promote only the groups' nonviolent ends."[57] This is because

---

50 *Id.* at 12–13.

51 18 U.S.C. § 2339A(b)(1) (2012).

52 *Tunis*, 49 Am. Crim. L. Rev. 285 (2012).

53 8 U.S.C. § 1189(a)(8) (2012).

54 18 U.S.C. § 2339B(a)(1) (2012).

55 Humanitarian Law Project, 561 U.S. at 16–17.

56 *Id.* at 29 (noting that by removing a previous "humanitarian" exception from a related anti-terrorism provision, Congress "considered and rejected the view that ostensibly peaceful aid would have no harmful effects").

57 *Id.* at 36.

the Congress determined that foreign terrorist organizations "are so tainted by their criminal conduct that *any contribution to such an organization* facilitates that conduct.[58]

In short, a defendant charged with a violation of the material support statute may not defend himself by:

> (1) challenging the designation of a group as an FTO, (2) challenging the constitutionality of the FTO designation process, (3) arguing that he did not intend or know that his actions would support illegal terrorist activities, or (4) arguing that his actions did not or will not support any illegal terrorist activities.[59]

Accordingly,

> the most one can do is argue that he did not do it, or that he did not know the organization was an FTO or engaged in terrorism. Beyond that, there will be no room for debate. What we are left with is a statute that all but guarantees conviction upon the defendant entering the courtroom.[60]

Finally, the United States Supreme Court sustained the propriety of the material support statute on the highly obeisant ground that

> evaluation of the facts by the Executive, like Congress's assessment, is entitled to deference. This litigation implicates sensitive and weighty interests of national security and foreign affairs.[61]

## IV. Impact upon the criminal justice system

The shift from a traditional law enforcement perspective to an intelligence-gathering approach, with the latter's need for secrecy, has had a lasting impact upon the criminal justice system in terrorism cases, as well as upon police surveillance tactics.

In a recent terrorism prosecution in Chicago,[62] the government informed the defense that it intended to introduce at the defendant's trial evidence it had obtained by means of electronic surveillance it had conducted under FISA,[63] which, as detailed above, does not have to satisfy the probable cause requirements mandated for criminal cases. The defense sought access to the classified materials submitted in support of the FISA warrant applications with the purpose of suppressing the evidence.[64]

---

58 *Id.* at 29 (quoting Antiterrorism and Effective Death Penalty Act of 1996, Public Law No. 104–132, § 301(a)(7), 110 Stat. 1214, 1247 (1996) (emphasis added by court)).

59 *Tunis*, 49 Am. Crim. L. Rev. 271 (2012).

60 *Id.* at 300.

61 Humanitarian Law Project, 561 U.S. at 33–34.

62 *United States v. Daoud*, 755 F.3d 479 (7th Cir. 2014).

63 *Id.* at 480.

64 *Id.* at 481.

The federal district court judge noted that no court had ever previously allowed such disclosure to the defense; however, the judge, after studying the classified materials, highlighted the fact that the defense attorneys had appropriate security clearances for the level at which the materials were classified.[65] In her ruling granting access to the defense, the judge pointed out that: (1) "the adversarial process is integral to safeguarding the rights of all citizens", (2) that the constitution presupposes "the right of the accused to require the prosecution's case to survive the crucible of meaningful adversary testing, (3) "the supposed national security interest at stake is not implicated where defense counsel has the necessary security clearances", and (4) "the probable value of disclosure and the risk of nondisclosure outweigh the potential danger of disclosure to cleared counsel."[66]

The government immediately filed an interlocutory appeal challenging the judge's ruling.[67] On appeal, the panel reversed the district court's ruling and barred the defense from seeing any of the classified materials.[68] The Seventh Circuit Court of Appeals held that FISA

> is an attempt to strike a balance between the interest in full openness of legal proceedings and the interest in national security, which requires a degree of secrecy concerning the government's efforts to protect the nation. Terrorism is not a chimera… . Conventional adversary procedure thus has to be compromised in recognition of valid social interests that compete with the social interest in openness.[69]

The reviewing court further dismissed the importance of the security clearances of defense counsel and found that disclosure could still harm national security interests:

> Though it is certainly highly unlikely that Daoud's lawyers would, Snowden-like, publicize classified information in violation of federal law, they might in their zeal to defend their client, to whom they owe a duty of candid communication, or misremembering what is classified and what not, inadvertently say things that would provide clues to classified material.[70]

Ultimately, the appellate court itself reviewed the classified materials at issue and determined that the government was accurate in its claim that disclosure would harm national security interests and that disclosure to the defense attorneys was not necessary.[71]

Interestingly, after the first public oral argument, the reviewing panel held an

> *in camera* hearing at which questions were put by the panel to the justice department lead lawyer on the case concerning the classified materials. Only cleared court and gov-

---

[65] *Id.*

[66] *Id.*

[67] *Id.*

[68] *Id.* at 485.

[69] *Id.* at 483.

[70] *Id.* at 484.

[71] *Id.* at 485.

ernment personnel were permitted at that hearing. The defendant's lawyers, before leaving the courtroom as ordered, objected to our holding such a hearing and followed up their oral objection with a written motion."[72]

The court further remarked that defense counsel's motion "cites no authority for forbidding classified hearings, including classified oral arguments in courts of appeals, when classified materials are to be discussed."[73]

Finally, the judge who authored the court's decision opined that the defense's objection to the classified oral argument

was ironic. The purpose of the hearing was to explore, by questioning the government's lawyer on the basis of the classified materials, the need for defense access to those materials (which the judges and their cleared staffs had read). In effect this was cross-examination of the government, and could only help the defendant.[74]

Several observations on this unusual case are in order. Initially, the change toward an intelligence-gathering model is more than evident in the lack of transparency that is now a hallmark of terrorism cases in United States courts. Evidence to be introduced at trial is secured through secret warrants based upon classified materials that the defense is – as evidenced by this case itself – never, as a matter of practice, granted access to. Then, a classified oral argument is held with only the government's lawyer present – with no opportunity for the defense to question the veracity of the state's claims or to advocate on behalf of its client.

The appellate court's dismissal of the value of the defense's security clearances is also very curious. The court hypothesized that counsel might – "Snowden-like" – break the law and publicly leak the classified information or otherwise forget their responsibilities or the nature of the material and make inadvertent disclosures.[75] But why is this same concern not equally applicable to the judges, their staff, or the government lawyers (all with clearances) who were present at the classified oral argument? What makes defense counsel any less trustworthy than government personnel?

Additionally, the authoring judge further belittled the defense's objection to being excluded from the *ex parte* classified oral argument, asserting that it was only for the defense's benefit anyway. But how do we know that? The defense attorneys were not present. Maybe what the government attorney told the judges was false and could have been exposed with minimal participation by the defense? In a system built upon adversarial testing, cross-examination, and distrust of government, secret court proceedings – whether at the trial level or on appeal – are anathema, and equal participation by both sides of the controversy, especially where the de-

72 *Id.*

73 *Id.*

74 *Id.*

75 *Id.* at 483.

fendant's liberty is at stake, is paramount, not only for the individual defendant but for the perception of the public as well.

Lastly, brief reference should be made to the type of surveillance that inevitably results from a system based upon an intelligence-gathering model, as opposed to the traditional law enforcement approach. One of the most illustrative examples in this regard is what has become known as the New York Police Department's (NYPD's) Muslim Surveillance Program,[76] in which the police department

> has dispatched teams of undercover officers, known as 'rakers,' into minority neighborhoods as part of a human mapping program, according to officials directly involved in the program. They've monitored daily life in bookstores, bars, cafes and nightclubs. Police have also used informants, known as 'mosque crawlers,' to monitor sermons, even when there's no evidence of wrongdoing. NYPD officials have scrutinized imams and gathered intelligence on cab drivers and food cart vendors, jobs often done by Muslims.[77]

The NYPD's intelligence unit also drafted

> an analytical report on every mosque within 100 miles of New York … . It mapped hundreds of mosques and discussed the likelihood of them being infiltrated by al-Qaida, Hezbollah and other terrorist groups. [Yet,] [i]f FBI agents were to do that, they would be in violation of the Privacy Act, which prohibits the federal government from collecting intelligence on purely First Amendment activities.[78]

Significantly, the CIA was "instrumental in transforming the NYPD's intelligence unit," which partnership "has blurred the bright line between foreign and domestic surveillance."[79]

## V. Conclusion

There is no doubt that the transition to an intelligence-led approach in the fight against terrorism has irreparably altered the manner in which law enforcement operates and in which the courts assess cases involving terrorism and national security. How far this shift in paradigms will permeate into the criminal justice system as a whole awaits the defining chisel of future events.

---

76 *Wasserman*, 90 N.Y.U. L. Rev. 1787 (2015).

77 *Apuzzo/Goldman*, Assoc. Press (Aug. 23, 2011).

78 *Id.*

79 *Id.*

## Bibliography

*Alda, Erik/Sala, Joseph L.*, Links Between Terrorism, Organized Crime and Crime: The Case of the Sahel Region. 3 International Journal of Security & Development 1–9 (2014).

*Apuzzo, Matt/Goldman, Adam*, With CIA Help, NYPD Moves Covertly in Muslim Areas, Associated Press (Aug. 23, 2011), available at http://www.ap.org/Content/AP-In-The-News/2011/With-CIA-help-NYPD-moves-covertly-in-Muslim-areas [last visited Sept. 18, 2016].

*Becker, Steven*, Closing the Door on Justice: Secret Evidence and the Lack of Transparency in Court Proceedings in the Wake of the "War on Terrorism." In: Steven Becker/Davor Derenčinović (eds.), International Terrorism: The Future Unchained? University of Zagreb Faculty of Law 2008, pp. 1–17.

– Increased Cooperation Between Law Enforcement and Intelligence Agencies After September 11, 2001. 76 Revue Internationale de Droit Pénal [International Review of Penal Law] 57–74 (2005).

– "Mirror, Mirror on the Wall ...": Assessing the Aftermath of September 11th. 37 Valparaiso University Law Review 563–626 (2003).

– Maintaining Secret Government Dossiers on the First Amendment Activities of American Citizens: The Law Enforcement Activity Exception to the Privacy Act. 50 DePaul Law Review 675–741 (2000).

*Becker, Steven/Cave Janus*, Increased Cooperation Between Law Enforcement and Intelligence Agencies After September 11, 2001. In: M. Cherif Bassiouni (ed.), 2 International Criminal Law. 3d ed. Martinus Nijhoff Publishers Dordrecht 2008, pp. 71–82.

*Cole, David*, Misdirected Snooping. Chicago Daily Law Bulletin 6, 24 (June 5, 2002).

*Dempsey, James*, Civil Liberties in a Time of Crisis. 29 Human Rights 8-10 (2002).

*Martin, Kate*, Intelligence, Terrorism, and Civil Liberties. 29 Human Rights 5-7 (2002).

*Sherman, Michael*, Symposium Issue: "9/11": Effects on U.S. Law: Featured Contributor: FOIA in the Aftermath of 9/11, 19 St. Thomas Law Review 281–295 (2006).

*Tunis, Brent*, Note: Material-Support-to-Terrorism Prosecutions: Fighting Terrorism by Eroding Judicial Review. 49 American Criminal Law Review 269–300 (2012).

*Wasserman, Matthew*, Note: First Amendment Limitations on Police Surveillance: The Case of the Muslim Surveillance Program. 90 New York University Law Review 1786–1824 (2015).

# US Courts, Jurisdiction, and Mutual Trust: *RJR Nabisco v. European Community*

*Mark A. Drumbl*

Combating organized crime, or any transnational scourge for that matter, requires co-ordination among states. Such co-ordination helps reduce transaction costs, minimize free-riders, diminish moral hazard, and incubate economics of scale. All of these elements weave together in the development of effective transnational regulation, prevention, and enforcement.

One way to achieve these outcomes is to negotiate multilateral treaties, for example the Convention against Torture, which involve commonly agreed-upon crimes and a commitment to domesticate these, with the added inclusion of 'prosecute or extradite' clauses within the procedural structure. Concatenated bilateral treaties also may achieve similar ends.

That said, one aspect of combating cross-border harms is the extent to which the courts of one state may unilaterally assert jurisdiction over criminal (or tortious, or other) conduct that occurs in another state. When courts are given authority to prosecute and punish, for example by a domestic statute, might that authority extend to harms committed outside the state? Note that these questions do not involve bilateral or multilateral negotiation among states, but rather unilateral assertions of legislative and judicial authority by one state over conduct that occurs elsewhere, in whole or in part, or that occurs in (over, across) multiple states.

This chapter surveys this question within the context of the jurisprudence of the United States Supreme Court. It asks and answers the following: What is the reach of US federal courts in terms of harms suffered or conduct undertaken *outside* of the US? This is a question that has arisen on several occasions in recent years in case-law. For the most part, the US Supreme Court has hesitated to allow US courts to assert jurisdiction over harms felt extraterritorially in the absence of Congress (the legislature) expressly providing for extraterritorial reach in the legislation that is being judicially enforced. That said, it seems that the US Supreme Court may be slightly more inclined to find extraterritorial reach in cases that involve criminal sanction for conduct that involves money laundering and material support to foreign terrorist organizations.

This chapter places these jurisprudential developments within the framework of the construction of mutual trust and international comity among nations and courts. Truth be told, invasive unilateral assertion of jurisdiction by the courts of one state into matters experienced within the territories of another state may roil comity and in fact bust trust. These concerns have animated US Supreme Court cases in divergent areas of the law, leading to a general reticence to exercise jurisdiction over disputes that lack a compelling nexus with the United States. On the other hand, it may also be possible to construct this reticence by the US Supreme Court as indicating a withdrawal from transnational adjudication as well as a restrictiveness on public interest litigation and access to justice, specifically in the context of plaintiff class action damages claims. In the end, this chapter posits that an optimal way forward may lie in the negotiation of new multilateral treaties along the lines of the Convention against Torture, as mentioned earlier, or in the area of reciprocal enforcement of judgments.

This chapter begins by discussing the general rules regarding extraterritorial reach as recently adjudicated by US federal courts. This chapter then details the specific case of the suppression of organized crime through a detailed case-study of the Racketeer Influenced and Corrupt Organizations Act (RICO), whose extraterritorial reach was adjudicated in 2016 by the US Supreme Court in a case entitled *RJR Nabisco, Inc. v. European Community*.[1] This chapter concludes with some broader reflections that return to the themes of mutual trust.

## I. General approaches to extraterritoriality

The US court system divides into federal courts and state (e.g. California, Montana) courts. Complex determinations emerge as to which band of courts has jurisdiction over which sort of claims, and also of transfer of claims from state courts into federal courts. These are beside the point, however, in that the focus of this chapter aims only at the federal court system and its enforcement of important pieces of legislation enacted by the federal Congress.

The federal system in the US begins with the federal district courts located within each state. There are 94 judicial districts. At the appellate level, the country is divided into judicial circuits. Twelve of these are geographic, clustered in regions of the country. There is a thirteenth circuit, the federal circuit, which is not geographic but thematic and hears specialized appeals (for example, those involving patent laws). The United States Supreme Court is the top court in the country in the federal system, though also has jurisdiction over certain matters from the state courts.

[1] *RJR Nabisco, Inc., et al. v. European Community, et al.*136 S.Ct. 2090 (2016).

In sum, the United States Supreme Court has developed firm presumptions against the extraterritorial application of US statutes in the absence of clear indication by Congress at the time of enacting the legislation that Congress intended for it to have extraterritorial reach.[2] Congress clearly has the power to declare US law as applying extraterritorially. It must do so affirmatively and unmistakably. If Congress is silent, or unclear, or falls short of the affirmative and unmistakable threshold, then the presumption is that the legislation does not apply extraterritorially. This presumption can be rebutted, however, and this aspect is the focus of considerable litigation.

As intoned in 2007 in *Microsoft v. AT&T* – 'United States law governs domestically but does not rule the world'[3] – the principle against extraterritoriality operates to avoid international discord when US law is applied to conduct in foreign countries. This principle also reflects the far more prosaic notion that Congress generally legislates with domestic concerns in mind; and guards against forum shopping and foreign plaintiffs coming to US courts to redress grievances, particularly in what have become known as 'foreign cubed' disputes, that is, disputes that concern foreign plaintiffs, foreign defendants, and harms felt in foreign places.

*Morrison v. National Australia Bank (NAB)*, a case decided by the US Supreme Court in 2010, provides a good introduction to the subject matter. The petitioners in this case were Australians.[4] Petitioners had purchased shared in the NAB, which then wrote them down and, hence, considerable monies were lost. Petitioners sought to recover for their losses. They sued in US Courts under s. 10(b) of the Securities Exchange Act of 1934, which provides a cause of action (and extensive treble damages) in such situations if proven to violate the statute. So the question in *Morrison* is whether the Securities Exchange Act provides a cause of action to foreign plaintiffs suing foreign defendants for alleged fraud (and misconduct/deception) in connection with securities traded outside of the US.

The Supreme Court ruled no. The Court began with the core presumption that, when it comes to Congressional legislation, unless a contrary intent appears it applies only within the territorial jurisdiction of the United States. The Court noted this was a canon of construction, not a formal limit on Congress' powers. Congress has the power to legislate extraterritorially if it says so.

In *Morrison*, plaintiffs had been successful at the lower court levels. The Second Circuit Court of Appeals had developed an approach that suggested that if the leg-

---

2 *EEOC v. Arabian Am. Oil Co. (Aramco)*, 499 U.S. 244, 248 (1991) (construing a statute only to reach conduct within the United States unless Congress affirmatively declares that the statute applies to conduct abroad).

3 *Microsoft Corp. v. AT&T Corp.*, 550 U. S. 437, 454 (2007).

4 *Morrison v. National Australian Bank*, 561 U.S. 247 (2010). Technically, Morrison was not a petitioner any more at the time of the litigation, but his name remains listed as such.

islation is silent in cases of extraterritorial reach it can be interpreted extraterritorially in certain factual situations. The Second Circuit had developed an 'effects test' and a 'conduct test' to determine the applicability of the Securities Exchange Act to a foreign securities transaction. The Second Circuit inquired whether the wrongful conduct had a substantial effect upon the US (territory) or a US national (citizenship); or whether the wrongful conduct occurred in the US.

The United States Supreme Court rejected this test as unpredictable, complicated, nuanced, unstable, and lacking in bright-lines. Justice Scalia reinforced the firmness of the presumption against extraterritorial enforcement. Instead, he developed what is called the *transactional test*. According to this test, a US court may exercise jurisdiction over a claim brought under section 10(b) of the Securities Exchange Act if: (1) the purchase or sale is made in the United States *or* (2) if the purchase or sale involves a security listed on a domestic US stock exchange. For Justice Scalia, and the Court, one of these two factual elements, if found, would establish jurisdiction even if the harms were felt elsewhere. The *Morrison* claim involved no securities listed in the US and all aspects of the purchases of remaining claims occurred outside of the US. Hence, there was no jurisdiction. The lawsuit was dismissed. A US court could not adjudicate it. The US was not an appropriate forum. The Act applies only to transactions involving services listed on domestic stock exchanges and to domestic transactions in other securities.

Justice Scalia was motivated by a variety of concerns, including the concept of comity among nations. According to Justice Scalia, extensive extraterritorial application of US law would undermine foreign law as applicable in foreign jurisdictions. Such a scenario might create overlapping judicialization and, if the US laws departed from the foreign laws, would trigger confusion among investors. In reaching this conclusion, Justice Scalia drew heavily from many *amicus* briefs that had been submitted in this dispute by a variety of foreign governments and international associations urging restraint in the assertion of extraterritorial jurisdiction by US courts. In this regard, then, Justice Scalia sought to better develop trust among states in the combatting of corporate fraud by drawing down the US position as some sort of 'global cop' or US courts as some sort of 'global forum'. Justice Scalia was also, at the time, acutely aware of the attraction that foreign plaintiffs embroiled in foreign harms could have for US courts, with availability of aggressive discovery procedures in the initial litigation stages and the possibilities of treble damages (or punitive damages). He wished to guard against US courts becoming the 'Shangri-La' of class action litigation for lawyers.

In 2013, the United States Supreme Court dealt with the issue of extraterritoriality in the *Kiobel* case, which involved the venerated Alien Tort Statute. The ATS dates from the First Congress (1789). It is a succinct instrument that reads as follows:

> The district courts shall have original jurisdiction of any civil action by an alien for a tort only, committed in violation of the law of nations or a treaty of the United States.[5]

The ATS lay largely dormant for two centuries. Beginning in 1980 with the Second Circuit Court of Appeals' judgment in the *Filártiga* litigation, however, plaintiffs turned to the ATS to pursue redress in US courts for atrocity crimes.[6] Plaintiffs did so in a broad variety of factual circumstances, including when allegations involved abuses committed outside the United States by non-US nationals against non-US nationals. By definition, plaintiffs pursuing ATS claims will be foreign nationals. In many instances, however, plaintiffs present some connection to the United States, either because they are physically present in, had moved to, or are non-residents living in the US. In any event, a first generation of ATS claims pursued individuals based on their alleged direct involvement in atrocity crimes. A second wave that began in the 1990's targeted corporations on theories of aiding and abetting in the commission of atrocity crimes. This latter wave proved more controversial jurisprudentially (*i.e.* regarding modes of liability) as well as politically (*i.e.* risking a chilling effect on investment in developing nations, dragging US courts into disputes with no connection to the jurisdiction, and interfering with the conduct of US foreign relations).

These controversies suffused the *Kiobel* case, decided in April 2013 on jurisdictional grounds regarding the extraterritorial application of US statutes.[7] Here, the US Supreme Court sharply curtailed the scope of future ATS claims by requiring proof of a compelling nexus with the United States:

> [E]ven where the claims touch and concern the territory of the United States, they must do so with sufficient force to displace the presumption against extraterritorial application. Corporations are often present in many countries, and it would reach too far to say that mere corporate presence suffices.[8]

The facts of *Kiobel* involved Nigerian citizens, albeit long-time legal residents of the United States on asylum grounds, who pleaded that Dutch, British, and Nigerian oil exploration and extraction corporations aided and abetted the Nigerian government in committing systemic human rights violations during the 1990's. All nine judges dismissed the case, holding that the factual context was too remote from the United States to justify letting the claim continue. Chief Justice Roberts – writing for a five justice majority – robustly applied the presumption against extra-

---

5 28 U.S.C. § 1350.

6 *Filártiga v. Peña-Irala*, 630 F.2d 876 (2d Cir. 1980) (involving a civil claim by two Paraguayan-citizen parents against a Paraguayan police officer who tortured and killed their son in Paraguay; the family initiated the claim after both parties had immigrated to the United States).

7 *Kiobel v. Royal Dutch Petroleum Co.*, 133 S.Ct. 1659, 1669 (2013).

8 *Kiobel v. Royal Dutch Petroleum Co.*, 133 S.Ct. 1659, 1669 (2013).

territoriality to the ATS. Justice Kennedy[9] and Justice Breyer (writing for himself and three others)[10] gestured in separate concurrences towards a slightly more generous approach to jurisdiction. Justice Alito, in contradistinction, drew a line that was even firmer than that of Chief Justice Roberts. In the *RJR* case that constitutes the next step of this chapter, Justice Alito adopted a somewhat more permissive approach when it came to the penal sanction.

What is the bottom line, then, when it comes to the ATS and extraterritoriality in the wake of *Kiobel*? Clearly, the range of claims that can be brought has narrowed. An ATS case cannot proceed if the asserted wrongful conduct has entirely occurred outside of the United States. A defendant's US citizenship, while relevant, is not on its own dispositive to satisfy the requirement that the litigation sufficiently touches and concerns the United States. As is evident from the case-law, however, it is far too early to sound the death-knell of ATS litigation. Claims will continue, in particular, where the underlying conduct (including manufacture, financing, managing, or developing) occurs in the United States, where the conduct was intended to impact the United States, and where the United States may be harboring an alleged wrongdoer. That said, in 2018 in *Jesner v. Arab Bank* the US Supreme Court ruled that a corporation cannot be sued as a defendant under the ATS.[11] This sharply limits recourse to the ATS. But that is an entirely different matter.

## II. Extraterritoriality and the suppression of organized crime

On June 20, 2016, the US Supreme Court decided *R.J. Reynolds v. European Community (and 26 Member States)*. This litigation implicated the well-known Racketeer Influenced and Corrupt Organizations Act (RICO). Among other things, RICO makes it unlawful to acquire or maintain an interest in an enterprise through a pattern of racketeering activity.

The facts of this dispute are as follows. The European Community filed suit under RICO alleging that RJ Reynolds (RJR, a cigarette company, which ceased operating as a united entity in 1999) participated in a global money-laundering scheme

[9] *Kiobel*, 133 S. Ct. at 1669 (Kennedy, J., concurring) ("The opinion for the Court is careful to leave open a number of significant questions regarding the reach and interpretation of the Alien Tort Statute. In my view this is a proper disposition.").

[10] *Id.* at 1671 (Breyer, J., concurring) ("I would find jurisdiction under this statute where: (1) the alleged tort occurs on American soil, (2) the defendant is an American national, or (3) the defendant's conduct substantially and adversely affects an important American national interest, and that includes a distinct interest in preventing the United States from becoming a safe harbor (free of civil as well as criminal liability) for a torturer or other common enemy of mankind.").

[11] *Jesner v. Arab Bank*, 138 S. Ct. 1386 (2018).

in association with various organized crime groups. Allegedly, drug traffickers smuggled narcotics into Europe and sold them for euros that – through transactions involving black-market money brokers, cigarette importers, and wholesalers – were used to pay for large shipments of RJR cigarettes into Europe. The European Community accused the RJR corporation of 'being part of a sprawling cigarette smuggling enterprise that deprived them of billions of dollars in customs and tax revenues', with the thrust of the complaint being that:

> Greatly simplified, the complaint alleges a scheme in which Colombian and Russian drug traffickers smuggled narcotics into Europe and sold the drugs for euros that – through a series of transactions involving black-market money brokers, cigarette importers, and wholesalers – were used to pay for large shipments of RJR cigarettes into Europe. In other variations of this scheme, RJR allegedly dealt directly with drug traffickers and money launderers in South America and sold cigarettes to Iraq in violation of international sanctions.[12]

The European Community alleged it was harmed

> in various ways, including through competitive harm to their state-owned cigarette businesses, lost tax revenue from black-market cigarette sales, harm to European financial institutions, currency instability, and increased law enforcement costs.[13]

The litigation had dragged on for 16 years. The European Community first sued RJR in the United States District Court for the Eastern District of New York in 2000. Three separate actions were involved. As the US Supreme Court noted, this dispute recurringly involves '[m]ultiple trips up and down the federal court system'.[14]

RICO defines 'racketeering activity' to encompass dozens of state and federal offenses, known as 'predicates.' When these predicates occur as part of *racketeering activity*, then, RICO applies as a separate set of offenses applicable to the case of organized crime.[15] This is a bit like the logic of crimes against humanity under article 7 of the Rome Statute of the International Criminal Court, namely, a series of underlying crimes are identified (murder, extermination, sexual slavery etc.) and, if committed as part of a widespread or systematic attack directed against a civilian population (with knowledge of the attack), can become persecuted as crimes against humanity.

Turning back to RICO, then, what are the predicates? These include murder, extortion, assassination of governmental officials, hostage taking, transacting in criminally derived property, securities fraud, and drug-related activities. If the predicates determine a pattern and that pattern indicates racketeering activity, then the

---

12 *RJR*, 136 S. Ct. at 2098.

13 *Id.*

14 *Id.*

15 *H.J. Inc. v. Northwestern Bell Telephone Co.*, 492 U.S. 229, 239 (1989) (specifying that 'a pattern of racketeering activity' requires at least two predicates committed within 10 years of each other).

additional separate criminal provisions in RICO are triggered. In terms of the specifics of the facts of the RJR dispute, then, *inter alia* § 1962 RICO makes it a crime to:

- invest income derived from a pattern of racketeering activity in an enterprise 'engaged in, or the activities of which affect, interstate or foreign commerce';
- acquire or maintain an interest in an enterprise through a pattern of racketeering activity;
- conduct an enterprise's affairs through a pattern of racketeering activity.

RICO also importantly provides a private *civil cause of action* (§ 1964(c)) for 'any person injured in his business or property by reasons of a violation' of any of these penal prohibitions. So, once again very loosely similar to the Rome Statute of the International Criminal Court, a possibility for private damage awards to restitute (or compensate) for the harms arise.

The claim brought by the European Community that the US Supreme Court had to decide upon was that RJR violated these provisions by engaging in a pattern of racketeering activities that included numerous predicate acts, such as money laundering, material support to foreign terrorist organizations, mail wire, wire fraud, and certain statutory violations.

In terms of previous decisions, at the District Court level RJR's motion to dismiss the law suit was granted because the District Court found that RICO does not apply to racketeering activity occurring outside US territory or to foreign enterprises. At the appellate level, the Second Circuit ruled differently, holding that RICO applies extraterritorially to the same extent as the predicate acts of racketeering that underlie the alleged violation. The Second Circuit found that certain predicates do apply extraterritorially in this case, and those predicates supported the separate claim of RICO liability. These predicates are: money laundering and material support of terrorism. The Second Circuit also held that RICO's civil action permits recovery for a foreign injury caused by the violation of a predicate that applies extraterritorially. The private damages claim was a weighty concern for RJR's corporate interests.

The Supreme Court granted *certiorari* (namely, leave to appeal) because of split outcomes among the courts below, specifically the Second Circuit in this litigation and the Ninth Circuit in *United States v. Chao Fan Xu*.[16]

At the Supreme Court, Justice Alito began with the general test as discussed earlier. Absent clearly expressed Congressional intent to the contrary, federal laws will be construed to have only domestic application. Hence, a two-step test arises.

---

16 706 F.2d 965 (C.A.9 2013) (holding that RICO does not apply extraterritorially).

1. Has the presumption against extraterritoriality been rebutted: does the statute give a clear, affirmative indication that it applies extraterritorially?
2. If not, then, does the conduct complained about touch and concern the US with sufficient force so as to oust the presumption against extraterritorial application?

RICO lacks any explicit mention of extraterritorial application. Justice Alito held, however and with all other judges on this point, that some of RICO's predicate offenses do apply extraterritorially, notably in this matter, money laundering and material support to foreign terrorist organizations.[17] This was an outcome that tracked the views of the Second Circuit. Other predicates could be alleged if they involved domestic commission of the underlying offenses, which was found to be the case for the three remaining alleged violations.[18]

Justice Alito began by noting that RICO is a 'rare statute that clearly evidences extraterritorial effect despite lacking an express statement of extraterritoriality',[19] but only in penal matters. This was not for the private lawsuit. Even if certain penal prohibitions apply extraterritorially, § 1964(c) (the private right of action) does not overcome the presumption against extraterritoriality. A private RICO plaintiff 'must allege and prove a domestic injury to its business or property'.[20] On this point, however, Justice Alito was joined only by three other judges (Justices Roberts, Kennedy, Thomas). Three judges (Justices Ginsburg, Breyer, and Kagan) dissented. (Note that only 7 judges took part in this adjudication: at the time there were only 8 appointees one of whom, Justice Sotomayor, had to recuse herself because she had sat on the Second Circuit). The dissent rooted within the facts[21] and also within the law.[22]

The bifurcation of the penal sanction and the plaintiff's damages remedy reveals, perhaps, a more liberal treatment of criminal liability in the extraterritorial context than of an ability, whether in tort or other remedial basis, to obtain private monetary damages. Clearly, on this latter note, there is some alignment with the reasoning in *Kiobel*. There also is alignment with the reasoning in *Morrison* in that, in *RJR*, the Court mentioned frustrations regarding securities fraud enforcement that France had evoked in its *amicus* brief in *Morrison*, noting that

---

[17] *RJR*, 136 S. Ct. at 2101–2 (noting other predicates not germane to this litigation that also apply to foreign conduct); see also *id.* at 2103 ('A violation of § 1962 may be based on a pattern of racketeering that includes predicate offenses committed abroad, provided that each of those offenses violated a predicate statute that is itself extraterritorial.').

[18] *Id.* at 2099 (mail fraud, wire fraud, and Travel Act statutes do not apply extraterritorially but the complaint states domestic violations of these predicates).

[19] *Id.* at 2103.

[20] *Id.*, at 2107–2108.

[21] *Id.* at 2114 ('All defendants are U.S. corporations, headquartered in the United States, charged with a pattern of racketeering activity directed and managed from the United States, involving conduct occurring in the United States.').

[22] *Id.* at 2112.

> [a]llowing foreign investors to pursue private suits in the United States … would upset that delicate balance and offend the sovereign interests of foreign nations.[23]

This alignment, to be sure, might engender disappointment from activists committed to the rights of victims to reparations and compensation. The monetary damages dismissal in *RJR* understandably proved far more newsworthy in the aftermath of the litigation.[24]

Still, *RJR* presents as a slightly more generous read of the extraterritorial reach (than in previous cases) when a penal statute involves criminal activity, notably group-based organizational conduct and, of course, anything to do with 'terrorism' – the power of a word.

## III. Conclusion

While reliance on domestic legislation to address extraterritorial harm may achieve some good, it is an unsettled proposition. Defendants in such cases may succeed in dismissing lawsuits on the basis that the court in question is exceeding the permissible boundaries of its jurisdictional reach. In any event, even if justifiable extraterritorial reach is found, U.S. courts may also turn to other doctrines – *forum non conveniens* or the political question doctrine – to refuse to exercise jurisdiction. The result is that, at most, reliance on national legislation to redress extraterritorial transnational harms is and should be limited. What then? Well, it may make better sense to think of international enforcement or transnational codification of law. As Professor *Sunčana Roksandić Vidlička* ably argues:

> A purely national enforcement of criminal law has all too often been ineffective when serious economic crimes are at stake […] Serious economic crimes can have disastrous consequences for human rights (constituting the *Rechtsgut* of the offence) and are often root causes of conflict.[25]

And, certainly, in terms of diversifying remedies to include reparations to victims, well, one lesson of *RJR* is that even an aggressive domestic penal statute may not be able to offer much in the way of results. Here, too, it seems that international consensus is the most reliable way forward. That said, such consensus may be difficult to obtain. This means, then, to come full circle that national legislatures who are deeply committed to recovery of damages (and enforcement of punishment) in cases of serious transnational violations of law would need, extrapolating from the

---

[23] *Id.* at 2107 (quoting Brief for the Republic of France as Amicus Curiae in Support of Respondents at 26, Morrison, 561 U.S. 247).

[24] *Adam Liptak*, 'Supreme Court Sides with R.J. Reynolds in RICO Case', New York Times (June 20, 2016),

[25] *Sunčana Roksandić Vidlička*, 'Filling the void – the case for international economic criminal law', Zeitschrift für die gesamte Strafrechtswissenschaft, Volume 129, Issue 3 (2017), pp. 883–884.

US experience, to affirm as much clearly when they enact domestic legislation. The problem of judicial imperialism thereby arises. So, once again, it seems that a return to the muddled and murky process of international negotiation, creation of international treaties and organizations, and development of multilateral rights for victims' compensation is the best way forward. Languid, perhaps, this method still persists as a viable path to build mutual trust. Such is an interesting lesson in an era where multilateral institutionalism increasingly is subject to scathing political attack.

# The Phenomenon of Terrorist Political Parties and Countermeasures for Their Suppression

*Aleksandar Marsavelski**

## I. Introduction

In the early 1990s, *Leonard Weinberg* wrote the first and foremost article about the conditions under which political parties turn to terrorist activities.[1] He argued that the links between terrorist groups and political parties have become common, often affecting each other's appearances and disappearances.[2] There are many examples of such links. Political parties labelled as terrorist include the Kurdistan Workers' Party (PKK), which is linked to Kurdish militant separatism, as well as radical Islamist political parties linked to the Islamic State of Iraq and the Levant (ISIS). ISIS itself could be considered a terrorist political party seeking to establish a pan-Islamic state. Donetsk Republic is another proto-state political party, which is classified as a terrorist organization by the Ukrainian authorities.[3] In China, Uyghur jihadists have established a terrorist organization called Turkistan Islamic Party aimed at seeking the independence of East Turkestan. Some terrorist political parties have been dissolved, such as Batasuna and its successors, which served as political wings of the recently dissolved Basque terrorist organization ETA. Other parties continue to exist after renouncing their terrorist activity, such as Sinn Féin, an Irish political party historically associated with the Irish Republican Army (IRA).

In *Weinberg*'s view, political parties that are most likely to stimulate the formation of terrorist groups share two things in common: (1) advocating grandiose political goals and (2) highlighting the illegitimacy of the dominating political order.[4] Both these characteristics create challenges in finding an adequate definition

* Assistant Professor, Faculty of Law, University of Zagreb. The research for this paper was funded by the Croatian Science Foundation project.

[1] *Weinberg* 1991, pp. 423–438.

[2] *Weinberg* 1991, p. 436.

[3] Separatist political parties Donetsk Republic and Peace for Luhansk have been banned in Ukraine and classified as terrorist organizations. In 2014, these parties won the general elections in the unrecognized Donetsk People's Republic and Luhansk People's Republic respectively.

[4] *Weinberg* 1991, pp. 436–437.

of terrorism in the context of freedom fighter vs. terrorist dilemma.[5] For example, Hamas won the majority of seats in the 2006 Palestinian Parliament elections as a result of Palestine's struggle for freedom from Israeli oppression, but it also killed hundreds of Israeli civilians, and many countries consider Hamas a terrorist organization, including the U.S. and the EU.

According to *Michels*, modern political parties are 'fighting organizations' in the political sense of the term, and as such they must conform to the laws of tactics.[6] In democratic settings, their strategy is generally non-violent, because it consists of election campaigns. In authoritarian settings, however, they can take recourse to violence to maintain or obtain political power. The former are those ruling authoritarian parties, while the latter are considered revolutionary or terrorist organizations. Many contemporary social democratic parties evolved from communist parties that had used violence to overthrow monarchs or otherwise change the form of government in their countries. Many conservative political parties also evolved from militant nationalist parties that had fought for national unification or for the secession of a particular nation. Many of them used similar means of struggle to what ISIS is using today. Take for instance the assassination of the *King Alexander I of Yugoslavia*, orchestrated by the Internal Macedonian Revolutionary Organization (IMRO), a militant political organization with a background of armed uprisings against the Ottoman regime a few decades earlier. Today, attacks on any European head of state as well as violent uprisings would constitute acts of terrorism.[7]

But why do political parties take recourse to terrorism? The criminological explanation for this lies in *Merton*'s concept of 'rebellion'.[8] Terrorist violence occurs when opposition parties reject legitimate means to change the government or where such means are not available, so their actions are directed towards a replacement of the political system that conforms with their ideology and enables them to obtain political power.[9] In authoritarian countries, this is often the only way to change the government.

While the international community has laid down important international rules to prosecute individuals for atrocities constituting war crimes, crimes against humani-

---

5 *Marsavelski* 2013.

6 *Michels* 1966, p. 78.

7 Even at that time, the assassination of *King Alexander* was an *occasio legis* for the League of Nations' 1937 Convention for the Prevention and Punishment of Terrorism. Two IMRO's successor parties were re-established in the 1990s in Bulgaria and Macedonia, of course without terrorist policies or activities.

8 According to *Merton* 1939, p. 678, 'rebellion occurs when emancipation from the reigning standards, due to frustration or to marginalist perspectives, leads to the attempt to introduce a "new social order".'

9 *Marsavelski* 2014, p. 505.

ty, genocide, and even terrorism,[10] the international law neglects liability of political parties for such atrocities, as organizational liability is generally still disputed. Yet even at Nuremberg, the Nazi Party was not left without punishment. The International Military Tribunal charged the bodies of the Nazi Party with all crimes under the Nuremberg Charter, while the Tribunal convicted three of its bodies as criminal organizations. The statutory jurisdiction of the International Criminal Court, however, accepts neither the crime of terrorism nor the criminal liability of organizations. Furthermore, the terror of the Nazi Party initially began through its military wing, the SA *(Sturmabteilung)*, which was also prosecuted at Nuremberg but acquitted due to lack of temporal jurisdiction.

## II. Military wings of political parties

*Michels* argues that there is a close resemblance between a fighting democratic party and a military organization.[11] Many political parties emerged in non-democratic settings where they could only function as armed political organizations fighting against an oppressive regime. Once the political party assumed state power, the military wing lost its function and was usually either dissolved or transformed into the national army.

The Italian Fascists were the first creators of political party military wings.[12] In the early 1920s *Mussolini*'s National Fascist Party established a military wing known as the Blackshirts, which was later integrated into the Italian armed forces. The SA of the Nazi Party was the most powerful military wing of a political party that ever existed. By the end of 1933 it counted 4.5 million men and was by far more powerful than the German army.[13] The reason for this unusual state of affairs was that the 1919 Treaty of Versailles did not permit Germany to have a military exceeding 100,000 soldiers.

According to the dominant view in the literature, a political party cannot be exclusively formed on the basis of the militia.[14] It also needs non-military bodies in order to be a real political party and not merely a terrorist organization or a guerrilla group. Military wings are a kind of private army wearing party emblems and

---

[10] Regardless of the legal classification, some of these atrocities can constitute what is called 'state terrorism' in the literature. See *Primoratz* 2004, pp. 113–127. See also *Derenčinović* 2005, pp. 125–145.

[11] *Michels* 1966, p. 80.

[12] See *Duverger* 1976 [1964], p. 38.

[13] *Nuremberg Judgment* (1946), para. 481. According to the 1933 census, Germany had 65 million inhabitants, which means that nearly seven per cent of the German population were members of the SA.

[14] See *Duverger* 1976 [1964], p. 37.

subjected to the same discipline and training as soldiers. This is why no one in the literature has so far considered ISIS a political party. But this does not mean it could not become one. For instance, the first war criminal convicted by the International Criminal Court, *Thomas Lubanga Dyilo*, led the militia group called Union of Congolese Patriots, which later registered as a political party in DR Congo.

Sometimes political parties try to conceal their military wing in order to avoid liability. In the 1980s, during the Basque conflict, the ruling Spanish Socialist Workers Party (*Partido Socialista Obrero Español*, PSOE) established an informal military wing called Antiterrorist Liberation Groups *(Grupos Antiterroristas de Liberación)*, known under the acronym GAL, which was engaged in a dirty war against the Basque Homeland and Liberty organization (*EuskadiTa Askatasuna*, ETA). The connection between PSOE and GAL was kept secret from the general public, although the group was under the control of the PSOE leadership, including the Minister of Interior *José Barrionuevo* who was convicted in 1996 on charges related to his involvement in the 'dirty war' against ETA.

In democratic settings political parties no longer need an armed struggle to acquire state power because they are allowed to contest elections. However, there are two basic types of political parties that tend to establish military wings even in democratic settings. The first type are undemocratic political parties, which refuse to contest elections, because they want to replace democracy with an authoritarian regime (e.g. Nazi, Islamist, or Communist regime). The second type are separatist political parties that want a part of the state territory to secede and to establish an independent state (e.g. Basque country, Kurdistan, Donetsk or Luhansk Republic).

If a party's military wing is closely linked to the party's leadership, terrorist attacks committed by the party's military wing are easily attributable to the political party. In some cases, however, it is difficult to estimate the closeness of the relationship between the political party and its military wing. Again, a good example for this is Hamas, which has a military wing called Al-Qassam Brigades. Even though the Al-Qassam Brigades are an integral part of Hamas, they have a significant level of independence in decision making,[15] which makes it difficult to estimate whether we can attribute their crimes to Hamas or treat them as a separate organization.[16]

---

[15] Some authors described Hamas' relationship with the Brigades as reminiscent of Sinn Féin's relationship to the military arm of the IRA and quoted a senior Hamas official: 'al-Qassam Brigade is a separate armed military wing, which has its own leaders who do not take their orders [from Hamas] and do not tell us of their plans in advance.' (*Kass/O'Neill* 1997, p. 267). Carrying the IRA analogy further, *Kass/O'Neill* 1997, p. 268, state that the separation of the political and military wings shielded Hamas' political leaders from responsibility for terrorism while the plausible deniability this provided made Hamas an eligible representative for peace negotiations as had happened with Sinn Féin's *Gerry Adams*.

[16] In addition to this, Al-Qassam Brigades operate on a model of independent cells, and even high-ranking members are often not aware of the activities of other cells, which allows the group to consistently regenerate after member deaths.

In order to prevent terrorist activities of political parties, it is necessary to demilitarize them by dissolving the party's military wing. This is a mechanism to defend democracies against undemocratic political parties that tend to use their military wing in an armed struggle to acquire state power. The author of the concept of militant democracy, *Karl Loewenstein*, discusses this:

> All democratic states have enacted legislation against the formation of private paramilitary armies of political parties and against the wearing of political uniforms or parts thereof (badges, armlets) and the bearing of any other symbols (flags, banners, emblems, streamers, and pennants) which serve to denote the political opinion of the person in public ... The military garb symbolizes and crystallizes the mystical comradeship of arms so essential to the emotional needs of fascism.[17]

But do such laws of militant democracies solve the problem of terrorist political parties, having in mind that most terrorist political parties are illegal anyway and that many operate in non-democratic settings? For example, ISIS can be seen as a terrorist political party dominated by its military wing. ISIS could meet the essential elements of a political party – it is an organized group of people with the purpose to obtain and hold governmental power.[18] The best way to prevent terrorist organizations such as ISIS is to create conditions in which people do not support such organizations. In the Middle East it is essential to maintain peace and stability and boost economic development so that people do not support radical fundamentalist alternatives such as the Islamic State.

The first political promotion of the modern conceptualization of an 'Islamic state' came with the foundation of a political party called Jama'at-i Islami (Islamic Party) in British India by the Pakistani Muslim theologian *Mawlana Mawdudi*, who became the most influential Islamic revivalist in North Africa and Central and Southeast Asia.[19] Following the partition of India in 1947, Jama'at-i Islami split into separate independent political parties in India, Pakistan, and later Bangladesh. In February 2013, the Parliament of Bangladesh amended the 1973 International Crimes Tribunals Act, allowing the government to prosecute organizations for wartime atrocities that took place during the 1971 Bangladesh war for independence. The amendment paved the way for the prosecution of the largest Islamist political party in Bangladesh, Jama'at-i Islami, which collaborated with the Pakistani military in atrocities, including those labelled as Bangladesh genocide.[20] Although there are no links between Jama'at-i Islami and ISIS, they represent the two major competing concepts of an Islamic state, one that promotes a modern nation state with Islamic values, and one that promotes a pan-Islamic fundamentalist state. But

---

[17] *Loewenstein* 1937b, pp. 648–649.

[18] Some western-centric political scientists note that only parties that contest elections are political parties. E.g. *Sartori* 1975, p. 64.

[19] Following the partition of India in 1947, Jama'at-i Islami split into separate independent political parties in India, Pakistan, and Bangladesh.

[20] During the 1971 Bangladesh Liberation War, members of the Pakistani military and supporting Islamist militias from Jama'at-i Islami killed up to three million [4][8] people.

had it not been for such a strong political promotion of the concept of an Islamic state in countries with predominantly Muslim populations, perhaps ISIS would just have been a marginal terrorist organization.

Prosecutions of political parties were not unprecedented. Apart from the previously mentioned Nuremberg trial of the Nazi party organizations, ruling regimes in authoritarian settings have organized a number of political trials in order to prosecute opposition parties. The legislation applied in these cases constituted what *Jakobs* later called *Feindstrafrecht* (criminal law for the enemy), as we shall see in the historical case we will analyse in the next chapter.

## III. An example of a political trial against a political party

*Louis Proal* made an interesting remark in his study of political crime, in which he stated that '[w]henever political parties wish to persecute their adversaries, they invoke the public safety, satisfying their private grudges under pretext of the security of the people.'[21] Indeed, throughout history, the notion of enemy of the people has been widely used to justify the suppression of the political opposition. The Soviet criminal law concept of 'enemies of the people' *(враги народа)* was developed as a legal ground for the largest state practice of political trials in history, described in detail in *Solzhenitsyn*'s famous book *The Gulag Archipelago*.

The first major Soviet political trial took place in Moscow in 1922 against the members of the Party of Socialists-Revolutionaries (PSR), which supported the White Army during the first part of the Russian Civil War (1917–1919). The prosecution disregarded the 1919 Amnesty Decree, arguing that it only covered those individuals who had no longer taken part in the counterrevolutionary activities of PSR.

The trial was set up to try twenty-two members of the PSR.[22] They were indicted on four groups of counts: the first three related to the participation of the PSR in the civil war against the Soviet regime and the fourth to participating in *Volodarsky*'s assassination and in the assassination attempt on *Lenin*.[23] The defendants agreed with the facts of the first three counts but argued that these were covered by the 1919 Amnesty Decree. With respect to the last accusation, they denied the Party's involvement in assaults on Bolshevik leaders by arguing that these were isolated acts of individual PSR members.

The principal provision on counterrevolutionary crimes used against the defendants in this case was Art. 60 of the Criminal Code, penalizing membership in any

---

21 *Proal* 1898, p. 162.

22 *Woitinsky* 1922, p. 50.

23 *Woitinsky* 1922, p. 62.

organization whose actions were oriented towards the perpetration of counterrevolutionary acts listed in Arts. 57, 58, and 59 of the Code. In this case the Tribunal considered the PSR as a criminal organization within the meaning of Art. 60.[24]

The trial itself was very political. At the very first session, the presiding judge announced that 'the court does not intend to handle the case from a dispassionate, objective point of view but would be guided solely by the interests of the Soviet Government.'[25] Albeit the defendants were only individual members, the prosecution attempted to propose a sanction that would directly affect the PSR: at the end of the trial, the prosecution wanted the accused to 'repent and disavow their party'.[26] However, the defendants 'did not ask to be pardoned, nor to have their party dissolved and cease to be considered a party'.[27] Most of the defendants were found guilty and sentenced either to death (12) or to imprisonment (9), but they did not plead guilty, unlike the defendants in later Soviet show trials. This judgment was submitted for examination to the *All-Russian Central Executive Committee* in Moscow, which commuted the verdict by imposing a conditional sentence:

> The verdict will not be executed if the Party of Socialists-Revolutionists actually abandons all underground, conspiratory, *terroristic*, and rebel activity, as well as all military espionage against the Soviet Government. If, however, the Party of Socialists-Revolutionists will continue in the future to wage armed war against the Soviet Government, it will inevitably bring about the execution of all the condemned inspirers and organizers of *counter-revolutionary terrorism* and rebellion.[28]

This 'conditional sentence' was a *de facto* dissolution of the PSR – because any activity in opposition by this party could easily be interpreted as underground, conspiratory, terrorist, or rebel activity. It is clear that the main purpose of this political trial was not to impose death penalties on individuals but to impose a 'death penalty' on the political party, which was in fact the 'enemy of the people'.

The PSR trial demonstrates the way in which criminal law can be abused for political purposes when applied to political parties, especially in 'terrorism cases'. While the institution of anti-terrorism measures that followed after the September 11 attacks brought 'a radical revolution in legal theory and practice unparalleled in modern times',[29] including laws for the enemy, these measures failed to adequately address the engagement of political parties in terrorist activities. The international community left the issue of political parties acting as terrorist organizations to be dealt with through the national constitutional processes of banning political parties.

---

[24] *Jansen* 1922, p. 128.

[25] *Jansen* 1922, p. 52.

[26] *Jansen* 1922, p. 81.

[27] *Solzhenitsyn* 1975, p. 356.

[28] *Solzhenitsyn* 1975, pp. 82–83. See also *Jansen* 1922, p. 131.

[29] *Becker/Derenčinović* 2008, p. vii.

## IV. The liability of political parties for terrorist offences

There are several models of liability of political parties for terrorist offences. The harshest form of liability is criminal liability, because, typically, the criminal justice system has the power to impose the harshest punishments on individuals and organizations. Attribution of criminal liability to a political party should occur only in exceptional circumstances – only when there is a clear link between the party and the crime committed and alternative modes of liability have proven to be ineffective responses.

In most jurisdictions worldwide, political parties are considered to be legal entities if they are legally registered as such. Legislative reforms introducing corporate criminal liability result in an automatic extension of the range of criminal liability to political parties. In the course of such reforms some states restricted or excluded the criminal liability of political parties or exempted them from certain sanctions. For example, the criminal codes of France, Croatia, and Macedonia exempt political parties from the punishment of dissolution and ban on performance of certain activities. The purpose of such exemptions is to avoid direct interference of the criminal justice system in political processes.

In the European Union political parties are already mostly regulated as legal entities. In 2003, the EU passed a regulation governing European political parties, which, *inter alia*, determined that every political party at European level must meet the condition of 'legal personality in the Member State in which its seat is located'.[30] Albeit this regulation does not directly affect national political parties, it would be difficult for EU Members States to have a two track regime in which European political parties are legal persons while national ones are not.

The EU directive on combating terrorism requires Member States to take the necessary measures to ensure that legal persons can be held liable for terrorist offences and to ensure effective, proportionate, and dissuasive sanctions for legal persons.[31] This does not necessarily mean that EU Member States are obliged to impose criminal liability on legal entities (including political parties) for terrorist offences, but most of them tend to do so. Others introduced at least administrative liability on legal entities for terrorist offences (e.g. Germany).

The possibility of holding political parties liable as criminal organizations is widely accepted in the legislation although rare in practice. Criminal organization statutes are typically applicable to parties that are illegal because their activities are

---

[30] Regulation (EC) No 2004/2003 of the European Parliament and of the Council of 4 November 2003 on the regulations governing political parties at European level and the rules regarding their funding, Art. 3 (a).

[31] Directive (EU) 2017/541 of the European Parliament and of the Council of 15 March 2017 on combating terrorism and replacing Council Framework Decision 2002/475/JHA and amending Council Decision 2005/671/JHA, Arts. 17–18.

unconstitutional (e.g. terrorist organizations, extreme left or right parties). Terrorist organizations have been recognized as a distinct form of criminal organizations, both in international conventions and in national legislations. Some criminal legislations, such as the German Criminal Code, exempt political parties from liability as criminal organizations, leaving it primarily to constitutional courts to respond to their illegal activities. Although Germany has such an exemption for criminal organizations, called the party privilege, the Code does not include the same exemption with respect to political parties as terrorist organizations. This is due to the negative experiences with the Red Army Faction in the past. The 1976 criminal law reform introduced in § 129a of the Criminal Code a new criminal offence of forming terrorist organizations *(Bildung terroristischer Vereinigungen)*, but the new statute did not include a party's privilege provision, again giving criminal courts the power to decide on crimes of political parties without bringing the matter first to the Constitutional Court. Constitutional party bans are the main alternative form of liability of political parties for terrorism, besides criminal and administrative liability.

## V. Constitutional ban of terrorist political parties: the example of Spain

Spain is the country most experienced in constitutional bans of terrorist political parties in Europe. The cornerstone of militant democracies, such as Spain, is the possibility to ban undemocratic political parties.[32] In particular, the concept of militant democracy is often understood as a fight against radical political parties.[33] Thus, its mechanisms are designed to suppress particular types of wrongful activities by political parties – mainly those related to political subversion in form of terrorism or hate crime.

In 2002, for the first time since its transition to democracy in 1977, Spain passed a law that opened the way for the Supreme Court to order the dissolution of certain political parties. The *occasio legis* for passing the new Organic Law 6/2002 on Political Parties[34] was a problem with political parties linked to ETA. In particular, the focus of concern was Batasuna, the radical Basque separatist party widely perceived to be the political wing of the terrorist group ETA.[35]

---

32 See *Thiel* 2009a, p. 403.

33 See *Sajo* 2004, p. 210.

34 *Ley Orgánica 6/2002 de Partidos Políticos*, 27 June 2002. The previous Law 54/1978 on Political Parties of 4 December 1978, which regulated the possibility of dissolution or suspension of political parties by a competent judicial authority in two cases: (1) if a political party acted as an unlawful association pursuant to the Criminal Code, and (2) if their organization or activities were contrary to democratic principles.

35 *Turano* 2003, p. 730.

According to Art. 1 of the Spanish Constitution, Spain is a state that advocates political pluralism as one of the highest values of its legal system. This harks back to the transitional period in which the Constitution of Spain was enacted. It was one year after the downfall of *Franco*'s single-party system, which had brought decades of terror and the suppression of the political opposition. The bitter taste of *Franco*'s *Law on Political Responsibilities*, which outlawed all opposition parties, was still present. Hence, political parties, being the main instrument of political pluralism, have a special position in the Spanish constitutional law. They are regulated in preliminary provisions at the very beginning of the Constitution:

> Political parties are the expression of political pluralism, they contribute to the formation and expression of the will of the people and are an essential instrument for political participation. Their creation and the exercise of their activities are free in so far as they respect the Constitution and the law. Their internal structure and their functioning must be democratic (Art. 6).

However, the Constitution does not have a specific provision on banning political parties; instead it generally regulates restrictions on the right of association. According to the Art. 22(2) of the Constitution, associations which 'pursue ends or use means classified as criminal offences are illegal', while Art. 22(5) prohibits 'secret and paramilitary associations'.

The conditions and procedure of banning a political party in Spain is now regulated in the Organic Law 6/2002 on Political Parties, a law the Basque government had unsuccessfully challenged before the Constitutional Court in 2002.[36] Pursuant to Art. 9(2) of the Law, the conditions for banning a party read as follows:

> [A] political party is declared illegal if its activity violates democratic principles, particularly when, with that activity, it aims at damaging or destroying the regime of freedoms or at hindering or eliminating the democratic system, through any of the following conducts, carried out repeatedly and seriously: the systematic violation of fundamental rights and freedoms, by promoting, justifying or excusing attacks against life or physical integrity of persons, or the exclusion or persecution of persons on the basis of their ideology, religion or belief, nationality, race, gender, or sexual orientation; the instigation, encouragement or legitimation of violence as a means to achieve political goals or to eliminate the necessary conditions for the exercise of democracy, pluralism and political freedoms; the political completion and support of the terrorist organizations' action to achieve their purposes by subverting the constitutional order or seriously disrupting public peace, by trying to subject public authorities, specific individuals or society's groups or the population in general to a climate of terror, or the contribution to multiply the effects of both terrorist violence and the fear and intimidation generated by it.[37]

It is clear that the new law, *inter alia*, expands the state power to ban groups that support violent acts committed by others even when they do not engage in violence themselves. This provision is followed by a very detailed description of types of conduct relevant for establishing the conditions for banning a political party (Art. 9(4)

---

[36] See *Pietro* 2010, p. 239.

[37] *Ley Orgánica 6/2002 de Partidos Políticos*, 27 June 2002, Art. 9(2) as cited in *Pietro* 2010, p. 231.

*Banned political parties in Spain under Organic Law 6/2002*

| **Political Party** | **Year of registration** | **Date of Supreme Court's declaration of illegality and subsequent decisions** |
|---|---|---|
| Basque Citizens *(Euskal Herritarrok, EH)* | 1998 | 27/1/2003 – Supreme Court<br>16/1/2004 – Constitutional Court<br>30/6/2009 – ECtHR |
| Popular Unity *(Herri Batasuna, HB)* | 1986 | 27/3/2003 – Supreme Court<br>17/1/2004 – Constitutional Court<br>30/6/2009 – ECtHR |
| Unity *(Batasuna)* | 2001 | 27/3/2003 – Supreme Court<br>21/1/2004 – Constitutional Court<br>30/6/2009 – ECtHR |
| Movement for Auto-determination (*Autodeterminaziorako Bilgunea, AuB)* | 2003 | 3/5/2003 – Supreme Court<br>9/5/2003 – Constitutional Court<br>1/7/2009 – ECtHR |
| Socialist Patriots *(Sozialista Abertzaleak, SA)** | 2003 | [20/5/2003 – Supreme Court order (RJ 2003, 4058)] |
| List of Citizens *(Herritarren Zerrenda, HZ)* | 2004 | 24/5/2004 – Supreme Court<br>27/5/2004 – Constitutional Court<br>30/6/2009 – ECtHR |
| All the Options *(Aukera Guztiak, AG)* | 2005 | 27/3/2005 – Supreme Court<br>31/3/2005 – Constitutional Court |
| Socialist Patriots *(Abertzale Socialisten)*** | 2007 | 4/5/2007 – Supreme Court<br>11/5/2007 – Constitutional Court |
| Union of Socialist Patriots *(Abertzale Sozialisten Batasuna, ASB)* | 2007 | 16/5/2007 – Supreme Court<br>11/4/2008 – Constitutional Court: the appeal is not admissible |
| Basque Nationalist Action *(Eusko Abertzale Ekintza – Acción Nacionalista Vasca, EAE-ANV)* | 1977 [1930] | 16/9/2008 – Supreme Court<br>29/1/2009 – Constitutional Court<br>15/1/2013 – ECtHR |
| Communist Party of the Basque Homelands *(Euskal Herrialdeetako Alderdi Komunista, EHAK)* | 2002 | 18/9/2008 – Supreme Court<br>29/1/2009 – Constitutional Court |
| Freedom *(Askatasuna)* | 1998 | 9/2/2009 – Supreme Court<br>13/2/2009 – Constitutional Court |
| Three Million Democracy *(Demokrazia Hiru Milioi, D3M)* | 2009 | 10/2/2009 – Supreme Court<br>13/2/2009 – Constitutional Court<br>30/6/2009 – ECtHR |

* successor of the banned party Batasuna

** founded because of the expected ban of Abertzale Sozialisten Batasuna (ASB)

of the Law).[38] Finally, Art. 9(4) of the Law provides the acts that must be taken into consideration when ascertaining and assessing the activities of a political party, including, *inter alia*: 'criminal convictions of its leaders, candidates, elected persons or members, for crimes established by the Penal Code, in the absence of any internal disciplinary action leading to the expulsion of the same convicted persons'.[39]

The Government and the Public Prosecutor's Office are entitled to seek a constitutional ban of a political party. In addition to these, the Congress of Deputies and the Senate may also call upon the Government to seek the banning of a political party. The case is then brought before the Special Chamber of the Supreme Court, including all the evidence relevant for banning the party (e.g. police reports, party statute). During this procedure, there is a possibility to impose precautionary measures pertaining to the activities of the political party. After the judgment is delivered, the parties can appeal to the Constitutional Court. If a party is banned, its activities stop immediately. After the Constitutional Court, the ultimate instance for the banned party is the European Court of Human Rights. In practice, Spanish courts have applied this procedure mainly to political parties linked with ETA. The table on the left presents the relevant information about these parties and subsequent bans during the first ten years of applying the Organic Law. It also shows a significant jurisprudence of the European Court of Human Rights (ECtHR) on such cases, which established legal standards that shall be analysed in the forthcoming chapter.

## VI. Freedom of political association in the ECtHR's jurisprudence

The Council of Europe has developed the most advanced international standards concerning freedom of political association and the extent to which restrictions are permitted. In 1999, following a survey on the practice among countries, the Venice Commission adopted a set of guidelines[40] on the dissolution of political parties, which recognized that:

> Prohibition or dissolution of political parties can be envisaged only if it is necessary in a democratic society and if there is concrete evidence that a party is engaged in activities threatening democracy and fundamental freedoms. This could include any party that advocates violence in all forms as part of its political programme or any party aiming to overthrow the existing constitutional order through armed struggle, *terrorism* or the organisation of any subversive activity.[41]

---

38 See *Pietro* 2010, pp. 231–232.

39 See *Pietro* 2010, pp. 232–233.

40 Guidelines on the Prohibition and Dissolution of Political Parties and Analogous Measures, adopted by the Venice Commission at its 41st plenary session in Venice, 10–11 December 1999, CDL-INF (2000) 1.

41 *Ibid.*, Explanatory Report, § 10.

The freedom of political association is part of a broader human right of freedom of association guaranteed under the major regional and international human rights documents.[42] The European Convention on Human Rights (ECHR) clearly states that freedom of association is not an absolute right and that restrictions are possible if two conditions are satisfied: (1) that the restriction is prescribed by law and (2) that such restriction is necessary in a democratic society.

The first condition is merely a formal requirement, and it is satisfied if the unlawful conduct and subsequent sanctions for political parties are *prescribed by law*. In the case of *Herri Batasuna and Batasuna v. Spain*, the European Court of Human Rights reiterated that the principle of legality can be considered as respected when measures adopted by a state are not only grounded in the national law but are also sufficiently accessible and foreseeable as to their effects, i.e. sufficiently precise in their wording to enable persons to adjust their conduct.[43] Furthermore, the Court underlined that the exceptions set out in Art. 11 are to be strictly construed.[44] With respect to the imposition of criminal sanctions against political parties, the Convention also provides special guarantees of the principle of legality under Art. 7(1). These guarantees are essential elements of the rule of law, in particular its two main aspects: non-retroactivity of criminalization and clarity of criminal legislation. On the other hand, the framers of the Convention also included an exception to the principle of legality in Art. 7(2) to enable punishing war crimes and other serious offences committed in war times.

The second is substantive in nature and needs to be interpreted. In determining the existence of a necessity, states have only a limited margin of appreciation, which goes hand in hand with the rigorous European supervision embracing both the law and the decisions applying it.[45] Only convincing and compelling reasons can justify restrictions on freedom of association, even more so where political parties are concerned, given the importance of their role in a democratic society.[46] According to the Court's jurisprudence, the phrase 'necessary in a democratic society' means that, to be compatible with the Convention, the interference must correspond to: (1) a pressing social need, (2) to be proportionate to the legitimate aim pursued, and (3) to conform to democratic principles.[47] Each of these standards shall be further elaborated.

---

42 See e.g. Art. 11 ECHR, Art. 16 ACHR, Arts. 20 and 23 UDHR.

43 *Herri Batasuna and Batasuna v. Spain* (2009), para. 56.

44 *Herri Batasuna and Batasuna v. Spain* (2009), para. 77.

45 *Herri Batasuna and Batasuna v. Spain* (2009), para. 77.

46 *Herri Batasuna and Batasuna v. Spain* (2009), para. 77. See also *United Communist Party of Turkey and Others v. Turkey* (1998), para. 46; *Socialist Party and Others v. Turkey* (1998), para. 50; *Freedom and Democracy Party (ÖZDEP) v. Turkey* (1999), para. 45; *Refah Partisi (Welfare Party) and Others v. Turkey* (2003), para. 100.

47 See e.g. *Socialist Party and Others v. Turkey* (1998), 25 May 1998, paras. 46–52.

First, in *Handyside v. UK*, the Court ruled that the word 'necessary' meant that there must be a *pressing social need* for the interference.[48] While evaluating whether such a 'pressing social need' exists or not, the Court grants national authorities a certain margin of appreciation: 'it is for the national authorities to make the initial assessment of the reality of the pressing social need.'[49]

Second, it is the evaluation of democratic necessity that has spawned the most significant principle of investigation into the reasonableness of human rights restrictions – the *principle of proportionality*.

Any measure taken against political parties affects the freedom of association and subsequently the democratic processes in the country concerned.[50] In particular, drastic measures, such as dissolution of a political party, may be taken only in the most serious cases.[51]

The statute and the programme of a political party cannot be used as the sole criterion for determining its objectives and intentions, but its content must be compared with the actions of party members and leaders as well as with the positions they defend.[52] However, in *Refah Partisi (Welfare Party) and Others v. Turkey*, the Court took the view that a state cannot be required to wait with an intervention until a political party has seized power and begun to take concrete steps to implement a policy incompatible with the standards of the Convention and democracy even though the danger to democracy is sufficiently established and imminent. The Court considered that where the national courts established the presence of such a danger, after detailed scrutiny subject to rigorous European supervision, a state may 'reasonably forestall the execution of such a policy, which is incompatible with the Convention's provisions, before an attempt is made to implement it through concrete steps that might prejudice civil peace and the country's democratic regime'.[53]

---

48 *Handyside v. UK* (1976), para. 48.

49 *Handyside v. UK* (1976), para. 48. See also *Janowski v. Poland* (1999), para. 30 ('States have a certain margin of appreciation in assessing whether such a need exists, but it goes hand in hand with a European supervision, embracing both the legislation and the decisions applying it, even those given by an independent court').

50 *Ouranio Toxo and Others v. Greece* (2005), para. 34.

51 *Herri Batasuna and Batasuna v. Spain* (2009), para. 78. See also *United Communist Party of Turkey and Others v. Turkey* (1998), para. 46; *Socialist Party and Others v. Turkey* (1998), para. 50; *Freedom and Democracy Party (ÖZDEP) v. Turkey* (1999), para. 45; *Refah Partisi (Welfare Party) and Others v. Turkey* (2003), para. 100.

52 *Herri Batasuna and Batasuna v. Spain* (2009), para. 80. See also *United Communist Party of Turkey and Others v. Turkey* (1998), para. 58. E.g., expressing a separatist ideology by demanding territorial changes in speeches, demonstrations, or political programmes do not *per se* endanger the territorial integrity and national security of a state, and thus it does not affect the protections under the Convention. See *United Macedonian Organisation Ilinden and Others v. Bulgaria* (2006), para. 76.

53 *Refah Partisi (Welfare Party) and Others v. Turkey* (2003), para. 102. See also *Herri Batasuna and Batasuna v. Spain* (2009), para. 81.

It is important to bear in mind that one precondition for such preventive interventions in political processes is the existence of a *pressing social need.* According to the Court's case law, the examination of the question whether the dissolution of a political party on grounds of a risk for democratic principles meets a pressing social need must concentrate on: (1) whether there was plausible evidence that the risk to democracy was sufficiently imminent and (2) whether, from acts and speeches imputable to the party, it is possible to draw a clear picture of a model of society incompatible with the concept of a democratic society.[54]

The Court has observed that the fact that activities of a political party are regarded by national authorities as undermining the constitutional order of the state does not mean that the party does not enjoy protection pursuant to Art. 11 and other protections granted by the Convention.[55] It is in the nature of political parties to influence the whole regime, in particular to make proposals for an overall societal model, which they put before the electorate, and to implement those proposals once they come to power.[56] The Court underlined that a political party may promote a change in the law and the constitutional order of a state under two conditions: (1) the means used must be in accordance with the law and democratic processes, and (2) the proposed change must be compatible with fundamental democratic principles.[57] Hence, a political party whose leaders incite violence or advocate a policy that does not respect democracy or whose purpose is to destroy democracy, including the rights and freedoms recognized in democracies, do not enjoy the Convention's protection against penalties imposed on those grounds.[58]

Some specific restrictions that can be considered necessary in a democratic society are already envisaged in regional human rights documents. We shall observe how these exceptions can be related to political parties, i.e. to freedom of political association. The exceptions relevant for the criminal responsibility of political parties are the following: (1) interests of national security or public safety, (2) prevention of crime, (3) protection of the rights and freedoms of others, (4) exclusion of members of the armed forces and the police.

First, the interests of national security or public safety can be at stake when an opposition political party engages in activities involving violence, in particular in case of terrorist acts. Once a political party takes recourse to terrorism, in any state

54 *Refah Partisi (Welfare Party) and Others v. Turkey* (2003), para. 104. See also *Herri Batasuna and Batasuna v. Spain* (2009), para. 83.

55 *United Communist Party of Turkey and Others v. Turkey* (1998), para. 27; *Socialist Party and Others v. Turkey* (1998), para. 29; *Presidential Party of Mordovia v. Russia* (2004), para. 28.

56 *Refah Partisi (Welfare Party) and Others v. Turkey* (2003), para. 87.

57 *Herri Batasuna and Batasuna v. Spain* (2009), para. 79.

58 *Herri Batasuna and Batasuna v. Spain* (2009), para. 80. See also *United Communist Party of Turkey and Others v. Turkey* (1998), para. 58; *Refah Partisi (Welfare Party) and Others v. Turkey* (2003), para. 100.

in the world, whether authoritarian or democratic, the party will be deemed a terrorist organization and subsequently dissolved. The intriguing question is whether a political party can be subject to such severe sanctions if it engages in activities involving less violence, such as violent public protests. There is no solid ground in arguing that a sanction for a political party organizing such a protest should be automatically dissolved. Furthermore, there are various circumstances that should be considered, in particular in democratic societies, because, otherwise, such sanctions would violate the proportionality inherent to the principle of necessity in democratic societies.

The second restriction, related to the prevention of crime, overlaps with the first regarding crimes that endanger the national security or public safety.

The third restriction generally relates to the protection of rights and freedoms of others. Crimes of political parties always affect the rights and freedoms of others, although their consequences need not always be direct. This depends on the type of crime. For instance, practicing systematic torture of political dissidents directly violates the human right to freedom from torture, while corruption indirectly affects the rights of all citizens.

These exceptions demonstrate the nature of the relationship between political freedoms and criminal responsibility of political parties: the freedom of political association does not legally prevent holding political parties criminally liable. Nevertheless, there is no doubt that the criminal responsibility of political parties as well as subsequent criminal sanctions have the potential to represent a practical restriction on the freedom of political association. However, it would never eliminate this freedom because, even in cases where a party is dissolved, the members can always establish a new political party. Therefore, this issue should be conceived in terms of whether or not we want to produce an effect that could marginalize certain actors from political life. When it comes to terrorist political parties, this is undoubtedly a desired effect.

## VII. Conclusion

Bringing political parties to court in order to determine their liability for criminal offences is a feature of the contemporary judicialization of politics.[59] This tendency has direct implications for the constitutional division of powers, which is the most plausible reason why, in many countries, it appears inconceivable to attribute criminal liability to political parties. Countries have introduced or maintained various legal obstacles to the prosecution or conviction of political parties, and most law enforcement bodies are unwilling to undertake criminal procedures and hold politi-

59 *Hirschl* 2008, p. 119.

cal parties criminally liable. The jurisprudence of the European Court of Human Rights clearly indicates that neither criminal prosecutions nor alternative sanctions on terrorist political parties, including party bans, would be incompatible with human rights standards.

But when it comes to terrorist political parties, jurisdictions worldwide find a way to impose sanctions. Listings of political parties as terrorist organizations spark controversy as such procedures are the result of government decisions rather than the outcome of court proceedings. To avoid this, international criminal law should follow the Nuremberg precedent and include the liability of terrorist political parties.

Bringing parties to court, however, is not always an ideal solution either. Various controversies linked to political trials throughout history have demonstrated the need for restrictions on the criminal responsibility of political parties in political settings where criminal proceedings risk being instrumentalized in confrontations with the opposition parties. Therefore, it is necessary to strike an adequate balance between the interests of justice and the need of preserving a functioning democratic system.[60] Having evaluated different models of criminal liability of political parties, we can conclude that each model has its advantages and disadvantages. It is an illusion to think that there is one model that fits all situations, because it also depends on the political system, the legal tradition (common law vs. civil law), the type of terrorist activity, and many other circumstances. After all, one man's terrorist organization is another man's freedom party.

## Bibliography

*Becker, Steven W./Derenčinović, Davor*, Foreword. In: S.W. Becker/D. Derenčinović (eds.), International Terrorism: The Future Unchained? Faculty of Law, University of Zagreb. Zagreb 2008.

*Derenčinović, Davor*, Državni terorizam. In: D. Derenčinović, Ogledi o terorizmu i antiterorizmu. Zagreb 2005.

*Di Pietro, Diana*, Does Terrorism Need Democracy? The Spanish Cases on Political Parties Accused of Being Linked with ETA before the European Court of Human Rights. In: G. Guarino/I. D'Anna (eds.), International Institutions and Co-operation: Terrorism, Migrations, Asylum. Naples 2010, pp. 225–276.

*Duverger, Maurice*, Political Parties: Their Organization and Activity in the Modern State. 3rd ed. Cambridge 1976 [1964].

*Hirschl, Ran*, The Judicialization of Politics. In: K.E. Whittington et al. (eds.), The Oxford Handbook of Law and Politics. Oxford University Press Oxford 2008.

60 *Marsavelski* 2014, p. 525.

*Jansen, Marc*, A Show Trial Under Lenin: The Trial of the Socialist Revolutionaries. Moscow 1922.

*Kass, Ilana/O'Neill, Bard E.*, The deadly embrace: the impact of Israeli and Palestinian rejectionism on the peace process. University Press of America 1997.

*Loewenstein, Karl*, Militant Democracy and Fundamental Rights, II. 31 The American Political Science Review 638–658 (1937).

*Marsavelski, Aleksandar*, The Crime of Terrorism and the Right of Revolution in International Law. 28 Connecticut Journal of International Law 243–295 (2013).

– Responsibility of Political Parties for Criminal Offences: Preliminary Observations, Challenges and Controversies. In: A.-M. Getoš Kalac/H.-J. Albrecht/M. Kilchling (eds.), Mapping the Criminological Landscape of the Balkans. Duncker & Humblot Berlin 2014, pp. 499–525.

*Merton, Robert*, Social Structure and Anomie. 3 American Sociological Review 672–682 (1939).

*Michels, Robert*, Political Parties: A Sociological Study of the Oligarchical Tendencies of Modern Democracy. 2nd ed. Free Press 1966.

*Primoratz, Igor*, State Terrorism and Counter-terrorism. In: Igor Primoratz (ed.), Terrorism: The Philosophical Issues. Palgrave Macmillan New York 2004.

*Proal, Louis*, Political Crime. T. Fisher Unwin London 1898.

*Sajo, Andras*, Militant Democracy and Transition towards Democracy. In: A. Sajo (ed.), Militant Democracy. Eleven International Publishing Utrecht 2004.

*Sartori, Giovanni*, Parties and Party Systems: A Framework for Analysis. ECPR Classics Colchester 2005[1976].

*Solzhenitsyn, Aleksandr*, The Gulag Archipelago. Harper & Row New York 1975.

*Thiel, Markus*, Comparative Aspects. In: M. Thiel (ed.), The 'Militant Democracy' – Principle in Modern Democracies. Ashgate Farnham 2009, pp. 379–424.

*Turano, Leslie*, Spain: Banning political parties as a response to Basque terrorism. 1 International Journal of Constitutional Law 730–740 (2003).

*Weinberg, L.*, Turning to Terror: The Conditions under Which Political Parties Turn to Terrorist Activities. 4 Comparative Politics 423–438 (1991).

*Woitinsky, Wladimir*, The Twelve Who Are to Die: The Trial of the Socialists-Revolutionists in Moscow. Berlin 1922.

## Case law

*Freedom and Democracy Party (ÖZDEP) v. Turkey* (1999), App. No. 23885/94, ECtHR GC Judgment of 8 December 1999.

*Handyside v. UK* (1976), App. No. 5493/72, ECtHR Judgment of 7 December 1976.

*Herri Batasuna and Batasuna v. Spain* (2009), App. Nos. 25803/04 and 25817/04, ECtHR Judgment of 30 June 2009.

*Janowski v. Poland* (1999), App. No. 25716/94, ECtHR Judgment of 21 January 1999.

*Nuremberg Judgment* (1946), IMT Judgment for the Trial of German Major War Criminals, 30 September and 1 October, 1946.

*Ouranio Toxo and Others v. Greece* (2005), App. No. 74989/01, ECtHR Judgment of 20 October 2010.

*Presidential Party of Mordovia v. Russia* (2004), App. No. 65659/01, ECtHR Judgment of 5 October 2004.

*Refah Partisi and Others v. Turkey* (2003), App. Nos. 41340/98, 41342/98, 41343/98 and 41344/98, ECtHR GC Judgment of 13 February 2003.

*Socialist Party and others v. Turkey* (1998), Case No. 20/1997/804/1007, ECtHR Judgment of 25 May 1998.

*United Communist Party of Turkey and Others v. Turkey* (1998), Case No. 133/1996/752/951, ECtHR Judgment of 30 January 1998.

*United Macedonian Organisation Ilinden and Others v. Bulgaria* (2006), App. No. 59491/00, ECtHR Judgment of 19 January 2006.

# Phasing the Syrian Crisis: from Peaceful Protests to Internationalized Conflict

*Cenap Çakmak*

## I. Introduction

Emerging as part of a series of peaceful and sporadic protests aimed at expressing dissatisfaction with the brutality and authoritarian practices of the Assad regime, the Syrian crisis has undergone different stages over time, evolving from popular demonstrations into an internationalized armed conflict that now involves the interests of major powers, states in the region, sub-state actors, and global terror networks. Although seen as part of the Arab Spring process that has marked a process of political change in some of the Middle East and North African (MENA) countries, the conflict now bears no association with this popular awakening whatsoever.

In some aspects, the Syrian crisis exhibits similarities with both past and ongoing civil wars; but there are also striking differences in terms of the actors involved in the conflict, the nature of the dispute, and the interests and ambitions raised in the process. Typically, a civil war involves two major factions: a central government and a rebellious group representing a part of society dissatisfied with the regime rule. Only a small portion of internal conflicts draw reaction from a third party, usually neighboring states. The Syrian conflict stands out with its internationalized nature, eventually attracting the attention of major powers, regional actors, and leading intergovernmental organizations. In international legal terms, the conflict is an armed conflict of non-international character, indicating that there are at least two parties that have to comply with the rules of international humanitarian law. But the political reality goes well beyond this legal characterization.

Relevant rules and principles of international law are applicable to most of the warring parties, whereas the Assad regime recognizes all opposition groups as terrorists, suggesting that they are subject to national law. Relatively moderate groups seem to have observed international humanitarian law, whereas Islamist extremists honor no boundary in their cause. The political nature of the conflict is further complicated by the intricacy of the positions and political interests of the actors on the ground. The regime seeks to maintain full control over the Syrian territory even if it means unusual concessions including military presence to unofficial allies; an international coalition of Western powers is mainly concerned about the eradication of the Islamic State (ISIS) in both Syria and Iraq. Some of the regional actors support the main opposition group, Free Syrian Army (FSA), whereas neighboring states, particularly Turkey, have their own exclusive concerns, i.e., border security.

The alliances are also shaped by the diversity of the actors and the interests which often appear to be irreconcilable. On one level, for instance, Turkey and the United States hold similar aspirations such as toppling Assad and supporting the FSA; but a visible schism is observed in their approaches vis-à-vis the Kurdish groups in the northern part of Syria. While the majority of Arab states express support for the FSA, they align with the US when it comes to a Turkish military offensive against the major pro-Kurdish groups. Russia and Iran lend extensive support to the Assad regime; however, there are slight disagreements in terms of how territorial integrity should be maintained and protected.

## II. Syria and the Arab Spring: unorganized sporadic protests and demonstrations

The popular uprisings in the Arab world against repressive regimes since 2011 have been exemplified in and/or exerted influence on Tunisia, Egypt, Libya, and then Syria. This so-called Arab Spring process was understood as a great opportunity by the majority of Arab citizens to express their opposition to brutal regimes. The reactions and protests in Syria that began after the arrest and the subsequent torture of a boy grew further when the boy was not released. It should be noted that the protests were unplanned and spontaneous for the most part.

What has been occurring in Syria is the last in the chain of popular movements in the Middle East. The riots were triggered by the failure of the Assad regime to keep its promises to introduce reforms and by mass arrests. It should be noted that what occurred in Syria is closely linked with political concerns, including the lifting of the martial law order – in effect since 1963 – as well as the recognition of political freedoms. A review of the ongoing conflict in Syria reveals that there are not too many similarities with the Arab Spring process. Unlike in the cases of Tunisia and Egypt, there is now a domestic struggle for power rather than consistent demands for rights and freedoms.

It is difficult to argue that the protestors had specific demands in mind in the initial stages of the opposition and reaction. Although it is possible to find some generic demands regarding fundamental rights and freedoms, the lack of systematic demands and a well-defined political stance to satisfy these demands should be noted. As might have been expected, the Assad regime failed to make reasonable accommodation for these unplanned and unorganized reactions. Instead, the regime opted to use brutality to address this problem, mostly for fear that the sentiments of the Arab Spring would spread to the region.

However, the protestors did not retreat; instead, they expressed their demands more loudly. Contrary to the expectations of the regime, the people voiced their demands more systematically and decisively. They now placed greater emphasis on the details of their demands, including the need for political reform. The Assad regime responded violently; to clarify, it should be noted that at this stage there was no organized opposition asking for the resignation of the Assad regime. Their only demand was political reform. In other words, the initial demands of the protestors were not so comprehensive as to demand a revolution.

At this stage, the international community's stance regarding the demonstrations was moderate, sometimes ethical and principled. It was noted that the Assad regime must respond positively to popular demands; thus, the international community acted on a normative basis. However, the Assad regime did not respond to the calls from international actors and instead escalated its violence against the protestors. However, the protestors did not back down. It should be emphasized that, at this stage, the street protests were the main form of demonstration by the opposition, and that the protestors were unarmed. Therefore, what occurred in Syria was that unarmed protestors took to the streets demanding freedom and reform, and the regime responded to these demands and protests with violence. The international community's stance vis-à-vis this brutality was mostly ethical and cannot be considered an intervention in domestic affairs.

In response to the growing brutality of the Assad regime, parts of the international community clarified their position and urged the regime to introduce reforms. It should be recalled that, at this stage, the removal of Assad from power was not the main goal. The international community asked Assad to introduce reforms rather than to abdicate. It should also be recalled that comprehensive talks were held with Assad to discuss these matters. In these talks, proponents of change stressed the initiation of a reform process to address the demands of the people.

However, the Assad regime failed to respond to these calls more strongly and adopted a harsher approach to the opposition groups. Despite these harsh measures, the international community continued to ask the Assad regime to consider introducing political reforms as an option. However, the US concluded that the Assad regime had no intention of introducing reforms and began to stress that Assad and his regime must leave. Turkey followed suit shortly thereafter and urged the Assad regime to step down, after concluding that the regime had no intention whatsoever of addressing the demands of the people.

This conclusion was not based on subjective considerations. Reports by independent human rights groups and by the UN Human Rights Council confirm that the Assad regime committed heinous crimes including crimes against humanity, which means that there was documented brutality and a campaign of massacres initiated by the regime; in addition, the documentation also indicated that the regime had no intention of giving up on this campaign any time soon. Because asking

Assad to step down required an alternative, actors that favored a regime change including the US and Turkey made efforts to ensure that an opposition would emerge. To this end, they tried to create an international front against the Assad regime and united certain opposition groups.

## III. Civil war in Syria

Government brutality and resilience of the opposition created a distinct environment where the Syrian crisis turned into a bloody civil war. Amidst diplomatic efforts to address the growing violence in the country and to achieve some form of stability, attention was paid to the individual crimes committed by the members of the warring parties in the conflict. Although it seems that the priority of the international actors is to put an end to the conflict and to make plausible plans for the overall outlook of the country in the aftermath of the conflict, how to deal with the individual crimes is also relevant to this endeavor, particularly because of the possibility that the leaders of the warring factions may face international prosecution.

There are now concrete discussions and even desires to hold Assad accountable for these crimes. But the list of the culprits may not be limited to Assad; many others on his side as well as members of the opposition groups, particularly the extremist jihadist factions, may also be referred to the national or international courts because of their involvement in criminal activities. For this reason, given that a great number of individuals may be summoned to the courtroom, the political outlook of the country will be most likely influenced by the judicial process that may follow the end of the conflict.

At this stage, it is apparent that since the start of the popular uprising in Syria, many international crimes which call for individual and collective responsibility have been committed. These offenses, which are prosecutable under international law by any state regardless of whether they were committed in their territories or under a competent international body in accordance with the principle of universal jurisdiction, may include crimes against humanity and war crimes. Crimes against humanity are offenses that can be perpetrated in times of peace and of war. Several reliable reports indicate that members of the Assad regime have been responsible for the commission of such crimes since the beginning of the riots. On the other hand, war crimes are offenses that can only be identified in times of armed conflict. Therefore, to report war crimes requires a proper armed conflict defined as such under international law.

It could be said that the upheaval in Syria turned into a civil war a long time ago. Into a civil war, where the clashing parties are required under international law, particularly international humanitarian law and the law of armed conflict, to observe the rules applicable to armed confrontations. Now some other reports indicate that both warring parties, the Assad regime and the opposition groups, could be held liable for the perpetration of international crimes, particularly war crimes. As noted above, international law assumes the role and authority to interfere in matters involving the commission of these offenses, as the perpetrators will not remain solely in the hands of the relevant national authorities. In cases where international crimes are committed, the jurisdiction of a national authority is extended to cover the prosecution of the individuals identified as culprits.

An evaluation of the situation in the Syrian domestic war is particularly crucial and relevant as this may be taken as a basis for an international action to deal with the conundrum in the country. It should be noted that the international community is not required – morally or legally – to interfere in the internal matters of a given country. A high number of casualties in a clash does not necessarily mean that the international society or any given state or institution should assume a role and initiate a military campaign to stop the killings. This may sound strange; but if it is fought properly and legally, a civil war cannot be considered a reason to intervene in the domestic affairs of the country where this war is taking place, unless the war is considered a threat to international peace and security.

The case in Syria is complicated from several aspects. It requires closer attention and analysis for a better understanding of the nature of the crisis and the probable measures that could be taken by the international community in connection with possible breaches of legal responsibilities of the parties and the applicable international legal rules. The crisis started as a popular uprising against the central government. The people asked for reforms and for recognition of their fundamental rights by the regime. They held peaceful protests and demonstrations, to which the government forces and the militia backing them responded with brutal force. At this stage, it was reported that regime forces committed some international crimes, particularly crimes against humanity.

However, things have significantly changed since the crisis was transformed into the form of a civil war with two major warring parties, the Assad regime and the Free Syrian Army, as well as other armed opposition groups. There is no central authority to decide whether or not the situation in Syria can be defined as a civil war; but there is widespread agreement – as evidenced by the statements and calls by relevant bodies including the Red Cross and the UN – that the parties are now fighting an internal war where they have, in addition to the responsibility to avoid crimes against humanity, now also responsibilities in connection with war crimes.

Verification of international crimes is extremely important as this may serve as a main basis for legitimate military action. Under current international law, military intervention is legitimized in case of a threat against international peace and security as determined by the UN Security Council. As an emergent international norm, responsibility to protect (R2P) may also be taken as a means of justification to prove the existence of such a threat. This norm basically suggests that they are inherently sovereign despite this fact. States are responsible to protect their people against genocide, crimes against humanity, war crimes, and ethnic cleansing. The norm further states that in case they fail to fulfill this obligation, the international community should take action to protect the people.

From this perspective, it could be said that when it is apparent that a state is unable or unwilling to protect its people against said situations, the international community is allowed to take any measure including military action. The widespread commission of international crimes, including, more recently, the employment of chemical weapons in Syria, may be viewed as a breach of this responsibility. Therefore, it could be argued that the international community has a moral and legal obligation to deal with the situation. However, past practice now shows that the UN Security Council has sole discretion to determine whether a state has breached its responsibility to protect its people.

## IV. Regionalization of the conflict and use of proxies

The Syrian crisis did not remain a conventional civil war; instead, it attracted attention from regional powers as well as global players with strong regional interests and visions. Even though the main line of division was drawn to separate the Assad regime from the moderate opposition, the alignments in the regionalization phase, in some cases, went beyond this designation and involved reliance on proxies to protect specific security interests and use the conflict as an opportunity to address their own national concerns.

The conflict was thus further complicated due to the involvement of the proxies, leading to a visible sectarian divide that became a major dynamic in the political alignments among the actors on the ground. But not all proxies have enjoyed support from a favorable regional player; the ISIS managed to become enemy of them all, with not a single ally, despite its strong rigid Sunni ideological basis. The same applies to al-Qaeda-linked terror organizations such as the al-Nusra Front.

Iran has been particularly active as a regional power in the Syrian conflict. Contrary to its political position vis-à-vis the uprisings in other parts of the MENA region, the Iranian administration sided with the Assad regime, which is considered a dictatorship in the West. Iran recognized Assad as a key factor in exercising control over the Shiite militia Hezbollah and in manipulating the political landscape of Lebanon. This Iranian policy remained the prominent reason in the formation of the ISIS and the subsequent irreversible sectarian divide in the Middle East. Apparently, Iran pursued a selective approach in the Arab Spring case, applying different sets of rules in almost identical situations mostly for sectarian purposes.

Iran supported Assad by sending Special Forces to Syria, a wild move first admitted by deputy head of Quds Force, *Ismail Gha'ani*, in an interview with the Iranian semi-official news agency ISNA in May 2012. Subsequently, when the situation started to slip out of control from Assad's hands, Iran not only helped in recruiting thousands of Shiite mercenaries, mainly from Pakistan and Afghanistan, but also increased the military presence of the Revolutionary Guards and Quds force in Syria. Iran also asked Hezbollah to dispatch its fighters to Syria and played a critical role in convincing Russia to send its forces in support of Bashar al Assad, which turned the tide of war decisively in Assad's favor.

Iranian interference in Syria became a catalyst in turning the overall regional situation into a sectarian conflict, and it affected the regional theatre of war. First, the Sunni states in the region, concerned about a rising Shiite influence in the Levant, started supporting defected personnel from the Syrian armed forces. The Sunni militias subsequently flocked to Syria, only deteriorating the overall situation. These groups not only started fighting the Syrian military and the Shiite militias but within themselves as well. The emerging sectarian divide in the region was thus taken to a point of no return, primarily due to Iranian and GCC intervention. Second, the widening sectarian gulf provided an opportunity for the Sunni militants to radicalize large segments of youths belonging to the Sunni sect from within and outside the region by highlighting the extremely grim humanitarian situation.

Turkey, as a neighboring country, also got involved in the crisis mostly for security reasons. Initially, Turkish authorities held hopes that they would be able to convince Assad to respond to the popular demands. Several official visits were made and close contact was established with the Syrian authorities. But the Assad regime was not responsive, resulting in Turkey suspending diplomatic ties with Syria. Subsequently, as part of an official position, Turkish authorities urged Assad to step down, because his administration was no longer legitimate by international legal standards. In addition to joining efforts to impose diplomatic and economic sanctions, Turkey also closed its embassy in Damascus and called for international involvement in the matter.

As a concrete move, on the other hand, Turkey established close ties with the main opposition in Syria, FSA, and hosted the Syrian National Council (SNC), all in an effort to put an end to Assad's rule. Military training was offered for the opposition fighters; additionally, Turkey assembled an initiative of Friends of Syria, an international political coalition that recognizes the Syrian opposition as the legitimate representative of Syria. In reference to normative responsibility, Turkey urged the international community, particularly the United Nations, to take action to address the humanitarian catastrophe. Acting in line with the responsibility discourse, Turkey offered refuge for the people who left Syria and provided extensive humanitarian support for them as well.

But Turkey's involvement apparently also deepened the sectarian divide; although indirectly, Turkey seemed to side with the Sunni groups and acted very cautiously when it came to the Shiites and Alawites in Syria. Yet it has been most ardent in the case of the Kurdish advance, particularly in the northern part of the country. Declaring the pro-Kurdish groups as terrorists, Turkey held offensives and deployed troops to deal with what it called terrorism. Neither the Arab world nor the West endorsed this bold action, leaving Turkey in a precarious position in terms of normativity, a claim that has been undermined by military action and contribution to the sectarian divide.

Saudi Arabia, another regional power indirectly involved in the conflict, acted out of fear of Iranian influence in the entire region. When the people raised demands in protest against the Assad regime, the Saudis saw it as a key opportunity to undermine Iranian influence through regime change; this is why they actively supported armed rebel groups that were seen as an antedote to the emerging Shi'ite Crescent. But despite the continuous efforts on the part of Saudi Arabia, Assad has remained in power and appears to be emerging from the war. It is likely the Saudi government did not anticipate that Syria still remains an essential element in Russia's Middle East foreign policy and that Russia would intercede militarily to the extent that it has. Saudi Arabia anticipated that the arms would enable the rebels to quickly overthrow Assad as Mubarak and Ben Ali had been in Egypt and Tunisia, respectively. Instead, the war in Syria has continued for much longer than it may have without the support and aid of the Saudis.

## V. Internationalization of the Syrian conflict

Established norms and practices of international law and international politics suggest that the Syrian crisis should be dealt with by the international society, as it obviously poses a threat to international peace and the way interstate relations have been tailored to fit the demands and needs of the players on the international political stage. However, the international society has failed to put an end to the crisis and to dictate a viable settlement. International crimes remain a big problem; the warring factions have not wavered in their positions and aspirations, and the regional powers involved in one way or another in the conflict are placing greater emphasis on the preservation of their security interests.

The crisis was further complicated by the involvement of non-regional powers, with different and often clashing interests, which eventually led to the inability of international organizations to function as facilitators for the settlement of the dispute. In other words, ironically, the internationalization of the conflict now seems to be a major factor for the state of irresolution in the Syrian crisis. From the beginning of the conflict, major powers, including the United States, Russia, and China, held contradicting political positions that exacerbated the crisis and blocked any potential operationalization of existing mechanisms once designed to cope with political distress in the international system.

In realization that the Syrian regime would not properly respond to the popular demands and would try to suppress the riots by reliance on brute force, the US administration slightly changed its initial position that can be characterized by indifference and neutrality, starting to urge the Assad regime to step down. The Obama administration, placing emphasis on the need to initiate a process of political change and to respond to popular demands, implied that the central government was responsible for doing that. In legal terms, the US objectively suggested that the Syrian government needed to fulfill its obligations under international law vis-à-vis the Syrian people or because this was its basis of legitimacy in the first place. In an official statement, the US administration, for instance, stressed that Syrian President Assad should lead the change or otherwise leave office. In the same statement the US administration further recalled that they were "working unilaterally, regionally, and internationally in order to try to build a broad-based approach to how to respond to the need to increase pressure on the regime."

In this and other similar statements, the US lent some credit and time to the Syrian government so that it could comply with its international legal obligations. However, when the US concluded that the Syrian regime had failed (and would continue to fail) to deliver its promises and honor these obligations, the US placed strong and decisive emphasis on the regime's responsibility to protect the people. Roughly speaking, in August 2011, the US changed its position from asking the Syrian government to be responsive to the popular demands to stressing that the regime is illegitimate because it is unable or unwilling to protect the people. This indicates that the conflict in Syria had turned, in legal terms, into an international problem which calls for attention by the international community. The involvement of the international community, particularly of members with the strongest interests, was justified by the principle of responsibility to protect, which implies that a government is responsible to protect its people from genocide, crimes against humanity, war crimes, and ethnic cleansing by virtue of being the sole sovereign entity in the territory of the state. Through its policy, the US reminded the Syrian government of that responsibility.

But a strong interference for the purpose of dealing with the atrocities has never been the most viable option in the case of Syria due to the fact that a number of issues had to be addressed prior to such an extreme action. The questions to be addressed included whether or not a military action would have been possible in the absence of an authorization by the UN Security Council, and, if such action had been possible, what potential source of legitimization could be invoked. More importantly, in the case of an intervention by the international community, attention must be paid to the protection of the people rather than the toppling of the repressive regime in order to maintain proper justification and legitimization.

It appears that the US' Syria policy has considered all these concerns and questions. According to the US administration, the Syrian government should be primarily held responsible for the human rights violations and extreme violence during the conflict, and it is obvious that the Syrian state and regime have been in breach of the responsibility to protect their people under international law. But this is not sufficient for the US or any other state to act unilaterally and rely on coercive measures against the Syrian regime. International law has established certain mechanisms for such violations and the failure to fulfill the responsibility as a sovereign state. But these mechanisms have not been exercised up to now in Syria for mostly political reasons. And yet, it is not possible to refer to illegitimate and illegal measures and means in order to overcome this impasse created by the obstructive attitude of China and Russia, particularly by relying on their power to veto a draft resolution at the UN Security Council. In other words, the end does not justify the means; for this reason, it is not reasonable to rely on illegal military means and measures. It is, instead, imperative to insist on a more consistent and legitimate attitude and approach.

Thus, it was almost impossible (and unreasonable) to develop a policy of intervention on a legal basis to respond to the humanitarian tragedy in Syria. In other words, the Assad regime, despite strong calls by the US administration, showed no intention of stepping down; and Russia and China further indicated that they would not change their position vis-à-vis the Syrian crisis. But despite this deadlock, the US tried some options for a legitimate course of action. These options primarily sought to ensure that the international community would become aware of the situation in Syria and respond to it decisively. As part of this policy, the US contributed to the measures and policies devised to alienate the Assad regime in the international arena. One example of this policy is the Friends of Syria, an *ad hoc* initiative that attracted at some point nearly 90 countries joining in efforts to condemn the Assad regime for the atrocities for which he was held responsible. This initiative was particularly important because it was designed to show that at least a substantial part of the international community had a stance vis-à-vis what was happening in Syria, sending a message to the Assad regime that it was no longer legitimate. From this perspective, this approach was consistent with the calls by the US administration that Assad must go because he has no future in the administration of Syria.

However, this relatively normative policy has in recent years been replaced by a perspective of *realpolitik*. Under this changed policy, the US, rather than zealously urging the regime to step down, paid greater attention to the eradication of ISIS and supported non-Islamist factions, mainly the Kurds, even if it meant strong disagreements with its NATO ally Turkey. Military support for the pro-Kurdish groups, particularly in the northern part of Syria, received tacit approval of Russia; and it seems that in return, the US no longer puts strong pressure on the Assad administration.

Russia, on the other hand, was initially in favor of finding a diplomatic solution for the conflict rather than resorting to military action. It supported the idea of political reforms to appease the opposition, as well as the ceasefire attempts negotiated by *Kofi Annan* as an UN-Arab League special envoy. Russia even backed the possibility of establishing a transitional government composed of members of the Assad regime and the opposition groups. This was a specific move against a scenario where the US was not able to influence the UN in determining the course of events.

However, in what seems to be a response to the US position, Russia placed strong emphasis on the legitimacy of the Assad regime, which was considered a potential facilitator of its interests in at least part of the region. Over time, Russia gradually solidified its role in Syria. In September 2013, it effectively prevented a potential US intervention ensuring the dismantlement of the Syrian chemical weapons. In 2015, however, Russia maintained strong military presence in the country, the first Russian military intervention since the end of the Cold War of the former Soviet area. It should also be noted that the only Russian military base preserved in the post-Cold War era outside the Soviet area is in Tartus, Syria, signifying the importance attached to the Syrian conflict. From this perspective, it is possible to argue that Russia sees its intervention in the Syrian crisis as an opportunity to amplify its influence in the Middle East by forging new partnerships and strengthening the existing ones.

Russia's interest in the Syrian crisis is also relevant to its ambition to prevent Syria from eventually becoming a failed state where extremists find refuge. Not only does the presence of fundamentalists in Syria raise concerns about regional and global security, but it is also taken as a real threat to Russian national security. The inflow of Chechens and Tatars in Syria as fighters on the side of religious extremist groups has also been a source of concern for Russia. But despite the multiple reasons of national security, Russia depicts the conflict in Syria as a confrontation between the regime and terrorist groups, and not a legitimate opposition. With this sort of depiction, Russia relied on the international support it received from prominent players, particularly China and India. On the other hand, although cautiously, Russia also maintained indirect ties with major strands of Syrian opposition, indicating that what it is really interested in is to promote its own national interests.

Due to the involvement of major powers in the conflict, which took action not for normative reasons but for national security purposes, the leading international organizations also failed to address the humanitarian catastrophe effectively in Syria. Despite resolutions adopted at the UN Security Council, the gravity of the humanitarian situation remained unchanged in Syria, proving that the Council has been ineffective in addressing the humanitarian challenges in the country. The tone of the resolutions specifically focusing on the use of chemical weapons, on the other hand, has grown stronger. Resolution 2118 (UNSC Resolution No. 2118, 2013), determining "the use of chemical weapons in the Syrian Arab Republic constitutes a threat to international peace and security," condemned "in the strongest terms any use of chemical weapons in Syria," and decided the Syrian state

> shall not use, develop, produce, otherwise acquire, stockpile or retain chemical weapons, or transfer, directly or indirectly, chemical weapons to other States or non-State actors.

Similarly, in resolution 2209 (UNSC Resolution No. 2209, 2015), the UNSC condemned "any toxic chemical, such as chlorine, as a weapon" and reiterated that "no party in Syria should use, develop, produce, acquire, stockpile, retain, or transfer chemical weapons."

The UN involvement in the Syrian conflict was not limited to the Security Council. The General Assembly also produced legal documents addressing the grave situation. However, the Assembly, particularly through the Human Rights Council (HRC), mostly focused on the human rights rather than the security aspect of the crisis. The HRC has been more active in addressing the human rights situation and the breaches of international human rights law and international humanitarian law in Syria. The Council's attention has been directed at the underlining responsibilities of the warring parties, particularly of the Syrian government. In its resolution 16/L, the HRC condemned widespread human rights violations committed by the Syrian government forces. Overall, the resolution urged the government to refrain from excessive violent measures against peaceful protests and demonstrations. Additionally, the Council dispatched a commission of inquiry

> investigate all alleged violations of international human rights law in the Syrian Arab Republic, to establish the facts and circumstances of such violations and of the crimes perpetrated and, where possible, to identify those responsible, to make recommendations, in particular, on accountability measures, all with a view to ensuring that those individuals responsible are held accountable. (A/HRC/16/L, 2011).

The UN and its organs often stressed the responsibility of the central government to protect the people against the repercussions and ensure that proper measures are taken to provide security for the population. Particular references included protection against crimes against humanity and war crimes. Both direct and indirect references to the R2P principle have been identified in the documents produced by the UN bodies, indicating that this principle is gaining wider recognition and acceptance by the international community. However, selectivity in the references and implementation of measures that could be regarded as relevant to the principle suggest that there is no ground to believe the R2P is part of international customary law, reflecting a consensus among members of the international society. Such a consensus appears to exist in terms of the use of chemical weapons, which has not been tolerated by the UNSC. Even states pursuing conflicting strategies and policies in Syria (for instance, Russia and the United States) have agreed that no party to the conflict should employ chemical agents, and proper investigations should be conducted to determine whether there has been such a violation. However, despite recognized and substantiated breaches of international law as documented by the UN, no effective measure has been taken so far to deal with the humanitarian crisis in the Syrian conflict.

# VI. Conclusion

This study offers an overall sketch of the stages in the Syrian crisis, reflecting the transformation from sporadic popular demonstrations to a bloody internal conflict and then to an international dispute that now requires the close attention of the entire international community and the adoption of decisive and strong measures. In this sense, this conflict is a litmus test of the international society which, by definition, is supposed to assume legal and normative responsibilities to save the Syrian state and nation, as well as protecting international peace and order. By identifying the stages in the conflict, the failures, shortcomings, and constraints of the international society in developing comprehensive norms to address major humanitarian situations and to discourage or end domestic political violence including civil war become more evident. A particularly complex problem is also observed in the implementation of the norms, which still depends on the willingness of the states and the accommodation of their interests, specifically in the field of security. Hence, the crisis and the state of irresolution carries the potential of eroding the credibility and the binding effect of international legal and moral norms that represent political progress in the history of the IR.

This is why this study aims to identify the stages in the conflict and to determine the dynamics that underline the move from one stage to the next. The compartmentalization of the conflict also displays the rapid change of the situation on the battle ground, with changing alliances as well as the involvement and elimination of different actors at different stages. Roughly speaking, the initial stage, quite unplanned and unexpected, is characterized by sporadic street demonstrations, where the protestors, obviously encouraged by the initial popularity of the Arab Spring reactions in other parts of the MENA region, expressed dissatisfaction with the Syrian regime, without demanding the toppling of the Assad government. The regime, appreciative of the delicacy of the situation, pledges to take some concrete steps at this stage but also shows no mercy or tolerance to the protestors. Mass campaigns of arrests are followed by reported cases of torture, disappearances, and summary executions. As expected, the outcome is that the protestors retreat; as a result, the central government maintains full control and remains immune to the spreading effects of the Arab Spring.

However, the brutal response by the government makes the people more resilient and organized. In the face of growing popular resentment, the Assad regime relies on violence, which breeds a similar reaction from the people. This second stage is characterized, unlike the initial stage of peaceful protests, by the government's exercise of violent measures and the use of violence by the protestors. At this stage, a visible political opposition emerges and grows, showing a sign of promise for success towards political change. The opposition draws attention and support and develops hopes that the change will be smooth and non-violent. This optimistic assumption is based on growing international support for the opposition and the deteriorating image of the Assad regime as a repressive government.

But the Assad regime remained firm and strong, relying on all measures available to sustain its rule. This led to the third stage in the conflict where the parties engage in a civil war. The opposition is able to assemble its own armed forces, specifically with the aid of those who defect the Syrian army, as well as a political coalition representing different segments of Syrian society, eventually managing to present itself as a competent political representative of popular interests. At this stage, the international legal obligations had been underscored for both parties, with the international community calling for compliance with international humanitarian law.

The conflict, however, did not remain a conventional civil war and was further complicated by the involvement of jihadist groups and sectarian proxies. Even though stakeholders of the conflict argued otherwise, the sectarian divide appeared to be an important dynamic in the alignments and political positions. This also attracted the attention of regional powers including Iran, Turkey, Saudi Arabia, and Qatar, each supporting groups they consider useful to advance their goals in Syria or to protect their national borders. This is therefore the stage at which the conflict is transformed from a civil war into a war of proxies.

Eventually, the proxy wars turned into an internationalized conflict due to the perceived threat posed by the sectarian divide, as well as the growing schism between the interests of the actors involved in the crisis. Major international institutions and states have become engaged, either out of a sense of normative responsibility or of the inherent tendency of protecting national interests. But despite the strong attention paid to the crisis, no working settlement has so far been reached, thereby revealing the constraints and shortcomings of the existing legal and normative mechanisms of global governance.

# The Geo-Strategic Importance of the Caucasus and the Radicalization Potential of Different Population Groups in the Region

*Dr. Dr. h.c. Eliko Ciklauri-Lammich*

## I. Introduction

In order to determine the threat of radical religious terrorism in the Caucasus, it is necessary to understand the region's historical and current ethnic and cultural situation. Many Islamic State fighters in Syria and Iraq came from southern Russian republics. There are numerous reasons for their radicalization. The large oil and gas reserves of the region are very important for the emergence of these conflicts. In addition, the Caucasus is a transit territory for raw energy resources in the form of pipelines for the West. We address some of the aspects that can be seen as causes of conflict. In addition to historical, political and religious backgrounds, we also look at ethno-national and geo-political aspects and put them in the foreground of our research.

## II. Ethnic majorities in the Caucasus Region

The subject of terrorism has been well researched in the scientific literature. There is a broad spectrum of causes and reasons which motivate a person or entire groups of people to commit such criminal acts.[1]

We address some of the aspects that can be seen as causes of conflict. In addition to psycho-social, political and religious backgrounds, we also look at ethno-national and geo-political aspects and put them in the foreground of our research. The effects of grievances, personal tragedies and suffering that entire populations have experienced can still be felt after hundreds of years.

---

[1] See for details *Albrecht*, in: Arnold/Zoche, Terrorismus und organisierte Kriminalität, pp. 17–31; *Getoš*, 94 (6) Monatsschrift für Kriminologie und Strafrechtsreform (2011), pp. 431–451; *Wildfang*, Terrorismus (2010).

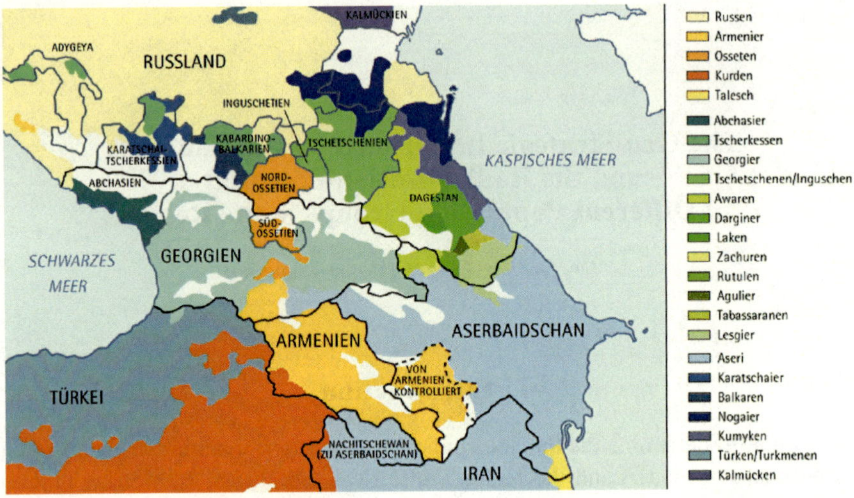


*Figure 1.* The area of the Caucasus: 440 000 km², 30.6 million people, more than 46 peoples and 75 languages

Such grievances include some of the conflicts that have existed in the Caucasus region for centuries, for example, discrimination on the basis of different nationalities or religious affiliations, the forced assimilation of Christian populations, the expulsion of Muslim ethnic groups from undemocratic regimes by occupying powers or international law, which in the history of the Caucasus, led to the resettlement or deportation of an entire people and religious groups.[2]

The wealth of peoples, the diversity of nationalities, religions and cultures, all of which come together in a relatively small geographical area, are particularly relevant factors in view of the enormous geo-strategic importance of terrorism.

Since the Middle Ages, significant and major trade routes have been running through the region, for example, the silk road stretching from China to the West. In the 19th century, France and the Kingdom of England became interested in gold and manganese on the Georgian territory, as well as in the oil and gas reserves of the Caspian Sea.

The large oil and gas reserves of the region are a crucial factor in the emergence of many conflicts. In addition, the Caucasus is a transit territory for raw energy resources in the form of pipelines for the West. There are currently three relevant

---

2 *Stadelbauer*, in: Auch (ed.), Lebens- und Konfliktraum Kaukasien, pp. 11–15.

*Figure 2*. Oil and Gas Pipelines on the territory of the Caucasus

oil and gas pipelines on the territory of the Caucasus, which meet at a junction on Caspian territory: Baku-Supsa, Baku-Norossiysk and Baku-Tbilisi-Erzurum. Several other pipelines are already being planned.[3]

## III. Insights into the history of ethnic diversity and the geo-strategic importance of the Caucasus

The Caucasus is one of the most diverse areas of the world, with an extremely varied geographical and ethno-national composition. Moreover, this part of the world has historically been a cultural and religious crossroads.

Geographically, the Caucasus is located between the Caspian and the Black Sea. It has a temperate climate that has so far shielded it from natural or ecological disasters. This is one reason why the region has historically attracted settlers from a broad range of national and ethnic groups. Thus, the region has experienced competition between various ethnic groups. This competition has resulted in territorial,

[3] *Picco*, East, West jockey for position in Caspian region; http://www.ucdenver.edu/academics/internationalprograms/CIBER/GlobalForumReports/Documents/East_West_Jockey_for_Position.pdf (as of 15 April 2019).

ethno-political, and religious disagreements, migration, deportation, exile, and even genocide.

The Caucasus, particularly the densely populated north (nowadays part of the Russian Federation), have historically been highly multicultural. This multinationalism created administrative units of the Russian Federation, such as the Kabardino-Balkaria Republic, the Chechen Republic, the Karachay-Cherkessia Republic, the Republic of North Ossetia-Alania, the Republic of Ingushetia, the Republic of Adygea, and the Republic of Dagestan. Nearly fifty ethnic groups populate a 355.000 sq.m. area of land that represents just 2.1% of the Russian Federation.[4] However, almost 15% of the country's population lives in this area and it is one of the fastest growing region of Russia (along with Tatarstan). Both the North and South Caucasus are rich in various precious natural resources, in particular manganese, gold, and other metals. The South Caucasus is considered one of the historical homelands of copper, iron, and non-ferrous metals: Dmanisi, in Georgia,[5] has historically been associated with the processing of natural resources, and the Caspian Sea is one of the most important centers of oil and gas reserves in the region.

Modern energy requirements and their effect on regional conflicts are well known.[6] Special attention has been paid to the Caucasus by a number of large industrial countries, including the US, Iran, Russia, Turkey, China, and member states of the European Union.[7]

## IV. Religion and its role in the Caucasus

There are many nationalities, ethnic groups, and religious confessions, in this region. The ancient Greeks controlled the entire Black Sea and founded many cities. The local population adopted Christianity in the fourth century. Besides Orthodox Christians (Georgians, Russians, Gregorian Armenians, Greeks), there are Catho-

4 *von Gumppenberg/Steinbach* (eds.), Der Kaukasus, pp. 177, 204–209.

5 *Huseinova*, Historical Encyclopedia Caucasus, "Chaschioglu", p. 382; see also Georgien-Nachrichten, Sakdrissi-Goldmine 5000 Jahre alt, www.georgien-nachrichten.com/kultur-georgien-culture-georgia/archaeology-dmanisi.

6 *Tirkia,* Atlantic Council, 11.2.2015: Rearticulating NATOs Strategy Toward Georgia, https://www.atlanticcouncil.org/publications/articles/rearticulating-nato-s-strategy-toward-georgia (as of 10 April 2019).

7 *Ebel/Menon*, Energy and conflict in Central Asia and the Caucasus, Lanham 2000; *Picco*, East, West jockey for position in Caspian region, http://www.ucdenver.edu/academics/internationalprograms/CIBER/GlobalForumReports/Documents/East_West_Jockey_for_Position.pdf; *Perović*, magazin. Zeitschrift der Universität Zürich, 4/2013, pp. 17–19.

lics, Protestants, Lutherans, and various sects closely connected to the Christian faith: Old Believers, Doukhobors, Adventists, Hollisters, etc.[8]

Around the seventh century, the Arabian conquest of the region resulted in the spread of Islam.[9] Depending on which empire was ruling, this region, consequently, came under Byzantine, Iranian, Arab, Mongolian, Ottoman Empire and finally Russian influence.

In 1557, the Kabardian and other Adyghe people were the first to come under Russian control. Following this, Russia started to settle the Slavic peoples, including the Cossacks. In this period, the competition between the Ottoman and the Russian empire influenced the Caucasus.[10] Often, religion was instrumentalized in order to carry out these conflicts.[11] In addition, the colonial policy of Russia was very strict, which created difficult living conditions for the Muslim population. Indeed, the Muslim population was compulsorily resettled on several occasions from today's Russian/Caucasian territory. Similar practices were also used by Muslim conquerors on the local Christian population. For instance, in the seventeenth century, Shah Abbas transferred 100.000 Georgian families from Georgian lands, in particular from Kakheti and Hereti, to Khorasani, Isfahan, and Fereydan (provinces of modern-day Iran). The majority compulsorily converted to Islam and were culturally assimilated (only a single group of Georgians who settled in Fereydan preserved the use of Georgian). During the 1970s, thousands of their descendants returned to Georgia.[12]

During World War II, in November 1944, the Crimean and North Caucasian Muslims were exiled (mainly Chechens, Ingush, Karatschai, Balkars, Kalmyks, Crimean-Tatars, Meskhetian-Turks from Georgia) as well as Germans (that had settled there) to Central Asia and Kazakhstan. Several ethnic mountain groups did not hide the fact that they considered Nazi Germany to be a liberating force from

---

8 http://www.Politscience.info/Filemanager/files/Kavk-shed-pol-8-religia-2017.pdf (as of 12 April 2019).

9 *Huseinova*, Historical Encyclopedia Caucasus, "Chaschioglu", p. 86; *Stigler*, in: Auch (ed.): Lebens- und Konfliktraum Kaukasien, p. 155; *Bobrowitsch/Babitsch*, Sewernyj Kawkas w Sostawje Rossijskoi Imperii, pp. 33–38.

10 *Perović*, Der Nordkaukasus unter russischer Herrschaft.

11 In 1853–1856, Turkey was defeated in the Caucasus by Russia. Russian troops in the south of the Caucasus played an important role in victory over the Turks, as they assisted the local Georgian troops who were fighting to protect their homeland from the Turks. After their defeat, Turkey was not able to regain a foothold in the region, *Stigler*, in: Eva-Maria Auch (ed.): Lebens- und Konfliktraum Kaukasien, p. 155; *Perović*, Der Nordkaukasus unter russischer Herrschaft, pp. 8–12.

12 *Muliani*, Jaygah-e Gorjiha dar Tarikh va Farhang va Tammadon-e Iran [The Georgians' position in the Iranian history and civilization]; *Armenakyan*, A Portrait of Armenian Women in Iran, https://chai-khana.org/en/a-portrait-of-armenian-women-in-iran (as of 28 February 2019).

the communist system and were, consequently, cooperative.[13] Upon the conclusion of the war and after Stalin's death, the majority of the deported population returned to their traditional lands.[14]

At that time, the territories and property of the deported minorities had long been distributed among the local people of the Communist state. This gave rise to new reasons for violent riots in the 70s and 80s between Ingush and Ossetians or later with Mesketi Turks in Fergana.[15]

Interestingly, German interests have long been associated with the Caucasus, with the first German colonists coming to Georgia in October 1817. Ultimately, the German colonists became entwined in broader geo-political disagreements between Russia and Germany (later the Soviet Union and Nazi Germany).[16] After the beginning of the Nazi invasion of the Soviet Union on 28 August 1941 and the rapid movement of the German armed forces, further resettlement of the German population in the Soviet Union and also from the Caucasus began.[17]

Muslim resettlement of the Black Sea region began in the middle of the 19th century. On the one hand, these refugees could not see their future in the Russian Empire, while, on the other hand, local Russian authorities forced them to leave their homeland and find shelter in the Ottoman Empire (a fact that the Ottomans were not pleased about). Many of these refugees died[18] and, while some eventually returned to their homelands (such as those of Abkhazian, Circassian, or Chechen origin), many others settled in Syria and Jordan. This is an important historical detail, as once the Soviet Union collapsed, many of the descendants of these exiled Muslims returned to the Caucasus to engage in jihad with other Muslim fighters. Their purpose was to fight against Russians, particularly in Chechnya, and to fight in the Abkhaz-Georgian conflict against Georgian Christians.[19] Later on, many

---

13 After the death of Stalin, all exiled refugees received the right to repatriation, with the Muslim Meskhetians being the only exceptions. The problem of returning Muslim Meskhetians to the homeland after the Farghana tragedy (June 1989) has gained more power. The government of Georgia took the obligation to step up gradual repatriation in 1999 and 2004, and in 2007.

14 *Bugaj*, Die Nationalitätenpolitik im Nordkaukasus während des „sozialistischen Experiments“, pp. 84–95.

15 *Politkovskaja*, Tschetschenien, pp. 150–186.

16 *Petersen*, in: Göttsch-Elten/Eisler (eds.): Minderheiten im Europa der Zwischenkriegszeit, pp. 163–191.

17 At the beginning of World War I, the anti-German "Black Hundred" organization emerged in present-day Ukraine. This organization campaigned for the removal of Germans from Moscow, St. Petersburg, Odessa, and other cities. The government adopted "Liquidation Laws", according to which Russian-Germans lost large areas on the Russian-Austrian and Russian-German borders.

18 *Quiring*, Der vergessene Völkermord, pp. 19–22.

19 *O'Loughlin/Holland/Witmer*, Eurasian Geography and Economics, vol. 52 issue 5, 2011, pp. 596–600.

jihadists returned to fight in the Iraqi and Syrian wars, fighting for al-Qaeda and the Islamic State.[20] This topic will be returned to later.

From the mid-eighteenth century, the whole of the North Caucasus fell under Russia's military interests and was ultimately conquered by Tsarist Russia. In 1801 and 1867, Russia abolished the eastern and western kingdoms of Georgia and, now that there was nothing stopping the further conquest of the South Caucasus, Azerbaijan and Armenia became part of the Russian Empire.[21] In this period of history, the small ethnic minorities of the North Caucasus did not have any nationality-based statehood, nor their own script as did the South Caucasus.

During every historical conquest, the invaders considered the Caucasian Gateway as an outpost of significant strategical importance. The role and importance of the Caucasus is still present.

The circumstances mentioned here created the premises, that the smaller ethnic groups identified themselves primarily on the basis of the language that they were speaking, and on the broader spectrum, the religious affiliation was the main unifying factor for different ethnic groups.

Historically, there has been a competition between the ethnic or national groups based on religious and ethno-political grounds that have manifested themselves in the form of deportation, expulsion and even genocide. These were usually activated during the world's crises, such as the world wars and revolutions.

As we have seen, the North Caucasus consists of various nations and ethnic groups, as well as different religions. The local inhabitants adopted Christianity in the fourth century and, apart from Orthodox Christians (Georgians, Russians, Gregorian Armenians/Armenian Apostolic Church, Greeks), they are represented by Catholics, Protestants, Lutherans and various religious sects that are close to the Christian faith. There are also many other religions like Judaism and Muslims – Sunnis, Shiites, Salafism Alevis, Bahai Kurds, Yesidien, Asyrie, Buddhists, Zoroastrianis, and various sects.

Part of the North Caucasus population were adherents of the Christian faith under the influence of the Georgian culture and were later islamized. Before the Arab invasions, this region was considered to be one of the most important centers of the Zoroastrian religion, and afterwards only the part of Ossetians/Alans living near the neighboring Georgia remained adherents of the Christian faith, while the other parts became adherents of the Sunni and of the Shia Islam. So basically, the inhabitants of a village of the same nationality consisted of Christians, Sunnis and Shiites. Only a fraction of these inhabitants were considered Salafist saints, or the adherents of the righteous Islam, creating a threat and tension in this relatively small area.

---

20 *Quiring*, Der vergessene Völkermord, Berlin 2013.

21 *Huseinova*, Historical Encyclopedia Caucasus, "Chaschioglu", pp. 86.

The South Caucasus is also distinguished by its religious diversity. 75% of the population of Azerbaijan consists of Shiites. The Sunni adherents in Azerbaijan mostly belong to the community of Dagestanis and represent 25% of the Muslim population. On the majority of Northern Caucasus territory, both Islamic schools are spread. Their adherents are scattered across Abkhazia, Adjara, Chechnya, amongst Kisti people, Circassia and Kabardia, and also Ossetians. Simultaneously, the northern part of the Caucasus has a long history of Judaism and the adherents of Buddhism can also be found. There are traditional Kurdish and Yezidi settlements in the South Caucasus, especially in Armenia and Georgia.[22]

The total area of the Caucasus is approximately 450 thousand square kilometers, with a population of 30.6 million people. However, it should be noted that a specific variety of Islam has formed in the Caucasus, which was strongly influenced by the local mountain traditions, and is actually considered as a fundamental basis for the coexistence of various ethnic national groups living there. So-called unwritten laws were based on the customs and traditions. Sufism is also widespread in the area, it was easily incorporated with the nature of the local population and natural religious beliefs. In conclusion, next to the Sunni Islam, the most prevalent religion is the Shia, followed by Alevites and the Baha'is.

Religion had always had a special significance for the Caucasus as a whole and the circumstances have not changed this. The nations, big or small, who have lived on these territories for centuries, consider it as the only means for preserving their identity as the various conquerors and Empires emerged upon them. After the collapse of the Soviet Union, nationalist and religious movements have emerged on the entire area, and they became the instrument which, in broader sense, provided the basis for the destructive processes, such as permanent civil wars and violent actions against minorities that transformed into violent conflicts, resulting in the death of hundreds of thousands of people and in millions becoming refugees.[23] Traditionally, several ethnic groups live on Georgian territory. These days, the country houses over 26 ethnic groups: 83.8% of the population are Georgians. In contrast to the northern Caucasus and Azerbaijan, in which the majority consists of Muslims, in Georgia, the Muslim population is a minority (approximately 10.7%) of the population, which amounted to 3.729.635 inhabitants in 2015.

Most of this Muslim population is due to compulsory conversion of Georgians in Ottoman times. By far the greater part of the originally Georgian population, forced to convert to Islam, lives on Turkish territory today, estimated at a few million people. Exact numbers have not been collected here.

---

22 http://www.politscience.info/Filemanager/files/Kavk-shed-pol-8-religia-2017.pdf (as of 15 April 2019).

23 *Gammer,* Musulmanskoe Soprotivlenije Zarizmu, p. 14.

Generally, Christianity is always equated with the Georgian identity, so the more Muslims there are, the higher the risk of losing the Georgian identity. Many young ethnic Georgian Muslims who were born or grew up after independence, are choosing Orthodox Christianity over Islam, despite their parents' objections, the reason being, 'I returned to my ancestors' religion'.[24]

They see it as a correction of historical troubles, referring to Adjara's population adopting Islam during the Ottoman Empire's rule over the region. It is also worth noting that the Muslim population of Georgia is quite diverse (including Azerbaijanis, ethnic Georgians, Kisti people and Avarians) and unifies various Muslim confessions (Sunnis, Shiites, Salafists). The majority in Georgia, about 80%, consider themselves Christians. Orthodox Christians in Georgia are considered the main political power. Muslim settlements, even though they are quite compact, are located close to the Christian settlements.

Many men, fighting for IS, used Georgia as a transit country on their way to Syria. Pankisi Gorge is a valley region in north-eastern Georgia, just south of Georgia's historic region of Tusheti. In recent years, Muslim communities in Georgia have likely been infiltrated by the Islamic State. An estimate from the Georgian Ministry for Internal Affairs put the total number of IS members at around a dozen. The most well-known Georgian fighting for IS, *Tharchan Batiraschwili*, was an officer in the Georgian Army. He is better known by the name of *al-Shishani*. He was born in 1986 in the village of Barkiani in Pankisi Gorge, a region settled by ethnic Chechens. He took part in the 2008 Georgian war against Russia, receiving a commendation. Later he was imprisoned for the illegal possession of a weapon. After his release, he joined the IS. The media has reported on the death of *al-Shishani* several times.[25]

Some of these individuals also rose to higher positions in the IS army. However, religious radicalism in Georgia is currently no longer a particular threat.

As an active participant in the fight against terrorism, Georgia has ratified several conventions, such as the European Convention on the Suppression of Terrorism on 15 March 2001, the International Convention for the Suppression of the Financing of Terrorism on 27 October 2002, the European Convention on the Prevention of Terrorism on 10 June 2000, and the Convention on Nuclear Terrorism on 4 June 2010.[26]

---

24 *Varshalomidze*, Ethnic Georgian Muslims in a Christian-dominated nation, Dec. 2017, https://www.aljazeera.com/indepth/features/2017/12/ethnic-georgian-muslims-christian-dominated-nation-171204110108701.html (as of 15 April 2019).

25 *Clifford*, Caucasus Survey, vol. 6, issue 1, p. 62–80, received 7 Aug 2017, accepted 30 Oct 2017, published online: 22 Nov 2017 (as of 15 March 2019).

26 Georgian Legislative Herald, https://matsne.gov.ge/ka/document/view/1221899? publication=0 (as of 15 April 2019). International Convention for the Suppression of the Financing of Terrorism – 10/01/2000 – Ratification Law No. 29(III)/01.

Additionally, there is also the Georgian Center for Strategy and Development (GCSD), a non-profit, non-partisan, non-governmental organization, which intends to support Georgia's national security, to strengthen the principles of effective and democratic governance of the country and to create conditions for Georgia's sustainable development. Based on the goals of the center, its work involves research, monitoring, advocacy and the implementation of educational projects.[27]

In the Global Terrorism Index 2017 of the Institute of Economics and Peace, Georgia ranks 77th in terms of terrorist threats.

Many Islamic State fighters in Syria and Iraq came also from southern Russian republics. There are numerous reasons for their radicalization.

Salaphite, also salaphite-jihadist movements have spread in the Caucasus region due to the double interactions amongst the Caucasus countries.[28] At the beginning of the 1990s, after the dissolution of the Soviet Union, the young Muslims received an opportunity to study Islam abroad (mostly in Egypt or Saudi Arabia). These youths brought the salaphite ideology back home, when they returned to take part in the Russian-Chechen war of the 1990s. Most of them had tight connections to jihadist organizations, which at that time were gaining power and influence. Therefore, many local Muslims were influenced by their ideology.[29]

The Chechen Wars (1994–1996 and 1999–2009) caused the further radicalization of militants within these former Soviet regions.[30] Radical Islamic – or Salafist – militants were particularly active during the Second Chechen War, acting with the primary goal of carving-out their own state to be ruled according to Islamic jurisprudence: the Sharia. Indeed, Islamic rule now exists in several mountainous regions of Chechnya and in certain areas of the Chechen capital, Grozny.

Many Chechens looked to religion for hope during the violence and decay of war. Moreover, the unrest weakened existing power structures, caused economic

---

27 http://gcsd.org.ge/en/about/ (as of 15 April 2019).

28 Beginning in the 1960s, the conservative Islamic doctrine of Wahhabism spread from Saudi Arabia outwards. At the time, the Soviet Union's information sources took note of this state-sponsored missionary policy and documented that the "Wahhabis" practiced a militant form of Islam, directed by a foreign state; *Quiring*, Pulverfass Kaukasus, pp. 10–22. During Gorbachev's Perestroika era (1985–1989), missionaries from abroad brought Wahhabism into predominantly Muslim-populated regions of the Soviet Union. They were particularly active in the Fergana Valley, Chechnya, and Dagestan: these areas have since become hotspots of religious unrest and conflict. *Yaffa*, Putin's Dragon. Is the ruler of Chechnya out of control?, The New Yorker (31 January 2016) https://www.newyorker.com/magazine/2016/02/08/putins-dragon (as of 15 April 2019).

29 *Ovchinsky*, Fünf Jahre „Krieg“ gegen Terrorismus und die neue Weltunordnung: Analysebericht – M.: INFRA-M, 2006.

30 https://worldpolicy.org/2011/08/29/islam-rises-from-chechnyas-ashes/ (as of 15 April 2019).

misery and disorientated an entire generation. This societal breakdown saw a previously primarily atheist society transition into a deeply religious one.

Additional victim of the increasing violence was the centralized education system. With its breakdown, a weakening of the state's central power began to take place, particularly in isolated mountainous regions. At the same time, large amounts of money from sponsors abroad flowed into these regions. These funds were used to construct Muslim religious centers and Koran schools. The power vacuum resulted in the creation of "safe zones" for Wahhabis and Salafists: within these enclaves, they were free to create their own propaganda and promote further radicalization.[31] The shift towards a radical Islamic society has had a particularly negative impact on the female inhabitants of the towns and villages, as the only option they now have is to visit Koran schools.[32] Consequently, for young women who want to leave the region, one their best perspectives is to marry a "real man" – a warrior for the "only true religion" – with whom they can leave their village and help build the Islamic State. If necessary, the wives of these fighters are willing to die for this cause: be it with or on behalf of their husbands.[33]

A particular phenomenon within the region are the so-called "black widows".[34] As the name suggests, these women are often dressed in black because they have lost a husband or a son to fighting. Since the early 2000s, *Ibn al-Chattab*, an Arab and a comrade-in-arms of Chechen leader *Shamil Basayev*, has set about turning black widows into "holy warriors" in a training center in the Caucasus. To do so, he hired arab jihadists to pass on their knowledge of warfare. The FSB (Russia's principal security agency) estimated that there were about 150 black widows in 2004. Nineteen black widows were involved in the 2002 theatre hostage drama in Moscow, with this "heroic widow battalion" being praised by Islamic militants. In July 2003, two "martyrs" blew themselves up at an open-air concert in Moscow: a terrorist attack that claimed a dozen lives. In February 2004, a black widow detonated a bomb in the Moscow metro, killing thirty-nine passengers. Only seven months later, two black widows ignited explosives in two separate airplanes, killing almost 100 passengers. Statistically seen, few countries have experienced as many female suicide attacks as Russia.[35]

---

31 *Foertsch, Volker/Lange, Klaus* (eds.), Islamistischer Terrorismus: Bestandsaufnahme und Bekämpfungsmöglichkeiten, https://www.hss.de/fileadmin/migration/downloads/Berichte_Studien_86_Terror.pdf (as of 15 April 2019).

32 *Swirszcz*, Nationalities Papers The Journal of Nationalism and Ethnicity, vol. 37, no. 1, 2009, pp. 59–88.

33 https://d-w-d-f.weebly.com/die-schwarzen-witwen.html (as of 15 April 2019).

34 *Adler*, Ich sollte als schwarze Witwe sterben.

35 The Soufan Group (December 2015), Foreign Fighters: An Updated Assessment of the Flow of Foreign Fighters into Syria and Iraq, http://soufangroup.com/wp-content/uploads/2015/12/TSG_ForeignFightersUpdate3.pdf (as of 15 April 2019).

What started 25 years ago as an ethno-national struggle for independence in Chechnya has turned into a jihad under the influence of the IS.

Major drivers creating incentives for participation in Salafi-jihadist movements in the North Caucasus include the state security services' harsh crackdown on all aspects of the Salafi movement, corruption, nepotism and bleak socioeconomic futures for the youth, and corroboration between government agencies and "official" religious authorities.[36]

These drivers existed independently of the Syrian and Iraqi civil conflicts and the rise of ISIS, and created networks of Salafi-jihadists in the North Caucasus as early as the Second Chechen War (1999–2001). During the 2000s, the insurgent jamaat diffused from the Chechen Republic to the other republics of the North Caucasus (especially, Dagestan, Ingushetia and Kabardino-Balkaria).

The Syrian conflict and the rise of ISIS and other Salafi-jihadist groups attracting foreign fighters caused an outflow of Salafi-jihadist followers from the North Caucasus to participate in the conflict in the Middle East. While precise and methodologically sound calculations are difficult to find, authorities estimate that at least 1,000 individuals from the Russian North Caucasus have left to fight in Syria and Iraq.[37] Moreover, evidence suggests that security services in the North Caucasus republics have even encouraged travel by foreign fighters, allowing them to leave the country freely in the hope that they will not conduct attacks on Russian territory.

As early as 2013, ISIS launched a large-scale propaganda offensive in Russia via the Internet and social media. In it, it uses feelings of discontent, anger and powerlessness against local and federal authorities by addressing and denouncing discrimination against ethnic minorities in Russia and arbitrariness towards non-traditional forms of Islam. In recent years, Moscow has tried to get the problem under control primarily by intelligence and military means.

## V. Would ISIS fighters return to the Caucasus?

The weakness of the terrorist group operating under the umbrella of the IS has several reasons. First, Russia has achieved some success in recent years in neutralizing leaders and members of the militant uprising in the North Caucasus. Furthermore, *Dokku Umarov*, head of the "Caucasian Emirate", was killed by special forces back in 2013, as well as later his two successors. There was also an exodus of fighters and violent Salafists from the North Caucasus to Syria and Iraq, which has led to difficulties in recruiting new fighters. Important sources of financing from

---

36 *Quiring*, Pulverfass Kaukasus, pp. 115–120.

37 *Weiss*, Russia's Double Game with Islamic Terror, http://www.thedailybeast.com/articles/2015/08/23/russia-s-playing-a-double-game-with-islamic-terror0.html (as of 15.4.2019).

abroad dried up, and since the collapse of IS in Syria and Iraq, it is likely that any fighters will return to Russia.

About 40.000 Islamic State supporters came to Syria and Iraq. According to a study of the Soufan Center and the Global Strategy Network, 5.500 fighters have returned to their home countries.[38]

Due to strict treatment of returnees in their countries of origin in the Caucasus or Russia, there is little chance that they will return there, but some of them do so.[39]

## VI. Conclusion

In transition societies with fragile democracy and economic misery, there is a danger that the cultural and religious diversity of the people will be exploited and abused. Despite all the odds, it is hoped that the situation in this beautiful part of the world will ease. Economic and democratic development are vital for the security and coexistence of the many different nationalities and religions in the Caucasus.[40] Furthermore, economic and political stability contribute to peace in the region. With support from the international community and organizations, it is hoped that positive development can be achieved in the Caucasus region.

## Bibliography

### Books and Articles

*Adler, Sabine*, Ich sollte als schwarze Witwe sterben – Die Geschichte der Raissa und ihrer toten Schwestern, Munich 2005.

*Albrecht, Hans-Jörg*, Terrorismus und Organisierte Kriminalität: Beziehungen, Zusammenhänge und Konvergenz. in: Harald Arnold/Peter Zoche (eds.), Terrorismus und organisierte Kriminalität. Theoretische und methodische Aspekte komplexer Kriminalität. Berlin, Münster 2014.

*Armenakyan, Nazik*, A Portrait of Armenian Women in Iran, https://chai-khana.org/en/a-portrait-of-armenian-women-in-iran (as of 28 February 2019).

---

38 https://www.washingtonpost.com/gdpr-consent/?destination=%2fgdprconsent%2fdestination%3d%252fgraphics%252f2018%252fworld%252fisis-returning-fighter%3f&utm_term=.1e22dc9dda21 (as of 15 April 2019).

39 For example, *Akhmed Chatayev*, an ISIS operative who masterminded the Ataturk Airport bombings in 2016 and was later shot by security forces in Georgia, together with two of his accomplices. They were already planning new terrorist attacks.

40 *Ruge*, in: Auch (ed.): Lebens- und Konfliktraum Kaukasien, Humanitäre Aspekte und Prävention von Konflikten im Transkaukasus, p. 190.

*Bobrowitsch, W./Babitsch, I.*, Sewernyj Kawkas w Sostawje Rossijskoi Imperii. Moscow 2004.

*Bugaj, Nikolaij*, Die Nationalitätenpolitik im Nordkaukasus während des „sozialistischen Experiments“, in: Eva-Maria Auch (Hrsg.), Lebens-und Konfliktraum Kaukasien, Großbarkau 1996, p. 84–95.

*Clifford, Bennett*, Georgian foreign fighter deaths in Syria and Iraq: what can they tell us about foreign fighter mobilization and recruitment? Caucasus Survey, vol. 6, issue 1 p. 62–80, Published online: 22.11.2017 (as of 15 March 2019); https://doi.org/10.1080/23761199.2017.1399701.

*Ebel, Robert/Menon, Rajan,* Energy and conflict in Central Asia and the Caucasus, Lanham 2000.

*Foertsch, Volker/Lange, Klaus* (eds.), Islamistischer Terrorismus: Bestandsaufnahme und Bekämpfungsmöglichkeiten, Munich 2005, Berichte & Studien der Hanns-Seidel-Stiftung vol. 86, https://www.hss.de/fileadmin/migration/downloads/Berichte_Studien_86_Terror.pdf.

*Gammer, Moshe*, Musulmanskoe Soprotivlenije Zarizmu, Moscow 1998.

*Getoš, Anna-Maria*, Terrorismus entmystifizieren. Innovative Gewaltforschung als Schlüssel zum Verstehen politischer Gewalt. 94 (6), Monatsschrift für Kriminologie und Strafrechtsreform, (2011) pp. 431–451. doi:10.1515/mks-2011-940602/.

*Huseinova, Irada*, Historical Encyclopedia Caucasus, “Chaschioglu”. Baku 2010.

*Muliani, S.*, Jaygah-e Gorjiha dar Tarikh va Farhang va Tammadon-e Iran. The Georgians’ position in the Iranian history and civilization], Esfahan: Yekta 2001.

*O’Loughlin, John, Holland, Edward C., Witmer, Frank. D.* W., The Changing Geography of Violence in Russia’s North Caucasus, 1999–2011: Regional Trends and Local Dynamics in Dagestan, Ingushetia, and Kabardino-Balkaria. Eurasian Geography and Economics, 52 (5), 2011, p. 596–630; https://doi.org/10.2747/1539-7216.52.5.596.

*Ovchinsky, V.S.*, Fünf Jahre „Krieg“ gegen Terrorismus und die neue Weltunordnung: Analysebericht – M.: INFRA-M, 2006 (Пять лет “войны” с терроризмом и Новый мировой беспорядок: Аналитический доклад/В.С. Овчинский. – М.: ИНФРА-М, 2006, Russian).

*Perović, Jeronim*, Der Nordkaukasus unter russischer Herrschaft. Geschichte einer Vielvölkerregion zwischen Rebellion und Anpassung, Vienna 2015.

*Perović, Jeronim*, Porträt seines Forschungsprojektes zur Energiegeschichte: Treibstoff der Macht, Interview mit Jeronim Perović, magazin. Zeitschrift der Universität Zürich, 4/2013, pp. 17–19.

*Petersen, Hans-Christian*, The Making of Russlanddeutschtum. Karl Stumpp oder die Mobilisierung einer ‚Volksgruppe‘ in der Zwischenkriegszeit, in: Silke Göttsch-Elten/Cornelia Eisler (eds.): Minderheiten im Europa der Zwischenkriegszeit. Wissenschaftliche Konzeptionen, mediale Vermittlung, politische Funktion, Münster, New York 2017, pp. 163–191.

*Picco, Giandomenico*, East, West jockey for position in Caspian region, International Journal of Social Sciences and Humanity Studies vol. 4, no. 1, 2012, http://www.ucdenver.edu/academics/internationalprograms/CIBER/GlobalForumReports/Documents/East_West_Jockey_for_Position.pdf (as of 15 April 2019).

*Politkovskaja, Anna S.*, Tschetschenien. Die Wahrheit über den Krieg, Cologne 2003.

*Ruge, Reiner,* Humanitäre Aspekte und Prävention von Konflikten im Transkaukasus in: Eva-Maria Auch (ed.): Lebens- und Konfliktraum Kaukasien, Gemeinsame Lebenswelten und politische Visionen der kaukasischen Völker in Geschichte und Gegenwart, pp. 190–209.

*Quiring, Manfred*, Der vergessene Völkermord. Sotschi und die Tragödie der Tscherkessen. Mit einem Vorwort von Cem Özdemir, Berlin 2013.

– Pulverfass Kaukasus. Nationale Konflikte und islamische Gefahren am Rande Europas Berlin 2016

*Stadelbauer, Jörg*, Der Kulturraum Kauakasien. Forschungsdefizite an der Schnittstelle zwischen Osteuropa und dem Orient, in: Eva-Maria Auch (ed.): Lebens- und Konfliktraum Kaukasien, Gemeinsame Lebenswelten und politische Visionen der kaukasischen Völker in Geschichte und Gegenwart, Großbarkau 1996, pp. 11–20.

*Stigler, Johanna,* Zwischen Separation und Assimilation. Die Integration der kaukasischen Juden in ihr ethnisches Umfeld. in: Eva-Maria Auch (ed.): Lebens- und Konfliktraum Kaukasien. Gemeinsame Lebenswelten und politische Visionen der kaukasischen Völker in Geschichte und Gegenwart, Großbarkau 1996, pp. 155–161.

*Swirszcz, Joanna*, The Role of Islam in Chechen National Identity, Nationalities Papers The Journal of Nationalism and Ethnicity, vol. 37, no. 1, 2009, pp. 59–88, published online: 20 November 2018, https://doi.org/10.1080/00905990802373637.

*von Gumppenberg, Marie-Carin von/Steinbach, Udo* (eds.), Der Kaukasus. Geschichte – Kultur – Politik, Munich 2008.

*Yaffa, Joshua*, Putin's Dragon. Is the ruler of Chechnya out of control?, The New Yorker, 31. January 2016, https://www.newyorker.com/magazine/2016/02/08/putins-dragon.

*Weiss, Michael* (2015), Russia's Double Game with Islamic Terror, http://www.thedailybeast.com/articles/2015/08/23/russia-s-playing-a-double-game-with-islamic-terror0.html (as of 15 April 2019).

*Wildfang, Anne*, Terrorismus. Definition – Struktur – Dynamik. Berlin 2010.

## Internet Sources

Georgian Center for Strategy and Development, http://gcsd.org.ge/en/about/.

Georgien-Nachrichten, Sakdrissi-Goldmine 5000 Jahre alt. Archäologen graben ältestes Goldbergwerk aus, https://www.georgien-nachrichten.com/kultur-georgien-culture-georgia/archaeology-dmanisi.

Georgian Legislative Herald, matsne.gov.ge/ka/document/view/1221899? publication=0 (as of 15 April 2019). International Convention for the Suppression of the Financing of Terrorism – 10/01/2000 – Ratification Law No. 29(III)/01.

https://d-w-d-f.weebly.com/die-schwarzen-witwen.html.

http://www.politscience.info/Filemanager/files/Kavk-shed-pol-8-religia-2017.pdf (as of 12 April 2019).

https://www.washingtonpost.com/gdprconsent/destination=%2fgraphics%2f2018%2fworld%2fisis-returning-fighter.

https://worldpolicy.org/2011/08/29/islam-rises-from-chechnyas-ashes/.

The Soufan Group (December 2015), Foreign Fighters: An Updated Assessment of the Flow of Foreign Fighters into Syria and Iraq, http://soufangroup.com/wp-content/uploads/2015/12/TSG_ForeignFightersUpdate3.pdf (as of 15 April 2019).

*Tirkia, Mariam*, Atlantic Council, 11.2.2015: Rearticulating NATOs Strategy Toward Georgia, https://www.atlanticcouncil.org/publications/articles/rearticulating-nato-s-strategy-toward-georgia (as of 10 April 2019).

*Varshalomidze*, *Tamila*, Ethnic Georgian Muslims in a Christian-dominated nation. A large number of people see Islam as alien to the Georgian national identity, Dec. 2017, https://www.aljazeera.com/indepth/features/2017/12/ethnic-georgian-muslims-christian-dominated-nation-171204110108701.html (as of 15 April 2019).

# Part 3
# Summary

# Aiming for a New Architecture of Security Law

*Dr. Marc Engelhart*

## I. Introduction

The contributions in this book sketch some of the many aspects and players involved on the international and national level in the so-called fight against terrorism. They analyze the different national solutions and point out many of the existing problems on all levels especially the problems to find appropriate solutions. The discussion on terrorism is part of a larger one on security law and its structures and features, dealing with many of the threats to modern society from economic risks to risks of undermining democracy and statehood.

The problems for security law in regard to fighting terrorism originating from the Islamic State (IS) are well depicted by the following case: "IS Wife." This was the occupation given by 16-year-old Elif Ö. on her Facebook profile from Syria to reconnect with family and friends in mid-April 2015. She had disappeared from her home near Munich in early March. Her family already assumed that she had gone to Syria because she had become increasingly radicalized in the year before. Elif posted almost daily until her account was closed. She wanted to encourage other women to follow in her footsteps: to keep fighters in Syria company, to manage their households, and to produce offsprings for the theocratic regime.

The case of Elif Ö. was one of many successful recruiting efforts by the IS in Germany and other (Non-)European countries (see also the contributions in this book on the specific situation in the Caucasian region by *Ciklauri-Lammich* and in Syria by *Çakmak*). These recruits became foreign fighters or otherwise supported the IS. All the years, there was the fear in the home countries, that foreign fighters might come back to their home countries and might plan and conduct terrorist attacks. Now with the IS coming to an end, at least concerning their control of larger territories, a much larger number of the recruits want to come back to their home countries. Some of the women now have children born in IS territory. These developments create many practical and legal problems.The challenges for the security agencies in this regard are enormous. Previously inconspicuous juveniles and adults had become conspicuously religious and attracted to the extremist and violence-prone fight waged by the IS against the "infidels" in the Near East and, in isolated cases, also in the West. When these persons come back, decisive questions are, if they have committed prosecutable crimes abroad, still are radicalized and ready to fight, hence if they constitute a security risk and, if yes, how to deal with such risks. It is the duty of the intelligence services to monitor such general threats. The police have the responsibility to protect against concrete acts of violence. And, once radicalization has led to criminal offenses, such as the support of terrorist groups, which is a criminal offense that is frequently committed at an early stage (and often includes the support of foreign terrorist groups), the prosecution authorities come into play. The above-mentioned examples stand for the typically complex and conflict-laden conflicting situation involving different authorities and areas of the law that have recently been grouped together under the umbrella term "security law." The term is a product of the modern state's obligation to afford its citizens an effective and comprehensive protection against concrete danger and, increasingly, also against potential threats inherent in the global "risk society."

## II. The structures of modern security law

The use of the term "security law" suggests a uniform system concealed behind this development. On closer look, however, it becomes apparent that the primary purpose of this terminology is to capture and simultaneously obscure the overlaps between the areas of criminal law, police law, and intelligence law. Thus, the subject matter central to the architecture of security law is the functional connections between and the boundaries separating these three areas of the law and any overlaps, be they authorized or unauthorized.

That said, the borderlines seem to be clear. In some national legal systems, such as in German law, it is a common and plausible tradition to distinguish between criminal law, on the one hand, and police and intelligence law, on the other, using repression and prevention as the dividing line. The function of criminal law is to use repressive measures to process wrongful acts committed in the past; by contrast, the objective of police law and intelligence law is to prevent future violations of the law. This is the backdrop to the disparity in requirements, especially in terms of the procedural measures of an interventional nature, regarding the prerequisites for interventions and the scope of the measures themselves. The threshold for intervention reflects this: Criminal law requires a concrete suspicion (*konketer Tatverdacht*); police law, a concrete or abstract danger (*konkrete/abstrakte Gefahr*); and intelligence law merely a (sufficiently substantiated) situation of endangerment. The extensive expansion of the areas of law in recent decades has further reduced the dichotomous distinction between prevention and repression.

## A. Expansion of criminal law

### 1. The focus on prevention in substantive criminal law

Even in its basic conception, criminal law was designed to deal not only with acts of the past but also to foster prevention. This becomes particularly evident in the legal reasons for punishment – general prevention and special prevention –, which are recognized purposes of criminal law and, as such, essential grounds for legitimizing punishments. Numerous institutions of the General Part of the German Criminal Code are based on the idea of prevention. One example is attempt and, in particular, withdrawal from the attempt under § 24 StGB (the German Criminal Code, hereafter "CC"). It is recognized that withdrawal from an attempt takes the notion of victim protection into account in that it prevents further loss or injury. The concept of prevention is particularly clear in the event of preventive custody under §§ 66 ff. CC, a measure aimed at protecting society from future acts being committed by a dangerous offender. As such, it exemplifies the incorporation of a risk prevention law into the Code.

Moreover, criminal law has increasingly embraced prevention in recent decades. This led to the coining of the terms "preventive criminal law" and "security criminal law." Traditional criminal law was expanded and turned into a tool employed to fight acts society disapproves of.

This development is reflected in the "modern" category of endangerment offenses (see *Vervaele* in this book on anticipative criminalization). A notable example for the extension of the classic repertoire of offenses was to accept the endangerment of collective protected legal interests as worthy of protection. This allowed the legislator to create numerous criminal offenses that can take place well in advance of a concrete violation of individual protected legal interests and are instead focused on the (potentially) dangerous nature of the act (that is, on mere risk). They are a manifestation of the risk society *Beck* already described in the 1980s, which caused a shift in criminal law away from the protection of legal interests and towards risk management. The offenses that belong to this area of the law, which is aptly called "risk criminal law," include a wide range of subject matters (e.g. environmental, economic and sex offenses) but the most dynamic development took place in regard to terrorist offenses: supporting a terrorist organization under § 129a CC is one of the "older" examples whereas receiving "instruction" in a foreign terror training camp (§ 89a CC) is a more recent one (see also for the situation in the UK *Lowe*, in the USA *Becker* and *Drumbl*, and also *Marsavelski* on the specific aspect of terrorist political parties). These offense definitions make it possible to apply criminal law measures against radicalized individuals ready to commit violent acts – such as the above-mentioned Elif Ö. – before they have a chance to harm others in an attack. This means that offenses have been introduced into the criminal law whose substantive legal purpose – due to the fact that they are far removed from the legal interest – is to avert a danger, which is primarily the responsibility of the police (because it is future-oriented). Thus, the prosecution of crime and danger prevention, which also continues to cover such risks, coexist in these legal areas.

A state focused on risk in the area of criminal law is inevitably faced with ever-increasing safeguarding demands as well as security levels. As a result, the state, whose "only" obligation, by tradition, was to safeguard liberty, turns into an all-round safety provider and welfare state (the *Vorsorgestaat*). The concept of taking safety precautions relies heavily on the approach of *governing through crime*, which is frequently proclaimed in the supranational context. This in turn begs the following question: To what degree can the approaches to *governance*, which, until recently, were more oriented towards public law, also be applied to criminal law, particularly as regards the use of criminal law in multi-level systems and for the legitimation of supranational sanctioning power. This development is also key for the extension of national criminal law because the supranational concepts of criminal law are significantly more comprehensive (have a broader understanding of criminal law) than that of e.g. German criminal law. Supranational requirements may subsequently prompt a further expansion of the functional limits of criminal law.

### 2. The expansion of the law of criminal procedure

Like substantive criminal law, the law of criminal procedure has also been progressively expanded and turned into an all-encompassing law of intervention whose objective is prevention. One example is the expansion of criminal investigative measures into so-called preliminary work (*Vorfeld*), in other words, into the area of preventive police work (investigations in advance of criminal activity; in German, *Vorfeldermittlungen*). In addition, the Code of Criminal Procedure meanwhile provides a plethora of frequently covert investigative measures in the telecommunication area, which were originally reserved for the police or the secret service or should have been restricted to them because of their intrusive nature. For this reason, the phrase such as "policialisation of criminal procedures" (*Verpolizeilichung des Strafverfahrens*; similar the term for introducing secret surveillance measures: *Vergeheimdienstlichung des Strafverfahrens*) seem appropriate. As in substantive law, the resulting focus in terms of content lies increasingly on the prevention of future violations of protected legal interests and not only on the prosecution of violations already committed.

### 3. Privatization trends and alternative mechanisms

The expansion of criminal law and the law of criminal procedure into the area of prevention is often accompanied by a shift towards other regulatory mechanisms. For example, economic criminal law, in particular, provides not only comprehensive sanctions for endangerment and risk creation but also embraces the vigorous privatization of compliance. The development of compliance, which originated in the US in 1980s, boosts the idea of prevention by assuming that the *good (corporate) citizen* will actively follow the rules as part of his or her duty rather than taking it for granted in the tradition of *v. Liszt*. Companies are required to implement compliance measures as part of their duty to prevent crimes. Private actors have also been extensively entrusted with enforcing rules and regulations and with investigating violations. Here internal investigations in part are replacing official investigations by the authorities. In such a system, the state can take on a guiding function with incentives such as recognizing cooperation and compliance efforts, e.g. offering the possibility of deals to put a swift end to proceedings, etc.

One area of growth enjoying expansion particularly in European and international law is the area of property sanctions that are neither a fine nor a financial penalty (see the contribution in this book by *Serafin*). This is very important for the fight against terrorism financing, organized crime, and corruption (see for an example the contribution in this book on the illicit trafficking in cultural property by *Campbell/Paul*). For example German law provides for the measures of confiscation and the so-called extended confiscation: The courts do not count these as criminal law sanctions in the strict sense: The culpability principle does not apply, and in extended confiscation (to ease the rules of evidence) no proof of a concrete act or of the unequivocal origin of an object involved in a crime is required. Because the law provides for gross confiscation (*Bruttoabschöpfung*), which means that expenditures incurred are not deducted, the impact of this measure is punitive in the many cases in which the amount confiscated exceeds the amount actually present. Thus, confiscation serves as an example of how a criminal sanction, which is technically considered the quintessential sanction, is complemented or replaced by measures under property law, with reduced evidentiary requirements particularly for the police, in order to confiscate de facto gained assets. This demonstrates a clear trend to at least take assets if the offender cannot be brought under criminal law (to the full extent). *Civil asset forfeiture* under US law is one example of how extensive these measures can be: There, the police are authorized to confiscate an item suspected to be involved in a crime and need to release it only if the person in question can prove that this is not the case. Thus, the law no longer "prosecutes" the offender but rather the alleged or potential objects of crime.

## B. Expansion of the police

The expansion of substantive and procedural criminal law has been accompanied by a steady expansion of police law and intelligence law. This is most evident at the federal level in Germany (see the contribution in this book by *Miller*). In the past two decades, the law enforcement powers of the federal police force have been continuously extended, and its human and material resources have been substantially increased. The Federal Criminal Police Office, in particular, has evolved from an agency whose responsibilities used to be communication and coordination of the different state police authorities into a comprehensive police unit with jurisdiction for serious transnational crime. This development continues to blur the borderline between law enforcement duties and preventive police work. Terrorism is an area where this is particularly evident. The Federal Criminal Police Office and the police forces at state level have had jurisdiction for the criminal prosecution of terrorism since the 1970s. In 2009, the Office was also assigned counterterrorism tasks. These preemptive powers include measures such as online computer searches and video surveillance not equally provided for law enforcement under the Code of Criminal Procedure at that time. Due to the fact that information gathered for preventive purposes may also be used for criminal prosecution to a large extent, the Office has far-reaching possibilities to combat terrorism based almost equally on either preventive or repressive powers. This development shows that one of the main questions nowadays is not only what powers should be given to the police but also under what conditions or thresholds an exchange of information should take place. In addition, the example of online computer searches shows the pacemaker function of police law as criminal procedure law in 2017 introduced it as a new repressive investigation measure.

## C. Expansion of the intelligence services

There has also been an expansion of the intelligence services, like that of the police. In Germany, the different agencies, the Offices for the Protection of the Constitution at the federal and state levels, the Federal Intelligence Service (BND), and also, to some extent, the Military Counterintelligence Service (MAD) have been given wide-ranging powers for gathering intelligence, particularly on terrorist objectives but also on other cross-border crime, such as drug trafficking or money laundering. Strategic telecommunication surveillance provides the Federal Intelligence Service under the Art. 5 G 10 Act the possibility to conduct (investigations in advance absent any suspicion of wrongdoing. Despite the principle of earmarking (that information may only be used for the purpose it was collected for), the exchange of data is permitted in many cases; thus, information obtained by the intelligence services can be transmitted to the police and the public prosecutor's office. This may ultimately result in a criminal proceeding without the government having a concrete suspicion, a situation not allowed under "traditional" criminal procedure. The more the agencies are tasked with collecting information on criminal behaviors the more frequent these cases become in practice. Since September 11, 2001, the cooperation between the police and the intelligence services has been enhanced in terms of organization by establishing joint central facilities, where staff from different agencies work next door to each other, and by sharing data. This means there are neither serious legal nor practical obstacles for close cooperation.

## III. Dangers of the development and problem identification

The legal areas mentioned above were essentially expanded without any systematic analysis and coordination of existing measures. Thus, many measures, taken by themselves, appear to be reasonable and timely adjustments to the new possibilities and threat scenarios associated with technological advances and internationalization. Viewed positively, a look at the entire security architecture reveals that the new possibilities opened up a wide range of procedures and measures to combat the risks. The other side of the coin, however, is that the borderlines between the tasks and the powers in criminal law, police law, and intelligence law are becoming blurred. This results in overlapping competences and an unclear distribution of responsibilities. What citizens may expect of a certain agency and how this may be achieved is becoming vaguer. The rights owed to the affected person and the way in which his or her fundamental rights can be effectively protected is not clear in many cases or do not correspond with the powers of intervention. The legislator is often faced with a dilemma: To be sure, criminal law is the law that affords the affected person the most protection due to its comprehensive protective principles, which are steeped in history and most clearly defined. Yet, whenever the legislator does take recourse to criminal law, the law is expanded far beyond its original scope. In this way, the legislator frequently creates a danger prevention law that bears the label of criminal law.

The development in terms of the police and the intelligence services contravenes a separation principle considered crucial after WW II, namely separating information gathering without executive power (intelligence services) from executive power without comprehensive information gathering rights (police). Formally, the separation principle is adhered to because police agencies and intelligence services are not joined in one agency; in terms of substantive law, however, the thriving exchange of information means that, in practice, the idea of the principle is only partly observed. As in some countries police and intelligence powers are given to one authority the question arises, how useful the separation principle is at all and what its features should be.

The problems of an unclear structure of police and intelligence powers and authorities became glaringly exposed in the context of the investigations into the homicide offenses, bomb attacks, and bank robberies committed by the far-right organization known as "National Socialist Underground" (NSU) in Germany. The examination of the cases at the federal and state levels involved a myriad of agencies in the police and intelligence services as well as public prosecutors' offices. Investigative work was not efficiently distributed and coordinated to match the respective competences, and the information exchange between the authorities was inadequate. These shortcomings interfered with the timely solution of the cases and possibly even with the prevention at least of some of the incidents. Moreover, the way in which the Federal Office for the Protection of the Constitution handled the management of undercover liaison officers proved to be so poor that it raised doubts as to whether such powers should be given to the intelligence services at all. The legislator has partially responded to these deficiencies by drawing on the "tried-and-true" instrument of expanding the federal agencies, particularly the Office of the Prosecutor General and the Federal Office for the Protection of the Constitution.

The fact that the legislative response consists in almost standardized (extension of relevant competences, authorities and sanctions) and selective (reactive case-by-case legislation) regulations points to a general problem of security law: its complexity. In light of the diversity of instruments, actors, and procedures, not just the legislator is faced with the difficult question of whether this does not warrant a reform of the system as a whole rather than piecemeal measures. Academia also faces a similar challenge; most research addresses individual aspects of security law (such as combating terrorism, the expansion of the federal agencies, the separation principle, or specific surveillance measures). An analysis of the entire system and its evolution is rare. In the majority of cases, research is conducted from the point of view of repressive criminal law or from a public law, prevention-oriented perspective. The powers of the intelligence services and their influence on criminal procedure have only most recently caught the attention of researchers, mainly because they already substantially influence criminal proceedings in practice.

## IV. Comparative research as a tool for ongoing development

### A. Approach

What could be a way out of the existing dilemma approaching security law? A first step is to take the whole picture into account. This means to analyze, evaluate, and continue to develop the design of security law in terms of the boundaries and the overlaps of its preventive and repressive aspects. This especially means to review and analyze key system-relevant developments in substantive and procedural law. It is neither enough to look at changes in substantive law without taking into account the various procedural aspects nor is it, vice versa, enough to adjust and especially expand investigations measures without considering the effect on substantial law. Expanding everything without a critical impact assessment leads to unlimited policing. Therefore an emphasis has to be placed on the preventive nature of criminal law (especially the creation of new preparatory or even preemptive offenses) and the preventive aspects of the law of criminal procedure and on how these features overlap well into police law, intelligence law and even extension into the law of war.

On the basis of such research one can develop and evaluate models of how the boundary between prevention and repression should be drawn, and try to design an ideal type. Possible models to be taken into account might involve legal systems such as German law with a distinct separation of criminal law, police law and intelligence law as well as systems from the common law area (United Kingdom and the US) where such a difference between these areas those not exist to the same extent. Moreover, the speedy development of the European and International law systems warrants to take them into account, too, e.g. in a kind of multi-level functional comparison. In detail, in view of the tension between repression and prevention approaches also have to take into account and to provide sufficient rule of law safeguards, especially in the area bordering on criminal law (and where traditionally lower guarantees have been accepted). In this process justice has to be done to basic principles such as legal certainty and also to sound concepts for limiting the exercise of sovereign power.

## B. Initial considerations

The approach of German law, which is to distinguish between repressive criminal law and preventive police and intelligence law, is only rudimentarily shared by the law in the UK and the US. Common law distinguishes between *criminal law* and *policing* by tradition. However, while the police are principally charged with ensuring compliance with the law in general (*law enforcement*), there is no clear distinction between preventive and repressive purposes with respect to their tasks or powers. Furthermore, police authorities typically carry out many tasks which, from a German point of view, would fall within the ambit of the intelligence services and include numerous very intrusive covert investigative measures. For example, the FBI also has jurisdiction for *national security*, including any investigative work it involves. Any distinction comes mainly at the organizational level, where a specific internal unit may be assigned with criminal prosecution. This ultimately allows for a relatively swift adjustment of measures to a given situation within one agency (sometimes even without changing the legislation) and especially without having to inform outside agencies.

Since the attacks of September 11, 2001, the US and the UK have focused on expanding their criminal law as well as their police and intelligence law, particularly in the counterterrorism area (see the contributions by *Lowe* and *Becker* in this book). In England, for example, the competences of the police were significantly expanded by introducing the option of detention without charge. The Counter-Terrorism and Security Act 2015 reintroduced the option of an immediate passport seizure for up to 30 days and a re-entry ban for the UK for a maximum term of up to two years (*temporary exclusion order*). These measures only apply on suspicion of terrorism. In addition, there are specific *terrorism prevention and investigation measures*, such as house arrest or the mandatory requirement to reside at a specified location, which provide extensive options for proceeding against terrorism suspects. Measures such as these equip the police with a more flexible approach against persons such as Elif Ö., who are considered a risk but where the level of suspicion does not rise to the level of committing an offense. The main challenge now associated with these measures is to ensure sufficient judicial review of the suspicion, which is often based on secret intelligence information, in order to guarantee effective legal safeguards.

The questions raised at the national level are similar to those raised at the supranational level (see the contributions in this book by *Derenčinović*, *Munivrana Vajda/Roksandić Vidlička* and *Vervaele* on the international level as well as *Ligeti/Lassalle* and *Paulussen* on the European level). Here, the delimitation of criminal law from preventive danger prevention measures is a key issue, particularly in terms of counter-terrorism objectives. In the last two decades, European law and the law of the UN have evolved into an independent intervention and sanction law. From a German vantage point, measures such as maintaining terrorist lists or fighting piracy include elements of both criminal law and police law. The classification is very important for the transposition into national law but is rarely clear and unambiguous, not least because "criminal law" and "police law" have their own international (and, world-wide, nationally different) terminologies. This is unfortunate, because a qualification as criminal law is principally commensurate with far-reaching rights and guarantees for the affected persons, unlike (administrative) police law, which does not recognize them to the same degree. To avoid this, there are first indications that very intrusive measures will be given a standard similar to the procedures and rights in criminal law. This denotes a shift away from the difficult question of classification, as is often already the case in UK and US national law. It means a change in perspective, away from the classification as "preventive/repressive" towards an approach primarily focused on protected interests and interventions – the impact on affected persons and, in turn, any necessary legal safeguards take center stage. This may prove to be the point of departure for a contemporary understanding of a sanctioning regime.

# Schriftenreihe des Max-Planck-Instituts für ausländisches und internationales Strafrecht

The main research activities of the Max Planck Institute for Foreign and International Criminal Law are published in the following six subseries of the “Schriftenreihe des Max-Planck-Instituts für ausländisches und internationales Strafrecht” (Research Series of the Max Planck Institute for Foreign and International Criminal Law), which are distributed in cooperation with the publisher Duncker & Humblot:

- “Strafrechtliche Forschungsberichte” (Reports on Research in Criminal Law)
- “Kriminologische Forschungsberichte” (Reports on Research in Criminology)
- “Interdisziplinäre Forschungen aus Strafrecht und Kriminologie” (Reports on Interdisciplinary Research in Criminal Law and Criminology)
- “Publications of the Max Planck Partner Group for Balkan Criminology”
- “Series of the Max Planck Institute for Foreign and International Criminal Law and Bahçeşehir University Joint Research Group”
- “Sammlung ausländischer Strafgesetzbücher in Übersetzung” (Collection of Foreign Criminal Laws in Translation)

These publications can be ordered from the Max Planck Institute at <www.mpicc.de> or from Duncker & Humblot at <www.duncker-humblot.de>. Two additional subseries are published: “research in brief” contains short reports on results of research activities, and “Arbeitsberichte” (working materials) present preliminary results of research projects. These publications are available at the Max Planck Institute.

Detailed information on all publications of the Max Planck Institute for Foreign and International Criminal Law can be found at <www.mpicc.de>.

---

Die zentralen Veröffentlichungen des Max-Planck-Instituts für ausländisches und internationales Strafrecht werden in Zusammenarbeit mit dem Verlag Duncker & Humblot in den folgenden sechs Unterreihen der „Schriftenreihe des Max-Planck-Instituts für ausländisches und internationales Strafrecht“ vertrieben:

- „Strafrechtliche Forschungsberichte“
- „Kriminologische Forschungsberichte“
- „Interdisziplinäre Forschungen aus Strafrecht und Kriminologie“
- „Publications of the Max Planck Partner Group for Balkan Criminology“
- „Series of the Max Planck Institute for Foreign and International Criminal Law and Bahçeşehir University Joint Research Group“
- „Sammlung ausländischer Strafgesetzbücher in Übersetzung“

Diese Publikationen können direkt über das Max-Planck-Institut unter <www.mpicc.de> oder über den Verlag Duncker & Humblot unter <www.duncker-humblot.de> erworben werden. Darüber hinaus erscheinen in der Unterreihe „research in brief“ zusammenfassende Kurzbeschreibungen von Forschungsergebnissen und in der Unterreihe „Arbeitsberichte“ Veröffentlichungen vorläufiger Forschungsergebnisse. Diese Veröffentlichungen können über das Max-Planck-Institut bezogen werden.

Detaillierte Informationen zu den einzelnen Publikationen des Max-Planck-Instituts für ausländisches und internationales Strafrecht sind unter <www.mpicc.de> abrufbar.

Max-Planck-Institut für ausländisches
und internationales Strafrecht

Selected criminal law publications:

S 164 *Yukun Zong*
**Beweisverbote im Strafverfahren**
Rechtsvergleichende Untersuchung zum deutschen, US-amerikanischen und chinesischen Recht
2018 • 487 Seiten • ISBN 978-3-86113-779-5 € 44,00

S 163 *Huawei Wang*
**Die strafrechtliche Verantwortlichkeit von Internet-Service-Providern**
Ein deutsch-chinesischer Rechtsvergleich
2019 • 228 Seiten • ISBN 978-3-86113-781-8 € 35,00

S 162 *Alejandra Castillo Ara*
**Normbefolgungsunfähigkeit im Strafrecht**
Eine vergleichende Analyse des deutschen und US-amerikanischen Rechts
2019 • 254 Seiten • ISBN 978-3-86113-782-5 € 35,00

S 161 *Ulrich Sieber/Valsamis Mitsilegas/Christos Mylonopoulos/ Emmanouil Billis/Nandor Knust* (eds.)
**Alternative Systems of Crime Control**
National, Transnational, and International Dimensions
2018 • 343 Seiten • ISBN 978-3-86113-786-3 € 44,00

S 156 *Ulrich Sieber / Nicolas von zur Mühlen* (eds.)
**Access to Telecommunication Data in Criminal Justice**
A Comparative Analysis of European Legal Orders
2016 • 771 Seiten • ISBN 978-3-86113-796-2 € 58,00

S 155 *Jennifer Schuetze-Reymann*
**International Criminal Justice on Trial**
The ICTY and ICTR Case Referral Practice to National Courts and Its Possible Relevance for the ICC
2016 • 232 Seiten • ISBN 978-3-86113-797-9 € 35,00

S 154 *Carl-Wendelin Neubert*
**Der Einsatz tödlicher Waffengewalt durch die deutsche auswärtige Gewalt**
2016 • 391 Seiten • ISBN 978-3-86113-799-3 € 41,00

S 150 *Ulrich Sieber/ Benjamin Vogel* (eds.)
**Terrorismusfinanzierung**
Prävention im Spannungsfeld von internationalen Vorgaben und nationalem Tatstrafrecht
2015 • 237 Seiten • ISBN 978-3-86113-805-1 € 35,00

Max-Planck-Institut für ausländisches und internationales Strafrecht

Selected criminal law publications:

S **128.5.1** *Ulrich Sieber / Konstanze Jarvers / Emily Silverman* (eds.)
**National Criminal Law in a Comparative Legal Context**
**Volume 5.1: Grounds for rejecting criminal liability**
2016 • 410 Seiten • ISBN 978-3-86113-800-6 € 43,00

G 126 **Strafgesetzbuch der Tschechischen Republik –**
**Trestní zákonik České republiky**
Deutsche Übersetzung von Susanne Altmann
Einführung von Helena Valková, Josef Kuchta, Petr Bohata
Zweisprachige Ausgabe
2017 • 430 Seiten • ISBN 978-3-86113-789-4 € 50,00

G 125 **Die türkische Strafprozessordnung – Ceza Muhakemesi Kanunu**
Deutsche Übersetzung und Einführung von Mehmet Arslan
Zweisprachige Ausgabe
2017 • 289 Seiten • ISBN 978-3-86113-792-4 € 48,00

Selected criminological publications:

K 181 *Maria Walsh*
**Intensive Bewährungshilfe und junge Intensivtäter**
Eine empirische Analyse des Einflusses von Intensivbewährungshilfe auf die kriminelle Karriere junger Mehrfachauffälliger in Bayern
Berlin 2018 • 233 Seiten • ISBN 978-3-86113-269-1 € 35,00

K 180 *Linn Katharina Döring*
**Sozialarbeiter vor Gericht?**
Grund und Grenzen einer Kriminalisierung unterlassener staatlicher Schutzmaßnahmen in tödlichen Kinderschutzfällen in Deutschland und England
Berlin 2018 • 442 Seiten • ISBN 978-3-86113-268-4 € 42,00

K 179 *Michael Kilchling*
**Opferschutz innerhalb und außerhalb des Strafrechts**
Perspektiven zur Übertragung opferschützender Normen aus dem Strafverfahrensrecht in andere Verfahrensordnungen
Berlin 2018 • 165 Seiten • ISBN 978-3-86113-267-7 € 32,00

Selected publications from the criminological and interdisciplinary publication series:

BC 2 *Sunčana Roksandić Vidlička*
**Prosecuting Serious Economic Crimes as International Crimes**
A New Mandate for the ICC?
Berlin 2017 • 530 Seiten • ISBN 978-3-86113-264-6 € 44,00

BC 1 *Anna-Maria Getoš Kalac, Hans-Jörg Albrecht, Michael Kilchling* (eds.)
**Mapping the Criminological Landscape of the Balkans**
A Survey on Criminology and Crime
with an Expedition into the Criminal Landscape of the Balkans
Berlin 2014 • 540 Seiten • ISBN 978-3-86113-248-6 € 44,00

I 25 *Chenguang Zhao*
**The ICC and China**
The Principle of Complementarity and the National Implementation of International Criminal Law
Berlin 2017 • 245 Seiten • ISBN 978-3-86113-266-0 € 35,00

I 24 *Ulrich Sieber* (Hrsg.)
**Strafrecht in einer globalen Welt**
Internationales Kolloquium zum Gedenken an Professor Dr. Hans-Heinrich Jescheck vom 7. bis 8. Januar 2011
Berlin 2016 • 200 Seiten • ISBN 978-3-86113-259-2 € 30,00

I 23 *Hans-Jörg Albrecht* (Hrsg.)
**Kriminalität, Kriminalitätskontrolle, Strafvollzug und Menschenrechte**
Internationales Kolloquium zum Gedenken an Professor Dr. Günther Kaiser am 23. Januar 2009
Berlin 2016 • 176 Seiten • ISBN 978-3-86113-258-5 € 30,00

I 22 *Claudia Carolin Klüpfel*
**Die Vollzugspraxis des Umweltstraf- und Umweltordnungswidrigkeitenrechts**
Eine empirische Untersuchung zur aktuellen Anwendungspraxis sowie Entwicklung des Fallspektrums und des Verfahrensgangs seit den 1980er Jahren
Berlin 2016 • 278 Seiten • ISBN 978-3-86113-257-8 € 35,00

I 21 *Tanja Leibold*
**Der Deal im Steuerstrafrecht**
Die Verständigung gemäß § 257c StPO in der Systematik des formellen und materiellen Rechts
Berlin 2016 • 254 Seiten • ISBN 978-3-86113-256-1 € 35,00